The Ultimate Guide to Collectible

LEGO® SETS
Identification and Price Guide

Ed Maciorowski
Jeff Maciorowski

Published by

Krause Publications, a division of F+W Media, Inc.
700 East State Street • Iola, WI 54990-0001
715-445-2214 • 888-457-2873
www.krausebooks.com

To order books or other products call toll-free 1-800-258-0929
or visit us online at www.krausebooks.com

LEGO, the LEGO logo, the Brick and Knob configurations and the Minifigure are trademarks of
The LEGO Group of Companies. ©2015 The LEGO Group. LEGO® is a trademark of the LEGO
Group of companies, which does not sponsor, authorize, or endorse this book.

The publisher is not sponsored or associated with The LEGO Group of companies. This identification and price guide is the result of the authors' independent research reporting on the secondary market and is intended to provide information for collectors.

Cover credits: The *Star Wars* Ultimate Collection Series 10179 Millennium Falcon photo is
courtesy of Dave Watford. The *Star Wars* Ultimate Collection Series 10026 Special Edition Naboo
Starfighter photo is courtesy of Ed Maciorowski and Jeff Maciorowski. The word STAR WARS and
its associated trademarks are owned by Disney/Lucasfilm and licensed to The LEGO Group, and
are used in this book solely for identification purposes.

ISBN-13: 9781440244827
ISBN-10: 1440244820

Cover Design by Nicole MacMartin
Designed by Nicole MacMartin
Edited by Kristine Manty

Printed in China

10 9 8 7 6 5 4 3 2 1

ACKNOWLEDGMENTS

My brother, Jeff, and I, talk quite frequently about our journey into the world of LEGO. Who would have known that a simple LEGO set bought over 40 years ago by my parents would have evolved into a book about LEGO sets and bricks? Honestly, it's been a surreal, yet extremely positive experience, but then again, why shouldn't it be? I mean, after all, the book and our website are all about LEGO bricks, the most iconic toy of all time. So I guess we will start there, thanking The LEGO Group for producing the most wonderful, infinitely creative, geometrically perfect, sometimes simplistic, sometimes awe inspiring, always high quality, fun, and iconic LEGO brick and the multitudes of sets created with it.

We, of course, would like to thank Kris Manty, Paul Kennedy, and Krause Publications for giving us the opportunity to write this book. Jeff and I want to thank the book's designer, Nicole MacMartin, and any BrickPicker.com members and LEGO fans who submitted photos and information for it. We would like to thank the BrickPicker community, especially the moderators, who work for free and are our eyes when we can't be there. It is a privilege to have a chance to converse with such a wide variety of extremely intelligent individuals from around the world. The one

thing that LEGO bricks seem to attract is smart and gifted individuals. Two special people Jeff and I would like to thank is Huw Millington and Dr. Dave Watford of the legendary LEGO website, www.Brickset.com. They have been very supportive of our site when others were not.

Finally, Jeff and I would like to thank our sublime and extremely understanding wives, Liz and Jane. They have dealt with our LEGO obsession with the patience of two saints. It's quite difficult to accept the fact that there are thousands of LEGO sets stored in the finished basements or closets of our homes or new packages arriving at the front door on a daily basis. Also, they are generous of the time that they give to us to attend to BrickPicker site matters.

On a personal and final note, I would like to thank my son, Maximillian, most of all. He was the reason why I took a hiatus from LEGO collecting and noticed the huge increases in prices when I came back, thus giving us the reason to create BrickPicker. His passion and zest for life gave me a focus and a strength that I never thought I possessed.

I hope you all enjoy the book and feel free to stop by the www.BrickPicker.com site to check out the latest LEGO values and information.

The authors would like to thank the following people, who gave permission to use some of their photographs in this book:

Dr. Dave Watford, United Kingdom, gimmelego.blogspot.com; Ryan Hafer, Perry, MI, theplasticbrick.com; Roger (Flickr: Starstreek007), www.flickr.com/photos/starstreak007; Hamid (Flickr: KatanaZ), www.flickr.com/photos/10335017@N07/sets/; Zip250, www.flickr.com/photos/45313042@N08/albums; Christopher Gearhart, Mundelein, IL, Bigbudlego Productions; Anthony DeMarzio III, Philadelphia, PA, DeMarzio Enterprises; Luis Baixinho, Portugal, Spain; Telgar Sandseeker, Sainte Luce Sur Loire, France; Tomasz Bak, Olsztyn, Poland, legosoul.wordpress.com; Tim Ropp, Columbus, OH, MostlyTechnic, www.flickr.com/photos/mostlytechnic/; Matthieu Cousin, Paris, France; Techlug.fr, St. Bonnet de Mure, France, www.techlug.fr; Brent Manchester, Milton, WV; NMR, Sherbrooke, Canada; Nick Martin/Ace Kim, www.fbtb.net.

CONTENTS

INTRODUCTION

LEGO bricks. For over 50 years, these tiny pieces of plastic have won over the hearts and minds of millions of children and adults across the world. The popularity of these building bricks has grown exponentially over the years, with LEGO being named the "Toy of the Century" by the British Association of Toy Retailers and originally by *Fortune* magazine in 2000. This popularity has helped LEGO become the number one toy maker in the world in 2013, and outperform rival toy maker, Mattel, in terms of revenue and profit. But the profits don't stop with The LEGO Group or other retailers.

I have been a fan and collector of LEGO bricks and sets for almost 40 years, but it wasn't until about the last seven that the secondary LEGO marketplace caught my attention. With the advent of the internet and auction sites like eBay, a huge market for retired sets has developed over the past decade or so. I was amazed at the values of some of the more exclusive and rare LEGO sets. Even regular non-exclusive sets, many with standard features, designs, and brick types, increase in value after retirement. It was this growth in value of retired LEGO sets that started me and my brother, Jeff, on a quest to track these values in an accurate and updated manner.

eBay has played a huge role in the growth of the LEGO secondary market. The site has become a multimillion-dollar marketplace for vintage and retired items, and is the largest marketplace for new and used LEGO sets and pieces on the planet. On any given day, there are tens of thousands of transactions that deal with LEGO sets and pieces. Terapeak market research collects this sales data from eBay and we aggregate that data into our price guide, filtering out bad listings and removing outliers. We aggregate data from thousands of completed eBay LEGO auctions on a monthly basis. The data in this book is the most recent sales information that was available before the book went to press.

THE BASICS

There have been approximately 10,000 LEGO sets created over the past 50 years. What makes a set a valuable collectible is that each one has a limited production run — some a couple of months, some several years. The more unique and rare a set, usually the higher the value it has. The one factor that works differently from other collectibles is age. Older is not always more valuable. Some sets will plateau and may even drop in value over time. LEGO sets are valuable because of a connection of a potential buyer to a set. Many current fans are unfamiliar with old sets and place little value on

them, yet some newer sets can fetch thousands of dollars. A potential buyer might have wanted a set as a child and could not afford it, so when they get older and have some extra discretionary income, they pay top dollar for that retired set. Other sets are bought by collectors who are completists and enjoy collecting entire themes. There are many reasons why sets are valuable. They are iconic toys, are creative, and exceptionally produced, but they mostly create a bond with fans and future buyers.

For our purposes in this book, we are sticking with sets that were created and released from 2000 and after, but we do include prices and analysis for a handful of pre-2000, or vintage, sets. Besides being more relative to many fans and collectors, sets that were created after 1999 are on a different level of creativity and complexity. In addition to a change in set design, bold business decisions by LEGO to add licensed movie/TV properties such as *Star Wars*, *Harry Potter*, and *The Lord of the Rings*, have paid off considerably. The first and foremost of these more elaborate, licensed themes is the *Star Wars* Ultimate Collector Series, which launched in 2000. The UCS sets are more complex builds and accurate in appearance. They are large sets, designed with adult fans in mind. But even the smaller, more cost-effective licensed sets help drive new fans to LEGO. With every new *Star Wars* or *Harry Potter* movie, children flock to the stores to buy new sets based on it. Non-licensed themes also benefited from the more intricate designs and larger set sizes. The largest retail LEGO set ever produced (piece count), the 10189 Taj Mahal, is a beautiful rendition of one of the "Wonders of the World." LEGO is no longer a toy for just children, and this change in philosophy helped pave the way to The LEGO Group's financial success today. Now adults are buying sets for themselves and this practice drives up prices on many new and retired sets.

The fact that all LEGO sets do retire at some point creates a limited time to buy them from primary retailers. Short-term resellers and long-term investors capitalize on this and will stock up on new sets, waiting for a LEGO set to retire or go EOL (end of line), then will proceed to list these retired sets on eBay at a price higher than the manufacturer's suggested retail price. Some resellers even "flip" sets short term, basically reselling a hot or popular LEGO set before they retire. This usually occurs around Christmas or when a popular set is in short supply.

The main goal of this book is to show current market prices on many of the most popular sets in recent history. You might be surprised at what you read. That set purchased for Little Johnny three years ago might be worth more now used than you paid for it new. You will find that all sets are not created equal and that there are themes that appreciate well and others that do not. Also, the size of sets with regards to piece count and weight can also play an important factor in the value. LEGO bases their MSRPs on the weight of a set, for the most part. The more ABS (acrylonitrile butadiene styrene) plastic used to produce a set, the more it will cost at retail and on the secondary market. LEGO minifigures also play a major role in the value of set, and these peanut-sized plastic people produce huge profit potential. Many of the most valuable and profitable LEGO sets are because of a rare minifigure or it contains multiple minifigures.

HOW TO USE THIS BOOK

Each chapter in this book is based on a major LEGO theme and organized alphabetically. The most important themes are included, but a few less popular themes, such as Prince of Persia, Atlantis, and World Racers, are discussed briefly in the Miscellaneous chapter. Within each chapter, we list and analyze the top sets of a theme from the standpoint of profitability and Return on Investment (ROI). According to Investopedia.com, the definition of ROI is as follows:

A performance measure used to evaluate the efficiency of an investment or to compare the efficiency of a number of different investments. To calculate ROI, the benefit (return) of an investment is divided by the cost of the investment; the result is expressed as a percentage or a ratio. The return on investment formula:

$$ROI = \frac{(\text{Gain from Investment} - \text{Cost of Investment})}{\text{Cost of Investment}}$$

For our ROI calculations, the cost of investment is the MSRP of the LEGO set and the gain from investment is the current market price according to our data. We also include a basic list that ranks a multitude of sets from a theme according to their Return on Investment from MSRP. By analyzing some of the top sets from each theme, a smart and savvy LEGO fan might be able to pick out qualities that make certain sets valuable and qualities that produce investment "losers." There is a separate price guide in the back of the book that lists more sets in each theme and their values.

Values of LEGO sets can range greatly, even if they are the same set. It is not an exact science. Determining the exact value depends on the set itself. How rare is it?

HOW SETS ARE VALUED

For simplicity, we break down the value of LEGO sets into two categories: new and used. While many collectors know there are variations of each category, unless a set is inspected and checked for completeness, it is hard to value it accurately. We acquire our data from Terapeak Market Research. They purchase auction data from eBay directly. We then purchase that data from Terapeak and break down, aggregate, and filter data into a convenient price guide, removing anomalies and outliers from the final figures. The price guide is updated monthly, which is a long time in the world of LEGO reselling and investing. Huge fluctuations and price swings can occur over the course of 30 days, if a set retires or if LEGO makes major announcements. This guide gives you the most up-to-date prices prior to publishing that is possible. But, as with any price guide, it is just that: a guide. There can be price variations within a new or used set because of condition of the set itself. Unless otherwise noted, the values of sets discussed in this book are in MISB/MIB condition.

$$$$$

NEW; MISB
(MINT IN SEALED BOX)

Set is brand new with a box in excellent condition and factory sealed. Limited shelf wear is acceptable. Sets in this condition bring the most money. The better the box condition, the more the set is worth, but the difference between a perfect box and one with slight wear is small.

How popular is it? How badly does a buyer want one? Many sets have an emotional tie to a particular buyer, and they are willing to pay over and above the going rate for a set because they want it. It's that simple. Use our prices as a guide. Things change quickly in the LEGO world. Sets get retired. Sets get remade. What was once rare becomes commonplace when newer versions are produced. The bottom line is that these little plastic ABS bricks are valuable. Even sets that are incomplete can be sold for more money than was originally paid for at retail. Keep your sets in good condition. Save the boxes and instructions. Store them carefully. If possible, keep your valuable sets and pieces separate from the rest of your LEGO collection in case you ever want to resell your collection. Most importantly, enjoy your LEGO sets and bricks. They are a wonderful toy that stimulates the imagination and, quite possibly, your bank account.

WHY INVEST IN LEGO BRICKS?

As mentioned, the main purpose of this book is to discuss the values of a multitude of LEGO sets from 2000 to the present, but you have to understand that the values on the secondary market are, to a certain degree, a result of LEGO "investing." Without adult LEGO fans collecting, building, and stockpiling many popular sets, the demand and values of many recent ones may be much lower than they currently are on the secondary market. If there is no demand for sets, there will no reason for prices to increase the way they have. The process of LEGO designing,

producing, and retiring a set, then repeating the process over and over again for hundreds of sets on an annual basis, is paramount to the success of LEGO investing. But why should people invest in LEGO sets?

For one, it's a classic toy of impeccable quality that can be made into an infinite amount of creations. A LEGO brick from 50 years ago can be interchanged with a brick from today and the colors, fit, and finish are all the same. Another reason why LEGO sets are investment options is that they are extremely popular. The LEGO Group has posted year over year profits for the last eight years and is currently the world's number one toymaker. Probably the most important reason these are serious investment options is that they are produced in limited quantities, with each individual set having a limited production run and then retired. The fact that sets are retired creates a collectible, and in some cases rare, item.

Here are some things a novice should look for when choosing LEGO sets for investments:

- LEGO sets with rare pieces and minifigures. Minifigures are often called the "currency" of the LEGO world and are highly collectible and popular. Some individual minifigures can sell for tens, if not hundreds, of dollars.
- Licensed sets can appreciate very well after retirement and many contain valuable and highly collectible minifigures.
- Large sets, with 1,000 pieces or more, seem to exhibit strong returns on investment. The largest set of any LEGO theme can be the safest choice.

$$$$
NEW;MIB
(MINT IN BOX)

Box is in excellent condition with minimal shelf wear, but factory seals are broken or removed. Contents sealed in factory plastic baggies and all parts ccounted for. Instructions/stickers are in new condition. No stickers applied. For all purposes, an MISB that has been opened. This type of set is worth slightly less than the MISB – less than 5 percent in most cases.

$$$
NEW;NIB
(NEW IN BOX)

Box is damaged or destroyed. Contents sealed in factory plastic baggies. Set is complete, with all pieces, sticker sheets, instructions. Set never built. There are variations, depending on condition of the box and instructions. Set will be valued less than the average new price. Sets can sell for top dollar if the potential buyer is just interested in buying and building the set.

$$
USED
COMPLETE SET

Complete with box, instructions, and all pieces. Pieces are clean and in excellent condition. Box is in good condition with some shelf wear and minor damage. Used sets built for display by adult collectors usually are more valuable than sets that have been played with. If the sticker sheet is intact and stickers never applied, the set's value will increase.

$
USED
INCOMPLETE SET

Least valuable set. Box, pieces, and/or instructions missing. Depending on condition/what's missing, the value can vary greatly. Missing boxes can reduce the value, usually by around 10 percent. The value of a set missing pieces and/ or minifigures depends on what is missing. Sets missing minifigures can lose half their value, if not more.

- LEGO sets with a low Price Per Piece ratio, usually around $0.07 a brick (based on MSRP), can be profitable. Sometimes new LEGO sets are "parted" out and resold to fans as individual pieces. This is a huge market and helps many fans and builders acquire pieces they could not buy otherwise.
- Sets with short production runs usually equate to rarity, thus are more valuable. Many have a two-year production run, so anything less is optimal.
- Collector or limited edition sets can appreciate to higher levels than unmarked sets.
- Small sets and polybags can also show strong returns, and those with rare minifigures or small seasonal or holiday sets are solid choices.
- Unique sets can also be profitable in the long term.

There are also certain themes and subthemes that usually provide positive returns, such as the *Star Wars* Ultimate Collector Series. It is based on some of the iconic characters and vehicles of the movies, but unlike many of the simpler, non-UCS *Star Wars* sets, the UCS sets are highly detailed and complex builds, and designed for the adult collector and wallet. They are large sets with large price tags, but usually appreciate very well. One example of this superior growth is the 10179 UCS Millennium Falcon, which had an MSRP of $499.99. Current values for this set are $3,500+ on eBay and other auction sites. Another theme that is an outstanding investment is the LEGO Modular Buildings theme. These sets are also designed for adult builders and based on buildings found on an everyday city or town street. The 10182 Cafe Corner sold for $139.99 in 2007 and now is selling for over $1,600 on eBay, which computes to over 1,000 percent in ROI. That is incredible.

LEGO investing works with many different types and sized sets. Many smaller sets can exhibit even greater returns. A $9.99 set like 7884 Batman's Buggy: The Escape of Mr. Freeze has grown over 1,300 percent in ROI and is valued at over $130 in the secondary market. Gems like these can be found in different places. eBay is an excellent start for both new and used sets, and Craigslist and garage sales have been prosperous for some. For newer sets, LEGO Shop at Home, Amazon, Target, Walmart, and Toys R Us are the traditional LEGO retailers.

Variety in LEGO investing depends on condition also. Used sets can make excellent investment choices and many people will pay top dollar for a rare, retired, and previously built set in excellent condition. A used 10189 Taj Mahal sells for over $1,100 on eBay, which is amazing. There is also variety in investing styles: long term (investors), short term (flippers), and a combination of those two. Long-term investors will hold sets for two years or longer, ignoring many daily fluctuations in stock and prices, hoping to cash in a large profit in the future. Flippers try to take advantage of lack of supply and seasonal market conditions to buy and sell sets quickly for a small profit. Both methods have their advantages and disadvantages, as does investing in the large array of LEGO styles, themes, and conditions.

There are some drawbacks to investing in LEGO sets as well. Storing the boxes is a major negative. They can take up huge amounts of space and are susceptible to sun and water damage. Stack them the wrong way and they can be crushed from the weight of the other sets. The selling, packaging, and shipping process can also be time consuming and arduous. There are also fees, commissions, and taxes to take into account when you sell a LEGO set. All these potential negatives must be considered before entering the world of LEGO investment. This, plus the fact that the set that is invested in is not guaranteed to appreciate. Even with potential pitfalls, thousands, if not millions, of fans will venture into the hobby and/or business of LEGO collecting, investing, and reselling. Many will be successful and experience positive returns on their original investment year after year.

The future looks bright for the LEGO secondary market. The continued production of new, creative, and stylish LEGO sets that retire and become collectible, coupled with the enduring quality of the brick, will enable the secondary market to prosper.

SUPPORTIVE COMMUNITY

When my brother, Jeff, and I created BrickPicker.com in 2011, we discovered that there were thousands of like-minded individuals who realized there is serious money to be made in collecting, stockpiling, and reselling LEGO sets, if you choose the appropriate ones to buy and time the market correctly.

I have enjoyed the past four years on the BrickPicker. com forums meeting all types of people, from all parts of the world. The one consistent trait of fans, builders, collectors, investors, flippers, and resellers is that most are of high intelligence. Accountants, computer programmers, stock brokers, engineers, retailers, business owners, and more make up the BrickPicker membership, and we all share ideas and methods.

Our LEGO Price Guide was our original idea for the website, but it has since morphed into a Price Guide/LEGO Investing Guide. We work hard to give members multiple tools and data to help them make smart investment choices, and our blogs and forum help educate and entertain all manners of fans and investors, from the novice to the experienced. Even if you are not interested in reselling LEGO sets, there is plenty of up-to-date information to make a visit worth your while. Just checking current secondary market prices for your collection is of value. The one area that BrickPicker.com shines, though, is finding deals on new and used sets. Our network of thousands of fans helps keep the community informed to special sales and discounts at major LEGO retailers throughout the country, and other countries for that matter. We have the most up-to-date LEGO sales information on the planet. Good luck in your LEGO collecting or investing quest. Jeff and I look forward to meeting you on the BrickPicker.com forums.

CHAPTER 1

ADVANCED MODELS

ADVANCE MODEL SETS HAVE BECOME

While the majority of LEGO sets are designed for children and young adults, it can be argued that The LEGO Group's decision early in the new Millennium to design and produce larger and more complex sets reinvigorated sales and renewed interest from a new source: adult fans of LEGO.

Prior to 2000, there were a handful of LEGO sets that were larger than 1,000 pieces and what I would call advanced models because of their more complex build, including the 5571 Giant Truck (1,757 pieces), the 8448 Super Street Sensation (1,457 pieces), the 8880 Super Car (1,343 pieces), the 8480 Space Shuttle (1,308 pieces), and the 1280 Barcode Multi-Set (1,280 pieces). Not really an overly impressive bunch of sets, in my opinion, and most were created with Technic bricks. But better days, and sets, lied ahead. But before we discuss some of the most iconic LEGO sets of all time, let us examine the qualifications of an advanced model.

The vast majority of LEGO sets produced are small- to mid-sized sets. Sets that have one to 100 pieces in them make up more than half of

THE
OF COLLECTORS
BACK
AND RESELLERS
BONE

PRODUCING GREAT PROFITS ON THE SECONDARY MARKET, AND SOME OF THE CURRENT PRICES ARE EXTRAORDINARY.

the 9,000-plus sets ever created. This can be explained by the large amount of polybags created every year. Polybags are those soft, clear, and colored bags that small sets and promotional items are sold in.

The Collectible Minifigures Series sets are sold in a similar packaging, so that adds quite a few small sets on an annual basis. The bottom line is that each year, LEGO has a set inventory of between 500 to 700 sets and small boxed sets and polybags make up more than half. There is an inverse relation between sets produced and their size; quite simply, the bigger the set, the less that is produced.

This relates to the Advanced Models theme because given that they are usually the largest sets produced every year, they are also quite rare ... thus valuable.

For all intents and purposes, an Advanced Model LEGO set should contain around 1,000 pieces or more. While there are a few exceptions to this rule, many of the current Advanced Model sets range from 1,000 to 2,500 pieces, with a handful higher than that.

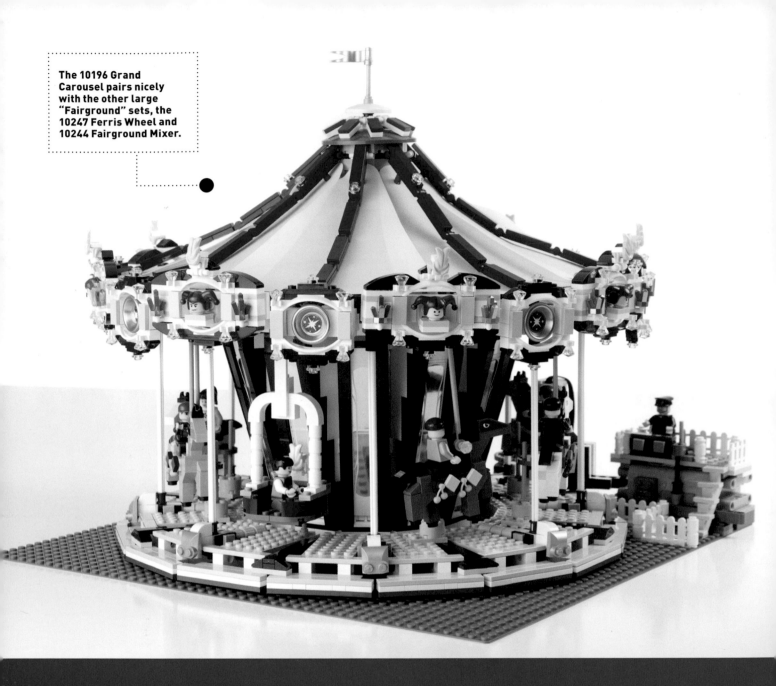

The **10196 Grand Carousel** pairs nicely with the other large "Fairground" sets, the **10247 Ferris Wheel** and **10244 Fairground Mixer.**

Another basic qualification is build complexity and brick type. LEGO sells many large containers of generic bricks for children, but these are not meant to be used in any sort of elaborate builds, so these LEGO "buckets of bricks" do not qualify to be Advanced Models. Although some Technic sets are huge, the finished model is not as detailed or complete as an Advanced Model externally and so these sets do not qualify as Advanced Models, either. Technic sets are generally based on the working internals of a vehicle or machine, with little in the way of exterior detailing. They are fun to play with, but sometimes a person has to use their imagination to visualize the vehicle a Technic set is supposed to resemble. An Advanced Model is an accurate, smaller-scale replica of a well-known building, landmark, car, truck, boat, plane, creature, or whatever the geniuses at the LEGO Design Team can come up with, and is meant to have little playability.

Advanced Models have complicated building techniques

and higher MSRPs, and have some creative elements to it as well, such as the Modular Buildings sub-theme. Historically speaking, the Advanced Model theme is comprised of some earlier ones including the Sculptures theme and Large Scale Models. They all represent a similar type of set, but the Advanced Models nomenclature is used for our purposes.

While the addition of this theme might not have single-handedly catapulted LEGO into the top toymaker in the world, I believe that the Advanced Models of the past 15 years, starting with the 3450 Statue of Liberty, brought many LEGO fans back from their "Dark Ages" and back into the fold.

I believe LEGO was intuitive and had great foresight when they decided to up the complexity of their sets to cater to adult fans. These exclusive sets have become the backbone of collectors and resellers, producing stellar profits on the secondary market. Some of the current prices of these sets are extraordinary. The future for this theme is bright, as LEGO designers will never run out of ideas and fans will never get tired of buying these sets.

10196 GRAND CAROUSEL

▶ **Year Released: 2009**
▶ **No. of Pieces: 2,363**
▶ **Minifigures: 9**
▶ **Retail Price: $249.99**

As noted on the box, the 10196 Grand Carousel comes with Power Functions, which enables the carousel to spin under battery power.

In 2009, LEGO released the 10196 Grand Carousel to the world. Up until this time, there was nothing like it. With its 3,263 pieces, it is one of the largest LEGO sets ever released and one of the most intricate. It is a replica of the typical carousel that you see at many county fairs or amusement parks, and is a beautiful set. It is a wonderful combination of red, dark red, medium blue, white, tan, and gold bricks, giving it a unique appearance. Not only is it tastefully colorful, the set contains some unique pieces and building techniques that are utilized to create special carousel decorations and features, such as upside down golden beards that resemble fleur-de-lis and a cloth material that replicates the canvas roof of the carousel. Cool court jester heads are incorporated in the design as well, giving it a fun and classic feel.

The 10196 Grand Carousel is definitely a set designed for adult LEGO builders or experienced young builders. The build is straightforward, yet highly complicated, with multiple parts needing to be aligned properly for the whole structure to function correctly. There are multiple moving parts on this set, including the entire carousel structure, which spins round and round, and each of the carousel's horses/cars/seats rotating up and down with each revolution of the main structure. The whole carousel is operated and moved by LEGO's Power Functions motor and battery pack. Many frustrated builders have partially assembled this set, only to pack it up in the box to store it in a closet or resell it on eBay or another auction site. For those fans who have the wherewithal to complete it, they are treated to a special set that exhibits wonderful display attributes and a playability that is not often found on large Advanced Model sets. Two other important features are that it contains nine

minifigures, which is a nice bonus on any set, and it comes with a LEGO "sound brick" that creates a recognizable carousel-like melody, which is also unique to this set.

Value wise, this set proverbially spins circles around most other ones; current value exceeds $2,200 and seems to be accelerating. The 10196 Grand Carousel is grand, indeed, appreciating over 800 percent from the MSRP. Even though many have complained of the difficult build and fragile nature, collectors are still flocking to this set in droves. One possible reason could be the release of the 10244 Fairground Mixer in early 2014. The 10244 Fairground Mixer is a technically creative set that replicates a county fair "Mixer" or "Scrambler" ride. It is the first of a rumored new theme of amusement park ride models being discussed on various LEGO forums. A new large Ferris Wheel is being discussed at the time of this writing as well. If the rumors are true, many fans who are "completists" would most likely want to pay handsomely to acquire a fantastic set like 10196 Grand Carousel to complete the LEGO amusement park. If you have a 10196 Grand Carousel, consider yourself lucky. It is a rare set in MISB form and had a short production run of a little more than a year, which in LEGO circles is quite short. Even used values are five times the MSRP of $249.99.

$ ▶ **New: $2,278** ▶ **Used: $1,215**

The 10177 Dreamliner comes with a display base and specifications plaque that is similar to *Star Wars* UCS plaques.

10177 BOEING 787 DREAMLINER

▶ **Year Released: 2006**
▶ **No. of Pieces: 1,197**
▶ **Minifigures: 0**
▶ **Retail Price: $79.99**

Timing in life is everything, and this is no different with LEGO sets and their values on the secondary market. Take the 10177 Boeing 787 Dreamliner for instance. Released in 2006 with a production run of about a year and a half, the Dreamliner is an Advanced Model that looks like a *Star Wars* Ultimate Collector Series 7191 X-Wing Fighter model, mounted in flying position on a black stand with the traditional UCS specifications plaque. If this set was released today instead of eight years ago – basically before the LEGO secondary market blossomed – it is possible that this would have been one of the most popular investing sets to date.

Based on the real life, twin-engined, long range, mid-sized airliner created and launched by Boeing in 2007, the 10177 Boeing 787 Dreamliner is a 1,197-piece set that sold for $79.99 at retail.

This translates into less than $0.07 per brick on average, which in the LEGO world, is an excellent value. The most recent comparable set would be the 10226 Sopwith Camel that had a retail price of $99.99 and 883 pieces, far from the bargain of the 10177 Boeing. This set is highly desirable as a display piece for a den or office, and can be removed from the stand and actually flown around a room with a little help, giving it a WHOOOSH factor, which is always a bonus. The set is an accurate replica of the commercial jetliner and many collectors and resellers would salivate to get their hands on a similar set in today's market.

Current values are north of $500. For a set that retailed for less than a fifth of that, the growth has been quite strong. Any set with a Return on Investment of over 500 percent from retail is no slouch, but you have to wonder what kind of growth this set would see if it was released today, with new LEGO collectors and resellers out there looking for a highly collectible, cost effective and visually appealing set to build, play with, and display. Recently, the 10177 has plateaued in value. This sometimes happens with sets that have been retired for awhile, but they can also begin to appreciate again after a lull, so never write off any large set as an investment.

$ ▶ **New: $544** ▶ **Used: $243**

The 151-foot copper-clad beauty, the Statue of Liberty, that welcomed countless immigrants to this wonderful country was turned into a 33-inch LEGO Lady in 2000. At the time, the 3450 Statue of Liberty was the largest LEGO set ever created, coming in at 2,882 pieces, most green in color. Along with the other more intricate sets launched in 2000, such as the *Star Wars* Ultimate Collector Series 7181 Tie Defender and 7191 X-Wing Fighter, the 3450 Statue of Liberty illustrated The LEGO Group's new philosophy of designing and producing sets for the mature mind and wallet and signified a major upgrade in set complexity.

The 3450 Statue of Liberty is a "WOW!" set that usually requires an experienced builder to complete it. I have had the pleasure of building this set, and it is quite tedious and confusing to say the least. It is a vertical build, which many LEGO busts and character replicas usually are. A vertical build is when the instructions are viewed from the top down instead of the traditional side-angled perspective. What makes matters worse is that the vast majority of bricks are in the rare sea green color, thus causing mass confusion if even one piece is misaligned. You can be steps past your initial error and realize you have to tear it all apart and start again.

This set is not for children. It is also 100 percent display and 0 percent play, unless you consider the original construction "play," which some people do. It is one

SPOTLIGHT

3450 STATUE OF LIBERTY

▶ **Year Released: 2000**
▶ **No. of Pieces: 2,882**
▶ **Minifigures: 0**
▶ **Original Retail Price: \$198.99**

15

Putting *LADY LIBERTY* [on a Pedestal]

In the photo of the 3450 Statue of Liberty, you can see the basic model in sea green and the tan-colored base that the statue replica sits on. The tan brick creation is a 3,000+- piece MOC (My Own Creation) of the actual Statue of Liberty base or pedestal. This MOC was created several years ago by talented builders after fans and collectors complained about the set looking incomplete without a proper pedestal. I was lucky enough to acquire one at a reasonable price (\$500). They are currently selling for close to \$2,000 and that is without Lady Liberty herself! As you can see, not only standard LEGO sets appreciate, custom sets and creations do nicely in the secondary market as well.

The 3450 Statue of Liberty was sold with two different box configurations: one in full color and the other in black and white. This was not the only set of the time period that came with multiple box designs. The 10018 Ultimate Collector Series Darth Maul and the 10019 Ultimate Collector Series Rebel Blockade Runner also had boxes in color and black and white. It would appear that the earliest versions of these sets came with the black and white box, and colored versions were released in later production runs. There is no real difference in values of either box type as far as we can determine, but it is an interesting tidbit nonetheless.

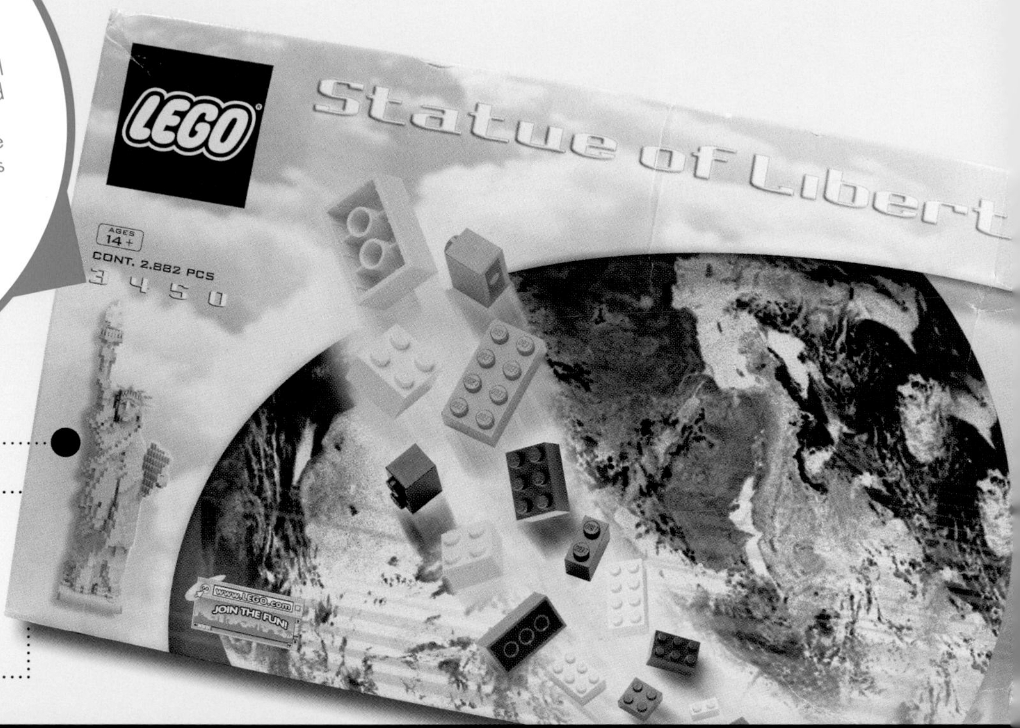

Finding a 3450 Statue of Liberty in MISB condition is truly rare and valuable.

of the finest LEGO sets in terms of display attributes that there is, so lack of playability is not a major negative concern for most people. Several points on the pieces themselves: they are on the smaller side, making the build process a lengthy one; the pieces are 99 percent sea green, which is a major bonus because of the rarity of bricks in that color, but for those people trying to "part out" this set and build it from a secondary LEGO source like eBay, it can be a very costly endeavor.

The 3450 Statue of Liberty listed for $199.99 MSRP back in 2000, a fair price for a set of this magnitude. The Price Per Piece ratio is under $0.07 a brick, so it is one of the most cost effective LEGO sets ever produced. Recent sold auctions for the 3450 Statue of Liberty on eBay have it passing the $1,800 mark for a new set; even the used values are in the $1,000 range. This set has appreciated over 800 percent from retail prices. That is quite impressive and because it is such a rare set, these prices probably will continue to climb. Highly collectible LEGO sets released early in the new Millennium were rarely "hoarded" by collectors or even the early resellers. A set like the 3450 Statue of Liberty was bought to be built in most cases and many of the current ones available for sale are previously built sets. A MISB 3450 Statue of Liberty is a rare animal, and those who have one should treasure it. It is one of the most iconic LEGO sets produced of all time and I still appreciate looking at it every day when I walk into my office. God Bless America!

$ ▶ New: $2,181 ▶ Used: $1,054

VW Beetle 1960 - Charlotte

Engine	:	4 cylinder Boxer, aircooled
Capacity	:	1192 ccm
Horsepower:		34 bhp at 3600 rpm
V-max	:	115 km/h
Length	:	4070 mm
Wheelbase	:	2400 mm
Weight	:	740 kg

10187 VOLKSWAGEN BEETLE

▶ **Year Released: 2008**
▶ **No. of Pieces: 1,626**
▶ **Minifigures: 0**
▶ **Retail Price: $119.99**

The 10187 Volkswagen Beetle's doors, trunk, and engine compartments all open and close.

For their 50th Anniversary celebration in 2008, LEGO gave fans a choice of which one of four classic cars they wanted turned into a LEGO model: Aston Martin DB5, Ford Mustang, Volkswagen Beetle, or Delorean. The Volkswagen Beetle won. Who can really argue about voting for the iconic Beetle? As ugly as it is, it is probably the one car that is known in every continent in the world and was honored by LEGO for this reason.

The 10187 Volkswagen Beetle is a large Advanced Model display set that does have some play qualities as well. Being that it is a replica of a car, the model does roll on real rubber tires and the trunk and doors of the car open to expose internal engine and interior pieces. As for the exterior features, the curves of the real life Volkswagen Beetle are made completely with ordinary LEGO bricks. There are no "special" bricks used to make the rounded hood, truck, and roof.

The 10187 Volkswagen Beetle has 1,626 pieces. The MSRP was $119.99, which makes it pretty

reasonable on the Price Per Piece scale. The current value is well over $700, with a Return on Investment of over 500 percent, which is exceptional in comparison to many other LEGO sets. Heck, it might be possible to buy an actual Volkswagen Beetle for less than $700. Used values for this set are in the $400 range, so that might be an option for some collectors.

Regardless of some small idiosyncrasies of the 10187 Volkswagen Beetle, the set is of high quality and displays and plays well, a nice feature for any Advanced Model.

$ ▶ **New: $763** ▶ **Used: $410**

10184 TOWN PLAN

- ▶ **Year Released:** 2008
- ▶ **No. of Pieces:** 1,981
- ▶ **Minifigures:** 8
- ▶ **Retail Price:** $149.99

In 2008, LEGO released the 10184 Town Plan that was promoted as an anniversary set to fans of the world. Here is what LEGO.com stated about the set:

Celebrate the 50th anniversary of the modern LEGO brick with this special-edition update of the classic Town Plan set! Completely redesigned with the best of modern bricks, details and design, the all-new Town Plan features a 1950s-style gas station with pumps, car wash and garage, a town hall with a newly-married couple, a movie theater with ticket booth, seats and posters, 2 automobiles, 8 minifigures, rare LEGO colors and elements, and more. Includes a letter from company owner Kjeld Kirk Kristiansen, who appeared as a kid on the original Town Plan box and returns on this one! Includes 3 gold bricks to celebrate the 50th anniversary of the LEGO brick!

What makes the 10184 Town Plan so special is it has almost 2,000 pieces, including three gold metallic bricks not found in any other set; the eight minifigures are exclusive to the set; and rumor has it that it is a limited release

set, but only LEGO itself truly knows the actual production numbers. In addition to the special bricks and minifigures, also included is a letter from company owner Kjeld Kirk Kristiansen commemorating the 50th anniversary of the LEGO brick. Besides the 10179 Millennium Falcon, this is the only set I know of that has any sort of special letter or document inside from LEGO or its owner. The 10184 Town Plan is one of the most highly rated sets by AFOLs and offers a quality design and building experience. LEGO fans love sets that display and play well, and this set does not disappoint on any level.

But all is not perfect. Where this set does disappoint is in the appreciation and growth department. Current values have hovered around $400 for some time. With the original MSRP priced at $149.99, the current $400 value is acceptable, but certainly not stellar in any way considering the special nature of the 10184 Town Plan. Maybe this is an opportunity for some savvy collectors to look at an older set as an investment option. Comparing the value of the 10184 Town Plan to other similar Advanced and Large Scale Models makes me think that there could be room for this set to appreciate in the future. Maybe if more fans learn of the unique qualities of this set, there would be a higher demand for it, thus higher secondary LEGO market values.

$ ▶ **New: $394** ▶ **Used: $255**

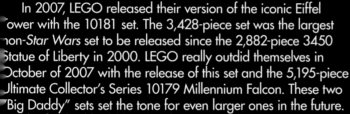

In 2007, LEGO released their version of the iconic Eiffel Tower with the 10181 set. The 3,428-piece set was the largest non-*Star Wars* set to be released since the 2,882-piece 3450 Statue of Liberty in 2000. LEGO really outdid themselves in October of 2007 with the release of this set and the 5,195-piece Ultimate Collector's Series 10179 Millennium Falcon. These two "Big Daddy" sets set the tone for even larger ones in the future.

The finished build height of 42 inches makes the 10181 Eiffel Tower the tallest of all LEGO sets, almost hitting four feet! As a display set, it is wonderful and maybe one of the most impressive models ever sold to the masses. Words cannot describe this model when seen in person. It is definitely a WOW set. The base is made up of four 32-inch x 32-inch stud LEGO baseplates, which in itself is huge for any LEGO model. Also, it is quite fragile and must be kept out of the reach of children and pets, as it would be quite difficult to rebuild if it was accidentally knocked over.

Speaking of children, this set was not designed for them. Period. The building techniques utilized are highly advanced and repetitive. The 3,000-plus pieces are mostly dark bluish gray, which makes assembly a difficult proposition for those with limited patience. The set is broken down into three main sections: the base, which includes the four leg sections and first level restaurant section; a mid section, which includes the secondary viewing platform; and the upper section is the long and narrow structure, which includes the upper viewing platform and the state-of-the-art telecommunications apparatuses. The upper section also includes a nice replica of the French flag. Advanced builders with the fortitude to complete the set are rewarded with a grand and majestic display piece that is the focal point of any room it is in.

The 10181 Eiffel Tower is not highly "hoarded" by resellers and collectors, and many of the current sets in existence were bought by individual fans, thus making the set somewhat rare. This could be one of the reasons why it has reached such stratospheric values, nearing the $1,800 level as of this writing. That is almost an 800 percent Return on Investment from the original retail price of $199.99, which is incredible, or, as the French would say, INCROYABLE! Few LEGO sets of such size and stature have appreciated to such levels.

▶ **New: $1,742** ▶ **Used: $681**

SPOTLIGHT

10181
EIFFEL
TOWER

▶ **Year Released: 2007**
▶ **No. of Pieces: 3,428**
▶ **Minifigures: 0**
▶ **Original Retail**
   Price: $199.99

The finished 10181 Eiffel Tower is 42 inches tall, making it the tallest LEGO set to date.

10213/10231 SHUTTLE ADVENTURE/EXPEDITION

▶ **Year Released:** 2010
▶ **No. of Pieces:** 1,204
▶ **Minifigures:** 3
▶ **Retail Price:** $99.99

In the early 1980s, the National Aeronautics and Space Administration developed a low Earth orbit, partially reusable spacecraft known as the Space Shuttle. The Space Shuttle fleet was used to launch numerous satellites, space probes, and even the Hubble Telescope over the 135 missions flown from 1981 to 2011.

In 2010, LEGO honored the Space Shuttle with the creation of the 10213 Shuttle Adventure, which is an accurate version of the real life shuttle. It is not an officially licensed NASA set, so markings on the model and the box are rather generic and not exactly like the real life Space Shuttle. Nonetheless, the 10213 Shuttle Adventure is well done. With 1,204 pieces, it is a playable, large display set, which is rather unique in the Advanced Models theme. It has a high WHOOOSH Factor and displays well in a bedroom or den. Although it is a well-made set, LEGO chose to revise it in 2011 and created the 1,230-piece 10231 Shuttle Expedition. LEGO designers tweaked the 10213 Shuttle Adventure set by making small changes to the engine, landing gear, main fuel tank, and satellite/Canada arm, and renaming the set. The changes were made to help improve small design flaws of the original set.

The growth of these two Shuttle sets is quite remarkable. You would think that the original 10213 Shuttle Adventure would have performed better than the replacement 10231 Shuttle Expedition for several reasons: It is the older set that was retired sooner and replaced with a newer set; the original Shuttle had a short production run of a year, which in the world of the LEGO secondary market, is rather short. The 10231 Shuttle Expedition had a longer production run, about a year and a half. Usually in the LEGO

The external fuel tank and rocket boosters detach from the main shuttle and the landing gear and shuttle bay doors are functional, giving the set(s) a multitude of play options.

secondary world, similar sets that are rarer and have been retired earlier are valued higher than the other sets it's compared to, but in this case, the newer Shuttle version is currently more valuable by around 20 percent. Maybe it was the arguable improvements that LEGO implemented that have proven to be the reason for the higher values of the 10231 model. Maybe the changes to the 10213 Shuttle Adventure brought added attention to the newer version, opening the eyes of LEGO investors and collectors. Whatever the reasons, both sets, which were $99.99 at retail, are approaching the $300 mark after a short time in retirement, illustrating that large Advanced Models that can fly around a room can also fly into the Stratosphere in both the real world and LEGO secondary market.

$ ▶ **New: $229** ▶ **Used: $143**

10155 MAERSK CONTAINER SHIP

▶ **Year Released:** 2010
▶ **No. of Pieces:** 990
▶ **Minifigures:** 0
▶ **Retail Price:** $119.99

Since the 1970s, The LEGO Group has had a partnership with a fellow Danish company, the Maersk Group, which specializes in many types of transportation and energy-related fields. LEGO has produced many Maersk-related sets over the years, and each is in the classic Maersk light blue color; most also have limited production runs, making them somewhat more rare and valuable than the typical set.

The 10155 Maersk Container Ship is a remake of the 10152 Maersk Sealand Container Ship from 2004. They were both promotional releases. From a build standpoint, the 10155 Maersk Container Ship is 990 pieces, and as noted, many are light blue, a color somewhat rare in nature, making them slightly more valuable than some traditional brick-colored bricks. Overall, the set design and build is somewhat basic and not overly impressive for an Advanced Model, in my opinion. The ship really does not look to scale and compared to the newer 10241 Maersk Line Triple E set, it looks

The special "Maersk" light blue bricks are rare and valuable to custom LEGO builders.

rather rudimentary.

The Maersk sets limited production runs usually helps increase appreciation and values after retirement. The set has shown solid growth over the past couple of years, more than doubling its original MSRP of $119.99. These Maersk sets seem to require a certain type of collector to take an interest in them. This lack of interest affects the long-term growth and reduces the overall values. While the 10155 is not a poor performer, it certainly hasn't performed as well as other large Advanced Model sets.

$ ▶ **New: $257** ▶ **Used: $146**

DESIGN IMPROVEMENTS

The Maersk LEGO sets have definitely stepped up their complexity and overall design quality over the past few years. Starting with the 10219 Maersk Train in 2011 and, more significantly, the 10241 Maersk Line Triple E in 2014, these sets are much more accurate in appearance and sought after by LEGO collectors. The 10241 Maersk Triple E, in particular, is an excellent rendition of the real life overseas container ship. The set is labeled for "expert" builders and has over 1,500 pieces. The 10241 Maersk Triple E has what looks to be the specifications plaque from an Ultimate Collector's Series set, which is a wonderful finishing touch and makes for a professional display in any office or den.

▶ **The 10241 Maersk Line Triple E has a design improvement over the earlier Maersk models and is more popular with collectors.**

MAERSK LINE

10189
TAJ MAHAL

- ▶ Year Released: 2008
- ▶ No. of Pieces: 5,922
- ▶ Minifigures: 0
- ▶ Original Retail
  Price: $299.99

The "Big Daddy" of the LEGO Universe, the 10189 Taj Mahal, is the largest set ever produced, with 5,922 pieces. The set is the LEGO replica of the white marble mausoleum located in Agra, Uttar Pradesh, India.

While it might not be the tallest set (10181 Eiffel Tower) or the heaviest set (Ultimate Collectors Series 10179 Millennium Falcon), the 10189 Taj Mahal spells "BIG" nonetheless. The vast majority of the pieces are on the smaller side, and white, which makes for long and repetitive building sessions.

The basic structure is broken down into six large sections and put together like a large Modular building. Being that it is an Advanced Model, advanced building techniques are used. One such technique is SNOT (Studs Not On Top) and this is used creatively on the center dome structure of the model. It is actually quite sturdy for such a decorative finishing touch, but it completes the model appropriately. The 10189 Taj Mahal will take most experienced LEGO builders at least 20 hours to complete. The internal plastic baggies that store the pieces from the factory are not numbered like newer set versions, so much of the time constructing this model is wasted on sorting and locating bricks, which is probably the most "unfun" part of any assembly project.

LEGO designers did a fabulous job of adding details to the Taj Mahal by utilizing many common brick types in repeating patterns.

The 10189 Taj Mahal makes a wonderful display. The finished product is quite detailed, with an assortment of ornate pieces that cover the entire structure. It is definitely a set for more advanced builders, but it is not as difficult as some Technic sets or other Advanced Models, like the 10181 Eiffel Tower. This set needs some space to spread out, with six 16-inch x 32-inch stud baseplates making up the foundation of the set. As for playability, there really isn't any besides the original build, and like many of the Advanced Models, there are no minifigures. It was designed to sit on a desk or shelf and look pretty sitting there ... and that it does with undeniable flair and panache.

The 10189 Taj Mahal not only is a grand set in person, it is worth several "grand" on the LEGO secondary market, reaching the $2,000 level

recently. It is only the second LEGO set to surpass the $2,000 level, appreciating over 500 percent from its MSRP of $299 in 2008. The set is continuing to appreciate at a steady clip, raising about 20 percent in the past year alone. That is quite an incredible feat for a LEGO set that has been retired for over four years. Most sets will show most of their gains in the first two to three years after retirement, yet the 10189 Taj Mahal is still exhibiting strong growth on the LEGO secondary market. As with the 10181 Eiffel Tower, this set was not highly hoarded and MISB sets are quite rare. Many of these sets have been opened and built, but a quality used 10189 Taj Mahal still sells for over $1,000. Either way, if you can acquire one of these sets, consider yourself fortunate.

$ ▶ **New: $2,394** ▶ **Used: $965**

10226/3451
SOPWITH CAMEL

▶ **Year Released:** 2012
▶ **No. of Pieces:** 883
▶ **Minifigures:** 0
▶ **Retail Price:** $99.99

Most everyone knows the legendary Sopwith Camel from Charles M. Shulz's classic comic, *Peanuts*. Snoopy would pretend to be a famous World War I fighter pilot and fight the infamous Red Baron in his Sopwith Camel (in actuality, his doghouse).

In real life, the Sopwith Camel is a British single-seat biplane fighter that had a powerful rotary engine, twin synchronized machine guns, and a short and highly maneuverable fuselage. These features helped it shoot down over 1,200 enemy fighters in World War I, more than any other fighter of the time. Because of this illustrious history, LEGO honored the Sopwith Camel by producing three models after it: the 3451 Sopwith Camel in 2001, the 10226 Sopwith

Camel in 2012, and the 40049, a promotional polybag that was released in 2012 with 65 pieces for $4.99.

The 3451 and 10226 sets come with 574 and 883 pieces respectively. The 3451 Sopwith Camel cost $49.99 at MSRP, and the 10226 cost $99.99. From a build standpoint, the 10226 Sopwith Camel is light years ahead of the older 3451 version. Being almost double the piece count, the 10226 is almost double the size. The detail is nicely done, and creative moving parts were added to the newer version including a rotating propeller and engine cylinders, hinged tail rudder, functioning wing ailerons and tail flaps that can

Features include a rotating propeller, hinged tail rudder, and tail flaps that can be controlled from the cockpit.

be controlled from the cockpit. This version also contains some rare dark green, tan, and silver bricks. The original 3451 Sopwith Camel has much less detail and moving parts and is more of a display piece. Both are attractive models and do have some WHOOOSH factor that gives it playability, especially the 10026 set. The difficulty of the builds are rather high, in particular the 10226, due to the fact that there are belts and strings incorporated in the design.

Current values of the MISB 3451 Sopwith Camel sets sold on eBay are around $170, giving it a Return on Investment of well over 200 percent. This is not bad, but considering the set has been on the LEGO secondary market for almost 14 years, it is nothing special, either. I think the 10226 Sopwith Camel has much more potential. As of this writing, it has not been officially retired by LEGO, but has been unavailable for purchase at MSRP by primary retail stores since about October of 2014. Nevertheless, even without the "retired" designation, the 10226 Sopwith Camel has shot up past $150 on the secondary market in a couple of months. This often happens with recently soon-to-be-retired LEGO sets. The 10226 has all the qualities of a set that will appreciate exceptionally well, so if you have the chance to pick one up at a reasonable price, it might pay off handsomely in the future.

The 10226 Sopwith Camel is a remake of the 3451 Sopwith Camel that was released in 2001.

$ ▶ **New: $164** ▶ **Used: $70**

The 10182 Cafe Corner was the first Modular Building released and is the most valuable.

10182 CAFE CORNER

▶ **Year Released:** 2007
▶ **No. of Pieces:** 2056
▶ **Minifigures:** 3
▶ **Retail Price:** $139.99

The 10182 Cafe Corner, released in 2007, is the first Modular Building, and also the most valuable of all the current ones. It set the standard for all of the Modular Buildings to follow. With its dark red roof and yellow and white awnings, the 10182 Cafe Corner is a real looker. The set came with three minifigures and contains three floors, which is a common trait of all of the Modular Buildings. A neat feature of the different floors is that they are removable, giving builders access to the interior components of the set. The 10182 Cafe Corner has few internal decorations to speak of, but later Modular Buildings have furniture, counters, and various adornments.

The 10182 Cafe Corner is currently reaching the $1,700 range. That is really amazing because the original MSRP was only $139.99, giving it over a 1,100 percent Return on Investment to date. What makes this set even more incredible is that it was released before LEGO investing and reselling became as

MODULAR BUILDINGS

Out of all the themes and subthemes produced over the past 15 years for advanced builders and adult tastes and pocketbooks, the *Star Wars* UCS sets are probably the most well known and heavily invested in. But a close second, in my opinion, are the sets in the Modular Buildings subtheme, currently made up of the eleven featured here.

This subtheme was developed after fans took a survey in 2006 and requested that LEGO produce more city and regular town buildings, structures with more architectural detail, buildings that are minifigure scale, etc.

From 2007 to present, the Modular Buildings subtheme has won over the hearts and minds of fans throughout the world. LEGO was intuitive in their design of these sets. Not only are they complete buildings in that they have floors, four walls and a roof, but they attach to one another with mating Technic pieces, so builders can connect multiple Modular Buildings together and create a city street.

Unlike many other sets that stand alone, the Modular Buildings look better together, all lined up in a row. This entices collectors to want to buy multiple Modular Buildings to complete a city block. This desire to have a complete set has driven up the values of some of the original Modular Buildings to astronomical numbers. As of this writing, the handful of Modular Buildings that have been officially retired or are sold out and close to retiring have increased dramatically in value.

widespread as it is today. Many resellers did not get a chance to hoard this set, so many collectors want the corner Modular to complete their city street and will pay top dollar to do so. The set has been a slow uptick in values for a long time. Where it will stop and plateau is anyone's guess, but it is my belief that with each new Modular Building that is released, the 10182 becomes more wanted, and valuable.

$ ▶ **New: $1,671** ▶ **Used: $736**

10190 MARKET STREET

- ▶ **Year Released:** 2007
- ▶ **No. of Pieces:** 1,248
- ▶ **Minifigures:** 3
- ▶ **Retail Price:** $89.99

The 10190 Market Street, also released in 2007, was designed by Adult Fan of LEGO Eric Brok as part of the LEGO Design by Me program. The program ended in 2011, but LEGO produced eight AFOL designs, besides this one: 5524 Airport; 5525 Amusement Park; 5526 Skyline; 10183 Hobby Train; 10191 Star Justice; 10192 Space Skulls; and 10200 Custom Car Garage.

Although part of the Factory theme, many consider the 10190 Market Street a Modular Building.

The 10190 Market Street lacks, from a design and build standpoint, but it was designed by a non-LEGO designer, so I can understand the shortcomings. It's a rather odd-looking building,

but many enjoy the Victorian and/or eclectic style. Also, the fact that Brok is from the Netherlands helps explain the taste in building style. By itself, it looks OK in my eyes, yet once added to the other Modular Buildings, it kind of looks out of scale or incomplete. The set only has 1,248 pieces, making it the smallest Modular Building by far. While the aesthetics can be debated, the Return on Investment on this set cannot. It is STELLAR, with over 1,600 percent in real terms: The current value is in the $1,500 range, but the original MSRP was only $89.99, making the 10190 Market Street one of the best LEGO investments of all time, if not *the* best. I consider myself lucky having one because of the rarity.

$ ▶ **New: $1,562** ▶ **Used: $666**

The sand green bricks of the 10185 Green Grocer are the color of money and are valuable.

10185 GREEN GROCER

- ▶ **Year Released:** 2008
- ▶ **No. of Pieces:** 2,352
- ▶ **Minifigures:** 4
- ▶ **Retail Price:** $149.99

The 10185 Green Grocer is the third Modular Building created. Unlike the first two sets, it has internal details, which include items such as a refrigerator, radiator, and Grandfather clock, in addition to food items and shelves. From an appearance perspective, the 10185 is one beautiful LEGO set, made up of sea green, tan, and gray bricks. The classic Brownstone architecture and internal window curtains are a pleasing combination of stylish elements that work

10197 FIRE BRIGADE

▶ **Year Released: 2009**
▶ **No. of Pieces: 2,231**
▶ **Minifigures: 4**
▶ **Retail Price: $149.99**

Starting around the time the 10197 Fire Brigade was released, the LEGO secondary market was just starting to hum, and set prices were starting to explode enough for me to notice and begin discussing the possible creation of an online LEGO price guide and investing forum. No other LEGO set of the time was more

highly collected than the 10197 Fire Brigade. It is an outstanding looking set, with some great playability features not found on previous Modular Buildings. Based on a 1930s fire station, the set also includes a replica of a 1930s fire truck and some nice interior details that give some play options.

> The 1932 address number on the front of the 10197 Fire Brigade represents the year that LEGO was founded.

The 2,231-piece set does a nice job honoring the fire stations of old, with its brick fascia and golden trim pieces, and really stands out when placed next to other Modular Buildings, with its dark red bricks and American flag. The set had a four-year production run, from 2009 to 2013, which is quite a long time for a LEGO set. It has been retired for a year and has basically doubled in value from the original MSRP of $149.99 to the $300 range currently. The growth has been solid and steady. I am curious to see how quickly (or not) the 10197 Fire Brigade appreciates, with so many sets being in storage units and investor's closets. This could dictate the future of how other Modular Buildings are stockpiled by resellers and investors.

$ ▶ **New: $298** ▶ **Used: $248**

well together. Unlike the haphazard 10190 Market Street and garish 10182 Cafe Corner, the 10185 is considered the most attractive Modular Building by many collectors.

The build is straightforward and fun, and geared toward adult builders, but some talented young builders can complete this set with a little effort. Value wise, the 10185 Green Grocer is worth a lot of "green," hitting the $800 level recently and exhibiting over 400 percent Return on Investment. While not exactly at the levels of the 10182 or 10190, it certainly is no slouch. I think the 10185 Green Grocer will suffer slightly from reseller "hoarding," unlike the first two sets.

$ ▶ **New: $905** ▶ **Used: $631**

CLOSE-UP

Creative use of bricks helps create the Shop sign of the 10211 Grand Emporium.

10211 GRAND EMPORIUM

▶ **Year Released:** 2010
▶ **No. of Pieces:** 2,182
▶ **Minifigures:** 7
▶ **Retail Price:** $149.99

The 10211 Grand Emporium is in LEGO limbo as of this writing — it is neither available for MSRP from primary retailers, nor has it been officially retired by LEGO. Until there is official notification, sometimes the values of semi-retired sets take a while to increase on the secondary market. Current values for this set are over $200, but look for the price to climb quickly after official retirement notification. As with the 10197 Fire Brigade, this set was highly stockpiled by investors and resellers, so only time will tell how high this set will appreciate.

At almost 2,200 pieces, it is a stunning and tastefully done corner Modular Building. It is quite large and comes with seven minifigures, a few which are used as window displays in the store. There are also other interior store displays and touches that finish off the set very well.

$ ▶ **New: $200+** ▶ **Used: $183**

The 10218 Pet Shop breaks into two separate buildings.

10218 PET SHOP

▶ **Year Released:** 2011
▶ **No. of Pieces:** 2,032
▶ **Minifigures:** 4
▶ **Retail Price:** $149.99

As of this writing, the 10218 Pet Shop is not retired and is still available at retail for $149.99. Released in May 2011, it is a 2,032-piece replica of a mom and pop pet store and makes for a quality inner "filler" Modular Building, which means that it is rather plain and unobtrusive, but every city street or block needs some regular filler buildings to make it look realistic. As with the other Modular Buildings, the 10218 Pet Shop will probably be a smart purchase and increase in value after it retires.

$ ▶ **New: $168** ▶ **Used: $132**

10224 TOWN HALL

▶ Year Released: 2012
▶ No. of Pieces: 2,766
▶ Minifigures: 8
▶ Retail Price: $199.99

The 1891 on the front of the 10224 Town Hall represents the birth year of the founder of LEGO.

This is the seventh Modular Building to be released in order, yet it appears to be the sixth Modular Building to be retired and is no longer available at retail. The set was released in March 2012 and while it has not received the official retired tag from LEGO as of January 2015, on the surface, it would appear to be retired. This would mean the set retired before the 10218 Pet Shop, released a year earlier. Now, it doesn't seem like a big deal to most LEGO fans, but in the world of collecting, investing, and reselling, it *is* a big deal. Most LEGO sets are "first released, first retired." The 10224 Town Hall bucked this trend and disappeared from the LEGO brick and mortar shelves months before a similar set that was released before it. This early retirement is a positive occurrence for those lucky people who acquired one or multiple 10224 Town Halls.

The set is the largest of the Modular Buildings, with over 2,700 pieces. It is an attractive brick red/orange/ brown color, with traditional Greek and Roman columns and finials. It is the centerpiece of any city street. It is also the most expensive at $199.99 retail. It also has eight minifigures, the most of any Modular Building. It is the Big Daddy of LEGO Modular Buildings, and with that, there are big expectations, especially when a set of this stature retires early. The early retirement is important because there is less of a set produced, and stockpiled. Rare means money in any collectible hobby, and the 10224 might be more rare than most. Secondly, the set might be less "hoarded" by LEGO investors and resellers, which could help later increase values in the secondary market cycle. There is a possibility that the 10224 Town Hall can reach levels of the earlier Modular Buildings because of the early retirement.

BUILDING TECHNIQUES

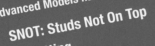

Advanced Models have these basic advanced building techniques:

- SNOT: Studs Not On Top
- Offsetting
- Letterings
- Diagonal Striping
- Micro-Striping
- SNIR: Studs Not In Row
- Mixed Cylinder Curving

While not really important to LEGO secondary market values, if these terms are mentioned within a discussion of a particular set, you can assume that the LEGO set was designed for the experienced LEGO builders of the world and that less experienced builders or children should avoid these sets if possible. These techniques require patience and a delicate touch.

$ ▶ New: $323 ▶ Used: $205

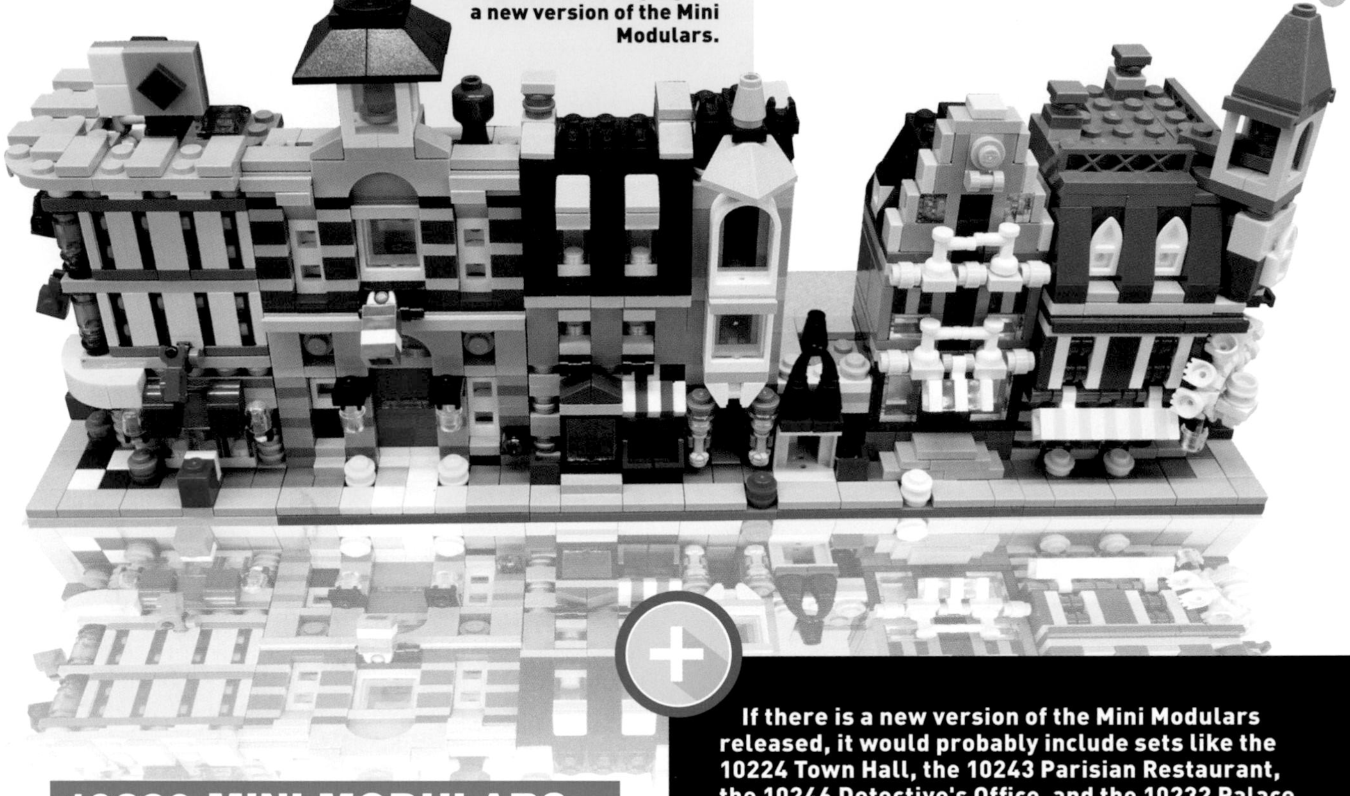

Because there have been new and different regular scale Modulars released since the 10230 Mini Modulars, collectors are hoping for a new version of the Mini Modulars.

If there is a new version of the Mini Modulars released, it would probably include sets like the 10224 Town Hall, the 10243 Parisian Restaurant, the 10246 Detective's Office, and the 10232 Palace Cinema. Values of the 10230 Mini Modulars would then skyrocket because LEGO collectors would want to pair the two together.

10230 MINI MODULARS

▶ Year Released: 2012
▶ No. of Pieces: 1,355
▶ Minifigures: 0
▶ Retail Price: $79.99

Jamie Berard, the LEGO designer of the 10182 Cafe Corner, 10185 Green Grocer, and 10197 Fire Brigade, to name a few, was playing around one day and created a mini version of one of his Modular Buildings. Thus, the 10230 Mini Modulars were born.

The 10230 Mini Modulars is a quarter-scale replica of the 10182 Cafe Corner, 10185 Green Grocer, 10190 Market Street, 10197 Fire Brigade, and the 10211 Grand Emporium. Made up of 1,355 pieces, the set sold for $79.99 at retail. The 10230 was a LEGO VIP Shop at Home exclusive for most of its retail life, making it somewhat exclusive. It eventually became available at more retailers right before being retired in December 2013.

It is a well done set, accurate, and cute. When a LEGO set gets a mini version, it is usually a great honor, and the 10230 Mini Modulars does a fantastic job honoring the larger sets. Investment wise, it has almost doubled in value since its retirement, making it a strong performer. I'm looking forward to the next version that mimics the rest of the current Modular Buildings.

$ ▶ New: $143 ▶ Used: $105

Each Mini Modular can be separated from the others.

▲ The 10230 Mini Modulars consist of miniature versions of the 10211 Grand Emporium, the 10197 Fire Brigade, the 10185 Green Grocer, the 10190 Market Street, and the 10182 Cafe Corner (from left on the front box cover).

MICRO MODULARS

LEGO did not stop at "Mini" Modulars. In October of 2014, in celebration of Toys R Us' Bricktober month-long event, LEGO released four "Micro" Modulars. They consisted of:

- 40180 Bricktober Theater
- 40181 Bricktober Pizza Place
- 40182 Bricktober Fire Station
- 40183 Bricktober Town Hall

While they are called Modulars, they are not replicas of any existing sets. They are completely new creations, designed for the Toys R Us October LEGO event. These sets are even smaller and simpler in scale than 10230 Mini Modulars. Due to the popularity of the full-sized Modular Buildings, these Micro Modulars will probably appreciate well. They were exclusive to Toys R Us with purchases above a certain dollar amount, so they should be rather rare, and collectible

Modulars that are Unretired and Still Available at Retail

Besides the 10218 Pet Shop, there are three other Modular Buildings that are still available at retail: The 10232 Palace Cinema, the 10243 Parisian Restaurant, and the 10246 Detective's Office. Here is a brief breakdown of each:

10243 PARISIAN RESTAURANT

▶ 2,419 pieces
▶ $159.99 MSRP

▶ Released in January 2014
▶ Replica of a romantic restaurant you would find on the streets of Paris
▶ BEAU!!! That's "beautiful" in French. Gorgeous set.
▶ Highly detailed. Looks best by itself. Too pretty to place next to another Modular
▶ Strong growth after retirement is expected

10232 PALACE CINEMA

▶ 2,196 pieces
▶ $149.99 MSRP

▶ Released in March 2013
▶ Reminiscent of Grauman's Chinese Theater
▶ Highly stylish, only two floors, includes a vehicle
▶ Interior details replicate a movie theater
▶ Strong growth after retirement expected

10246 DETECTIVE'S OFFICE

▶ 2,261 pieces
▶ $159.99 MSRP

▶ Released in January 2015
▶ Modeled after an old-school pool hall, barbershop, and office building
▶ Two separate buildings, one contains the pool hall and detective's office, while the other has a barbershop (Al's) and some extra rooms
▶ Detailed with some nice touches such as an antique mirror and window graphics
▶ Once again, another potential investment winner after retirement

CHAPTER 2

ARCHITECTURE

SETS IN THIS THEME ARE HIGHLY COLLECTIBLE AND OBTAINABLE, ENABLING MANY LEGO COLLECTORS, RESELLERS, AND INVESTORS ON A BUDGET THE ABILITY TO GET INVOLVED IN THE HOBBY WITHOUT BREAKING THE BANK. OF THE SETS THAT HAVE RETIRED, ALL HAVE APPRECIATED WELL.

In the early days of LEGO, there were little variations in bricks, such as slopes, round pieces, and plates. But in the 1960s, the "plate" brick was created and enabled fans to build scale models of buildings and structures with more accuracy, thus helping in the creation of the vintage "Scale Model Series," which were sets and models based on fans' dream houses. This gave many young architects and designers the tools to let their imagination go wild. One of these "LEGO inspired" architects was Adam Reed Tucker. Mr. Tucker used bricks to replicate some iconic buildings, like New York City's Empire State Building. LEGO designers realized that small-scale models of famous world landmarks and buildings could be reproduced in bricks with amazing accuracy. In 2008, LEGO, in conjunction with Tucker, released replicas of the Sears Tower and John Hancock Center of Chicago, which was the start of the current

These sets are quite different than traditional ones. The boxes are designed in a classy black finish, with gray and white accents, and not bold and bright colors of conventional boxes. The instruction manuals are also of higher quality and produced to look like a spined book, instead of a pamphlet.

Since Architecture sets are small-scale models, many are low in piece count and size, designed for adult tastes, and adorn a desk or shelf with elegance and style.

Of the more than 20 sets produced at this writing, only a handful have been marked as retired by LEGO. The sets that have retired have appreciated very well, showing a solid Return on Investment. The majority of the Architecture sets are relatively low price wise, with most under $50. There are a few larger Architecture sets in the $100 to $200 range, but that is the high end of the theme. If you are looking for something classic and a bit unconventional to build or save,

21021 MARINA BAY SANDS

▶ **Year Released: 2013**
▶ **No. of Pieces: 602**
▶ **Minifigures: 0**
▶ **Original Retail Price: $75**

The 21021 Marina Bay Sands is a replica of the gorgeous resort and casino that sits on Marina Bay in Singapore and is over 600 feet tall and has parks, pools, and gardens on top of the structure. It really is quite exquisite. The LEGO set is exquisite as well ... at least the growth so far. The 21021 Marina Bay Sands is not even retired as of yet and the current value has just reached $500 on the LEGO secondary market. This 602-piece set sold for approximately $75, which is over 600 percent Return on Investment. I say approximately because this set was never sold through conventional LEGO retailers in the United States, Great Britain, Europe, or Australia, so money conversion is approximate. Regardless, that kind of return is incredible for a set that is not retired.

This set was only sold in Singapore and surrounding areas in Asia, but mainly was available in one of the Marina Bay Sands gift shops. In addition to the rarity of this set, it was also marked as a "Limited Edition" on the box by LEGO itself, making it even more exclusive and valuable. Future growth is questionable, considering the number of pieces and it has already seen tremendous appreciation, but you never know what a particular collector will pay for such a rare set.

$ ▶ **New: $536** ▶ **Used: $299**

As the icon on the front of the 21021 Marina Bay Sands box indicates, this is a "Limited Edition" set and thus, more valuable.

The back of the 21021 Marina Bay Sands box has a photo of the spectacular real life structure and points of interest.

21001 JOHN HANCOCK CENTER

▶ **Year Released: 2008**
▶ **No. of Pieces: 69**
▶ **Minifigures: 0**
▶ **Original Retail Price: $19.99**

The 21001 John Hancock Center was one of the original Architecture sets released in 2008. The set is a replica of the 100-story, 1,500-plus-foot John Hancock Center in Chicago, IL. The John Hancock Center is a black building with white antennae and trim. In LEGO form, the set consists of 69 pieces, mostly black. As with any Architecture set, the set includes the stylish box and instruction manual. This is one underwhelming LEGO model, honestly, but the performance of the 21001 John Hancock Center since its retirement in 2011 is quite dramatic. The current value on the LEGO secondary market is slightly over $100, which is five times the MSRP of $19.99. That is quite an impressive increase, and those savvy collectors and investors who acquired multiples of this set years ago have benefitted greatly. This set is a great example of a low-cost LEGO set that is perfect for investors on a tight budget.

$ ▶ **New: $114** ▶ **Used: $60**

21000 SEARS/ WILLIS TOWER

▶ **Year Released: 2008**
▶ **No. of Pieces: 69**
▶ **Minifigures: 0**
▶ **Original Retail Price: $19.99**

The 21000 Sears/Willis Tower are two identical sets with different names, but the same LEGO set number. Halfway through the production of the set, the real building was sold and the name changed from the Sears Tower to the Willis Tower. The 21000 Sears Tower production run was from 2008-2011; the 21000 Willis Tower production run was from 2011-2013. The Sears/ Willis Tower is another Chicago skyscraper, standing over 1,700 feet to the tip of the antenna towers. The set itself is basic and black, with some white accents. Performance of the 21000 Sears Tower has been solid, almost tripling in value. The newer 21000 Willis Tower has not performed as well, but it only retired about a year ago, so with time, stronger growth is possible.

$ ▶ **New: $59** ▶ **Used: $30**

21016 SUNGNYEMUN

- ▶ **Year Released:** 2012
- ▶ **No. of Pieces:** 325
- ▶ **Minifigures:** 0
- ▶ **Original Retail Price:** $34.99

21008 BURJ KHALIFA-DUBAI

- ▶ **Year Released:** 2011
- ▶ **No. of Pieces:** 208
- ▶ **Minifigures:** 0
- ▶ **Original Retail Price:** $24.99

The 21016 Sungnyemun is a 325-piece set that is a recreation of the Eight Gates in the Fortress Wall of Seoul, South Korea. Also known as the *Gate of Exalted Ceremonies* in English terms, this is a set that flew under the radar all the way to retirement. The 21016 Sungnyemun was available at retail for less than a year, resulting in a set that many LEGO collectors, investors, and resellers failed to buy. A rather attractive set, the 21016 Sungnyemun has quadrupled in value from its original $34.99 price tag. Current values are in the $150 range, but the price has seemed to level off recently. It has been retired for two years, so quite possibly it has hit its peak value and plateaued. Time will tell if "completist" investors who want to complete their Architecture collection will cause the prices to increase or if interest in the set will fade with newer and more creative sets being released.

The tallest and possibly the most beautiful skyscraper in the world, the Burj Khalifa was honored in June 2011 with a LEGO version, the 21008 Burj Khalifa-Dubai. The real version was built in Dubai, United Emirates, and rises over 2,700 feet into the atmosphere. It is an impressive piece of architecture and engineering. The 208-piece LEGO set is basically made up of 100 or so 1-inch x 1-inch light gray cylinders. Certainly not a creative build, but from a distance, the set does resemble the real thing. Current values have reached $50 on the LEGO secondary market and that is double the MSRP of $24.99, which is solid growth over the past year and a half. This is another indicator that Architecture sets are reasonably priced and are reasonable choices for LEGO investment.

$ ▶ **New: $146** ▶ **Used: $46**

$ ▶ **New: $53** ▶ **Used: $25**

What Architectural-themed discussion would be complete without the mention of arguably the most famous American architect of all time, Frank Lloyd Wright? LEGO honored the famous architect and interior designer with three LEGO sets: the 21004 Solomon Guggenheim Museum, the 21010 Robie House, and the 21005 Fallingwater.

Wright designed and/or built over 1,000 structures in his life, many of which are iconic in nature and "one with nature." Wright tried to design buildings that were in harmony with nature and mankind and he called it "organic architecture." Wright also was an author, penning over 20 books, and an educator as well.

Through the creative use of common bricks, LEGO designers were able to recreate the round architecture and the illusion of windows on the 21004 Solomon Guggenheim Museum.

21004 SOLOMON GUGGENHEIM MUSEUM

▶ Year Released: 2009
▶ No. of Pieces: 208
▶ Minifigures: 0
▶ Original Retail Price: $39.99

Also known as the "Guggenheim," the Solomon R. Guggenheim Museum is the well known modern and contemporary art museum in New York City. The LEGO replica was released in 2009, retired in 2013, and sold for $39.99 at retail. The set consists of 208 pieces and is currently selling for close to double MSRP on the LEGO secondary market.

$ ▶ New: $77 ▶ Used: $44

21010 ROBIE HOUSE

▶ **Year Released: 2011**
▶ **No. of Pieces: 2,276**
▶ **Minifigures: 0**
▶ **Original Retail Price: $199.99**

The Frederick C. Robie House was honored by LEGO in 2011 with the creation of the 2,276-piece 21010 Robie House set. The largest Architecture set to date, it is a small scale version of the United States National Historic Landmark, which celebrates the most famous version of a "prairie-style" home, which is the first architecture style that was considered an American original. The set listed for $199.99 at retail and current values are approaching $300 at a brisk pace. The largest set of any theme usually appreciates well and that seems to be true in this case also.

$ ▶ **New: $293** ▶ **Used: $235**

The 21010 Robie House is the largest Architecture set produced to date, with 2,276 pieces.

21005 FALLINGWATER

▶ **Year Released: 2009**
▶ **No. of Pieces: 811**
▶ **Minifigures: 0**
▶ **Original Retail Price: $99.99**

Often referred to as the most beautiful American home or structure by many in the architecture field, Fallingwater (or the Kaufmann Residence) was reproduced in LEGO bricks in 2009 and consists of 811 pieces. The set does a nice job of imitating the waterfall and stream that flows through the center of the structure. The real life Fallingwater is truly an amazing feat of engineering and a sight to see. The set is available at retail for $99.99 as of this writing, but retirement might be close, so keep an eye on this. It might be a solid investment and collection choice for LEGO Architecture fans.

$ ▶ **New: $118** ▶ **Used: $78**

CHAPTER 3

BATMAN

THIS LICENSED THEME BETWEEN THE LEGO GROUP AND DC COMICS HAS TURNED OUT TO BE A GREAT MOVE FOR COLLECTORS AS WELL, AS BATMAN SETS HAVE DEVELOPED INTO SOME OF THE BEST INVESTMENTS.

The Caped Crusader ... The Dark Knight ... Bruce Wayne ... Batman. Whatever you call him, he is arguably one of the most famous and popular Superheroes of all time. The Batman character was first seen in the DC Comics comic book, *Detective Comics #27*, in May of 1939.

Since then, there have been numerous versions of the character, from comics to TV to the big screen. Multiple famous actors have also had the privilege to play the Superhero, including George Clooney, Michael Keaton, Christian Bale, and most notably, Adam West, who starred in the 1960s campy TV version, *Batman*. There is a new *Batman* movie coming out in 2016, *Batman vs. Superman: Dawn of Justice*, which is a sequel to the 2013 movie, *Man of Steel*. It will star Ben Affleck as Batman and include other superheroes such as Superman and Wonder Woman. The new movie will only reinforce the current strong interest in the Batman franchise.

Several years ago, LEGO was smart enough to work a licensing agreement with DC Comics

IT'S A LEGO INVESTOR'S 'MUST HAVE' TYPE OF SET

to acquire the rights to the Batman franchise. This has worked out to be truly a wonderful arrangement for The LEGO Group and the franchise, as Batman LEGO sets have developed into some of the best investments and collectibles. It appears that almost any LEGO set with a Batman minifigure appreciates very well. It's a LEGO investor's "must have" type of set, along with the Modular Buildings, Ultimate Collector Series Star Wars sets, and large Creator and Advanced Model sets. From the smallest polybag to a large 1,000-piece set, anything related to Batman seems to appreciate well, some with record Return on Investment. With the new Batman movie, this trend will most likely continue.

Please note: Some of the Batman sets discussed here are actually from the LEGO Superheroes: DC Comics theme and are not in the "Batman" theme. But for simplicity and to illustrate the popularity of Batman LEGO sets, we have chosen to put all sets containing a reference to Batman into one category.

POW! BAM! POP! This pint-sized powerhouse has appreciated over 1,300%!

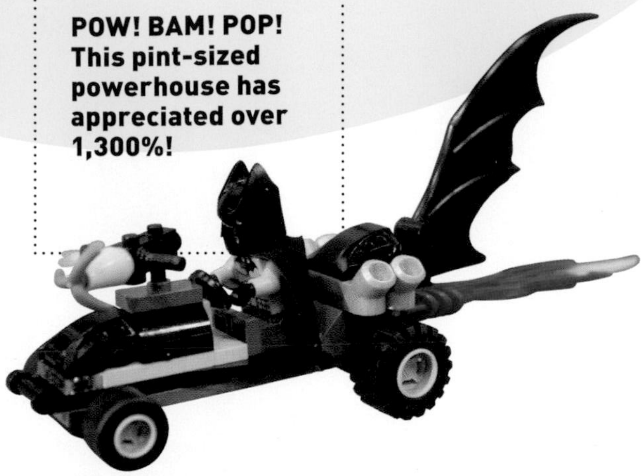

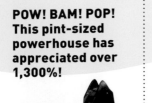

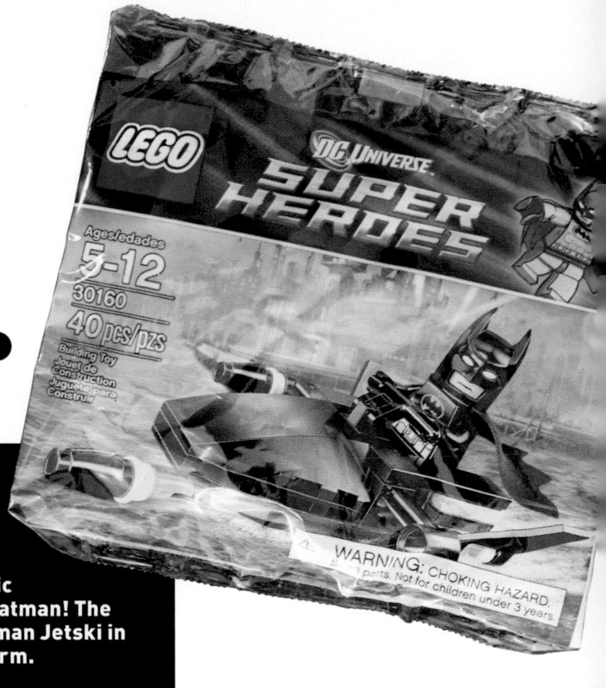

Holy plastic baggies, Batman! The 30160 Batman Jetski in polybag form.

7884 BATMAN'S BUGGY: THE ESCAPE OF MR. FREEZE

- ▶ **Year Released: 2008**
- ▶ **No. of Pieces: 76**
- ▶ **Minifigures: 2**
- ▶ **Retail Price: $9.99**

This is an amazing set, from a growth standpoint. Why? Who knows. The 7884 Batman's Buggy: The Escape of Mr. Freeze is only 76 pieces. None of its two minifigures (Batman and Mr. Freeze) is exclusive to the set. The design of the set is uninspiring. The pieces are not special. The set had a short production run of about six months, which could have helped its tremendous appreciation.

The set's current value is around $150, which is almost fifteen times more than the retail price of $9.99. This equates to over 1,300 percent in growth since 2008. The 7884 is in record territory for LEGO set growth for really no other reason than a short production run and being a Batman set. This might be the best example of how a low-priced set can be a great investment.

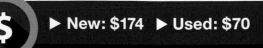

$ ▶ New: $174 ▶ Used: $70

30160 BATMAN JETSKI

- ▶ **Year Released: 2012**
- ▶ **No. of Pieces: 40**
- ▶ **Minifigures: 1**
- ▶ **Retail Price: $4.99**

LEGO collecting comes in all shapes and sizes, and the smallest collectible set is called a polybag. They are little plastic bags filled with less than 100 pieces, sometimes as few as five or six pieces. Some valuable sets come in small packages, such as the 30160 Batman Jetski. Originally selling for $4.99 in 2012, the set has tripled in value over the past two years. While you might not get rich owning one of these polybags, it is possible to buy multiples and not empty your bank account.

This set in particular has two things going for it. First, it is a Batman set with a Batman minifigure. Although it is not a super rare minifigure, it is a Batman replica and Batman equates to money in LEGO form, especially minifigure form. Secondly, this set was exclusive to Toys R Us in the United States and *The Sun* newspaper in Great Britain, thus limiting its availability and quite possibly helping it increase its value.

$ ▶ New: $19 ▶ Used: $16

The two exclusive minifigures of the 6860, Bruce Wayne and Bane, should help this set appreciate well.

6860 THE BATCAVE

▶ **Year Released:** 2012
▶ **No. of Pieces:** 690
▶ **Minifigures:** 5
▶ **Retail Price:** $69.99

$ ▶ **New: $78** ▶ **Used: $47**

7783 THE BATCAVE: THE PENGUIN AND MR. FREEZE'S INVASION

▶ **Year Released:** 2006
▶ **No. of Pieces:** 1,071
▶ **Minifigures:** 7
▶ **Retail Price:** $89.99

$ ▶ **New: $554** ▶ **Used: $330**

There have been two main Batcaves released in the last ten years: the 7783 The Batcave: The Penguin and Mr. Freeze's Invasion in 2006, and the 6860 The Batcave in 2012. The original 7783 set has 1,071 pieces and seven minifigures, four of which are exclusive. The 6860 set has 690 pieces and five minifigures, two of which are exclusive.

The growth of the 7783 set is quite strong, appreciating over 500 percent from the original MSRP of $89.99. The smaller 6860 Batcave was just recently retired and should be a solid investment choice for collectors. While it might not be as large or have as many exclusive minifigures as the 7783, the 6860 is still a Batman set and will probably outperform sets of similar size in other themes. On a personal note, I would like to see LEGO design a super-sized Batcave, which would really honor such a fictional icon.

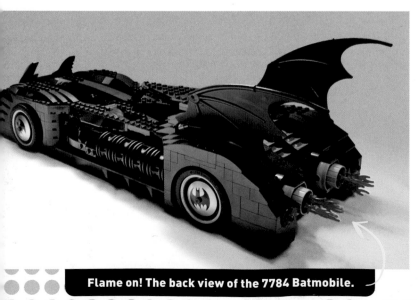

7784 THE BATMOBILE: ULTIMATE COLLECTOR EDITION

- ▶ **Year Released:** 2006
- ▶ **No. of Pieces:** 1,045
- ▶ **Minifigures:** 0
- ▶ **Retail Price:** $69.99

$ ▶ **New: $380** ▶ **Used: $211**

Flame on! The back view of the 7784 Batmobile.

Batman's vehicles over the years have played a huge role in defining the character and attracting the attention of millions of fans across the world. These vehicles also help LEGO create sets that are varied and playable.

The most quintessential Batman vehicles are the Batmobiles, including the versions in the pre *Dark Knight* movies, and the *Dark Knight* Batmobile, known as The Tumbler. We will leave out the Adam West Batmobile at this point, but LEGO did give this version some love and it is discussed later in the book.

Both versions are unique in their own ways and LEGO did them justice with the 7784 The Batmobile: Ultimate Collector Edition, released in 2006 with 1,045 pieces for $69.99, and the 76023 The Tumbler, released in 2014 for $199.99 with 1,869 pieces; it is currently still available at retail.

The 7784 version looks to have plateaued around the $400 range, which is over 400 percent growth from the MSRP of $69.99. That is solid growth. The 7784 does not include a minifigure or Ultimate Collector Series plaque, which I think hurts its performance in the LEGO secondary market. Regardless, it is a must have for any serious LEGO Batman fan. It is a close replica to the earlier Batmobile versions, and some of the pieces of the 7784 are rare. The 76023 set is a classic in the making. It is fantastic and highly playable and displayable with its minifigures and UCS plaque. It has rare pieces, such as the huge rubber tires, but most of all, it's damn cool. I highly recommend this set to any LEGO enthusiast.

FRONT VIEW.

The box art of the 76023 The Tumbler is quite impressive and needs to be seen in person to appreciate it.

76023 THE TUMBLER

▶ Year Released: 2014
▶ No. of Pieces: 1,869
▶ Minifigures: 2
▶ Retail Price: $199.99

$ ▶ New: $269 ▶ Used: $210

4526 BATMAN

▶ Year Released: 2012
▶ No. of Pieces: 40
▶ Minifigures: 0
▶ Retail Price: $14.99

$ ▶ New: $26 ▶ Used: $13

LEGO's Constraction subtheme combines Technic, Bionicle/Hero Factory, and conventional pieces to create large play figures. Two such sets are the 4526 Batman and 4527 The Joker. Both sold for $14.99 MSRP and were released in late 2011. These sets are somewhat different than most, so I thought it was prudent to include them. Growth wise, the 4526 Batman

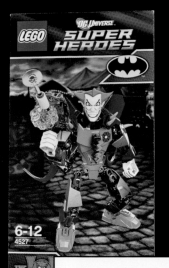

has doubled in value since retirement, and the 4527 The Joker has seen moderate growth to the $20 range. These sets were highly discounted, so the growth figures might actually be better considering a person's "buy in point." Regardless, these sets are unique and playable and look awesome displayed together.

The 7785 Arkham Asylum and the 10937 Batman: Arkham Asylum Breakout are a couple of the larger sets based on the fictional DC Universe prison for the criminally insane.

The 7785 set was released in 2006 with 860 pieces for $79.99. The 10937 set was released in 2013 for $159.99 and consists of 1,619 pieces. The 7785 has seven minifigures, four which are exclusive to this set. The 10937 has eight minifigures, five which are exclusive to the set. The 7785 Arkham Asylum has quite a few printed rare pieces that were included with the set, possibly helping increase its value in the LEGO secondary market. For all intents and purposes, both sets are retired. The 10937 Arkham Asylum recently disappeared from retailer's shelves and looks to be done at this writing. Values and growth for the 7785 Arkham Asylum are moderate, with the set peaking around $350, with a Return on Investment of over 350 percent. The 10937 set has seen some strong growth post retirement to the $250 range and looks to continue this rapid pace. From a build standpoint, both are creative and playable LEGO sets that display well.

4527 THE JOKER

▶ Year Released: 2011
▶ No. of Pieces: 57
▶ Minifigures: 0
▶ Retail Price: $14.99

$ ▶ New: $20 ▶ Used: $10

10937 BATMAN: ARKHAM ASYLUM BREAKOUT

▶ Year Released: 2013
▶ No. of Pieces: 1,619
▶ Minifigures: 8
▶ Retail Price: $159.99

$ ▶ New: $251 ▶ Used: $122

7785 ARKHAM ASYLUM

▶ Year Released: 2006
▶ No. of Pieces: 860
▶ Minifigures: 7
▶ Retail Price: $79.99

$ ▶ New: $369 ▶ Used: $244

CHAPTER 4

BIONICLE

WHILE THE VALUE OF BIONICLE SETS NEVER REACH HIGH LEVELS, THEY DO OFFER SOLID APPRECIATION. MANY OF THESE SMALL SETS HAVE EXCEPTIONAL GROWTH RATES, AND ARE A PERFECT CHOICE FOR COLLECTORS AND INVESTORS ON A BUDGET.

THE THEME THAT SAVED LEGO.

While that point can be argued, any LEGO historian will tell you that The LEGO Group was in poor financial shape in the late 1990s and the company was stagnant. LEGO had to shake things up. One way they did this was by designing sets that were targeted to adult fans, and with higher detail, complex builds, higher piece counts, and higher MSRPs. A second way was to create the Bionicle theme, an acronym for Biological Chronicle. The Bionicle theme is a series of sets that are a combination of existing Technic pieces and newly engineered components that create large, action-figure-styled models. The introduction of pieces with ball and socket qualities was a first for LEGO and enabled designers to create man-like models, with pivoting appendages. Thus, the new "Constraction" type of design was launched and helped change the face of LEGO for years to come.

LEGO took this new Bionicle theme that was launched in the United States in 2001 and ran with it, and was extremely smart about marketing these sets. The LEGO Group utilized comic books, television shows, and movies to promote the story of the Bionicle. Basically, it's the enduring story of Good vs. Evil and the characters that make up each side. The Good characters consist of the Toa, while the Bad characters consist of the Makuta, Piraka, and Barraki, to name a few. The Bionicle-themed sets became one of LEGO's best selling lines through early parts of the new millenium and started LEGO on its path to be the number one toy maker in the world. The Bionicle theme ended in 2010 and was replaced with a similar type of theme, the Hero Factory, which is based on robotic "heroes" that were created by robots to help protect them from evil beings and other robots. The Bionicle theme has been relaunched for 2015 and has replaced the Hero Factory theme.

The overall growth of Bionicle sets is positive on the LEGO secondary market, with some showing nice Returns on Investment. What you really don't see with Bionicle sets is stratospheric values, but they are steady gainers.

10204 VEZON & KARDOS

▶ **Year Released: 2006**
▶ **No. of Pieces: 670**
▶ **Minifigures: 0**
▶ **Original Retail Price: $49.99**

$ ▶ **New: $275** ▶ **Used: $145**

Many Bionicle sets are similar in appearance. A part or special piece or two is swapped out. A color scheme is changed. A new head is added, and maybe a new weapon. There are literally hundreds of Bionicle sets that are so similar, it is hard for the layman to tell the difference. Another issue is the naming system. "Toa" this …"Mata" that … it makes for a confusing discussion for non-Bionicle enthusiasts. For this reason, I will discuss only one Bionicle LEGO set, the 10204 Vezon & Kardos, as well as the three smaller sets used to build it: 8733 Axonn, 8734 Brutaka, and 8764 Vezon & Fenrakk, shown on the following pages.

The 10204 Vezon and Kardos is the "Big Daddy" of Bionicle sets, with its 670 pieces, and the highest valued set at this writing as well, almost reaching the $300 mark. In fact, no other Bionicle set is anywhere near this in value on the LEGO secondary market. It is the biggest, baddest, and most valuable Bionicle set of all time.

What makes the 10204 Vezon & Kardos an interesting set is that the three smaller Bionicle sets mentioned above are used to build it. There is also a main head or skull piece required to complete the model, and it's found only in the main set, but you can make all four Bionicle models with the main 10204 Vezon & Kardos set, if so desired. The set comes with four sets of instructions to complete all four models, so that is a neat option. Bionicle sets often give LEGO fans many creative combination options in lesser sets also. Many times a collector can buy two different sets and combine them into a larger Bionicle model. Sets are usually within the same subtheme and color class, and instructions are sometimes within one of the sets or online on the LEGO site. This is a really nice feature that helps promote LEGO's online activity and helps entice LEGO fans to purchase more than one Bionicle set.

Vezon and Kardos are the biggest, baddest, and most valuable Bionicle set.

The Bionicle theme has been revived for 2015. To date, none of the new Bionicle sets have come close to the sheer size and nastiness of the 10204 Vezon & Kardos.

Once completed, the 10204 Vezon & Kardos is jaw-dropping ... literally. The massive mouth of the dragon-like Kardos is filled with eleven vicious teeth. Kardos also comes with large clawed hands and feet, wings, and a long serpent tail — quite a scary sight, honestly. The companion model of the set is the smaller, but no less scary, Vezon. He comes with a ragged black cape and sickle. All in all, this is an impressive and evil LEGO model that displays well and has high playability, as with most Bionicle sets. Value wise, this set has plateaued around the $300 mark, and I really don't see any reason for it to continue to climb. Any future large-scale Bionicle sets should be looked at with interest. This set has performed well from a low MSRP and large Bionicle sets are a rare bird, so there could be potential for profit from a large, collectible set.

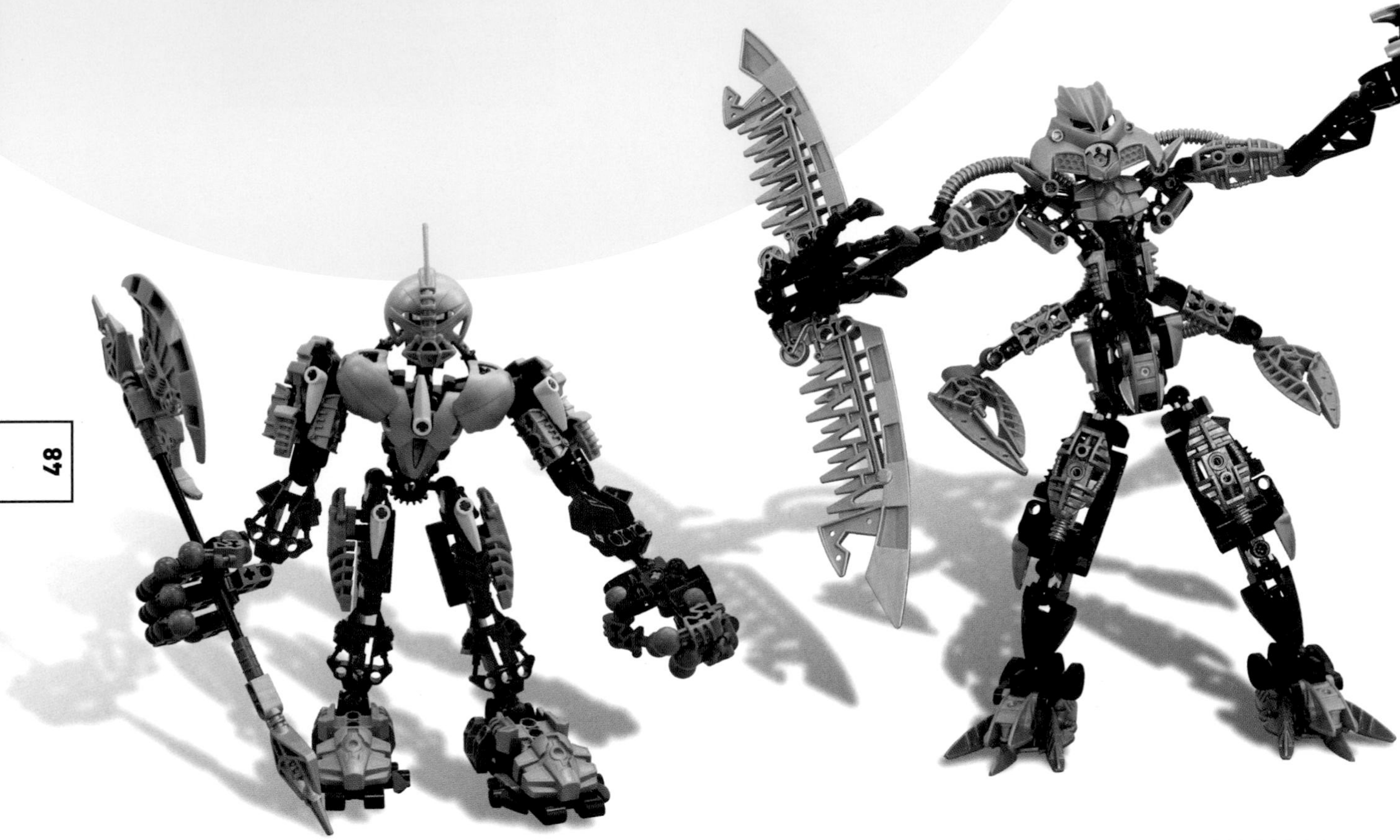

8733 AXONN

▶ Year Released: 2006
▶ No. of Pieces: 196
▶ Minifigures: 0
▶ Original Retail Price: $19.99

$ ▶ New: $84 ▶ Used: $52

8734 BRUTAKA

▶ Year Released: 2006
▶ No. of Pieces: 193
▶ Minifigures: 0
▶ Original Retail Price: $19.99

$ ▶ New: $94 ▶ Used: $49

8764 VEZON AND FENRAKK

- ▶ Year Released: 2006
- ▶ No. of Pieces: 281
- ▶ Minifigures: 0
- ▶ Original Retail Price: $29.99

$ ▶ New: $76 ▶ Used: $49

Fenrakk, the big, bad Bionicle Buddy of Vezon, resembles some sort of prehistoric puppy dog. Awesome creature.

The "Caped Crusader," Bionicle style!

MASKS HAVE COLLECTIBLE POTENTIAL

Bionicle "masks" are another potential collectible opportunity. Some of the Bionicle "mask sets" released in the original Bionicle production run have appreciated very well. A Bionicle mask is basically the face covering Bionicle creatures put over their inner face/head piece. LEGO released box sets of various Bionicle masks to give Bionicle fans options to upgrade their creations. Sets like the 8598-1:Kanohi Nuva and Krana Pack, 8525-1:Masks and 8599-1:Krana-Kal have Returns on Investment of close to 1,000 percent. Spectacular!

CHAPTER 5

CAS**T**LE

CASTLE SETS MAY BE SLOWER TO APPRECIATE IN VALUE, BUT THEY HAVE A FUN PLAYABILITY FACTOR AND ALSO SUPPLY THE MOC COMMUNITY WITH MANY UNIQUE BRICKS AND PIECES.

The Castle theme has been a backbone of The LEGO Group's product line since the 1970s. One of the first sets that I bought as a child almost 40 years ago was the 375 (Yellow) Castle set. LEGO bricks are the perfect medium to produce classic Castle architecture and structures, so it's no surprise that this theme has been extremely successful among many fans, collectors, and builders.

All of the Castle subthemes are similar in build and design, and many of the sets consist of structures made with special "Castle bricks," which are large plates and wall pieces that are much larger than traditional bricks. The Castles over the years have also had different color schemes, from yellows, grays, and blues, to blacks and reds. Castle sets usually come with a plethora of minifigures, all adorned with shields and helmets, swords, and crossbows. Also, horse and dragon maxifigures have been included in many sets over the last 35+ years, and the trend will most likely continue in future sets. Castle sets also supply the MOC community with

many unique bricks and pieces. Since many of the Castle-themed elements are based on wood products, such as drawbridges, ramps, catapults, wagon wheels, bricks were created to give the impression of old and antique objects. Even many of the wall plates are embossed with stone stickers and paint to give items a rustic feel.

The price-per-piece cost on many Castle sets is reasonable in most cases. Many of the larger Castle sets come with a whole ABS plastic army. These sets are generally popular with children, although there is a growing community of older Castle fans building spectacular MOCs of castles and keeps. Value wise, Castle-themed sets do appreciate, but at a slow to moderate pace. These sets are usually designed for play and not for mature builders and tastes. They are popular among the younger crowd, for the most part, but do not really reach very high values on the LEGO secondary market. If you like kings and knights, castles and keeps, and are not looking for an uber investment collectible, this theme is for you.

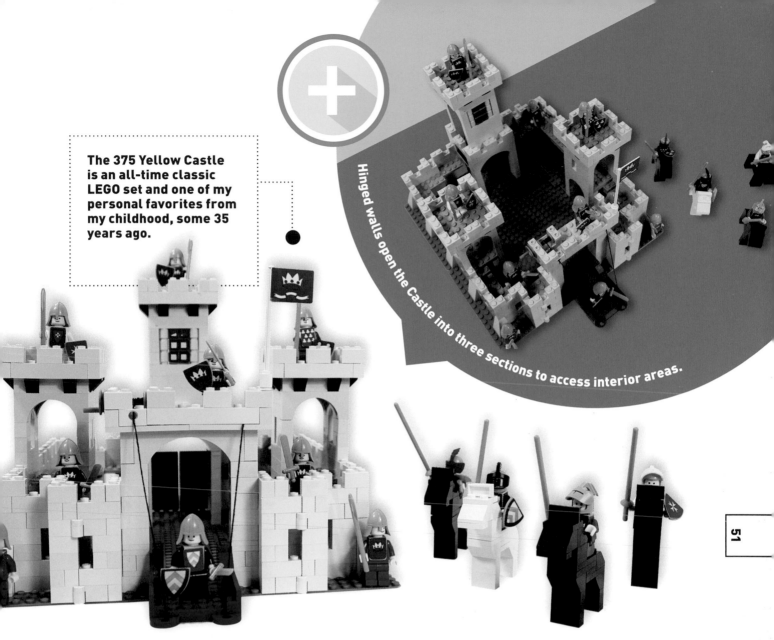

The 375 Yellow Castle is an all-time classic LEGO set and one of my personal favorites from my childhood, some 35 years ago.

Hinged walls open the Castle into three sections to access interior areas.

375 (YELLOW) CASTLE

▶ **Year Released: 1978**
▶ **No. of Pieces: 767**
▶ **Minifigures: 14**
▶ **Retail Price: $NA**

An all-time classic Castle set, the 375 (Yellow) Castle is an old-school LEGO building at its finest. Released in 1978, I bought this set when I was ten years old — prime LEGO building years. This was one of the sets that really got me hooked on LEGO. I loved all the yellow bricks this set supplied for my MOCs. It consisted of 767 bricks and was a large set for the time. I would equate it to any of the large

Advanced Models of today. It also included 14 minifigures, still impressive to this day. Honestly, the set is so old, we don't even have an MSRP for it. Not only that, it is so rare, we don't even have any sold listings that were for new sets. A new 375 (Yellow) Castle would be a rare find and could sell for thousands of dollars in MISB condition. Who would pay that, you may ask? Some wealthy LEGO fan or collector who had one as a child and wants to build one again. It happens every day in the LEGO Universe and is what keeps the secondary market profitable and healthy.

$ ▶ **New: $1,347** ▶ **Used: $153**

Dragon maxifigures play an important role in the collectability of Castle sets, and those that have them appreciate to higher values than those without dragons.

7094 KING'S CASTLE SIEGE

▶ **Year Released: 2007**
▶ **No. of Pieces: 973**
▶ **Minifigures: 10**
▶ **Retail Price: $99.99**

This is at the top of the Castle price guide at this writing. The 7094 King's Castle Siege is a 973-piece set released in 2007 for $99.99. Current values are approaching the $300 mark. The quintessential Castle set, the 7094 King's Castle Siege checks all the boxes for a Castle set: large "Castle bricks," drawbridge, horses, knights, dragon, king, and … skeleton army? Yes, skeleton army. The great thing about LEGO sets is that you can throw in an occasional skeleton, zombie, or ninja and have a set that attracts the kids and parents' dollars. It is a combination that has worked well over the years in various themes, especially the Ninjago theme of late. Overall, the 7094 King's Castle Siege is a good representation of the Castle theme; it's a nice with good value and moderate appreciation.

7093 SKELETON TOWER

▶ **Year Released: 2007**
▶ **No. of Pieces: 398**
▶ **Minifigures: 5**
▶ **Retail Price: $49.99**

The 7093 Skeleton Tower is one of the best performing Castle sets from a Return on Investment perspective. It has an ROI of over 300 percent since its release in 2007 and retirement in 2008. The set is has 398 pieces, sold for $49.99, and has five minifigures and one maxifigure. Current values on the LEGO secondary market are well north of $200. It had a relatively short production run, which probably helped in its growth. A cool set with some skeletons, bones, teeth, and a dragon, the 7093 Skeleton Tower is a good example of how fantasy mixes well with the Castle theme. Although recent Castle sets have returned to the traditional "knights in shining armor" era, Castle sets that mix in some supernatural elements seem to be popular amongst fans and better investment choices.

$ ▶ **New: $276** ▶ **Used: $151**

$ ▶ **New: $223** ▶ **Used: $82**

10193 MEDIEVAL MARKET VILLAGE

▶ **Year Released: 2009**
▶ **No. of Pieces: 1,601**
▶ **Minifigures: 8**
▶ **Retail Price: $99.99**

The 10193 Medieval Market Village is one of those sets that a long-time LEGO collector and investor cannot figure out. It is a gorgeous set, with a highly detailed and accurate medieval model with a generous amount of pieces (1,601) and minifigures (8) for the MSRP of $99.99. What I cannot figure out is why this wonderful set has only appreciated to approximately $150 since it was marked as retired two years ago.

The 10193 Medieval Market Village is a beautiful set, both in the box and built. The old Tudor houses of the set are wonderfully recreated by LEGO designers. The set was also a good value, with over 1,600 pieces for $89.99.

Similar sized and well-done sets from other themes have much better returns to date. One such reason for this slow growth is the long production run. Most sets have production runs of two to three years, with three years even being on the longer side. This set had five years, and thousands of investors, collectors, and resellers stockpiled it, so I guess there is a glut on the secondary market. This could be a good lesson for anyone thinking of investing on the next popular set with a long production run.

$ ▶ **New: $155** ▶ **Used: $120**

CASTLES THEMES
THROUGH THE YEARS

The Castle theme has had numerous versions and subthemes over the years:

- **Black Knights**
- **Black Falcons**
- **Wolfpack Renegades**
- **Dragon Masters**
- **Royal Knights**

- **Dark Forest**
- **Fright Knights**
- **Forestmen**
- **Lion Knights**
- **Knights' Kingdom**

- **Castle (2007)**
- **Kingdoms**
- **Castle (2013)**

CHAPTER 6

CITY [cars, boats, trucks, & planes

THE CITY THEME HAS BEEN THE BACKBONE OF LEGO THEMES FOR YEARS AND HAS INTRODUCED MILLIONS OF CHILDREN TO THE LEGO BRICK ON AN ANNUAL BASIS, YET AS COLLECTIBLE SETS, THEY ARE IGNORED BY INVESTORS. BUT THERE ARE SOME CITY SETS THAT HAVE POTENTIAL.

The City theme is another one of The LEGO Group's foundation themes. Launched in 1978, the City-themed sets are quite often the first traditional LEGO sets that many young fans are introduced to. Based on everyday life, these sets concentrate on various jobs and careers in local communities and sometimes around the globe. Sets can be related to by every age group and gender — everyone knows who a police officer is or what a fire truck looks like, so this theme connects with all manner of fans.

As with the Castle-themed sets, the City sets are usually reasonably priced, with a good mix of minifigures and parts. They are also below average as collectibles. City sets are constantly remade with newer versions. There is always a LEGO Police Station or Fire Station available for sale it seems. New

versions of sets come out every couple of years and most are similar to the older versions. This is done because there is a constant supply of young fans being introduced to sets on an annual basis, and LEGO wants the new fans to have the opportunity to purchase them at all times.

A few of the subthemes do make better investments than others, and we will analyze that with a breakdown of some of the major sets of the theme. It would appear vehicles play an important role in these sets, from replicas of local garages to full-blown rocket launching pads, but this makes complete sense because this is a theme designed for children ... and kids love their trucks, cars, boats, and planes. All in all, the City-themed sets are great for everyday play, but there are much better choices for collectible LEGO sets.

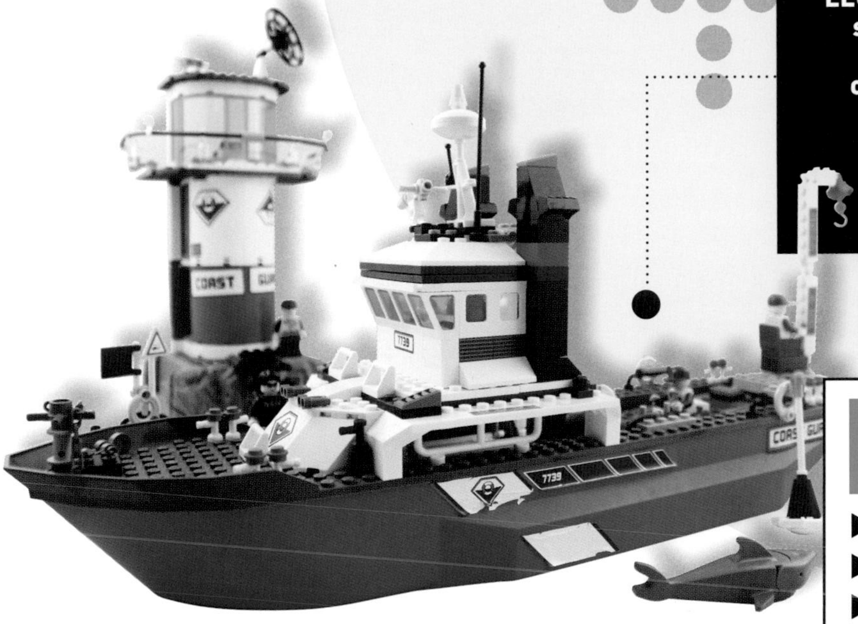

LEGO City Coast Guard sets are some of the better performers of the theme and the 4210 Coast Guard Platform is an example of this.

4210 COAST GUARD PLATFORM

- **Year Released: 2008**
- **No. of Pieces: 469**
- **Minifigures: 4**
- **Retail Price: $49.99**

$ ▶ New: $226 ▶ Used: $84

LEGO City Coast Guard sets and other ones similar to it, like the new Arctic City sets, deal with similar types of designs and all include base camps, boats, helicopters, and planes. I call them the City "Adventure" sets. The 4120 Coast Guard Platform and the 7739 Coast Guard Patrol Boat and Tower have both appreciated well from their retirements in 2009. These multipurpose sets that give LEGO fans many options of play do well and are quite popular. As with any LEGO City set, remakes are always a possibility, and that has been the case with the Coast Guard set. Regardless, the older City Coast Guard sets have doubled and tripled their MSRPs. If you like variety, these Adventure sets are a good choice for fun and profit.

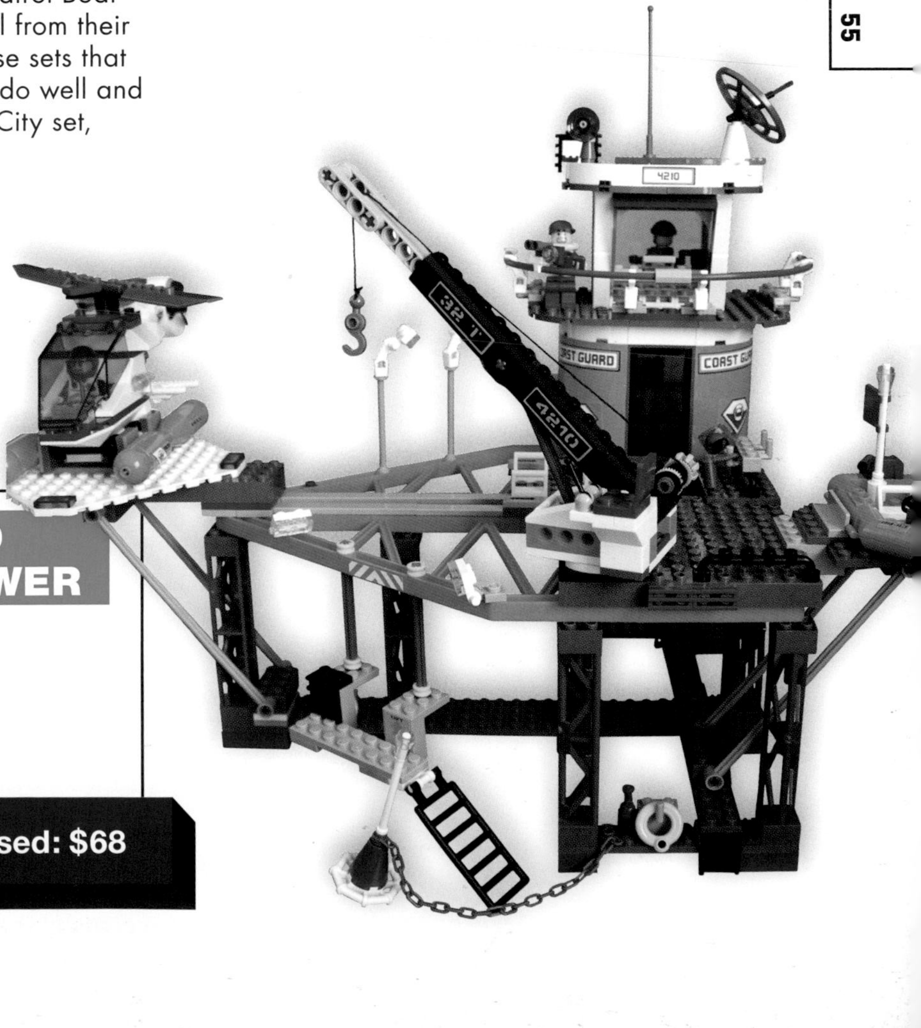

7739 COAST GUARD PATROL BOAT & TOWER

- **Year Released: 2008**
- **No. of Pieces: 444**
- **Minifigures: 4**
- **Retail Price: $59.99**

$ ▶ New: $195 ▶ Used: $68

he Emergency Services City sets consist of many of the Police, Fire Department and Hospital/Doctor sets. As noted, many of these types of sets are in constant supply from primary retailers, albeit a different version every couple of years. This constant supply of the foundation sets of the City theme never really let the sets become a rare and unique item after being retired. Look at the values of these three sets. The 7744 Police Headquarters has little more than doubled in value from its $89.99 MSRP. It has been retired over four years, but there is a new 60047 Police Station it has to compete with, so growth is somewhat stunted. A similar situation is going on with the 7945 Fire Station: A new one is available, the 60004 Fire Station, once again keeping the older 7945 set at double MSRP after years of retirement. The 7892 Hospital has shown the best growth, quadrupling its MSRP of $49.99 to the $200 level. One reason for the stronger growth is there hasn't been any recent replacements for the set, so there is no hospital currently for sale on the primary LEGO market. That will probably soon change, though, and a new hospital set would probably sell well.

7945 FIRE STATION

▶ **Year Released:** 2007
▶ **No. of Pieces:** 600
▶ **Minifigures:** 4
▶ **Retail Price:** $59.99

$ ▶ **New: $116** ▶ **Used: $66**

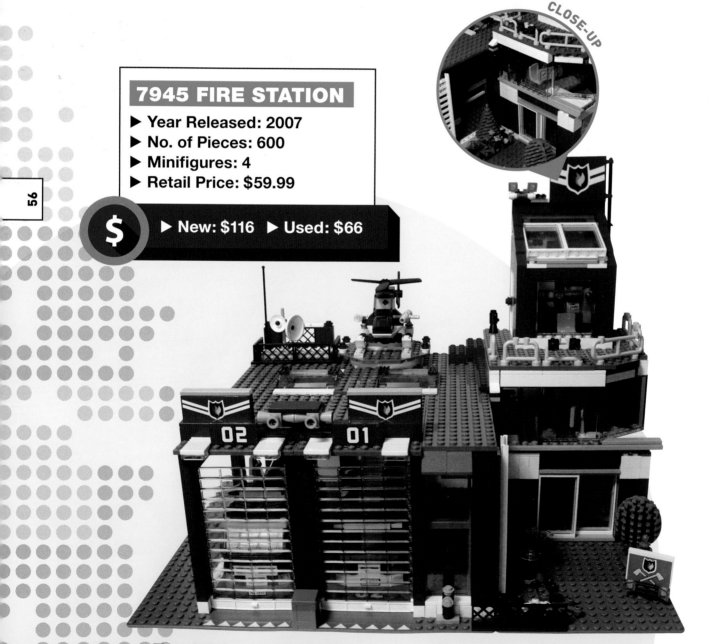

CLOSE-UP

There have been at least fourteen versions of the LEGO Fire Station since 1970.

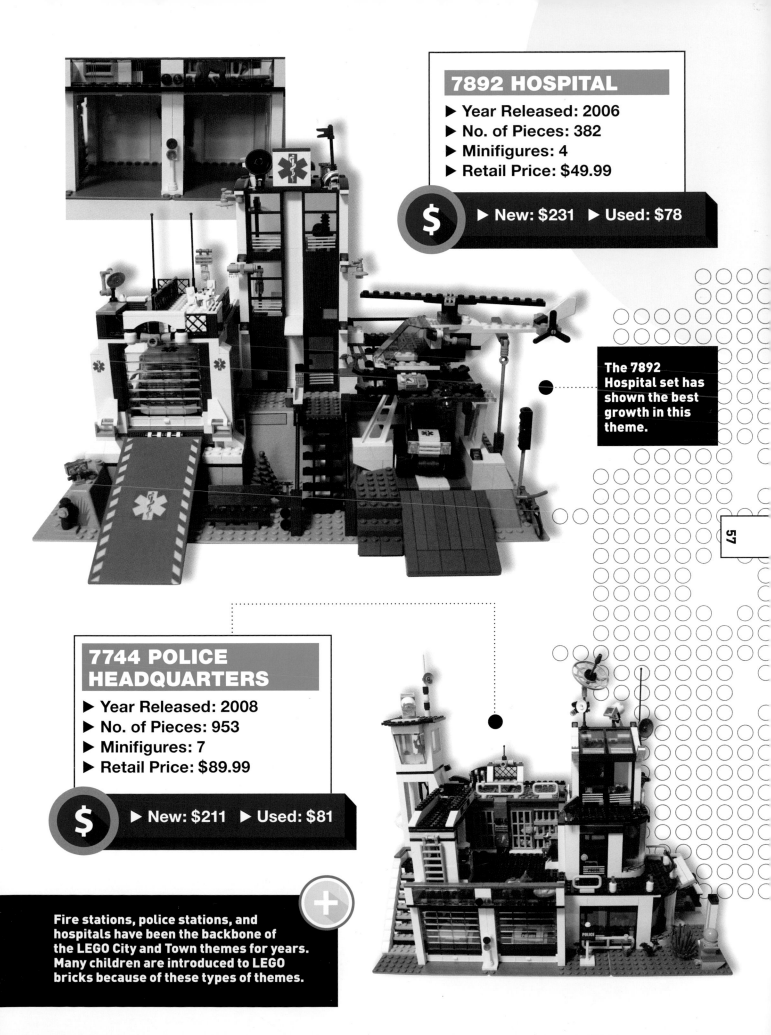

7892 HOSPITAL

▶ Year Released: 2006
▶ No. of Pieces: 382
▶ Minifigures: 4
▶ Retail Price: $49.99

$ ▶ New: $231 ▶ Used: $78

The 7892 Hospital set has shown the best growth in this theme.

7744 POLICE HEADQUARTERS

▶ Year Released: 2008
▶ No. of Pieces: 953
▶ Minifigures: 7
▶ Retail Price: $89.99

$ ▶ New: $211 ▶ Used: $81

Fire stations, police stations, and hospitals have been the backbone of the LEGO City and Town themes for years. Many children are introduced to LEGO bricks because of these types of themes.

3182 AIRPORT

▶ **Year Released: 2010**
▶ **No. of Pieces: 703**
▶ **Minifigures: 5**
▶ **Retail Price: $99.99**

$ ▶ **New: $275** ▶ **Used: $163**

7893 PASSENGER PLANE

▶ **Year Released: 2006**
▶ **No. of Pieces: 401**
▶ **Minifigures: 4**
▶ **Retail Price: $39.99**

Airports and airplanes are also solid collectible choices for the LEGO City fan. The 3182 Airport and 7893 Passenger Plane have both illustrated strong growth since retirement. The 3182 Airport was released in 2006 and listed for $99.99; current values on the secondary market are reaching $300. The 401-piece 7893 Passenger Plane has really exploded in growth for a City set and has also almost reached the $300 level. But the 7893 Passenger Plane was a $39.99 set at MSRP, giving it almost a 600 percent Return on Investment. I would imagine that airplanes are popular because they have a high WHOOOSH Factor when flying them around a room. Also, the parts that make up LEGO planes are somewhat large and expensive, so that aids in potentially parting out a City plane set. Anything that flies, floats, or rolls seems to appreciate.

$ ▶ **New: $271** ▶ **Used: $119**

7898 CARGO TRAIN DELUXE

▶ **Year Released: 2006**
▶ **No. of Pieces: 856**
▶ **Minifigures: 5**
▶ **Retail Price: $149.99**

LEGO train sets are some of the most solid, collectible sets produced, and the train sets within the City theme are no different. There are multiple train sets within the top tier of City set values. LEGO makes a ton of options for trains, from extra track to power functions and remote controls. The 7898 Cargo Train Deluxe is a 856-piece set released in 2006 for $149.99 and has since doubled in value — and then some. There are multiple other City train sets showing similar returns. What is neat is that they all interchange with one another, and the train tracks are universal to most trains throughout the LEGO Universe.

$ ▶ **New: $352** ▶ **Used: $212**

7905 BUILDING CRANE

▶ **Year Released: 2006**
▶ **No. of Pieces: 701**
▶ **Minifigures: 3**
▶ **Retail Price: $69.99**

The 7905 Building Crane is the cream of the Construction category of the City theme. Another quality set released in 2006, the 7905 Building Crane comes with 721 pieces and has appreciated about 400 percent from its MSRP of $69.99. It is quite a unique set, and there haven't been any comparable sets to reduce the value of it on the secondary market. It is over two feet tall, is an accurate replica of a large construction crane, and is quite usable. Overall, it's a cool and unique set that is a must have for any LEGO City Construction fans. Even if you are not a City fan, you will admire this set for its display and play qualities and design characteristics.

$ ▶ **New: $349** ▶ **Used: $194**

CHAPTER 7

CREATOR

MOST SETS IN THE EXPANSIVE CREATOR THEME HAVE AVERAGE GROWTH, BUT SOME ARE STRONGER. MOST ARE ALSO DESIGNED FOR PLAY AND NOT DISPLAY.

The LEGO Creator theme includes many types of sets and creations. It is not a licensed theme and concentrates on set designs from all sorts of sources, from cars and trucks to planes, spiders, dinosaurs, buildings, and whatever else you can think of.

The Creator sets are usually based on reality and not on fantasy or supernatural items. They can be as small as a 20-piece polybag or a huge 3,000-piece Advanced Model set.

While many of the larger Modular Buildings and Advanced Models are thrown into this class, this change was recent, and for the purpose of this book, we will separate the two, and focus on Creator sets that are a middle-of-the-road type of LEGO set, which is not too complex or expensive, but

more advanced than City or Duplo sets.

A popular option for the Creator theme is the Three-in-One sets. These sets enable the LEGO fan to build three models from the same pieces. For example, the 5892 Sonic Boom Creator set can be used to make a fighter jet, a propeller driven airplane and jet boat from the same pieces. This is a nice option and gives some of the Creator sets plenty of playability. For the most part, the basic Creator sets this chapter features are for play and not display. The larger Creator sets, currently marked as "Expert" on new LEGO boxes and have been classified into the Advanced Models theme, are all about display. The growth of the mid-grade Creator sets is average in most cases, but strong in some instances.

PLENTY OF
PLAY
ABILITY

4957 FERRIS WHEEL

▶ **Year Released: 2007**
▶ **No. of Pieces: 1,063**
▶ **Minifigures: 0**
▶ **Retail Price: $69.99**

The 4957 Ferris Wheel is a Three-in-One set that gives builders the option to create a large Ferris Wheel, crane, or drawbridge, with the Ferris Wheel being the main design. This is a 1,063-piece set released in 2007 for $69.99 — a real value. The production run was a year, which is relatively short and helps up the rarity factor. Current values are in the $350 range, up over 400 percent from retail.

There is a new 10247 Ferris Wheel being released in 2015, and it will probably be bigger and better than this version. It is my understanding LEGO is doing an Amusement Park theme, and the new 10247 Ferris Wheel will team up with the 1,746-piece 10244 Fairground Mixer. There will probably be more amusement ride-based sets released in the future to create an entire park.

 $ ▶ **New: $357** ▶ **Used: $184**

4954 MODEL TOWN HOUSE

▶ **Year Released: 2007**
▶ **No. of Pieces: 1,174**
▶ **Minifigures: 0**
▶ **Retail Price: $69.99**

The 4954 Model Town House is a beautiful 1,174-piece set and another Three-in-One that enables builders to create three different house designs. Unlike many LEGO house sets, the main house design is a complete model, with four walls and a roof. It is accurate in appearance and would make a valuable addition to any LEGO collector's town or city display. It also includes a scale car and a garage. There are no minifigures in the set, but it does look to be minifigure scale. The set was released in 2007 for $69.99 and had a short production run of a year. Growth of this set has been strong, breaking the $300

THE 4958 MONSTER DINO

▶ **Year Released: 2007**
▶ **No. of Pieces: 792**
▶ **Minifigures: 0**
▶ **Retail Price: $89.99**

The 4958 Monster Dino is one carnivorous and cool set. The 792-piece set released in 2007 for $89.99 had a short production run of a year. The set is a mix of LEGO Technic pieces and conventional bricks and has Power Functions and a sound brick that roars. The Power Functions enable it to move and has a remote control to operate it. There is a lot of value for $89.99, and the set is also a Three-in-One Creator set and gives the LEGO builder three options (dino, spider, and alligator) to build. Value wise, the 4958 Monster Dino has broken the $200 mark, almost two and a half times its MSRP price.

A remote-controlled Dinosaur that walks and bites and glows in the dark ... What else does a LEGO fan want?

 **$** ▶ **New: $220** ▶ **Used: $143**

barrier for over a 300 percent Return on Investment. The Creator "house" sets are some of the most popular LEGO sets in existence and have a huge following among the younger crowds because of their reasonable prices and mid-level build difficulty. The Creator houses are overall solid investments as well.

$ ▶ **New: $318** ▶ **Used: $209**

CHAPTER 8

DINO

LEGO AND DINOSAURS ARE A GOOD FIT, AND THE SETS IN THIS THEME HAVE PERFORMED WELL AND APPRECIATED NICELY SINCE RETIREMENT. THE *JURASSIC WORLD* MOVIE SHOULD HELP RENEW INTEREST IN THIS THEME AS WELL.

Dino sets are some of my personal favorites. I was the only first grader in the United States who knew how to spell Tyrannosaurus Rex. I knew that dinosaurs were cool before *Jurassic Park* was written, so when two of my most favorite things are combined — LEGO and dinosaurs — I pay attention.

The Dino theme is a small one, with only seven sets, ranging from 80 pieces to 793 pieces. The production run was also short, lasting about a year.

There have been multiple dinosaur-related themes over the years:

Dino Island (2000)
Dinosaur (2001)
Dino Attack (2005)
Dino 2010 (2010)
Dino (2012)

Each of the themes are relatively small in number and had short production runs. Models of the later sets are similar to one another. The dinosaur maxifigures have gotten increasingly realistic in appearance since the basic dinosaurs in the Dino Island theme of 2000.

The current Dino theme has performed amazingly well in comparison to others in the LEGO universe. All seven sets have appreciated nicely since the retirement in 2013. Earlier dinosaur themes have not performed that well, so the current sets' success is quite a surprise. The 5887 Dino Defense Headquarters is the largest of the Dino theme at 793 pieces and is also the most valued on the secondary market, tripling its retail price of $99.99 to reach the $300 level. The large T-Rex maxifigure is really a piece of work and makes the set special in my opinion. All of the Dino-themed sets have at least one large maxifigure, which helps the values of smaller sized sets in the theme. For example, the 5882 Ambush Attack is the smallest set, with a MSRP of $11.99, but it has the best Return on Investment, at almost 300 percent. LEGO maxifigures are valuable and many times can be parted out from new sets and sold for close to what the set cost. It doesn't make sense, but it happens every day on the LEGO secondary market. From a build standpoint, these sets are fun and for play, with basic building techniques employed.

One last point: LEGO has purchased the licensing rights for the new *Jurassic Park* movie, *Jurassic World*, released in 2015, and will be producing related sets named after it. At this writing, six sets are being released. It would appear that it will be a small theme in numbers, similar to the Dino theme. LEGO collectors and resellers should take note of this since the Dino theme prices might plateau because of these new dinosaur sets. On a positive note, LEGO fans will have another opportunity to purchase sets based on dinosaurs, and if past history is an indicator of future returns, then the new *Jurassic Park* theme might be an excellent choice for fans who want a set that is great for kids, but will also increase in value after retirement.

The 5887 Dino Defense Headquarters is the most valuable of the Dino-themed sets.

Small sets with maxifigures included are often highly collectible.

The Tyrannosaurus Rex maxifigure is currently selling for $100 on LEGO secondary market sites.

5882 AMBUSH ATTACK

▶ **Year Released:** 2012
▶ **No. of Pieces:** 80
▶ **Minifigures:** 1
▶ **Retail Price:** $11.99

$ ▶ **New: $45** ▶ **Used: $15**

5887 DINO DEFENSE HEADQUARTERS

▶ **Year Released:** 2012
▶ **No. of Pieces:** 793
▶ **Minifigures:** 4
▶ **Retail Price:** $99.99

$ ▶ **New: $291** ▶ **Used: $179**

CHAPTER 9

FRIENDS

DESPITE **CONTROVERSY** THAT THE FRIENDS THEME GIVES INTO GENDER STEREOTYPES, THIS HAS BECOME ONE OF THE BEST-SELLING THEMES OF RECENT YEARS.

The LEGO Friends theme was launched in January of 2012 amid a flurry of controversy. The criticism levied against The LEGO Group was that the Friends theme was geared toward girls and gave into gender stereotypes. The LEGO Group countered that the Friends theme was a result of intensive research and massive requests from parents to produce sets that young girls would enjoy building. Their research indicated that, while boys have a tendency to concentrate on external characteristics of a model, girls illustrate a tendency to focus on the internal features of a model or playset. The Friends-themed sets have designs developed around the inside of buildings, with an emphasis on role play. The controversy helped promote the theme so much, it became one of the best-selling themes of recent times. The theme has helped LEGO become the number one toy maker in the world, and that sales success looks to continue.

The Friends theme is based on the life and times of five main characters in the fictional land of Heartlake City: Emma, Olivia, Stephanie, Mia, and Andrea. The minifigures are similar in size to conventional minifigures, but are more realistic in appearance, with smoother contours and features.

The LEGO models themselves are like typical buildings and vehicles, but done in colorful bricks. A whole new color palette of bricks was created for the Friends theme, including pink, aqua, purple, yellow, and blue. These bright colors have become popular amongst LEGO custom builders of MOCs. In fact, these bright bricks bring a premium on many LEGO sites that sell individual parts. Also, in addition to new brick colors, a bunch of smaller creatures, such as horses, deer, cats, dogs, and dolphins were produced to be pets and friends of the Friends Five. The Friends sets are all about play, and the models are straightforward and designed for younger builders.

DEVELOPED AROUND THE INSIDE OF BUILDINGS, WITH AN **EMPHASIS ON ROLE PLAY.**

Friends sets are somewhat unique in the LEGO collectible world. Most are similar in design and presentation, and unless you really follow the theme closely, one set can easily be confused with another. They are all in the same colors, so every set has some sort of white or pink, blue, purple, violet, or some other pastel color.

That said, some Friends sets do appreciate better than others. A set like the 3187 Butterfly Beauty Shop has quadrupled in value from its $24.99 MSRP. It has 221 pieces and a short production run of eleven months.

The 41023 Fawn's Forest is another example of a small polybag set appreciating well. This $4.99 set at retail has hit the $20 mark on the LEGO secondary market. As with most LEGO themes, the largest sets of any theme will most likely be the most valuable collectibles. This will probably be no different with the larger Friends sets.

Sets like the 1,080-piece 3185 Summer Riding Camp, the 1,115-piece 41058 Heartlake Shopping Mall, the 695-piece 3315 Olivia's House, and 612-piece 41015 Dolphin Cruiser will all probably do well once retired.

41015 DOLPHIN CRUISER

▶ Year Released: 2013
▶ No. of Pieces: 612
▶ Minifigures: 3
▶ Retail Price: $69.99

$ ▶ New: $63 ▶ Used: $54

41023 FAWN'S FOREST

▶ Year Released: 2013
▶ No. of Pieces: 35
▶ Minifigures: 0
▶ Retail Price: $4.99

$ ▶ New: $20 ▶ Used: $NA

3187 BUTTERFLY BEAUTY SHOP

▶ Year Released: 2012
▶ No. of Pieces: 221
▶ Minifigures: 2
▶ Retail Price: $24.99

$ ▶ New: $104 ▶ Used: $41

Olivia's House is one of the better collectible sets of the Friends theme.

3315 OLIVIA'S HOUSE

▶ Year Released: 2012
▶ No. of Pieces: 695
▶ Minifigures: 3
▶ Retail Price: $74.99

$ ▶ New: $70 ▶ Used: $46

I would not consider Friends sets true collectible LEGO sets. The best collectible LEGO sets are rare, display well, and designed for adults. Friends sets are none of those. Many of the sets are generic in nature. They are extremely popular as a theme in general, but they are more of a short-term phenomena. By that I mean many of the Friends sets have increased values on the LEGO secondary market because of short-term shortages of product that resellers take advantage of. This often happens with popular themed sets like Friends around Christmas. Long term, many of these sets will be remade, with a new name or other small changes. The Friends sets are much like City sets in that LEGO wants to constantly introduce new, young fans, especially little girls in the case of Friends sets, to the theme.

The largest sets of any theme usually appreciate well on the LEGO secondary market and the 3185 Summer Riding Camp and 41058 Heartlake Shopping Mall will be no exceptions.

3185 SUMMER RIDING CAMP

▶ **Year Released: 2012**
▶ **No. of Pieces: 1,112**
▶ **Minifigures: 4**
▶ **Retail Price: $99.99**

$ ▶ **New: $177** ▶ **Used: $94**

LEGO will constantly remake these small- to mid-sized popular "core" sets every couple of years to keep things consistent.

But there is no arguing that the Friends theme is a powerhouse and one of the best-selling themes of the past decade. The sets are fun, creative, colorful, buildable, and great for both girls — and boys. While many Friends sets will never see high values in the secondary market, many will appreciate in a moderate to above average manner. I don't think LEGO had "collectibility" in mind when the Friends theme was created, but there are always a few sets that surprise investors with superior growth and maybe one day a Friends set will reach stratospheric levels.

41058 HEARTLAKE SHOPPING MALL

▶ **Year Released: 2014**
▶ **No. of Pieces: 1,120**
▶ **Minifigures: 4**
▶ **Retail Price: $109.99**

$ ▶ **New: $104** ▶ **Used: $80**

CHAPTER 10

HARRY POTTER

BASED ON THE POPULAR MOVIES, THE *HARRY POTTER* SETS HAVE ALWAYS BEEN ONE OF THE MORE SUCCESSFUL THEMES, BOTH ON THE PRIMARY AND SECONDARY LEGO MARKETPLACES. MANY OF THE ORIGINAL SETS HAVE SOLID INVESTMENT RETURNS, AND MANY OF THE RECENT RELEASES ARE INCREASING IN VALUE.

Early in the new millennium, LEGO began a strong push to create sets based on licensed themes, including the *Star Wars* theme, which became one of the most popular of all time, if not *the* most popular.

A second major licensed theme is *Harry Potter*, based on movie adaptations of author J.K. Rowling's book series.

The LEGO *Harry Potter* theme came in two waves: one from 2001 to 2007, and the second from 2010 to 2012. Basically, with the exception of a few sets, the second wave of *Harry Potter* sets are based on many of the original ones that were released from 2001 to 2007.

Overall, there have been fifty *Harry Potter*

50
HARRY POTTER
SETS RELEASED

sets released, and this doesn't count the multitude of promotional polybags.

The *Harry Potter* theme and sets have always been one of the more successful themes, both on the primary and secondary LEGO marketplaces. Many of the original sets have solid Returns on Investment, and many of the recent releases are on a steady pace upward in value.

LEGO did a great job with many of these sets, and some of the structures and minifigures are some of the best ever produced. There were plenty of accurate and creative sets released through the years, many with unique pieces and minifigures. They are attractive in appearance and their build difficulty is minimal.

It seems many of the smaller- to mid-sized sets have appreciated at a faster pace than some of the larger sets. One possible reason for this is that many of the larger sets are remakes from the first wave of *Harry Potter* sets, while some of the smaller- to mid-sized sets are one-and-done types, which means only one version of a set was made.

The 4766 Graveyard Duel has EIGHT minifigures in a 548-piece set, which is quite a lot for any LEGO set.

4767 HARRY AND THE HUNGARIAN HOMTAIL

▶ **Year Released: 2005**
▶ **No. of Pieces: 265**
▶ **Minifigures: 3**
▶ **Retail Price: $29.99**

The 4767 Harry and the Hungarian Homtail is another example of a small- to mid-sized LEGO set that has appreciated well over the past ten years. Like the 4766 Graveyard Duel, the 4767 Harry and the Hungarian Homtail was released in 2005 with a MSRP of $29.99. It has 265 pieces, three minifigures, and a dragon maxifigure. Two of the minifigures are exclusive to this set. The dragon maxifigure, the Hungarian Homtail is also exclusive to this set and one of the better LEGO maxifigures created at the time. As with the 4766 Graveyard Duel, this set also has exploded in growth over the past ten years, almost reaching the $300 level. That is also close to ten times the MSRP, which is amazing for any LEGO set, regardless the size. Small LEGO sets with maxifigures in them are excellent collectible options.

$ ▶ **New: $278** ▶ **Used: $185**

4766 GRAVEYARD DUEL

▶ **Year Released: 2005**
▶ **No. of Pieces: 548**
▶ **Minifigures: 8**
▶ **Retail Price: $29.99**

Great things come in small packages, and such is the case with the 4766 Graveyard Duel. This is a 548-piece set that was released in 2005. What is amazing with this set is that it contains eight minifigures, six of them exclusive. Eight minifigures in any $29.99 LEGO set is an amazing value, and to have six of them exclusive to the set is unheard of. LEGO sets with scary elements and monsters seem to appreciate well, and this is definitely the case with the 4766 Graveyard Duel. The set is approaching *ten times* MSRP, which is almost $300. This is an amazing Return on Investment and one of the best examples of how some small- to mid-sized LEGO sets can be fantastic collectibles and investments.

$ ▶ **New: $285** ▶ **Used: $141**

4841 HOGWARTS EXPRESS

▶ Year Released: 2010
▶ No. of Pieces: 646
▶ Minifigures: 5
▶ Retail Price: $79.99

$ ▶ New: $253 ▶ Used: $162

10132 MOTORIZED HOGWARTS EXPRESS

▶ Year Released: 2004
▶ No. of Pieces: 708
▶ Minifigures: 4
▶ Retail Price: $119.99

$ ▶ New: $599 ▶ Used: $352

What LEGO theme would be complete without a train? Well, *Star Wars* maybe, but for many "non outer space" themes, there is always some sort of train set in the lineup it seems. For *Harry Potter* fans, it is the 4841 Hogwarts Express. A stylish and accurate model of the movie train, the 4841 Hogwarts Express is a 646-piece set with five minifigures, three which are exclusive to the set. The set had a relatively short production run of a year and sold for $79.99 at retail. The 4841 Hogwarts Express recently reached $250, and growth has been above average, with a Return on Investment of over 200 percent. The 10132 Motorized Hogwarts Express is another quality train set that was released in 2004 and is a good example of how a LEGO builder could motorize the 4841 Hogwarts Express with current power functions parts and accessories.

Minifigures wait to board the 10132 Express.

4842 HOGWARTS CASTLE

- ▶ **Year Released:** 2010
- ▶ **No. of Pieces:** 1,290
- ▶ **Minifigures:** 11
- ▶ **Retail Price:** $129.99

$ ▶ **New: $378** ▶ **Used: $275**

BACK VIEW

4867 BATTLE FOR HOGWARTS

- ▶ **Year Released:** 2011
- ▶ **No. of Pieces:** 466
- ▶ **Minifigures:** 7
- ▶ **Retail Price:** $49.99

10217 DIAGON ALLEY

- ▶ **Year Released:** 2011
- ▶ **No. of Pieces:** 2,025
- ▶ **Minifigures:** 12
- ▶ **Retail Price:** $149.99

The 4842 Hogwarts Castle set is the fourth and last version of the iconic Hogwarts Castle and the largest. Containing 1,290 pieces and eleven minifigures, four of which were exclusive to this set, it was a good deal at $129.99 retail. The 4842 is a well done set and displays quite nicely. Another Harry Potter set, the 4867 Battle for Hogwarts, can be added as an extension to the 4842 set to make a large castle. The 4842 Hogwarts Castle has almost reached the $400 level as of this writing, and the Return on Investment is close to 200 percent. This is one of the larger and premier Harry Potter sets of the entire theme, so growth should continue to be steady, unless there are new movies released, with a new Hogwarts Castle recreated in LEGO bricks.

> **The 4842 Hogwarts Castle offers all sorts of playability features and combines nicely with the 4867 Battle for Hogwarts to make a supersized castle.**

The 10217 Diagon Alley is the largest Harry Potter set, with the finished model consisting of 2,025 pieces. It also has more minifigures, with twelve, half of them being exclusive to the set.

This set is wonderful. The buildings are excellent recreations of the movie Diagon Alley, and the plethora of minifigures is more than generous. This was highly thought of by LEGO collectors and investors during its two-year production run that ended in January of 2013. Even with all the love for this set from fans, the growth has been surprisingly subdued. Although it has doubled since retirement, a LEGO set with such characteristics and stature surely should have appreciated to higher levels at this point. The only reason I can figure for the slower growth is to the high degree it was stockpiled.

$ ▶ **New: $176** ▶ **Used: $107**

$ ▶ **New: $314** ▶ **Used: $242**

CHAPTER 11

HERO FACTORY

WITH BRAIN-SUCKING ALIENS, LASERS, ROCKETS, FLAMES, AND OTHER COOL FEATURES, SETS IN THE HERO FACTORY THEME MAINLY APPEAL TO CHILDREN, BUT THEY ALSO PRODUCE MODEST GAINS FOR COLLECTORS.

The Hero Factory and Bionicle themes are almost identical. Hero Factory was released in 2010 as a replacement for the Bionicle theme. In 2015, the Bionicle theme made a comeback and replaced the Hero Factory theme. The Hero Factory's sets, designs, and pieces are all almost duplicates of the Bionicle theme. They are both Constraction types with a heavy emphasis on Technic parts. The only real difference between the two is the story behind the characters and theme. The Hero Factory story is based on a population of robotic creatures living on an asteroid in a city called Makuhero City. In the center of the city, there is a huge factory that produces robotic "heroes" that protect the populace from various evil robots and creatures. Each Hero has their own abilities and weapons to help fight anything from fires to brain-sucking aliens.

As with the Bionicle theme, Hero Factory targets young boys who like to play with action figures and LEGO sets. The theme has been successful for LEGO and produces moderate gains for collectors and resellers. Many of the Hero Factory sets are

CREEPY COOL & CREATIVE

similar in nature, and unless you are an eight-year-old boy who watches the *Hero Factory* show on the Cartoon Network, a non-fan can get confused by the multitude of sets released each year. Many Hero Factory sets have short production runs, with new characters arriving each year and older ones disappearing from shelves. Most sets are packaged in a cool, large, resealable polybag, but some of the larger sets come in the traditional LEGO box.

For the most part, Hero Factory sets produce moderate gains on the LEGO secondary market. They are quite popular with kids, and many adults like myself also enjoy them. They are creepy, cool, and creative, and some are downright nasty. The Hero Factory set, and Bionicle sets for that matter, are the polar opposite of the Friends-themed sets. There are no cute bunnies or puppies in this theme. There are brain-sucking aliens, spikes, teeth, lasers, cannons, swords, rockets, flames, and whatever else a young boy loves. Two of the biggest and baddest of the Hero Factory theme are also two of the best investments as well: the 6203 Black Phantom and the 2283 Witch Doctor.

6203 BLACK PHANTOM

▶ Year Released: 2012
▶ No. of Pieces: 124
▶ Minifigures: 0
▶ Retail Price: $19.99

The 124-piece 6203 Black Phantom is an evil villain in the Hero Factory saga, but his set is tops of the theme. Originally selling for $19.99, the set now sells well north of $100, for almost a 500 percent Return on Investment. One factor that could have played a role in this set's explosive growth is the fact that the 6203 Black Phantom had only a nine-month production run, which is short compared to usual production times.

Villains in any LEGO theme seem to appreciate well and the 6203 Black Phantom is a great example of that.

$ ▶ New: $116 ▶ Used: $52

2283 WITCH DOCTOR

▶ Year Released: 2011
▶ No. of Pieces: 331
▶ Minifigures: 0
▶ Retail Price: $29.99

The other "Bad Boy" of the Hero Factory, and probably the baddest, is the 2283 Witch Doctor. At 331 pieces, it is the largest Hero Factory character. It stands about a foot tall, is almost nightmarish in appearance, and makes for one "wicked" display. With the skull face, staff, and devilish spikes, the Witch Doctor is one evil-looking LEGO model. From a collectibles view-point, this set is a winner, appreciating to almost four times its MSRP of $29.99 since it was retired about two years ago. These sets prove once again that they are a good example that LEGO collecting and investing can be cost effective and affordable and most of all — profitable.

$ ▶ New: $115 ▶ Used: $59

CHAPTER 12

IDEAS/CUUSOO

THE SETS IN THIS LOVED THEME HAVE BEEN DESIGNED BY LEGO FANS THEMSELVES, PROVING THEY ARE A SMART AND CREATIVE BUNCH. MANY ARE SCIENTIFIC AND TECHNICAL IN NATURE, AND ALL HAVE TURNED OUT TO BE FINANCIALLY LUCRATIVE TO COLLECTORS AND INVESTORS.

The LEGO Ideas theme is one of my personal favorites and that of many other fans. The LEGO Ideas theme began life as LEGO Cuusoo and was based on a Japanese website that promoted people presenting new products that could be brought to production. The word cuusoo in Japanese means "imagination" or "fantasy."

In short, a potential LEGO MOC or custom model design is submitted to the Ideas program. Once the proposed model reaches 10,000 votes of approval from fans, it will be submitted to LEGO for further review. If accepted, the MOC is manufactured and sold by regular LEGO retailers. The person who submits the winning design gets a 1 percent royalty on each set sold.

What this has done to the overall quality of LEGO designs is amazing. The custom MOCs are a fresh breath of air to the entire LEGO community. There are hundreds of new and imaginative creations waiting for approval. Even if most will never make it to production, the new ideas often work their way back into traditional LEGO sets in subtle ways. The Ideas sets that do receive approval for production are some of the most unique in existence, not really fitting into any theme or category, but filling a niche in the LEGO Universe. Here are the current Cuusoo and Ideas sets that have been produced or will be produced as of this writing:

- 21100 Shinkai 6500 Submarine
- 21101 Hayabusa
- 21102 Minecraft Microworld
- 21103 Back to the Future Delorean Time Machine
- 21104 Mars Science Laboratory Curiosity Rover
- 21108 Ghostbusters 30th Anniversary Ecto-1
- 21109 Exo Suit
- 21110 Research Institute
- 21301 LEGO Birds
- # TBA The Big Bang Theory
- # TBA WALL-E
- # TBA Doctor Who and Companions

As you can see, many of the Ideas sets are based on scientific and technical themes. That does not mean that LEGO only approves these sorts of themed sets, but that is what is appealing to fans in general. I have always observed that many adult LEGO fans I have spoken with are highly intelligent and well educated, many working in engineering, computer, and accounting fields. This would explain the preference of these sorts of sets. These niche sets have turned out to be quite popular and financially lucrative to many collectors and investors.

21100 SHINKAI 6500 SUBMARINE

▶ **Year Released:** 2010
▶ **No. of Pieces:** 412
▶ **Minifigures:** 0
▶ **Original Retail Price:** $49.99

The 412-piece 21100 Shinkai 6500 Submarine was the first Cuusoo set to be released and was only released in Japan, making it exclusive. Based on the deep sea submersible that set world records for manned submarines, the 21100 Shinkai 6500 Submarine has exploded in growth, hitting the $400 mark, for a 700 percent Return on Investment from the $49.99 retail price (in Japan). That is amazing. Many LEGO investors outside of Japan ignored this set because you would have to buy from secondary sources, but those who realized its potential value and made the effort have been rewarded handsomely.

> The 21100 Shinkai 6500 Submarine was only released in Japan and is a very rare set.

$ ▶ New: $400 ▶ Used: $225

21101 HAYABUSA

▶ **Year Released:** 2012
▶ **No. of Pieces:** 369
▶ **Minifigures:** 1
▶ **Original Retail Price:** $49.99

The 21101 Hayabusa has recently retired and doubled in value from its $49.99 MSRP. While the growth is not as brisk as the first Cuusoo set, it is solid nonetheless. Meaning "peregrine falcon" in English, the 21101 Hayabusa was based on a Japanese unmanned spacecraft that was developed to land near the Earth asteroid 25143 Itokawa to study its composition, topography, spin, density, and other scientific data. This set was available throughout the US and Europe, so rarity is not a factor.

> Many LEGO Cuusoo/ Ideas sets are designed around technology and the 21101 Hayabusa is a prime example of that.

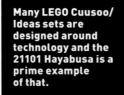

$ ▶ New: $109 ▶ Used: $62

21104 MARS SCIENCE LABORATORY CURIOSITY ROVER

▶ **Year Released:** 2014
▶ **No. of Pieces:** 295
▶ **Minifigures:** 0
▶ **Original Retail Price:** $29.99

The 21104 Mars Science Laboratory Curiosity Rover just recently disappeared from LEGO Shop @ Home and has shot up in value to over three times its MSRP of $29.99, to the $100 level. It had a short production run of about six months and was exclusive to LEGO stores and website. It looks like a relatively rare set on the secondary market and is another example of a low-cost LEGO set being an exceptional collectible and wonderful displays for an office or den.

$ ▶ **New: $99** ▶ **Used: $67**

21102 MINECRAFT MICROWORLD

▶ **Year Released:** 2012
▶ **No. of Pieces:** 480
▶ **Minifigures:** 0
▶ **Original Retail Price:** $34.99

One of the first Cuusoo and Ideas sets that made people notice the theme was the 21102 Minecraft Microworld. Based on the hugely popular *Minecraft* game, this was the first set of the new Minecraft theme, even though it can be considered an Ideas set as well. What made people notice this set was an inventory shortage a few years back before Christmas when it sold out at many retailers. LEGO resellers took advantage of the situation and sold the 21102 Minecraft Microworld for more than three times the retail price of $34.99. The set has since returned to more normal prices.

There are now, as of this writing, thirteen Minecraft Microworld and Minifigure Scale sets. It seems to be a popular theme among the younger crowd and will probably be decent collectible sets in the future.

$ ▶ **New: $46** ▶ **Used: $25**

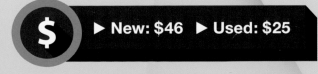

THE 21110 RESEARCH INSTITUTE

Recently, there was a shortage of the 21110 Research Institute right after the release of the set. There were rumors that LEGO was making it a short production run, so collectors and resellers went hog wild and bought up most of the existing inventory. Needless to say, it is possible LEGO underestimated demand and started reproducing these sets once again, but before they had the chance to sell more at retail, it was selling for five times its MSRP of $19.99. Many of these sets sold for well over $100 for a short time, but the price has since returned to $40.

21103 *BACK TO THE FUTURE* DELOREAN TIME MACHINE

▶ **Year Released: 2013**
▶ **No. of Pieces: 401**
▶ **Minifigures: 2**
▶ **Original Retail Price: $34.99**

The 21103 *Back to the Future* Delorean Time Machine has also just recently sold out at all primary retail sources. Current growth of the 401-piece set has been minimal, but it's early in the retirement cycle. A cool set that includes Marty McFly and Doc Brown minifigures, the 21103 *Back to the Future* Delorean Time Machine will surely appreciate well north of its $34.99 MSRP.

As you can see so far, all of the Cuusoo and Ideas sets have been on the smaller side. Many LEGO fans are hoping some of the larger MOC creations that have been submitted for approval will get the OK for production. Regardless, this theme is everchanging and the variety of LEGO sets produced is boundless. It has become one of The LEGO Group's most beloved themes because of the input fans have in deciding what will be produced. The future is bright with all of these sets, so for the LEGO collectors out there, pay attention to this theme. Each set is a potential collectible.

> To date, all of the Cuusoo/Ideas sets have been small to mid-sized sets, maxing out around 500 or so pieces.

$ ▶ **New: $45** ▶ **Used: $32**

CHAPTER 13

INDIANA JONES

THE SETS IN THIS THEME ARE HOMAGES TO SOME OF THE MOST EXCITING SCENES AND FEATURES OF THE MOVIES, AND MANY HAVE PERFORMED ABOVE AVERAGE. A RUMORED NEW MOVIE ON THE HORIZON COULD BOOST INTEREST.

Many of the LEGO licensed themed sets appreciate well on the secondary market, and the Indiana Jones theme is an example of positive returns on investment.

Indiana Jones is not a large theme; only eighteen sets were produced over a two-year period. They have been retired for about five years and without any new movies to stir interest in the theme, many LEGO collectors and investors have moved on to other sets. Regardless, the Indiana Jones sets have produced solid returns over the years. The theme has incorporated all four movies — *Raiders of the Lost Ark, Indiana Jones and the Temple of Doom, Indiana Jones and The Last Crusade*, and *Indiana Jones and the Kingdom of the Crystal Skull* — into the set designs, including important scenes, vehicles,

Of the eighteen sets, many key on most of the dramatic moments of the iconic franchise, including rolling boulders, out-of-control mine carts, and pilot-less Flying Wings.

The Indiana Jones theme is a solid, middle-of-the road theme, and many of the sets have performed above average over the past five years. Surprisingly, many of the larger sets in this theme have not reached high values and the smaller sets outperform them. Maybe the larger sets were based on less popular movies and that has affected values on the secondary market, or maybe the larger sets just don't stir the interest of LEGO collectors.

One potential bonanza for the current sets is the fact that there are rumors of a new *Indiana Jones* movie coming to theaters in the near future, so it is quite possible that the older sets

The 7199 Temple of Doom has reached the $200 level for about a 150 percent Return on Investment. While that is not bad, it certainly isn't great after five years of retirement.

The largest set of the Indiana Jones theme, the 7627 Temple of the Crystal Skull, has performed even worse. Currently, the 7627 set sells for $150, and the Return on Investment is less than 100 percent after five years — not really anything special.

7627 TEMPLE OF THE CRYSTAL SKULL

▶ **Year Released:** 2008
▶ **No. of Pieces:** 929
▶ **Minifigures:** 10
▶ **Retail Price:** $79.99

$ ▶ **New: $149** ▶ **Used: $91**

7199 TEMPLE OF DOOM

▶ **Year Released:** 2009
▶ **No. of Pieces:** 652
▶ **Minifigures:** 6
▶ **Retail Price:** $89.99

$ ▶ **New: $227** ▶ **Used: $157**

Temple of Doom playset features.

Indy tries to dodge the bad guys.

7620 INDIANA JONES MOTORCYCLE CHASE

▶ Year Released: 2008
▶ No. of Pieces: 79
▶ Minifigures: 3
▶ Retail Price: $9.99

$ ▶ New: $55 ▶ Used: $31

You have to look at the smaller sets of the Indiana Jones theme to see better Returns on Investment on the secondary market. Sets like the 7620 Indiana Jones Motorcycle Chase and the 7624 Jungle Duel, both $9.99 at retail, have appreciated to over $40, for more than 400 percent Return on Investment.

7624 JUNGLE DUEL

▶ Year Released: 2008
▶ No. of Pieces: 90
▶ Minifigures: 3
▶ Retail Price: $9.99

$ ▶ New: $53 ▶ Used: $34

+ 'BUY-IN-POINT'

The phrase, "buy in point," refers to the price at which a LEGO collector, investor, or reseller buys a set. Many LEGO sets are discounted at some point during their time on primary retailer shelves and websites. While the Return on Investment (ROI) data in this book and on the BrickPicker.com site is based on Manufacturer's Suggested Retail Price, if a LEGO set is purchased for less than MSRP, the ROI could be greater than indicated in this price guide, and vice versa if a LEGO set is purchased at a price higher than MSRP.

LEGENDS OF CHIMA

THERE IS A HUGE VARIETY OF SETS IN THIS THEME, AND WHILE THEY MAY NOT BE THE BEST COLLECTIBLES, THEY WILL APPRECIATE IN VALUE. ENJOY THEM FOR THE FUN THEY ARE AND YOU MIGHT GET LUCKY AND PICK AN INVESTMENT WINNER.

In January of 2013, LEGO released the Legends of Chima theme and launched the *Legends of Chima: The Animated Series* on the Cartoon Network. Originally meant to replace the LEGO Ninjago theme, the Legends of Chima is designed for the younger generation.

The storyline is based around multiple "tribes" of humanlike creatures that resemble animals — anything from lions to spiders to gorillas. The sets resemble the animals they represent. For example, a "lion" tribe set, vehicle, or structure is gold in color, like a lion, and has lion-like features including a mane and large teeth. The other animal tribe subthemes also try to replicate the main animal in their designs.

While they are all certainly popular among the younger LEGO crowd, themes like Legends of Chima, Ninjago, Friends, Bionicle, Hero Factory, and City, among others, are not designed with the adult LEGO fan or collector in mind, and many of these sets have generic designs within the theme characteristics.

HUMANLIKE CREATURES THAT RESEMBLE *ANIMALS*

In order for any LEGO set to be valued as a collectible, it has to be unique in design, somewhat rare in production levels, and have adults as the primary target audience. Themes like Legends of Chima can become valuable on the LEGO secondary market, but there are limits. Many of these sets increase in value because of lack of inventory from primary retailers or because Little Timmy wants a set for Christmas, but the sets are not available and Mom and Dad need to go to eBay to buy one. There can be some strong growth early on in the life cycle of these sets, yet over two years or more, they seem to plateau quickly. There always can be exceptions to the rule, and there can always be a Legends of Chima set that hits extreme values, but if you are looking for collectible sets, you might want to look elsewhere. The Legends of Chima sets were designed for short-term resellers and flippers who utilize market inventory shortages to make a profit.

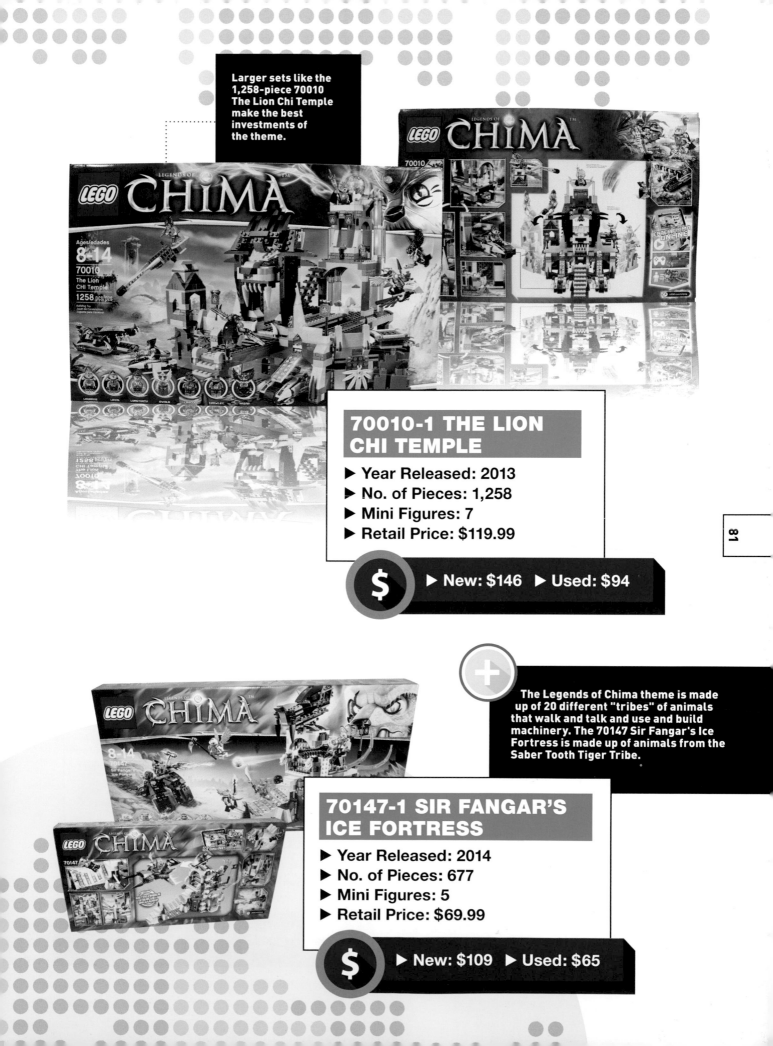

Larger sets like the 1,258-piece 70010 The Lion Chi Temple make the best investments of the theme.

70010-1 THE LION CHI TEMPLE

▶ Year Released: 2013
▶ No. of Pieces: 1,258
▶ Mini Figures: 7
▶ Retail Price: $119.99

$ ▶ New: $146 ▶ Used: $94

The Legends of Chima theme is made up of 20 different "tribes" of animals that walk and talk and use and build machinery. The 70147 Sir Fangar's Ice Fortress is made up of animals from the Saber Tooth Tiger Tribe.

70147-1 SIR FANGAR'S ICE FORTRESS

▶ Year Released: 2014
▶ No. of Pieces: 677
▶ Mini Figures: 5
▶ Retail Price: $69.99

$ ▶ New: $109 ▶ Used: $65

The impressive front gates of the 70146 Flying Phoenix Fire Temple. This part of the set remains stationary, while the Temple itself detaches and can be flown around the room.

70145-1 MAULA'S ICE MAMMOTH STOMPER

▶ Year Released: 2014
▶ No. of Pieces: 604
▶ Mini Figures: 6
▶ Retail Price: $89.99

$ ▶ New: $129 ▶ Used: $0

70146-1 FLYING PHOENIX FIRE TEMPLE

▶ Year Released: 2014
▶ No. of Pieces: 1,301
▶ Mini Figures: 7
▶ Retail Price: $119.99

$ ▶ New: $108 ▶ Used: $86

A phoenix-eye's view of the fire temple.

This set has seven minifigures, of which six are exclusive to this set. Li'Ella is one of them.

70014-1 THE CROC SWAMP HIDEOUT

▶ Year Released: 2013
▶ No. of Pieces: 647
▶ Mini Figures: 5
▶ Retail Price: $69.99

$ ▶ New: $129 ▶ Used: $47

A personal favorite of mine, the 70006 Cragger's Command Ship is potentially valuable for the rare olive green bricks included in the set.

70006-1 CRAGGER'S COMMAND SHIP

▶ Year Released: 2013
▶ No. of Pieces: 609
▶ Mini Figures: 6
▶ Retail Price: $79.99

$ ▶ New: $61 ▶ Used: $43

CHAPTER 15

THE LEGO MOVIE

BASED ON LEGO'S FIRST FORAY ON THE BIG SCREEN, THE SETS IN THIS THEME REVOLVE AROUND KEY SCENES AND ELEMENTS IN *THE LEGO MOVIE*. WHILE IT'S TOO EARLY TO JUDGE THE COLLECTIBILITY, THEY ARE FUN AND HAVE PLAYABILITY APPEAL.

The LEGO Group has done many things right since the new millennium. Prior to 2000, LEGO had a difficult time making a profit. *Fortune Magazine* named the LEGO brick the "Toy of the Century" right after the start of the new century, yet LEGO wasn't making a fortune. The LEGO Group's core philosophies and business model changed early in the new decade. LEGO began producing licensed sets such as *Star Wars* and *Harry Potter*. LEGO also started developing more detailed and complicated sets targeted at adult LEGO fans, builders, and collectors. LEGO also developed the Bionicle theme, which combined action figures with bricks. LEGO also got involved in TV and video games based on the Bionicles and other popular themes, like DC and Marvel Superheroes. Then, on February 7, 2014, LEGO took a gigantic leap, and chance, and got involved in the movie business by releasing their first big screen project: *The LEGO Movie*.

The LEGO Movie was a huge success, both critically and financially, earning close to $500 million worldwide. The movie was nominated for a Golden Globe Award, and also received an Academy Award nomination for the main theme song, "Everything is Awesome." In conjunction with the release of *The LEGO Movie*, LEGO released approximately thirty sets and promotional items relating to it. As with most licensed themes, *The LEGO Movie* sets revolve around important scenes, characters, and elements of the movie. To be quite honest, LEGO designers went above and beyond normal creativity standards with *The LEGO Movie* and its key components. There are some wild and crazy LEGO sets that are in the movie and produced for retail. It is still quite early in the collectors' cycle to judge the collectiblity and viability of many of these themed sets and to analyze prices and data. Most are still available at retail as of this writing and are sold by many major retailers. Only one set, the 70810 Metalbeard's Sea Cow, is a LEGO exclusive, and that is still sold at other large LEGO retailers. These sets are a lot of fun and playable for the most part. *The LEGO Movie 2* has been rumored for release in 2018, so there might be some renewed interest in these original sets in the future.

70810 METALBEARD'S SEA COW

- ▶ **Year Released: 2014**
- ▶ **No. of Pieces: 2,741**
- ▶ **Minifigures: 4**
- ▶ **Retail Price: $249.99**

By far, the 70810 MetalBeard's Sea Cow is the most collectible of the current *The LEGO Movie* sets, and with 2,741 pieces, it is one of the largest ever produced. It is an odd- looking sailing ship, with a "steampunk"-type flair and design. Many fans don't like the steampunk, science-fiction-meets-fantasy look, while others adore it. Either way, you cannot dispute it is one of the most detailed and crazy creative sets ever produced. In LEGO terms, the "greebles" are top notch. Almost every square inch is decorated in some fashion, from winged "Sea Cow" bowsprit to the highly adorned Captain's Quarters.

As a collectible, I like it a lot. Although its MSRP of $249.99 is high, you get a lot of set for the money. The future growth could depend upon the new LEGO movie coming out in 2018. If this set retires by then and it is in the new version, look out: it could explode in value. Even if it is not in the new movie, just the interest for *The LEGO Movie 2* will surely stimulate values of the original movie themed sets. I highly recommend this set as a collectible.

$ ▶ **New: $234** ▶ **Used: $191**

70816 BENNY'S SPACESHIP, SPACESHIP, SPACESHIP!

- ▶ **Year Released: 2014**
- ▶ **No. of Pieces: 939**
- ▶ **Minifigures: 7**
- ▶ **Retail Price: $99.99**

I love ... love ... love this set! Did I say love? The 70816 Benny's Spaceship, Spaceship, SPACESHIP! is a throwback to the Classic Space theme. Sets like the 497 Galaxy Explorer and the 6980 Galaxy Commander were some of my personal favorites as a child and young adult. I would spend hours on a Saturday or Sunday afternoon concocting all sorts of Space vehicles that looked like the 70816 Benny's Spaceship, Spaceship, SPACESHIP!. Although my creations were never as detailed or creative as this set is. I was not a LEGO "master builder" at the time. While many LEGO fans will laugh at this set and think it's ridiculous and overdone, older fans and collectors like myself will completely understand the design and appreciate it for what it is: a retrospective homage to a wonderful LEGO theme, Classic Space. This set, from a build and price point, is right on target: 940 pieces and seven minifigures (six exclusive) for $99.99. I look for the 70816 Benny's Spaceship, Spaceship, SPACESHIP! to be quite a collectible LEGO set at some point, especially if the spaceship is in the new LEGO movie. Regardless, it is an old-school favorite, and many old-school LEGO collectors will love to have one.

$ ▶ **New: $85** ▶ **Used: $70**

CHAPTER 16

THE LORD OF THE RINGS

WHILE *THE LORD OF THE RINGS* IS A BELOVED FRANCHISE IN NOVELS AND MOVIES, IT HASN'T FARED WELL IN LEGO FORM, BUT THE STANDOUT SETS FEATURED HERE HAVE THE POTENTIAL TO BECOME VALUABLE COLLECTIBLES.

J.R.R. Tolkien's *The Lord of the Rings* and *The Hobbit* are two of the best-selling novels ever written, and have been turned into six feature-length movies: *The Lord of the Rings* (2001), *Lord of the Rings: The Two Towers*, (2002), *Lord of the Rings: The Return of the King* (2003), *The Hobbit: An Unexpected Journey* (2012), *The Hobbit: The Desolation of Smaug* (2013), and *The Hobbit: The Battle of the Five Armies* (2014).

This fantasy novel and movie franchise is one of the most popular and highest-grossing in history, but popular books and movies don't always make for popular LEGO sets.

While the jury is still out on many of the sets in this theme, due to the fact that many are still available from primary retailers, the performance of sets that have retired or disappeared from shelves has not exactly lit the LEGO collectible and investment world on fire. This theme could have been done better, in my opinion. Many of the sets are underwhelming and designed around the minifigures, instead of buildings or vehicles. In the LEGO Universe, it is a good idea to have a variety of sets within a theme. There are many iconic structures and scenes that were left out of the current lineup, some which could have made

excellent and memorable LEGO sets. An Ultimate Collectors Series Minas Tirith could have been a spectacular set, or how about a chess set? Regardless, these sets will probably perform better than most, given some time.

It's really hard to put a finger on why such a beloved franchise does not translate well to LEGO sets. Possibly the designs are uninspiring. Many of the iconic scenes from the movies are hard to replicate in LEGO bricks. Many are large structures or rocklike in nature, which is almost impossible to scale down accurately.

Although LEGO castles sell well, the ones in these sets are not like your traditional King Arthur or LEGO Castle theme castles. These castle structures are more random and haphazard, utilizing the landscape around them to add to the castle's design. Even though this is more realistic, it is hard to convert into LEGO bricks unless massive MOC models are built.

One bright spot is that minifigures of the theme are a strong point, as are maxifigures. I think the Smaug Dragon maxifigure is one of the best LEGO maxifigures ever created. Minifigures make an important addition to any LEGO set. Time will tell on many of these sets.

79003 AN UNEXPECTED GATHERING

▶ **Year Released:** 2012
▶ **No. of Pieces:** 652
▶ **Mini Figures:** 6
▶ **Retail Price:** $69.99

A wonderful recreation of Bags End, the home of Bilbo and Frodo Baggins, this 652-piece set is a joy to build and admire. This set has recently disappeared from primary retailer shelves, so look for strong growth from this LEGO fan favorite. The set is highly detailed and accurate and has high playability features as well. Another must have for the *Lord of the Rings-The Hobbit* LEGO fan.

$ ▶ **New: $66** ▶ **Used: $47**

The Micro Scale Bag End was a miniature version of the 79003. It is a Limited Edition and was sold at the San Diego Comic Con in 2013 for $39.99. Current values are over $100 for an MISB set.

79018 THE LONELY MOUNTAIN

▶ **Year Released:** 2014
▶ **No. of Pieces:** 866
▶ **Mini Figures:** 5
▶ **Retail Price:** $129.99

This set was recently released when this book was being written, but it is valuable for one thing: the Smaug Dragon maxifigure. This maxifigure is currently selling for $70 or more on the LEGO secondary market. This set sells for $129.99! A great value can get even better with possible discounts. The Smaug Dragon could be the best maxifigure ever created for a LEGO set, and many of the pieces are somewhat rare.

$ ▶ **New: $128** ▶ **Used: $107**

Poor Bilbo Baggins gets a little crispy from the Smaug Dragon. The Smaug Dragon maxifigure is what makes The Lonely Mountain set valuable.

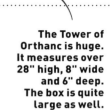

The Tower of Orthanc is huge. It measures over 28" high, 8" wide and 6" deep. The box is quite large as well.

10237 TOWER OF ORTHANC

▶ **Year Released:** 2013
▶ **No. of Pieces:** 2,359
▶ **Mini Figures:** 5
▶ **Retail Price:** $199.99

The largest of the sets at 2,359 pieces and a MSRP of $199.99, the 10237 Tower of Orthanc is on the cusp of retirement. It will most likely be the best collectible set produced in this theme because of its massive size and display qualities. This is an awesome and nasty looking LEGO set by any means, and a must have for any *Lord of the Rings-The Hobbit* enthusiast.

The imposing Tower of Orthanc will likely be the most valuable set produced in this theme.

$ ▶ **New: $237** ▶ **Used: $182**

Some creative LEGO fans will combine two 9474s and their minifigures to build a huge fortress and army.

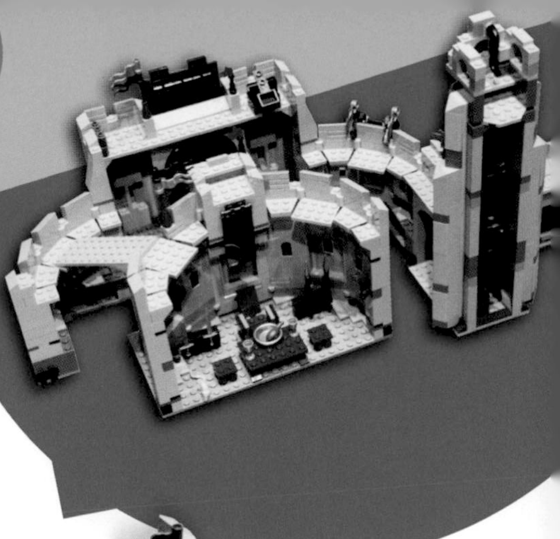

The back view of the set.

The Battle of Helm's Deep is a sure bet for steady future growth in value.

9474 BATTLE OF HELM'S DEEP

▶ Year Released: 2012
▶ No. of Pieces: 1,368
▶ Mini Figures: 8
▶ Retail Price: $129.99

A set that has been retired, the 1,368-piece and $129.99 9474 Battle of Helm's Deep is slowly appreciating in value. Many sets were discounted heavily at one point, so the current price of around $150 on the LEGO secondary market might be better for some investors and collectors than others who paid full MSRP. A popular and castle-like set with eight minifigures, look for this to continue a steady growth in value in the future.

$ ▶ New: $168 ▶ Used: $135

The King Theoden minifigure is exclusive to the 9474 Battle of Helm's Deep.

CHAPTER 17

MONSTER FIGHTERS

FRAUGHT WITH VAMPIRES, ZOMBIES, AND OTHER FRIGHTS THAT GO BUMP IN THE NIGHT, MONSTER FIGHERS IS A GREAT EXAMPLE OF A NON-LICENSED THEME THAT DOES EXTREMELY WELL ON THE LEGO SECONDARY MARKET.

What makes a great LEGO theme, especially when discussing values in the secondary market, is a question that is often debated on LEGO forums throughout the internet. Are licensed themes such as *Harry Potter* and *Star Wars* better investments than non-licensed themes such as Friends or Atlantis, or does it really not matter? In my opinion, there are winners and losers in each category, but the Monster Fighters theme is a great example of a winning non-licensed theme.

It was launched in May of 2013 and ended with the "semi-retirement" of the 10228 Haunted House in late 2014. I cannot officially claim that the 10228 Haunted House retired at this time, but for all practical purposes, it is.

The Monster Fighters theme, like many LEGO themes aimed at children, has a story behind it. The basic plot of the Monster Fighters story revolves around a vampire by the name of Lord Vampyre. Very creative. Lord Vampyre wants to make his wife happy and acquires a Moonstone for her. A Moonstone is a magical object that has mystical powers and when six

of them are placed together, legend has it that the moon will eclipse the sun and darkness will rule the Earth, enabling "monsters" to take over. A man by the name of Dr. Rodney Rathbone assembles a group of "monster fighters" to take on and destroy the creatures of the night. You can read more about this daring task in Dr. Rathbone's personal journal in a Monster Fighter video at LEGO.com.

It's a rather clever and amusing tale and one that many LEGO fans probably don't even know existed. It helps explain a lot of the individual sets and minifigures of the Monster Fighters theme and the reason behind many of the parts that make up the sets. Overall, there are nine regular sets and four polybags in the theme, making it one of the smaller themes to date. But many of the sets are doing quite well on the secondary market. The sets make excellent Halloween sets and it is possible that every October, they can find a new legion of fans who would love to acquire them, making them a solid choice for collecting and investing purposes.

MONSTER FIGHTERS 10228 HAUNTED HOUSE

▶ **Year Released: 2012**
▶ **No. of Pieces: 2,064**
▶ **Minifigures: 6**
▶ **Original Retail Price: $179.99**

The 10028 Haunted House opens up to expose various ghouls and ghosts, and could be called a "Demon Dollhouse."

The Monster Fighters theme has tugged at the heartstrings of many fans over the past two years. Based on the old-fashioned Saturday afternoon "Monster Movie," these sets are creepy, cool, and creative, with the 10228 Haunted House being the crowning jewel of the theme.

Released in September of 2012, this set one of the most unique ones I have encountered, and I often relate it to some supernatural "dollhouse." The 10228 Haunted House is a complete four-walled building that opens up on a pair of hinges and exposes the internal rooms and features of the toy, similar to many dollhouse designs, and is detailed on all four sides of the building.

The unique ability to open the model to expose internals in an easy manner lets children and adults have the ability to interact with the awesome interior decorations including kitchen, master bedroom, phonograph, and more. It also lets a collector add to the interior decorations. Sets like the 30201 Ghost or 5000644 Monster Fighters Promotional Pack can add wonderful touches to an already special and spooky interior. While the interior is detailed quite well, it is the exterior that really shines. The 10228 Haunted House is constructed in the rare sand green color, which is quite appropriate for any "haunted" structure. Randomly mixed in the green walls are some tan bricks with "brick" imprints. This technique makes the structure look weathered and dilapidated, which adds to the eerie appearance. The build of the set is straightforward and fun. There are a lot of creatively creepy details on the 10228 Haunted House that makes it an enjoyable project for all ages.

$ ▶ **New: $322** ▶ **Used: $235**

The front box reveals scenes of a zombie apocalypse in LEGO form.

9465 THE ZOMBIES

▶ **Year Released: 2012**
▶ **No. of Pieces: 447**
▶ **Minifigures: 4**
▶ **Original Retail Price: $39.99**

The less there is of a LEGO set, the better and more valuable it usually becomes, which is the case with the 9465 The Zombies. From a layman's point of view, the set is nothing special. It is a 447-piece set that was released in 2012 with a MSRP of $39.99. It looks like hundreds of other LEGO sets released in any given year. But the current value on the LEGO secondary market in the $180 range is surprising. That is about a 350 percent Return on Investment in two years' time.

Why such an increase in value? Zombies, and a short production run.

The set's key minifigures are "zombies,"

which in the world of LEGO collecting are like "plastic gold," and any set or collectible minifigure polybag that has a zombie included appreciates well. This set has three zombie minifigures and two of them are exclusive to it: the zombie bride and groom. The third zombie minifigure is a driver, which has been in four other sets, so it is not as valuable. When the set was released in July of 2012, it was basically retired or out of production by October of 2012. That is a short production run for any LEGO set, and coupled with the fact that this was a Target "exclusive" in the United States, this LEGO set was a rare one, indeed. At this point, the growth of the 9465 The Zombies has slowed dramatically, but it is still increasing at a slow pace. This is the type of set that a LEGO completist will want to obtain so that they can collect the entire Monster Fighters theme.

$ ▶ **New: $179** ▶ **Used: $134**

The back of the box illustrates the many secret compartments of the castle.

9468 VAMPYRE CASTLE

▶ **Year Released: 2012**
▶ **No. of Pieces: 949**
▶ **Minifigures: 7**
▶ **Retail Price: $99.99**

The 9468 Vampyre Castle is the second largest in this theme, with 949 pieces. It has recently disappeared from major retailers, and so it should take the typical post-retirement bounce in values like many other LEGO sets do.

The set uses the long time and tested Castle-themed bricks and parts in its design, giving it the classic look of past LEGO castles, albeit a little darker and scarier. The build is straightforward and designed for most LEGO fans above the age of 7 or 8. Within the walls of the Vampyre Castle are plenty of hidden compartments and features that you would find in a haunted castle, thus giving it a large playability factor. It folds out to expose the interior portions and displays well when retracted, making it a possible choice for Halloween displays through the years. It comes with seven minifigures, with the two Bat Monsters being exclusive to this set. The Vampyre Castle also contains a mount for the Moonstones and has all translucent bricks, except for the Mummies Moonstone. It also includes a vehicle to add to the fun factor, and appeals to all age

The set comes with seven minifigures, two of which are exclusive to it (Bat Monsters).

groups. Children will enjoy the playability features and adults will appreciate the scary display qualities that make it a seasonal point of interest. Overall, this is a popular set among LEGO fans, collectors, and investors, which should translate into a solid investment choice for those who own one.

$ ▶ **New: $137** ▶ **Used: $99**

9467 GHOST TRAIN

▶ **Year Released:** 2012
▶ **No. of Pieces:** 741
▶ **Minifigures:** 5
▶ **Retail Price:** $79.99

Trains seem to tickle the fancy of many LEGO enthusiasts. Maybe it's the fact that LEGO bricks are an excellent medium to produce train replicas or because hobby trains and LEGO sets both are smaller-scale replicas of real world creations. Whatever the reason, LEGO train sets are popular. Such is the case with the 9467 Ghost Train of the Monster Fighters theme.

Released in May of 2012, the 9467 Ghost Train sold for $79.99 at retail. The set contains 741 pieces and really wasn't a bargain Price Per Piece wise. The set was highly discounted during its year-and-a-half production run, eventually making it a good deal for many collectors and investors. The set contains many unique features such as glow-in-the-dark parts, train parts, and cool rubber wheels. Unlike many LEGO trains, this one rolls on rubber tires, giving it a more playability aspect. While this set can be converted to conventional train wheels, the parts would have to be acquired through aftermarket sources. Build wise, it is a fun set with some features that use bricks in a creative manner. The set comes with two Monster Fighters "fighters," Ann Lee and Frank Rock, that are not unique to this set, and three ghost minifigures that are unique to the set, making them somewhat valuable to the LEGO Halloween crowd.

The current value is nearing $100, and the positive growth should continue. The 9467 Ghost Train is a wonderful addition to any Monster Fighters LEGO collection. It plays and displays well and gets a few smiles in the meantime. Most of all, there is nothing similar to it in the LEGO world — and unique in the LEGO Universe is always a good thing.

$ ▶ **New: $97** ▶ **Used: $61**

Trains are popular in any theme, even ones from the Supernatural world.

GHOSTS
NOTHING TO BOO ABOUT

LEGO collectors have a soft spot for things that go bump in the night. Sets that contain zombies have proven to be popular and great investments in the secondary market, but not only zombies get the love — ghost minifigures are admired as well. Take, for instance, the 30201 Ghost polybag. This $3.50, 33-piece set has gone up over 600 percent in value from its MSRP, with current value just reaching the $25 mark.

The set contains one ghost minifigure that has the classic haunted movie "ball and chain" attached to it and a cool grandfather clock replica that would fit well in any of the larger Monster Fighter buildings. This is the perfect example of a set that is affordable and collectible.

CHAPTER 18

NINJAGO

SETS IN THEMES LIKE NINJAGO CAN APPRECIATE SHORT TERM AND MANY HAVE A POSITIVE RETURN ON INVESTMENT, BUT LONG-TERM POTENTIAL IS IFFY. BUT NINJAGO IS A FUN THEME AND CAN BROADEN YOUR LEGO COLLECTION.

Ninjago ... Masters of Spinjitzu. This is another example of a multiple-platform LEGO theme. Besides the brick aspect of the theme, the Ninjago franchise can be seen on The Cartoon Network and in video games. Released in 2001, the *Ninjago* TV series and LEGO theme were planned to end in 2014 and replaced by the Legends of Chima theme and TV show on the same network. But plans were changed and the Ninjago franchise will continue into 2015 and beyond, with a proposed *Ninjago* movie releasing in 2016 and possibly another in 2018.

Based on ninjas and a whole assortment of monsters and dragons, the Ninjago theme reminds me of the Power Rangers. Unlike earlier ninja LEGO themes, the Ninjago theme mixes in more modern technology and designs. tanks, mechs, and jet planes are mixed with traditional Japanese architecture and decoration. It is a combination that has given LEGO designers a ton of latitude when it comes to being creative and anything goes: ninjas, dragons, snakes, zombies, swords, rockets, spaceships, whatever. It's a fun theme and full of unique elements and minifigures.

Like the Legends of Chima, the Ninjago theme is targeted at young boys and the sets are not considered serious collectibles by many adults, probably because they are mass produced and available at any Target, Walmart, and Toys

BASED ON **NINJAS,** MONSTERS, **& DRAGONS**

R Us. But because of the popularity of the theme, especially several years ago when the cartoon originally launched, there were shortages of many sets around the holiday season, causing prices to spike upward — and thus a value increase on the LEGO secondary market. Resellers took advantage of stock shortages and sold many of these sets well above MSRP.

If you just examine the Ninjago theme as a popular one with children, you realize that many of these sets are not the above average LEGO collectible sets that some numbers indicate. Values increased on the secondary market because parents paid top dollar for sets that their children wanted, not because these sets were rare or highly unique. This has been illustrated by the fact that no Ninjago set has hit $200 on the secondary market as of this writing. The 2521 Lightning Dragon Battle and 2507 Fire Temple are closest, in the $190 range. This does not bode well for the long-term prospects of many of the sets, especially since these two have been retired for three years and can't crack $200.

Short term, though, many of the Ninjago sets do appreciate well, and exhibit a positive Return on Investment. Sets such as the 2260 Ice Dragon Attack, 30083 Dragon Fight, and 2509 Earth Dragon Defense, all have gains in the 300 percent range over the past few years.

The 30083 Dragon Fight small polybag has appreciated well.

30083 DRAGON FIGHT

▶ Year Released: 2011
▶ No. of Pieces: 31
▶ Minifigures: 1
▶ Original Retail Price: $3.49

$ ▶ New: $14 ▶ Used: $6

Most LEGO sets with dragons seem to increase in value.

CLOSE-UP

2507 FIRE TEMPLE

▶ Year Released: 2011
▶ No. of Pieces: 1,180
▶ Minifigures: 8
▶ Original Retail Price: $119.99

$ ▶ New: $191 ▶ Used: $144

The specialized head pieces of the various Dragons, such as the white-fanged 2260 Ice Dragon, are the most valuable bricks in the Ninjago theme.

2260 ICE DRAGON ATTACK

▶ **Year Released:** 2011
▶ **No. of Pieces:** 158
▶ **Minifigures:** 2
▶ **Original Retail Price:** $19.99

$ ▶ **New: $95** ▶ **Used: $41**

The 2521 Lightning Dragon Battle is the set that started the Dragon craze within the Ninjago theme.

2509 EARTH DRAGON DEFENSE

▶ **Year Released:** 2011
▶ **No. of Pieces:** 227
▶ **Minifigures:** 2
▶ **Original Retail Price:** $34.99

$ ▶ **New: $127** ▶ **Used: $58**

2521 LIGHTNING DRAGON BATTLE

▶ **Year Released:** 2011
▶ **No. of Pieces:** 645
▶ **Minifigures:** 4
▶ **Original Retail Price:** $79.99

$ ▶ **New: $193** ▶ **Used: $110**

CHAPTER 19

PIRATES
& PIRATES OF THE CARIBBEAN

COLLECTORS WHO BYPASS PIRATE-THEMED SETS MAY WANT TO RECONSIDER: SETS WITH SAILING SHIPS CAN APPRECIATE TO MODERATELY HIGH VALUES AND HAVE SOLID RETURNS ON INVESTMENT. PLUS, THE BUILT SHIPS DISPLAY WELL AND MAKE NICE CONVERSATION PIECES.

Ahoy, matey! Welcome to the LEGO Pirates theme. *The Pirates of the Caribbean* theme is included as well to help simplify matters. The original LEGO Pirates theme started in 1989 and has several iterations of the main theme since then. The most famous and popular variation was the release of the *Pirates of the Caribbean* theme in 2011, based on the big screen adaptation of the classic Walt Disney's Magic Kingdom ride, *The Pirates of the Caribbean*. The LEGO Pirates theme has always had its share of fans, both children and adult. There are multiple clubs and LUGS (LEGO User Group) that involve pirates and custom-built MOCs of pirate ships. For this theme, I will be discussing the main LEGO Pirates sets that contain a pirate or flagship, sail type of vessel. Land-based Pirates or *Pirates of the Caribbean* sets are just not that compelling or interesting to analyze.

The sailing ships of these themes can appreciate to moderately high levels and have solid Returns on Investment. While not the most popular LEGO theme of all time, there is a faction of pirate fans that love these ships and sets, but many collectors pass on them, probably to their detriment. The Pirates and *Pirates of the Caribbean* sets are good ones to diversify your collection with and do display quite well and would make a nice conversation piece in an upscale office or den.

One last note: The smaller Pirates and *Pirates of the Caribbean* sets that are non-ship related are really non-factors with this theme. While they can appreciate, I think there are better sets for your investment dollars, including these four main-masted sailing ship sets featured here.

LEGO designers excel at certain types of sets, including trains, spaceships, and masted ships. The above sets are polar opposites of one another. White vs. Black and Good vs. Evil are two obvious differences, but they are alike in one simple way: They are excellent display LEGO sets and will look great in any room or office.

10210 IMPERIAL FLAGSHIP

▶ **Year Released: 2010**
▶ **No. of Pieces: 1,664**
▶ **Minifigures: 9**
▶ **Original Retail Price: $179.99**

The largest ship of the themes, with over 1,600 pieces and nine minifigures, the majestic 10210 Imperial Flagship makes a wonderful display. Valued at over $500 on the LEGO secondary market, the set has the highest current value of any Pirates or *Pirates of the Caribbean* set. It seems to have peaked in value recently, and it has been retired for well over three years, so the Return on Investment of slightly under 200 percent is nothing to scoff at, but certainly doesn't put this set in the upper tier of LEGO collectibles.

$ ▶ **New: $521** ▶ **Used: $400**

4184 THE BLACK PEARL

▶ **Year Released: 2011**
▶ **No. of Pieces: 804**
▶ **Minifigures: 6**
▶ **Original Retail Price: $99.99**

Captain Jack Sparrow's ship, the 4184 The Black Pearl, is the smallest of the major sailing ships at 804 pieces and six minifigures. But of those minifigures, five are exclusive to the set. Even though the set is the smallest and lowest in cost at $99.99 MSRP, its current value is the highest on the LEGO secondary market at well over $300, exhibiting over 200 percent Return on Investment. What's also different about the current values of this set is that they are still growing, unlike many of the other ships in these themes, which seem to have plateaued. This is a cool ship that displays well, especially alongside the 4195 Queen Anne's Revenge.

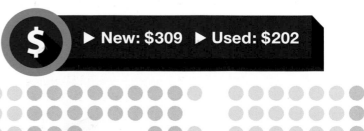

$ ▶ **New: $309** ▶ **Used: $202**

Maybe it's just me, but the happy red and white sails just don't match with the Skull and Crossbones flag.

10040 BLACK SEAS BARRACUDA

▶ **Year Released:** 2002
▶ **No. of Pieces:** 906
▶ **Minifigures:** 8
▶ **Original Retail Price:** $89.99

A remake of the 6285 Black Seas Barracuda from 1989, its nickname was the "Dark Shark." Both versions of the Black Seas Barracuda are pretty much identical, each a touch over 900 pieces with eight minifigures. This is the set that many pirate enthusiasts look at when speaking of the "classic" pirate ship of the theme. It sold for $89.99 at

retail, and current prices are well over $400, with almost a 400 percent Return on Investment — solid numbers for an older but iconic LEGO set.

$ ▶ **New: $649** ▶ **Used: $172**

4195 QUEEN ANNE'S REVENGE

▶ **Year Released:** 2011
▶ **No. of Pieces:** 1,097
▶ **Minifigures:** 9
▶ **Original Retail Price:** $119.99

A beautiful LEGO ship and the largest *Pirates of the Caribbean* set at over 1,000 pieces and a whopping nine minifigures, the 4195 Queen Anne's Revenge was a bargain at $119.99 MSRP. In fact, the set was available at a discount many times prior to retirement and I recall buying it for around $90. Many of the pieces are somewhat unique and rare, which is essential to LEGO antique ship MOCs and custom models. The set has reached the $300 level, for over 150 percent Return on Investment from retirement two years

ago. My favorite set in this theme, the 4195 Queen Anne's Revenge is stunning with the ruby red sails and antique detailing, making it a standout display set.

$ ▶ **New: $306** ▶ **Used: $204**

CHAPTER 20

SEASONAL

SEASONAL SETS ARE SOME OF THE BEST APPRECIATING COLLECTIBLE LEGO SETS IN EXISTENCE. NEW ONES ARE RELEASED ON AN ANNUAL BASIS AND OLD ONES ARE RETIRED QUICKLY. MANY SEASONAL SETS ARE QUITE SMALL AND HAVE LIMITS AS TO HOW HIGH THEY CAN APPRECIATE, THOUGH, BUT FOR THOSE ON A BUDGET, THESE SETS ARE TREMENDOUS VALUES.

As the title suggests, the sets of the Seasonal theme consist of ones from the different seasons of the year and also encompass many of the major holidays including Christmas, Easter, Halloween, Thanksgiving, and Valentine's Day.

For the most part, Seasonal sets are on the small side, from the tiniest boxes to the usual polybag. There is a subtheme, the LEGO Winter Village "collection," that includes larger sets that are based on multiple quaint houses and structures from a country village in wintertime. Many times these sets are included in the Advanced Models theme, but I am keeping them in the Winter Village theme. Besides the typical store-bought LEGO sets, some of the Seasonal ones are also promotional sets given away by LEGO in their VIP Program when certain purchase totals are reached.

Overall, the Seasonal theme is an enjoyable one for fans and collectors. The sets are affordable and appreciate well, albeit on a small scale. The Winter Village subtheme is the top of the Seasonal food chain and the sets are popular with collectors and resellers, especially when in short supply around the holiday shopping season. I highly recommend adding a few or more of these sets to your collection. Time your LEGO purchases correctly and take advantage of the LEGO VIP events and you might not even have to pay for a set.

40106 ELVES' WORKSHOP

▶ **Year Released:** 2014
▶ **No. of Pieces:** 107
▶ **Minifigures:** 2
▶ **Original Retail Price:** $3.99

$ ▶ New: $27 ▶ Used: $18

f the smaller sets of the Seasonal theme, many appreciate quite quickly. Sets like the 40029 Valentine's Day Box and 40053 Easter Bunny with Basket have quadrupled in value in a short time, from $4.99 MSRP to almost $20. Granted, many of the Seasonal sets never hit high values, but many do quadruple, so they are great for LEGO collectors on a budget.

An excellent example of how the free LEGO promotional items are great collectibles is the 40106 Elves' Workshop. This was a free item given away to LEGO VIP members if they bought a certain amount of LEGO sets during the 2014 holiday season. Current values of this set are close to $30, so these promotional items must be considered when timing and planning LEGO purchases to take advantage of the freebies and deals.

There are hundreds of these small Seasonal sets, many with Santa Claus, Easter Bunny, or Halloween Ghost or Goblin as a main character. Most do appreciate quickly in the short term and have low ceilings for maximum values, but they are cute, creative, and a lot of fun nonetheless.

My wonderful wife, Jane, bought me this gift several years ago for Valentine's Day. I think I bought her diamonds ...

40029 VALENTINE'S DAY BOX

▶ **Year Released:** 2012
▶ **No. of Pieces:** 51
▶ **Minifigures:** 0
▶ **Original Retail Price:** $4.99

$ ▶ New: $19 ▶ Used: $10

40053 EASTER BUNNY WITH BASKET

▶ **Year Released:** 2013
▶ **No. of Pieces:** 96
▶ **Minifigures:** 0
▶ **Original Retail Price:** $4.99

$ ▶ New: $18 ▶ Used: $0

WINTER SETS WINNERS

From a collectible standpoint, the Winter Village subtheme is where the action is. The sets started in 2009, and a new one has been released every year since.

The six sets released so far are all highly collectible, in that each one compliments the other. Many people love to collect and display these sorts of items around Christmas trees or on a table during the holiday season. As time passes and with each new Winter Village release, the older sets will become even more desirable to collectors the world over.

The sets themselves are adorable, with many creative design features that incorporate white and snow-like elements. These sets have all appreciated quite well after retirement and some do even before retirement, with inventory shortages before Christmas bumping up prices swiftly. A few of the sets have hit almost three to four times MSRP, which is outstanding.

10216 WINTER VILLAGE BAKERY

- ▶ Year Released: 2010
- ▶ No. of Pieces: 687
- ▶ Minifigures: 7
- ▶ Original Retail Price: $54.99

$ ▶ New: $161 ▶ Used: $128

10229 WINTER VILLAGE COTTAGE

- ▶ Year Released: 2012
- ▶ No. of Pieces: 1,490
- ▶ Minifigures: 8
- ▶ Original Retail Price: $99.99

$ ▶ New: $191 ▶ Used: $148

10235 WINTER VILLAGE MARKET

- ▶ Year Released: 2013
- ▶ No. of Pieces: 1,261
- ▶ Minifigures: 9
- ▶ Original Retail Price: $99.99

$ ▶ New: $139 ▶ Used: $66

At this writing, the 10245 Santa's Workshop is still available at retail, so now is as good as time as any to start your LEGO Winter Wonderland.

10245 SANTA'S WORKSHOP

▶ Year Released: 2014
▶ No. of Pieces: 883
▶ Minifigures: 6
▶ Original Retail Price: $69.99

$ ▶ New: $108 ▶ Used: $48

Winter-themed sets like the 10199 Winter Village Toy Shop often have good Price Per Piece ratios and include a large amount of minifigures, in comparison to sets in other themes. A LEGO fan gets a good bang for their buck!

10199 WINTER VILLAGE TOY SHOP

▶ Year Released: 2009
▶ No. of Pieces: 815
▶ Minifigures: 7
▶ Original Retail Price: $59.99

$ ▶ New: $230 ▶ Used: $171

The 10222 Winter Village Post Office is one of the better performing Winter sets, tripling from its retail price of $69.99 to well over $200 in a few years. Very impressive.

10222 WINTER VILLAGE POST OFFICE

▶ Year Released: 2011
▶ No. of Pieces: 822
▶ Minifigures: 7
▶ Original Retail Price: $69.99

$ ▶ New: $215 ▶ Used: $158

ADVENT CALENDARS

LEGO Advent calendars are classified by many collectors to the specific theme they are designed for. A LEGO City Advent Calendar is a City set, a *Star Wars* Advent Calendar is a *Star Wars* set, etc. That being said, you can make an argument to add the calendars to the Seasonal theme because they are only available during the Christmas season.

These calendars are interesting and fun. Released before Christmas for the past several years, they honor the old-school tradition of celebrating the "25 Days of Christmas" with special boxes and minisets/minifigures that can be added to each of the numbered days to keep track of how many days are left before Christmas. LEGO minifigures and minisets replace the candy or trinkets from non-LEGO Advent Calendars. The 75056 *Star Wars* Advent Calendar is a fan favorite, and with the Darth Santa minifigure, sure to be a highly collectible set at some point.

CHAPTER 21

SPACE

UNITRON **EXPLORIENS**
SPYRIUS **UFO**
ICE PLANET 2002
BLACKTRON ROCK RAIDERS
CLASSIC SPACE
ALIEN CONQUEST ROBOFORCE M-TRON SPACE (CITY)

MARS MISSION
GALAXY SQUAD
SPACE POLICE I,II,III
LIFE ON MARS **INSECTOIDS**
BLACKTRON FUTURE GENERATION

It was about thirty-six years ago when I was introduced to the LEGO Space theme. The set was the 497/928 Galaxy Explorer and I was hooked. The new fandangled pieces of the Classic Space theme just floored a nine year old. It was these pieces and sets that set me on my LEGO journey some four decades ago. What is funny is that the Space theme has seen multiple versions and subthemes over the years and hasn't really changed all that much. Here is a list of the different versions of the Space theme:

- Classic Space
- Blacktron
- Futuron
- Space Police
- M-Tron
- Blacktron Future Generation
- Space Police II
- Ice Planet 2002
- Spyrius
- Unitron
- Exploriens
- UFO
- Roboforce
- Insectoids
- Rock Raiders
- Life on Mars
- Mars Mission
- Space Police III
- Space (City)
- Alien Conquest
- Galaxy Squad

The Space theme is one of the pillars of LEGO's sales and community for over thirty-five years. Along with the City/Town and Castle themes, LEGO has been selling these simple and fun sets to millions of LEGO children and adult fans. Even the most recent Galaxy Squad subtheme is reminiscent of the older Space sets.

Since Space-themed sets are designed for children, they are some of the weakest sets to collect because they don't appreciate quickly in value, although some smaller sets in this theme do fairly well.

That being said, enjoy these sets. Buy them for your kids or yourself and stir up ancient memories of days gone by. Build them, fly them, roll them around the room. They are meant for play and not display.

A 487 set, MISB, could be worth thousands of dollars.

487 SPACE CRUISER

▶ **Year Released:** 1978
▶ **No. of Pieces:** 170
▶ **Minifigures:** 2
▶ **Retail Price:** $9.99

$ ▶ New: $0 ▶ Used: $92

493 COMMAND CENTER

▶ **Year Released:** 1978
▶ **No. of Pieces:** 189
▶ **Minifigures:** 4
▶ **Retail Price:** $0

$ ▶ New: $107 ▶ Used: $108

You have to remember that Space-themed sets are designed for children and not older fans. While many like myself enjoy the theme and relate to the sets, as a collectible, they are some of the weakest of all LEGO sets. While they do appreciate, they really don't do it quickly in comparison to other themes. Unless you can own a MISB Classic Space set such as the 497/928 Galaxy Explorer, 487 Space Cruiser, or 493 Command Center, which might sell for thousands of dollars because of their rarity, most Space sets have a problem breaking $200. Even the largest retired Space sets like the 70709 Galaxy Titan from the Galaxy Squad subtheme can't even break even and get back to MSRP from heavy discounts prior to retirement. Some of the smaller sets of the theme have shown decent appreciation. Sets like the 5619 Crystal Hawk from the Mars Mission subtheme have grown 400 percent in value: but to $20, from a MSRP of $3.99. That's great, but it also took six years to get there.

I am personally saddened by the growth of these sets on the LEGO secondary market. While many of them are remakes of earlier subthemes and sets, I'm surprised that they don't get more love from fans. I guess the *Star Wars* theme draws potential science fiction LEGO customers away from the Space- themed sets, but the bigger issue on the secondary market is that the Space sets are some of the most heavily discounted in the LEGO Universe. Many of the sets from the recently retired Galaxy Squad have been discounted close to 50 percent off. This might actually be advantageous to collectors due to the fact that if the buy-in point is lower than MSRP, the actual data in our price guide might be higher than indicated.

497/928 GALAXY EXPLORER

▶ Year Released: 1979
▶ No. of Pieces: 338
▶ Minifigures: 4
▶ Retail Price: $31.99

$ ▶ New: $0 ▶ Used: $219

Blue and gray bricks with yellow translucent windows are classic colors of this theme.

▶ The 497/928 Galaxy Explorer is the set that got me addicted to LEGO bricks. As a young man almost 40 years ago, this set and its new "space" bricks enabled me to create all sorts of spaceships and vehicles that I was unable to do so previously.

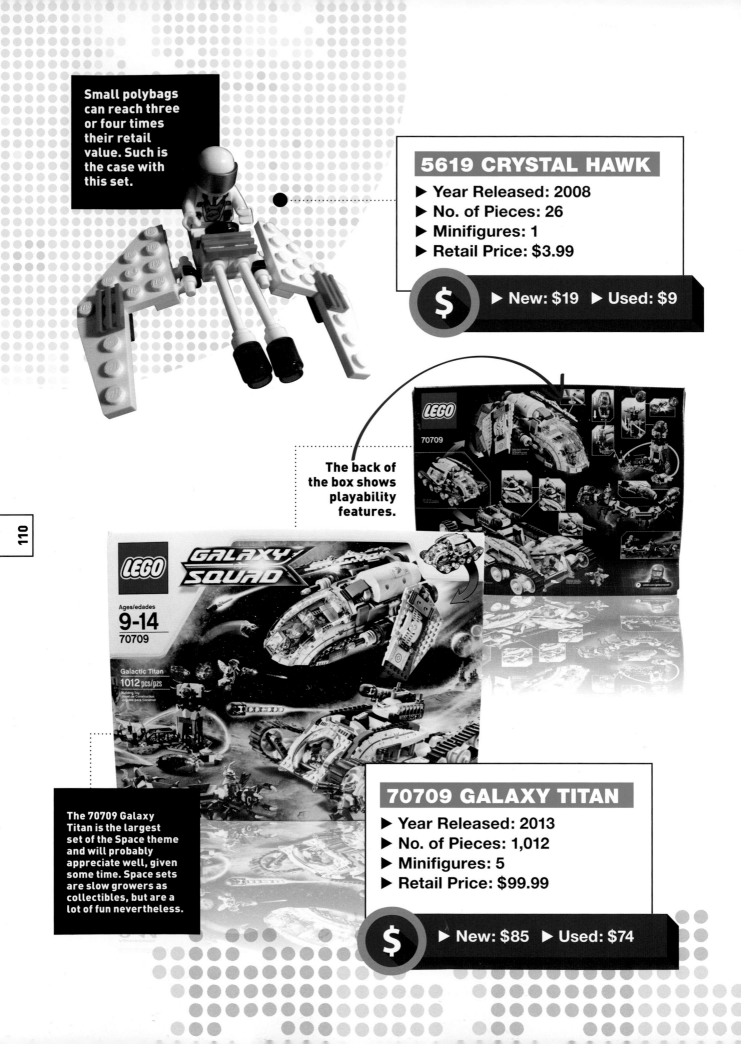

Small polybags can reach three or four times their retail value. Such is the case with this set.

5619 CRYSTAL HAWK

▶ Year Released: 2008
▶ No. of Pieces: 26
▶ Minifigures: 1
▶ Retail Price: $3.99

$ ▶ New: $19 ▶ Used: $9

The back of the box shows playability features.

LEGO GALAXY SQUAD

Ages/edades
9-14
70709

Galactic Titan
1012 pcs/pzs
Building Toy
Jouet de Construction
Juguete para Construir

The 70709 Galaxy Titan is the largest set of the Space theme and will probably appreciate well, given some time. Space sets are slow growers as collectibles, but are a lot of fun nevertheless.

70709 GALAXY TITAN

▶ Year Released: 2013
▶ No. of Pieces: 1,012
▶ Minifigures: 5
▶ Retail Price: $99.99

$ ▶ New: $85 ▶ Used: $74

CHAPTER 22

STAR WARS
ULTIMATE COLLECTOR SERIES

THE LEGO GROUP'S NEW PHILOSOPHY OF CREATING SETS THAT CATER TO ADULT TASTES, ABILITIES, AND BANK ACCOUNTS ORIGINATED WITH THE *STAR WARS* UCS SETS. THESE SETS HAVE EXPLODED IN MONETARY GROWTH OVER THE PAST 15 YEARS, AND THE LEGO SECONDARY MARKET IS ALL THE STRONGER FOR IT.

LEGO Dark Ages: A period of time in which a LEGO fan loses interest in their beloved bricks. It usually coincides with adolescence and early adulthood and ends when they are reintroduced to a particular set or theme that rekindles the love affair with the little plastic bricks.

Many adult fans of LEGO (AFOL) have this experience. My reawakening came when my brother, Jeff, and I were surfing the internet one day and came across the *Star Wars* UCS 10030 Imperial Star Destroyer for sale on eBay. I was amazed. It was a three-foot long, three hundred dollar, three-thousand-piece re-creation of the fantastic Star Destroyer from many of the early *Star Wars* films. I wanted it ... bad. I asked Santa Claus to bring it to me for Christmas that year and he agreed, making a 38-year-old man very happy, and so began my journey back into LEGO collecting and eventually LEGO investing.

The sets of the *Star Wars* Ultimate Collector Series have a tendency to do such things. The UCS sets are a subtheme of the larger *Star Wars* theme

SOME OF THE
MOST LOVED
& SOUGHT
AFTER SETS

consisting of 22 sets to date. For purposes of this book and because of the special nature of the sets, we will consider the UCS sets a theme unto itself. These sets comprise some of the most expensive and valuable LEGO sets ever produced. Even to this day, current UCS models are some of the most loved and sought after sets in production.

The UCS was launched in 2000, with the 7191 UCS X-Wing Fighter being the first release. What makes this set and following UCS sets so extraordinary is their complexity in build and accuracy in appearance, far exceeding earlier *Star Wars* sets and almost every other LEGO set ever produced. These sets were designed for the young adult and adult LEGO fans in the world. Even if you are not a *Star Wars* fan, you have to admire the engineering and design characteristics of the UCS sets.

The UCS sets are some of the largest ever released and costliest as well. Many would argue that this theme helped put The LEGO Group back in the black financially and has helped make LEGO the number one toy maker in the world.

THE 10179 MILLENNIUM FALCON

▶ **Year Released: 2007**
▶ **No. of Pieces: 5,192**
▶ **Minifigures: 5**
▶ **Retail Price: $499.99**

Note the small icon on the left bottom corner. This is a "First Edition" 10179 UCS Millennium Falcon, one of 20,000 made.

Photo courtesy of www.techlug.fr

Love it or hate it, the Millennium Falcon is the iconic vehicle from the most legendary movie series of all time. The creator of the *Star Wars* universe, George Lucas, based the design on a hamburger, with the cockpit being an olive to the side. The unique design — ugly yet lovable at the same time — has given the Millennium Falcon almost a cult-like following among *Star Wars* fans and many almost consider it another character in the film series. It is this affection that makes the Millennium Falcon the perfect candidate to be the greatest LEGO set ever produced.

Released in 2007 during LEGO's celebration of the 30th anniversary of *Star Wars*, the 10179 UCS Millennium Falcon was the shining star of the entire LEGO line that year. As a matter of fact, the 10179 is the all-time shining star of every retail LEGO set ever produced, in my opinion. It is also the largest set ever produced in sheer size and weight. At 5,192 pieces, it is second only to the 10189 Taj Mahal, which is 5,922 pieces. LEGO sets' size and value are gauged by the amount of ABS plastic in a set, and the 10179 UCS Millennium Falcon is by far the heaviest, at a little over 22 pounds of plastic. The finished model is almost three feet by two feet and is the size of a small table,

which, for a LEGO set, is quite large.

From a build standpoint, the 10179 UCS Millennium Falcon is a lengthy and time-consuming process. The instructions for this set are an actual book, not a pamphlet. If you haven't built one, it's a several-day process for most average builders and takes up an entire dining room table to separate and sort the 5,000+ pieces. This is a display set only; it has little playability. While the outside is highly detailed and covered with greebles, there is no interior portion of the model of any consequence. What it does have is five minifigures: Chewbacca, Princess Leia, Obi-Wan Kenobi, Luke Skywalker, and, of course, Han Solo. Minifigures in early UCS sets was a rare occurrence, although it seems that newer UCS sets are starting to include more minifigures. Only the Obi-Wan Kenobi minifigure is exclusive to this set. Overall, it is a dynamic looking set and recreates the movie version of the Millennium Falcon in LEGO bricks in such a way that it's hard to tell it's a LEGO set. There are also a few rare and expensive pieces with this set that makes it difficult to reproduce in the aftermarket without spending top dollar doing so. A large UCS specifications plaque finishes off the display.

The 10179 UCS Millenium Falcon was the first LEGO set to reach the $3,000 mark in value. Originally, the set sold for $499.99, making it the most expensive one ever sold to the general public. Besides the large size and piece count, the 10179 set has several other things going for it. For one, it is a LEGO *Star Wars* 30th Anniversary set which has special markings. Some of these 30th Anniversary sets had a bonus golden chrome C-3PO minifigure polybag

"What a piece of junk!"

— LUKE SKYWALKER REFERRING TO HAN SOLO'S YT-1300 CORELLIAN TRANSPORT SHIP, THE MILLENNIUM FALCON, IN STAR WARS IV: A NEW HOPE

A closeup of minifigures Han Solo and Chewbacca in the cockpit.

Photo courtesy of Telgar Sandseeker

Rear view of the Hyperdrive Engines that make the Falcon the "fastest piece of junk in the Universe."

Photo courtesy of Telgar Sandseeker

The 10179 Millennium Falcon.

Photo courtesy of Telgar Sandseeker

included. They were randomly placed in sets in 2007 and only 10,000 of these bonus polybags were produced. These C-3POs currently sell for $300+ on the LEGO secondary market. Another nice feature is that the first 20,000 released had a special "Certificate of Authenticity" included in the set that was numbered and came with a letter from LEGO stating that the set was a "First Edition" set. There was also a special notation on the box cover indicating it was a First Edition set. These first 20,000 sets can bring as much as $300-$400 more than a regular 10179 Millennium Falcon.

The growth of this set has been phenomenal, appreciating over 600 percent from MSRP, and it continues to appreciate. One has to wonder if the new *Star Wars* movies will have an effect on this set in particular. Rumors have it that the Millennium Falcon will be in the new movie, so it is quite possible a new version of the 10179 UCS Millennium Falcon will be released. If the newer version is smaller and less complex, look for the value of the set to continue to rise. Conversely, if there is another UCS Millennium Falcon released and it is close in build and pieces to the original, there could be a negative effect on the value of the older version. Time will tell. Regardless, it is the greatest LEGO set produced to date, in my opinion, and every serious LEGO collector should have one.

$ ▶ New: $3,450   ▶ Used: $2,064

10143 DEATH STAR II

▶ **Year Released: 2005**
▶ **No. of Pieces: 3,441**
▶ **Mini Figures: 0**
▶ **Retail Price: $269.99**

Although the 10143 UCS Death Star II is a set based on Death Star II in *The Return of the Jedi*, any discussion of a Death Star should include that classic dialog to set the mood. This is another of the large and in charge UCS LEGO sets, coming in at almost 3,500 pieces. It is a replica of the under construction, yet fully functional Death Star II. This set, like the 10030 UCS Imperial Star Destroyer, is a mass of dark and light gray LEGO bricks. The set has the traditional UCS nameplate, and as a bonus, the Super Star Destroyer Executor revolves around the equator of the Death Star II.

The build of this set is complex and tedious, making it an option for only experienced LEGO builders. There are so many gray bricks of similar nature, an inexperienced builder can easily make mistakes, and what should be a fun experience turns into a hair-pulling stress fest. That being said, the finished display is superb; a true gem in any LEGO collection. The value of this set has really hit astronomical levels, reaching the magical $1,500 mark recently. Its MSRP of $269.99 in 2005 was a fair price for a 3,500-piece set. Its ROI of over 400 percent from retail has really taken off over the past year. It is quite possible that the new *Star Wars* movies being released in 2015 has something to do with the recent interest in this set.

$ ▶ **New: $1,481** ▶ **Used: $767**

Obi Wan Kenobi: That's no moon... it's a space station.

Han: It's too big to be a space station.

Luke: I have a very bad feeling about this.

— *STAR WARS EPISODE IV - A NEW HOPE*

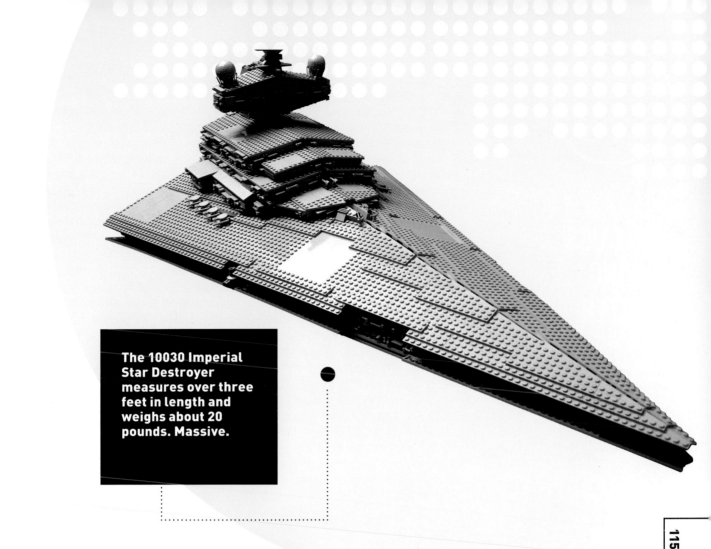

The 10030 Imperial Star Destroyer measures over three feet in length and weighs about 20 pounds. Massive.

10030 IMPERIAL STAR DESTROYER

▶ **Year Released: 2002**
▶ **No. of Pieces: 3,096**
▶ **Minifigures: 0**
▶ **Retail Price: $299.99**

Every *Star Wars* fan can recall the first time they watched the first action scene of *Star Wars Episode IV: A New Hope*. Right after the legendary opening crawl of yellow text, a white and red spaceship blasts onto the screen, the Rebel Blockade Runner. That was quite an action scene, and at the time (late 1970s), was quite impressive special effects. But what was chasing the Rebel Blockade Runner was even more impressive ... an Imperial Star Destroyer. At the time, it was the "Big Daddy" of *Star Wars* ships. This point also held true in relation to LEGO sets. In 2002, the 10030 UCS Imperial Star Destroyer was the biggest LEGO set ever sold at retail, coming in at 3,096 pieces, also making it the Big Daddy of LEGO sets at the time.

From a display standpoint, the set is just massive. It is approximately 3 feet in length and is the set that others are compared to. The 10030 UCS Imperial Star Destroyer is dead on in appearance, with multiple greebles (fine details) throughout the finished model. The set also includes a UCS plaque, which lists the ship's specifications, such as size, engine type, and weaponry. A small, in-scale replica of the Rebel Blockade Runner is also included as a wonderful finishing touch.

Value wise, this set has hit historical levels from its original $299.99 MSRP. Currently at over $1,500 in value, this has become one of the most expensive sets for sale in the LEGO secondary market, quadrupling its MSRP price. This set is a personal favorite of mine and is the reason why I got back into LEGO collecting.

$ ▶ **New: $1,527** ▶ **Used: $783**

7191 UCS X-WING FIGHTER

▶ **Year Released:** 2000
▶ **No. of Pieces:** 1,300
▶ **Minifigures:** 1
▶ **Original Retail Price:** $149.99

The year was 2000 and The LEGO Group was struggling to make a profit. Although their product was loved by millions of children, it wasn't translating into a successful business model early in the new millennium. Something had to change … and it did when The LEGO Group decided to start designing sets that appealed to an adult audience and were more complicated in build and accurate in appearance. The Ultimate Collector Series subtheme was created and includes many of the most iconic sets and characters of the *Star Wars* movies. They are also larger than standard LEGO sets and more expensive as well. The 7191 X-Wing Fighter was the first of these new UCS sets.

Every *Star Wars* fan recalls the final battle scene of *Star Wars IV: A New Hope*. Luke Skywalker takes on the dreaded Death Star in the iconic X-Wing Fighter, with R2-D2 as copilot, eventually destroying it with a single shot. The designers at LEGO did a tremendous job with this set, in my opinion. Containing 1,300 pieces, at the time of release, it was the seventh largest LEGO set ever sold to the general public and the star of the show, with its stylish black box and backlit image of the X-Wing Fighter. This is the first time LEGO made a statement with a box. Gone were the bright colors and childish imagery of earlier boxes and sets, replaced by a new, mature look for a new, mature type of set.

From a build standpoint, the 7191 UCS X-Wing Fighter was ahead of its time. When built, it was a close smaller-scale replica of the original movie ship. Unlike previous LEGO *Star Wars* re-creations, this set was dead on in appearance and coloration. It had an internal Technic gearing system that enabled the wings to move from a traditional closed position to the classic "X" position, which gave this set a playability element to it that many other UCS sets do not have. UCS sets, for the most part, are "display" sets. They are meant

The 7191 X-Wing Fighter was the first Ultimate Collector Series set to include a minifigure … in this case, R2-D2.

to be displayed in an office, den, or bedroom. Most come with a special UCS plaque that lists the name and specifications of a particular ship or character, and this set came with all the bells and whistles and looked wonderful sitting on a desk, but what was neat about it was the "WHOOOSH" Factor. What is a WHOOOSH Factor? It's when you take a LEGO set (or really any toy vehicle) and WHOOOOOOOOOSH it around a room, making engine noises and firing imaginary weapons. Five-year-old LEGO fans do it, and so do 55-year-old LEGO fans. The 7191 UCS X-Wing Fighter has the best WHOOSH factor in the LEGO world. One last point about the makeup of this set, it included an R2-D2 minifigure. For an early UCS, that was a unique feature.

From a monetary standpoint, this set has performed well over the past 14 to 15 years. Originally a $149.99 set, the 7191 UCS X-Wing Fighter has hovered around the $900 mark for the past several years, with a ROI of over 500 percent. What is interesting about these values is that this was the first UCS set produced and the first UCS remade. In 2013, a slightly larger and

more expensive UCS X-Wing was released, the 10240 UCS Red Five X-Wing Starfighter. For all intents and purposes, it is the same basic set. Older LEGO sets that are remade usually will decrease in value right before or soon after the new version is released. The 7191 UCS X-Wing Fighter bucked this trend and continued to increase in value long after the new Red Five version was released. To me, this positive growth trend speaks volumes to the quality of the original design, in that 15 years later, people are still willing to pay $900 for a LEGO set while there is a similar $200 version available.

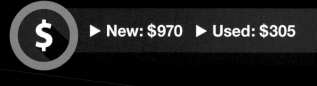

$ ▶ **New: $970** ▶ **Used: $305**

The 7191 UCS X-Wing Fighter was the first Ultimate Collector's Series set that has been remade. The new version, the 10240 UCS Red Five X-Wing Starfighter, is a slightly larger and more expensive set, but overall, the two sets are almost identical. New versions of sets sometimes will decrease or hold back the appreciation and values of the older versions. In the case of the 7191 UCS X-Wing and 10240 Red Five X-Wing Starfighter, the original 7191 UCS X-Wing has still exhibited growth after the 10240 UCS Red Five X-Wing was released, albeit, slower than previously recorded.

Raymus Antilles: This is a consular ship ... we're on a diplomatic mission ...

Darth Vader: If this is a consular ship, where is the Ambassador?

—STAR WARS EPISODE IV - A NEW HOPE

Although the 10019 Rebel Blockade Runner is not the sleekest-looking ship in the Rebel fleet, it is fast with its eleven ion turbine engines.

10019 REBEL BLOCKADE RUNNER

▶ **Year Released:** 2001
▶ **No. of Pieces:** 1,747
▶ **Minifigures:** 0
▶ **Retail Price:** $199.99

Every *Star Wars* fan can remember the first spaceship they saw explode onto the screen in *Episode IV: A New Hope*. The sleek white and red spaceship with eleven large ion turbine engines was known as a CR90 Corellian Corvette or a Rebel Blockade Runner in generic terms. The official name of the ship was the *Tantive IV*. The intense dialog referenced above occurred in the *Tantive IV* when Darth Vader made his first appearance in the original trilogy, setting the good vs. evil and action-packed tone

for all of the movies to follow.

In LEGO terms, the 10019 UCS Rebel Blockade Runner was launched in 2001 with a $199.99 MSRP. The set came with 1,747 pieces, which made it one of the largest LEGO sets to be released at the time. As with many of the *Star Wars* UCS sets, the 10019 Rebel Blockade Runner did not come with minifigures, but it did come with the traditional UCS plaque. From a build standpoint, the set had some unique pieces and colors that were not common in other sets. It is a fragile build and the eleven ion turbine engines seem to fall off easily under simple handling, but as with many UCS sets, it is meant for display and not for play. Prices for this set have recently reached the $1,000 plateau, and even after 10+ years on the LEGO secondary market, the 10019 Rebel Blockade Runner continues to appreciate steadily.

$ ▶ **New: $1,232** ▶ **Used: $589**

10029 REBEL SNOWSPEEDER

▶ **Year Released: 2003**
▶ **No. of Pieces: 1,455**
▶ **Minifigures: 0**
▶ **Retail Price: $129.99**

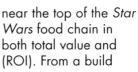

The iconic snow battle scene on the ice planet Hoth in *Episode V: The Empire Strikes Back* has to go down as one of the iconic battles of all time in the *Star Wars* Universe. The battle was the first major confrontation on screen that took place out of space and in a frozen "Earth" like environment. The only hope the Rebel Alliance had was the T-47 Airspeeder ... or, with reference to LEGO sets, the Rebel Snowspeeder.

The Rebel Snowspeeder does not play a major role in later films, yet many fans and LEGO collectors alike love this vehicle and have exhibited this love by pushing the current prices over $1,000. Originally sold for $129.99 in 2003, this 1,400+-piece set has proved to be a good investment for many LEGO collectors and investors. This set has produced a 700 percent ROI over the past 10 years, which puts it

The contrasting orange stripes on the white Snowspeeder stand out on the Ice Plant Hoth ... or on your desk.

near the top of the *Star Wars* food chain in both total value and (ROI). From a build viewpoint, the set is accurate in appearance and has a high playability factor as well. A fan can "WHOOOSH" the 10029 UCS Rebel Snowspeeder quite nicely around a room, making it even more fun to own. The set displays nicely with an attached UCS plaque. Overall, this is a set that is not flashy and gets little verbal attention from LEGO investors in LEGO forums, yet produces big-time returns – making it the perfect under-the-radar investment set.

$ ▶ **New: $1,084** ▶ **Used: $593**

10134 Y-WING ATTACK STARFIGHTER

▶ **Year Released: 2004**
▶ **No. of Pieces: 1,473**
▶ **Minifigures: 1**
▶ **Retail Price: $119.99**

The 10134 UCS Y-Wing Attack Starfighter was released in 2004 with a MSRP of $119.99, and has appreciated nicely over the past 10 years. It currently has reached the $800 level and a Return on Investment of over 500 percent from new. Actually, the 10134 UCS Y-Wing Starfighter has illustrated a higher ROI in comparison to the popular 7191 UCS X-Wing Fighter. The lower ROI of the 7191 X-Wing Fighter might be explained with the release of the newer UCS X-Wing, the 10240 UCS Red Five X-Wing Starfighter. Oftentimes, when a newer version of a LEGO set is released, the older version plateaus in value or even declines. Although the 7191 UCS X-Wing Fighter did not plateau or decrease in value after the Red Five version was launched, it is possible that the overall growth was reduced.

Although the 10134 Y-Wing gets little attention in comparison to the 7191 X-Wing Fighter, its growth on the LEGO secondary market has been similar.

As with other similar UCS sets like the 7191, 10029 UCS Rebel Snowspeeder and the 7181 UCS Tie Interceptor, the 10134 Y-Wing has both display and play qualities. You can easily pick one up and fly it around a room, giving it a high "WHOOOSH" Factor. The set has over 1,400 pieces and comes with the standard UCS display plaque. The build is straightforward, although the engines can be a bit tricky assembling. Overall, this is a solid build and investment.

$ ▶ **New: $842** ▶ **Used: $465**

Those beady orange translucent eyes give me the creeps every time I see this set in my office.

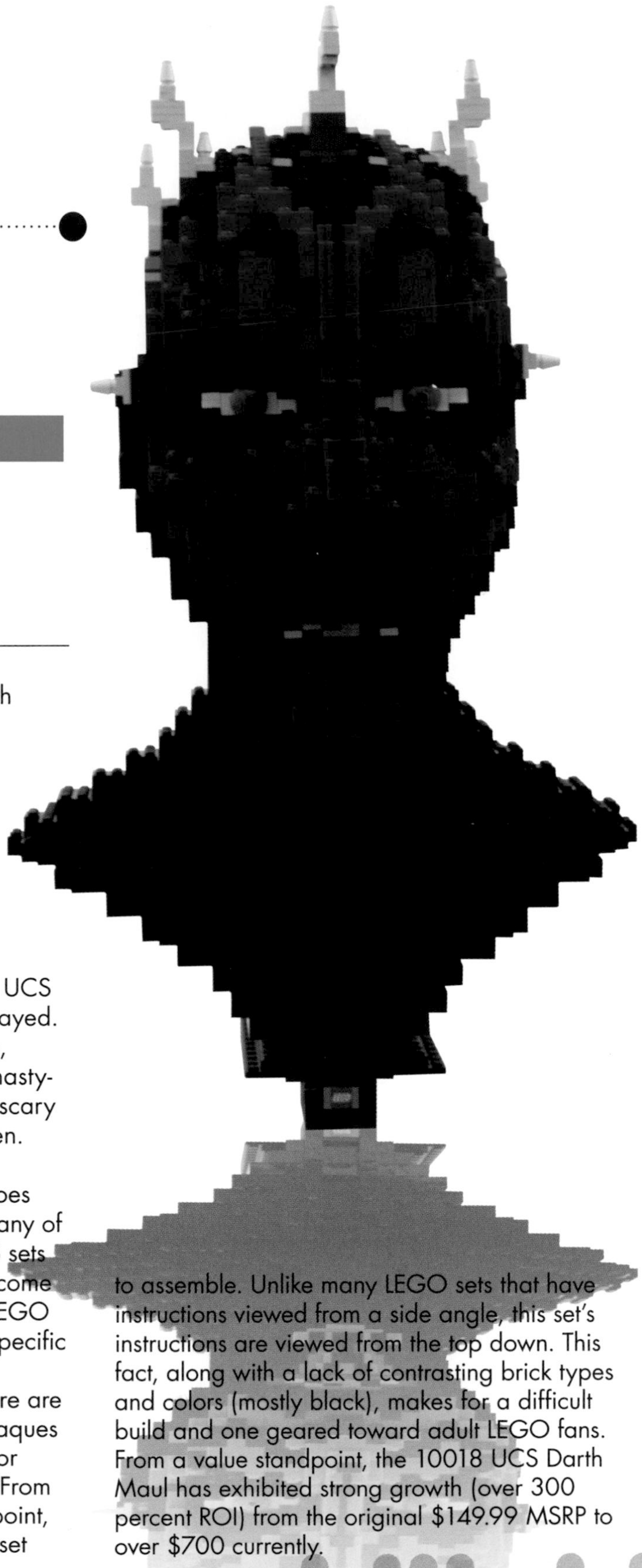

10018 DARTH MAUL

- ▶ **Year Released: 2001**
- ▶ **No. of Pieces: 1,868**
- ▶ **Minifigures: 0**
- ▶ **Retail Price: $149.99**

Released in 2001, the 10018 UCS Darth Maul is the most unique LEGO set ever produced, in my opinion. It is an actual LEGO "bust" of one of the most recognizable and evil *Star Wars* characters of all time, Darth Maul. Never before and never since has another LEGO set been designed or created for retail that replicates the head of a character on such a large scale. Comprised of more than 1,800 pieces, the UCS Darth Maul is an impressive set when displayed. With the black and red skin, multiple horns, and beady orange eyes, it makes for one nasty-looking LEGO model. It might even be too scary to display in some homes with small children.

The 10018 UCS Darth Maul is not your traditional UCS set. It is not a vehicle and does not come with a special UCS plaque that many of the other UCS sets have. It does come with a small LEGO "logo brick" specific to this set, but otherwise, there are no signs or plaques that describe or name the set. From a build standpoint, it is a difficult set to assemble. Unlike many LEGO sets that have instructions viewed from a side angle, this set's instructions are viewed from the top down. This fact, along with a lack of contrasting brick types and colors (mostly black), makes for a difficult build and one geared toward adult LEGO fans. From a value standpoint, the 10018 UCS Darth Maul has exhibited strong growth (over 300 percent ROI) from the original $149.99 MSRP to over $700 currently.

The 10018 is a realistic LEGO bust and difficult build. With basically only two brick colors, black and red, a builder can easily get confused with the top-down-vertical instructions.

$ ▶ **New: $836** ▶ **Used: $454**

This picture of the 10221 is quite appropriate. It looks like an upward-pointing arrow ... maybe it's referring to the future growth potential of this set.

10221 SUPER STAR DESTROYER

- ▶ **Year Released:** 2011
- ▶ **No. of Pieces:** 3,152
- ▶ **Minifigures:** 5
- ▶ **Retail Price:** $399.99

Super Star Destroyer. Sounds impressive, and it is. The ship in the movies, named *The Executor*, is almost 12 miles long, armed with over 2,000 types of weapons, and has a crew of almost 300,000! This movie ship is so impressive that it is utilized as Lord Darth Vader's personal flagship and is the premier command ship of the Imperial Navy.

Not only is the Super Star Destroyer a spectacular movie ship, the 10221 UCS Super Star Destroyer makes a majestic LEGO model as well. This sleek and stylish set is huge when complete, approximately 4 feet in length with 3,152 pieces. The model weighs almost 15 pounds when assembled because many of the pieces used are large plates and Technic beams, which are some of the largest LEGO pieces in existence. Another special feature of the set and one that is somewhat rare among older UCS sets is that it comes with five minifigures, three of which are exclusive: Darth Vader, Bossk, Dengar (10221 version, exclusive), IG-88 (10221 version, exclusive), Admiral Piett (exclusive). The minifigures are located in a special "command bridge" section that is hidden on the top of the set. Even though it is out of scale, it still is a creative way to incorporate minifigures into the design of the set, bringing some playability to a dynamic display model.

The 10221 UCS Star Destroyer is one of the more recently retired UCS sets. The original MSRP was $399.99, making it the second highest priced conventional LEGO set of all time, only behind the legendary 10179 UCS Millennium Falcon. What is amazing is that the set has been retired about half a year and has almost doubled the MSRP. Current eBay sales of the 10221 UCS Super Star Destroyer are in the $800 range and climbing. If this set performs in a similar fashion to the earlier "super" sized UCS sets like the 10179 UCS Millennium Falcon and 10030 UCS Star Destroyer, the future value of this set can rise into the Stratosphere.

> The 10221 Super Star Destroyer is 50 inches in LEGO form, but in the movie reality, a Super Star Destroyer can be miles long.

$ ▶ **New: $648** ▶ **Used: $510**

> The 7191 X-Wing Fighter and 7181 TIE Interceptor ushered in a new era of detailed and accurate *Star Wars* sets geared toward adult fans.

> Although not as well known as the other TIEs, the TIE Interceptor still is one wicked looking spaceship.

7181 TIE INTERCEPTOR

▶ **Year Released: 2000**
▶ **No. of Pieces: 703**
▶ **Minifigures: 0**
▶ **Retail Price: $99.99**

UCS 7181 TIE Interceptor is the companion model that was released along with the UCS 7191 X-Wing Fighter in 2000, the first year that the Ultimate Collector Series was launched. The UCS 7181 TIE Interceptor is a 703-piece set that sold for $99.99 new. The set is one of the least favorite of *Star Wars* LEGO UCS fans, maybe because the ship itself does not see major action in any of the movies. Unlike the more popular TIE Fighter or Darth Vader's TIE Advanced Fighter, which are more recognizable, the TIE Interceptors are more frequently seen in the *Episode VI, Return of the Jedi*.

The build and design of the set is straightforward and nothing special. It makes for a nice display, but I find the blue and black pieces are not accurate in appearance. It is a sharp-looking ship, with the angled and pointed wings, but the colors ruin it, in my opinion. The 7181 UCS TIE Interceptor has appreciated to over $600, which is over 500 percent ROI, but it is one of those sets that just does not get a lot of attention from LEGO collectors, regardless of the recent growth in value. The new *Star Wars* movies can bring a renewed interest in this set because it is the type of set that has not and probably will not be remade in UCS form, so some might consider it rare and unique. The box was quite stunning in my opinion and helps the value of the set, giving it a very classy and professional look. All in all, a solid UCS set that is overshadowed by larger and fancier sets.

$ ▶ **New: $697** ▶ **Used: $179**

All that is missing is Darth Vader in the cockpit of the 10175 Vader's TIE Advanced. Unfortunately, a Darth Vader minifigure won't fit without modifications.

Nice side view of the solar arrays, which are a source of power for the spacecraft.

10175 VADER'S TIE ADVANCED

▶ **Year Released: 2006**
▶ **No. of Pieces: 1,212**
▶ **Minifigures: 0**
▶ **Retail Price: $99.99**

In the climactic confrontation of the Battle of Yavin in *Episode IV- A New Hope*, Darth Vader makes a grand appearance in his TIE Advanced Starfighter, eventually being jettisoned into space from a few shots from Han Solo and his Millennium Falcon. The TIE Advanced Starfighter was a prototype of the new TIE fighter that was supposed to replace the conventional and current TIE Fighter in the Imperial Fleet. Armed with upgraded weapons, engines, and solar array wings, the TIE Advanced Starfighter is the pride of the Imperial Navy Starfighter corp.

LEGO honored the TIE Advanced Starfighter in 2006 by releasing the 1,212-piece 10175 UCS Vader's TIE Advanced, which is a spot-on replica of the movie craft. As with many of the UCS fighters like the 7191 UCS X-Wing and 10029 UCS Rebel Snowspeeder, the 10175 UCS Vader's Advanced has fantastic playability

as well as displayability. The WHOOOSH Factor is high with this LEGO model as is the overall accuracy and finish of the build. The set comes with the standard UCS plaque, which always seems to complete a set.

The 10175 UCS Vader's Advanced has appreciated well over the years, basically quintupling its original MSRP of $99.99. Current values are in the $500 range and increasing. As with many sets, the new movie launching late in 2015 seems to be stimulating growth within the theme.

$ ▶ New: $523 ▶ Used: $262

7194 YODA

▶ **Year Released: 2001**
▶ **No. of Pieces: 1,075**
▶ **Minifigures: 0**
▶ **Retail Price: $99.99**

The 7194 UCS Yoda set, released in 2001, is a different sort of set in the LEGO world. It is actually a whole body recreation of the legendary Jedi Knight, Yoda. Standing about a foot tall and comprised of over 1,000 pieces, it is not a super large set, yet the 7194 UCS Yoda makes an excellent impression upon *Star Wars* LEGO fans when seen on display. The set is a nice replica of Yoda and pairs well with the newer 10225 UCS R2-D2. The 7194 UCS Yoda does not come with the typical UCS plaque, but that does not take away from the overall display value of the set. Besides the movable head, there is no playability.

The value of the 7194 UCS Yoda has reached the $400 level with approximately a 300 percent ROI from MSRP. They are solid numbers for any investment, but compared to many of the other UCS sets, the 7194 is in the bottom half of those sets. It might be that the inferior growth in comparison to other UCS sets relates to the Yoda character in general. I believe most *Star Wars* fans will tell you they like Yoda and find him amusing, but if they

This Yoda set is a difficult top-down-vertical build because of the rotating head and delicate ears.

had to pick a favorite character, it would be Darth Vader, Luke, Han Solo, or one of the droids. Same thing with LEGO sets: they like the Yoda UCS set, but would probably spend their money on other more desirable UCS sets. Overall, this is a nice LEGO replica of one of the most recognizable movie characters of all time.

$ ▶ New: $451 ▶ Used: $195

COLLECTORS LIKE MINIFIGURE-SCALE SETS

According to many LEGO fans and collectors, one of the major shortcomings of earlier Ultimate Collectors Series sets was that they were not "minifigure scale." Simply defined, the finished models are not able to utilize a pilot minifigure(s) in the cockpit of the craft. These sets included:

- 10175 UCS Vader's TIE Advanced
- 7191 UCS X-Wing Fighter
- 7181 UCS TIE Interceptor
- 10129 UCS Rebel Snowspeeder
- 10134 UCS Y-Wing Starfighter
- 10215 UCS Obi Wan's Jedi Starfighter
- 10227 UCS B-Wing Starfighter
- 10240 UCS Red Five X-Wing StarfighterAlthough the 7191 UCS X-Wing Fighter and 10240 UCS Red Five X-Wing Starfighter did both include a R2-D2 minifigure, neither

included a Rebel Alliance pilot in the cockpit. The scale of the completed models is slightly off to make a minifigure fit in the cockpit of any of the above UCS sets.

This has shown not to be a major negative factor in the aftermarket values of these particular UCS sets, as indicated by the high returns on most, if not all, of the sets. That being said, LEGO seems to be addressing this issue with the new 75060 UCS Slave I. The infamous Boba Fett minifigure has a bird's eye view from the cockpit of the LEGO Slave I.

I think this new practice of including minifigures to properly scaled LEGO UCS models will be a boon to those future sets on the secondary market, since LEGO minifigures are often considered the "currency" of the LEGO Universe. Not only do minifigures increase values of older LEGO sets, it is a known fact that minifigures in new LEGO sets also increase the MSRP. LEGO fans love those little ABS plastic people.

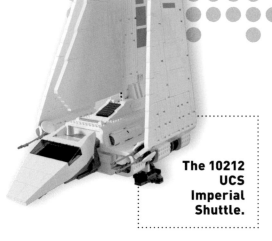

The 10212 UCS Imperial Shuttle.

10212 IMPERIAL SHUTTLE

▶ **Year Released:** 2010
▶ **No. of Pieces:** 2,503
▶ **Minifigures:** 5
▶ **Retail Price:** $259.99

The front of the 10212 Imperial Shuttle box shows the wings in "flight" position, while the back of the box shows the Imperial Shuttle with the landing gear down and wings up.

The official name of the 10212 UCS Imperial Shuttle is the Lambda class T-4a shuttle. Although not a major vehicle in the way of battle or action scenes in any of the movies, these attractive ships make their presence known nonetheless. Often utilized for transporting either the Sith Lord Darth Vader or the Emperor himself, the movie Imperial Shuttles often steal a scene with their gracefully folding wings moving into the landing position.

The LEGO recreation of the shuttle is a sight to see. It is a gorgeous set, reminding me of a swan in many ways. The mounting base for the replica is quite tall, enabling the folding wings to fully extend in either the flying or landing position. The ship can either use the UCS stand and plaque to be placed on or has landing gear that can be attached so it can sit like it would in the landing bay of a Star Destroyer or a landing pad on the Endor moon. Another cool feature of the ship is the LEGO Technic gear drive that operates the foldable wings, which is a useful and creative addition.

A final feature that is somewhat rare among UCS sets is that the 10212 UCS Imperial Shuttle comes with minifigures that actually fit into the cockpit and include Darth Vader, a Stormtrooper, Luke Skywalker (Jedi Knight, exclusive), Imperial

Officer (Imperial Shuttle Commander, exclusive), and Imperial Pilot (exclusive).

As indicated, three of these minifigures are exclusive to this set. Although they are not highly sought after minifigures, it still helps the resale value of this set on the LEGO secondary market. Speaking of resale values, the 10212 UCS Imperial Shuttle has performed moderately well over the past several years. The set retired approximately two years ago and has reached the $400 level, which is not bad considering the MSRP was originally set at $259.99. While not one of the fastest appreciating UCS sets, it still is respectable. The box seems quite small for such a large set, so maybe LEGO investors and resellers do not feel they are getting fair value for their money spent. Although the finished model is quite large and impressive, the box is not, and that is what sells a set many times in a brick and mortar LEGO store. Overall, this is a majestic display set, with some playability thrown in as well. Slow and steady growth in value looks to continue, with a possible boost in value from the new movie releasing late in 2015.

$ ▶ **New: $453** ▶ **Used: $333**

Naboo N-1 Starfighter™

size	11 meters long
engines	Twin J-type Nubian-221 engines for sublight speeds
hyberdrive	Nubian Monarc C-4 hyperdrive
crew	1 pilot and 1 astromech droid
weapons	Twin laser cannons and proton torpedo

The chrome pieces of the 10026 Special Edition Naboo are rare and valuable, helping the set appreciate to high values ... basically TEN TIMES the retail price!

10026 SPECIAL EDITION NABOO STARFIGHTER

▶ **Year Released: 2002**
▶ **No. of Pieces: 187**
▶ **Minifigures: 0**
▶ **Retail Price: $39.99**

Not all UCS sets are large, expensive, and made with thousands of bricks, such as the 10026 Special Edition Naboo Starfighter. Released in 2002, this UCS set only has 187 pieces complete. But where it lacks in size and piece count, it makes up for in rare pieces and style. This set contains numerous special pieces available only to this set and most of them are coated in chrome plating. Besides the rare parts, the Starfighter makes for a classy little display set, with its cool chrome and bright yellow pieces. It also includes the traditional UCS plaque, which finishes it off nicely. It would look at home on any *Star Wars* fan's desk or office.

With a low $39.99 MSRP, it is quite possible many fans initially ignored this set for other larger and more iconic vehicles and characters. That's too bad because this set has appreciated to almost $350 and has exhibited a Return on Investment of more than 700 percent since it retired. That is some bang for your investment buck and is a great example of how LEGO sets of all shapes and sizes can be top performers in the LEGO secondary market.

$ ▶ **New: $350** ▶ **Used: $159**

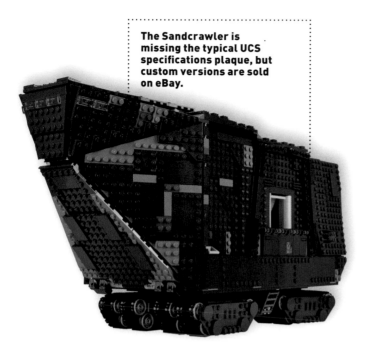

The Sandcrawler is missing the typical UCS specifications plaque, but custom versions are sold on eBay.

The 75059 has multiple doors and secret compartments to enable access to the detailed interior.

75059 SANDCRAWLER

- ▶ **Year Released: 2014**
- ▶ **No. of Pieces: 3,296**
- ▶ **Minifigures: 14**
- ▶ **Retail Price: $299.99**

The 75059 Sandcrawler, released in 2014, is still available at retail at this writing. The 75059 Sandcrawler is a 3,296-piece set with fourteen minifigures, nine of which are exclusive to the set. It is a wonderful, very "playable" replica of the Jawa's mammoth moving machine from

The 75059 comes with fourteen minifigures, nine of which are exclusive to the set.

Episode IV of the original trilogy. It is a remake of the earlier 10144 Sandcrawler (Non-UCS), which is a much smaller 1,669-piece set. What should be noted is that the 10144 Sandcrawler has "decreased" in value from well over $300 to about $260 currently. I wanted to bring this to your attention to illustrate the fact that LEGO sets do lose value, especially when a newer and better version of a model is released.

With regards to the 75059 Sandcrawler, the future is bright for this set. Although the 75059 Sandcrawler is still available at retail, this is an opportunity for many of you to buy a potentially profitable LEGO collectible. What you have to realize is that the chances of another Sandcrawler LEGO set being created in the near future is low, so a collector can have some confidence buying one of these large $299.99 UCS sets and not worry about a newer version affecting the current collectibles value. Most UCS sets are for display purposes only, as they are large and fragile, but the 75059 Sandcrawler is large and usable, with a multitude of minifigures and play options. But it also is an attractive display piece as well. The only thing it is missing in my mind is the typical UCS set plaque, but I have seen some creative people on eBay selling stickers to create one. This big, brown behemoth can make some green one day, so I recommend including one in your collection.

$ ▶ **New: $303** ▶ **Used: $250**

Front and back photos of the box of the 10174 Imperial AT-ST. Nothing flashy here.

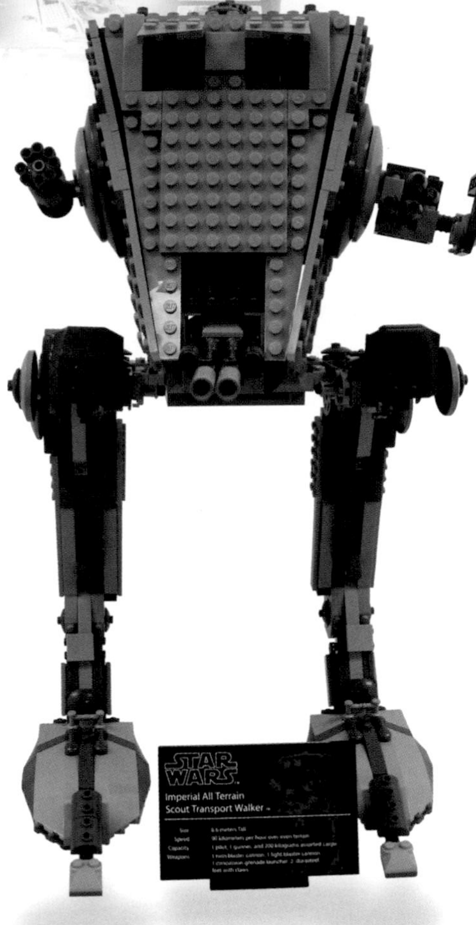

10174 IMPERIAL AT-ST

▶ **Year Released: 2006**
▶ **No. of Pieces: 1,068**
▶ **Minifigures: 0**
▶ **Retail Price: $79.99**

AT-ST — All Terrain Scout Transport, or, as some informally call it, the "chicken walker," due to its unique bird-like appearance and method of walking like a chicken. The Imperial AT-ST was meant to be a reconnaissance vehicle and played an important role in many battles of the *Clone Wars* and *Galactic Civil War*. Not as infamous or dangerous as its big brother, the AT-AT (All Terrain Armored Transport), the Imperial AT-ST, nonetheless, was included in some iconic on-screen battles, namely against the Ewoks in the *Battle of Endor*.

The LEGO version of the Imperial AT-ST is one of the more underrated UCS sets, in my opinion. With a MSRP of $79.99 and breaking the 1,000-piece mark, it was a nice bargain at retail. The 10174 set currently is valued around $300 and has grown over 250 percent since its release in 2006. Build wise, it is an accurate representation of the movie AT-ST, at least on the exterior. Unfortunately, the 10174 has no internal "greebles." Greebles, according to Wikipedia. com, are fine details added to the surface of a larger object that makes it appear more complex and, therefore, more visually interesting. The inside cockpit portion of the 10174 UCS Imperial AT-ST is non-existent. Too bad, because there is ample room to fit some Imperial Troopers/ Pilots and some control panels, and the added minifigures would have added some value to this set in the LEGO secondary market. As with most of the UCS sets, the 10174 UCS Imperial AT-ST has the UCS plaque.

$ ▶ **New: $291** ▶ **Used: $160**

Notice how the cockpit rotates to adjust to any and all flight positions, whether horizontal, vertical or angular.

10227 B-WING STARFIGHTER

▶ **Year Released: 2012**
▶ **No. of Pieces: 1,487**
▶ **Minifigures: 0**
▶ **Retail Price: $199.99**

The box is one of the best in the LEGO Universe, in my opinion. It's huge and well made, with beautiful graphics.

The B-Wing Starfighter, or affectionately known as the "Blade Wing" by the Rebel Alliance pilots, is one of the most heavily armed and largest of the Rebel Alliance fleet. It received its nickname because it looks like a "blade" cutting through outer space when it is in its vertical flying position.

The 10227 UCS B-Wing Starfighter makes quite an impression, and the almost 1,500-piece set is a beautiful rendition of the movie fighter. It is a large model and sits at an angle on its base and plaque setup. Even the cockpit rotates like the real movie version. But some LEGO fans have complained about poor build quality and that the set falls apart easily, but I have not experienced that.

This lack of interest in the ship itself could be the reason that the 10227 UCS B-Wing Starfighter retired in one year; most UCS sets are available at primary retailers for at least two years. Even more, the 10227 UCS

B-Wing Starfighter was put on sale by LEGO Shop @ Home for $99.99, which was half the original MSRP of $199.99. Amazing. A 1,500-piece UCS set discounted at 50 percent?! Best deal I have ever encountered from LEGO Shop @ Home.

The values have just reached the $200 level or basically MSRP, but considering that the set sold for half that a little over a year ago, the "real" appreciation of the set is quite impressive if you were one of the lucky ones to obtain the set at $99.99. The two main issues I have with it are that it is not minifigure scale, and the WHOOOSH factor is low due to the delicate nature of the build.

This is a quality sleeper/under the radar type of set that many people wrote off, yet it will continue to appreciate slow and steady over the next five to ten years.

$ ▶ **New: $209** ▶ **Used: $155**

10225 R2-D2

▶ **Year Released: 2012**
▶ **No. of Pieces: 2,127**
▶ **Minifigures: 1**
▶ **Retail Price: $179.99**

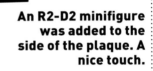

An R2-D2 minifigure was added to the side of the plaque. A nice touch.

Months ago, the 10225 R2-D2 was showing some signs of retirement, but many collectors and resellers insisted the set would remain available from primary retailers until the new movies were released late in 2015. Well, lo and behold, it looks like the 10225 R2-D2 has unofficially retired as of this writing.

In the course of about four months, the 10225 R2-D2 has appreciated by $100. In October of 2014, the value of the 10225 R2-D2 was around $180 on the LEGO secondary market ... basically equal to its MSRP of $179.99. Well, fast forward four months to January 2015 and the value of the 10225 R2-D2 on the LEGO secondary market has shot up to $280, or about a 60 percent jump in value in FOUR MONTHS! This is the perfect set to illustrate the value of LEGO collecting: When the right LEGO set retires, prices can explode on the secondary market. What makes a LEGO set a potential big gainer or the "right" type of set for big profit? Having a great design, displaying and/or playing well, uniqueness, and a huge fan base. One can also say rarity, but many quality LEGO collectibles are not rare, yet are still quite profitable after retirement. This is the situation with the 10225 R2-D2: it checks off those main points for a great collectible, but is not all that rare.

As with any sort of collectible, it becomes a lot more collectible and valuable after it is no longer available through traditional sources. Such is the case with many LEGO sets. LEGO collectors will procrastinate buying quality sets, hoping to "time" the market and buy right before retirement, but what happens is that sets can retire in a quick and random fashion at times and those procrastinators are left paying more than MSRP for the set. Sometimes LEGO collectors and resellers have budgetary or space constraints that prevent them from buying sets early, so it is understandable that some people will wait on buying a special set such as this ... and a special set this is. R2-D2 is an iconic *Star Wars* character. His image is everywhere and even if you don't like the movies, you can still like R2-D2. The LEGO model itself is spectacular. With over 2,100 pieces, the 10225 R2-D2 is a great replica of the legendary droid. With rotating head, retractable front foot/leg, retractable arm and cutting blade, the 10225 looks and works like the real thing. If you have the opportunity to obtain a 10225 R2-D2, do so. With the new movie releasing late in 2015 and in following years, the 10225 R2-D2 can find new fans who would love to own the set.

$ ▶ **New: $254** ▶ **Used: $179**

10240 RED FIVE X-WING STARFIGHTER

▶ **Year Released: 2013**
▶ **No. of Pieces: 1,558**
▶ **Minifigures: 1**
▶ **Retail Price: $199.99**

The 10240 Red Five X-Wing Starfighter is the first *Star Wars* UCS set that is a remake of an earlier set: the iconic 7191 UCS X-Wing Fighter from 2000. LEGO loves the X-Wing Fighter, with about fourteen versions of the famous craft made since 1999.

From the standpoint of a LEGO set, the

10240 Starfighter is a beautiful and accurate model, slightly larger than the 7191 UCS X-Wing Fighter it replaced. With functioning wings and cockpit that open and close, it has a high WHOOOSH Factor. It would have been great if it was minifigure scale, but it does come with a minifigure of R2-D2, who served as Luke Skywalker's X-Wing copilot many times. As of this writing, the set is still available at retail, but is showing signs of retiring. The 10240 is an excellent choice for a LEGO collectible set and if it can reach levels of the earlier 7191 UCS X-Wing Fighter ($900), many collectors and investors will be extremely happy.

$ ▶ **New: $213** ▶ **Used: $157**

The 10240 Red Five X-Wing Starfighter is a slightly larger remake of the 7191 X-Wing Fighter. Overall, a slightly improved version, except for the cockpit sticker, which is difficult to apply.

General Grievous is a creative combination of traditional and Technic bricks.

10186 GENERAL GRIEVOUS

▶ **Year Released: 2008**
▶ **No. of Pieces: 1,085**
▶ **Minifigures: 0**
▶ **Retail Price: $89.99**

General Grievous, the four-armed, lightsaber-swinging cyborg, makes quite an impression on any *Star Wars* fan. Half droid and half reptilian humanoid from the planet Kalee, General Grievous is the apprentice of the Sith Lord Count Dooku and is a barbaric and merciless beast. But he also is a tactical genius and conquers many worlds in his flagship, The Malevolence.

In 2008, LEGO honored this cruel and inhuman character with his own set. The 10186 UCS General Grievous is a 1,000-piece set comprised of a combination of traditional LEGO parts and Technic parts. The set had an MSRP of $89.99 and a short production run of about a year. From an appearance standpoint, the set is a close replica of General Grievous and makes an excellent display set with its decorative base and UCS plaque. The set is somewhat delicate, though, and the four lightsabers can become unwieldy. Playability is limited, even if it does look like an action figure.

Value wise, the 10186 UCS General Grievous has doubled in price to the $200 range. Much of the growth has occurred recently, possibly being related to the upcoming movies. Usually short production runs of a set help with secondary market values, but in this case, the short production run might have indicated a set that was a poor seller. *Star Wars* prequel trilogy LEGO sets sometimes under perform on the LEGO secondary market. Regardless, the 10186 General Grievous is a unique-looking set and reasonably priced, so there is still potential for some future growth.

$ ▶ **New: $189** ▶ **Used: $91**

75060 SLAVE I

▶ **Year Released:** 2015
▶ **No. of Pieces:** 1,996
▶ **Minifigures:** 4
▶ **Retail Price:** $199.99

Every once in awhile, there comes a LEGO set that really is well done and gets fans and collectors excited. Of recent memory, the 76023 The Tumbler was one of those electric LEGO sets that collectors know will be a home run after it retires. The 75060 Slave I is another such set. Released at the beginning of 2015, the 75060 Slave I has many chomping at the bit to get one. This 1,996-piece set currently sells for $199.99 from primary retailers.

The 75060 Slave I is accurate in appearance — from the weathered exterior to the greebles on the underside of the ship, the details are dead on. Another important factor is that this is one of the rare UCS sets that are playable, as it is minifigure scale and has four minifigures to play with. Many of these sets are not meant to be played

with, but the 75060 Slave I has many moving parts and compartments that give it that extra edge on other UCS sets. Boba Fett can fit into the cockpit; Han Solo and his Carbonite coffin have a mounting compartment in the Slave I. The 75060 Slave I is also sturdy when built, giving it a high WHOOOSH Factor. It also comes with a solid stand and plaque to display. All in all, this is a dynamic UCS set and a MUST HAVE for any *Star Wars* fan.

$ ▶ **New: $208** ▶ **Used: $177**

ORIGINAL MOVIES VS. PREQUELS

Out of the 22 Ultimate Collector's Series LEGO sets created, only four were based on the prequel trilogy:

- 10018 UCS Darth Maul
- 10026 UCS Special Edition Naboo Starfighter
- 10186 UCS General Grievous
- 10215 UCS Obi Wan's Jedi Starfighter

With two sets, the 7194 UCS Yoda and the 10225 UCS R2-D2, being based on characters from all six movies. Why such a huge difference? Simply put, *Star Wars* fans held the original trilogy films with higher regard than the prequels, and it would appear that the original movies had a greater influence on LEGO designers, thus creating the substantial difference in the amount of UCS sets produced for either

trilogy. Another indication of the increased interest in the original films and their related LEGO sets comes from the fact that these sets, as a whole, perform better on the LEGO secondary market than the prequel sets do.

LEGO sales and set popularity on the secondary market often mimics those of the primary LEGO retail market. If a particular LEGO set sells well on the secondary market, it probably sold well in the LEGO brick and mortar stores of the world before it was retired. It would make sense that The LEGO Group designs and produces sets that fans want, not ones that will collect dust on the shelves. I guess this explains why LEGO is constantly reissuing X-Wings, TIE Fighters, AT-ATs and Millennium Falcons ...They sell well!

PREQUEL TRILOGY	ORIGINAL TRILOGY
Episode I: The Phantom Menace	*Episode IV: A New Hope*
Episode II: Attack of the Clones	*Episode V: The Empire Strikes Back*
Episode III: Revenge of the Sith	*Episode VI: Revenge of the Sith*

There have been **6** *Star Wars* movies to date.

10215 OBI WAN'S JEDI STARFIGHTER

▶ **Year Released:** 2010
▶ **No. of Pieces:** 676
▶ **Minifigures:** 0
▶ **Retail Price:** $99.99

Although UC Series LEGO sets are some of the most iconic sets of all time and many are valued at high prices and continue to appreciate well, there is always a weak link in the chain, and the 10215 UCS Obi Wan's Jedi Starfighter is it.

Based on Obi Wan Kenobi's personal Delta 7 Aethersprite-Class Light Interceptor from the prequel trilogy of films, the 10215 Obi Wan's Jedi Starfighter was released in 2010 at a MSRP of $99.99. The set only has 676 pieces, which gives it a Price Per Piece (PPP) cost of almost $0.15 per piece, which is high in comparison to other LEGO sets. Granted, this particular set was heavily discounted by primary retailers, sometimes down to the $70-$80 range, but I guess even that was too high for some fans and investors to make the set attractive to them. Build wise, the set does have some quality and rare parts, though, and many LEGO investors and resellers use this set to "part out." The dark red and lime green bricks are somewhat rare in the LEGO Universe and bring a premium price on the LEGO secondary market. These rare brick colors do make for a unique build combination, though, and the finished UCS model is attractive and accurate in appearance. The 10215 UCS Obi Wan's Jedi Starfighter comes with the usual UCS specifications placard.

The current price of the 10215 UCS Obi Wan's Jedi Starfighter is a little over $100, which, after several years of being retired, is not much higher than the original MSRP. Even considering the discounted prices the set sold for previous to retirement, the growth of this set is weak. There could be several reasons for this poor appreciation: High PPP, the prequel

The completed LEGO model is over 18 inches long and 9 inches wide and includes some unique lime green bricks that nicely contrast the dark red and white bricks.

trilogy sets sometime under-perform, and the set lacks minifigures. Maybe the 10215 UCS Obi Wan's Jedi Starfighter was and currently is overshadowed by larger and more iconic sets like the 10221 UCS Super Star Destroyer, 10225 UCS R2-D2, and 10212 UCS Imperial Shuttle. Maybe LEGO fans and collectors just don't like the ship and/or set. It is quite possible an unloved LEGO set like this finds new life five to 10 years after retirement. There have been other LEGO sets that appreciate well years after an initial plateau (or even decrease in value) in growth. With the new movies landing in theaters late in 2015 and later in the decade, an ignored and reasonably priced UCS set like this might find some new fans.

$ ▶ **New: $113** ▶ **Used: $77**

SOME SETS VALUABLE FOR PARTS

LEGO sets are not only valuable as a complete used set and/or in Mint In Sealed Box/New In Box condition. Many LEGO sets are worth more for their individual pieces and minifigures than they are complete and sealed.

There is a large and prosperous secondary LEGO market practice of breaking new sets down into the individual bricks and reselling them for a profit. This is called "parting out" a LEGO set. Creative and industrious fans, collectors, and resellers have devised a huge industry, separate from LEGO altogether. There are various online "brick stores" that let small mom-and-pop resellers list their thousands of parted out LEGO bricks for sale.

Since The LEGO Group is in the business of selling complete sets and miscellaneous accessories and not individual bricks, LEGO, for the most part, does not have a retail option for fans and collectors to buy large quantities of the thousands of different types of bricks they are

currently producing or have produced in the past. They do offer customers their "Pick A Brick" walls in LEGO brick and mortar stores, but that brick selection is quite small and random, with maybe 40 to 50 different brick and color combinations in total. LEGO does offer fans the possibility of buying in small quantities or replace missing pieces, but nothing on any major scale.

So why do people need to buy LEGO bricks in bulk? For custom models, or in LEGO terms, MOCs. MOCs are "My Own Creation," which is a huge aspect of the LEGO secondary market. There are so many talented LEGO designers and builders out there, and many need mass quantities of bricks to complete their creations. The secondary LEGO market "brick stores" on sites like eBay, Brick Classifieds, Bricklink, and Brick Owl meet the needs of fans and builders and give them the opportunity to buy LEGO bricks from 50+ years of sets.

CHAPTER 23

STAR WARS
NON UCS [ULTIMATE COLLECTOR SERIES]

AS WITH ANY LEGO THEME, MINIFIGURES PLAY AN IMPORTANT ROLE IN *STAR WARS* SETS AND THEIR DESIGN, AND THIS THEME HAS SOME OF THE BEST IN THE BUSINESS. SOME *STAR WARS* MINIFIGURES CAN SELL FOR HUNDREDS OF DOLLARS ON THE LEGO SECONDARY MARKET.

LEGO and Lucasfilms worked out a licensing agreement in 1999 so that LEGO could produce *Star Wars*-themed sets. The two companies have extended that contract into 2022. The Walt Disney Company bought Lucasfilm in 2012 and will now have their logo on many of the sets. Disney will be releasing a new series of *Star Wars* movies starting late in 2015 and continuing them into the foreseeable future, thus keeping the *Star Wars* theme a large component in the LEGO line of sets.

The *Star Wars* theme has far and away been the most popular and bestselling licensed LEGO theme of all time. With well over 400 sets created over the past sixteen years, this theme has played a major role in the recent sales and profit bonanza of The LEGO Group and enabled LEGO to become the number one toy maker in the world.

Star Wars fans are passionate about their franchise, and many of them are passionate about LEGO bricks as well, and recently, older *Star Wars*-themed sets have found new life in the secondary market because of the increased interest from fans for anything *Star Wars*, especially items from *Episodes IV-VI*. With the inclusion of older characters like Luke Skywalker, Princess Leia, and Han Solo, both old and new sets will be in

prime position for some jaw-dropping returns over the next few years at the very least.

LEGO *Star Wars* sets can be broken down into four basic categories:

At the top are the Ultimate Collector Series (UCS) sets — the large and highly detailed sets designed for adults and used for display purposes. There is another chapter in this book dedicated to those special sets.

The other two categories are the non-Ultimate Collector Series sets — basically the vast majority of sets; these can include sets from all the movies and usually range from about 100-piece sets to a couple of thousand pieces

The third category is polybags and minisets, and a fourth minor category is *Star Wars* Technic sets.

Prices of LEGO *Star Wars* sets can range from a few dollars to a few thousand dollars and with all sorts of different growth patterns. Being that there are so many *Star Wars* sets produced annually and many are remakes of earlier versions, the return on investment for many sets can be lower than expected. For those of you who have an eye for unique LEGO sets and know the *Star Wars* characters and vehicles well, this theme can be fun and productive to collect.

The Boba Fett minifigure has specially printed graphics on the arms and legs and sells for over $200 on the secondary market.

10123 CLOUD CITY

▶ **Year Released: 2003**
▶ **No. of Pieces: 705**
▶ **Minifigures: 7**
▶ **Original Retail Price: $99.99**

The 10123 Cloud City comes with four minifigures, four which are exclusive to the set and very valuable.

I have discussed the importance of minifigures, and the 10123 Cloud City is the prime example of this. Released in 2003 with a $99.99 MSRP, the 10123 Cloud City is not a large set, with only 698 pieces and seven minifigures. It is a recreation of several of the more important scenes that take place on Cloud City in *The Empire Strikes Back*. It is a highly playable set that looks sort of haphazard, but what is amazing about it is that its current value on the LEGO secondary market is almost $1,000 — Return on Investment is almost 900 percent! Wow! What makes this set so special? The minifigures, some of which are selling for hundreds of dollars on the LEGO secondary market. The Lando Calrissian minifigure has sold for over $100, while the Boba Fett minifigure has sold for well over $200; even Princess Leia has sold for $50 or more. This set is also the only LEGO version of the iconic floating city, so that can play an important reason in the value increase as well.

$ ▶ **New: $975** ▶ **Used: $566**

The 7283 Ultimate Space Battle includes Obi-Wan Kenobi and Anakin Skywalker minifigures, two Buzz droids, two Jedi Starfighters, and a couple of Vulture Droids.

138

7283 ULTIMATE SPACE BATTLE

▶ **Year Released:** 2005
▶ **No. of Pieces:** 567
▶ **Minifigures:** 2
▶ **Original Retail Price:** $49.99

This is a unique set in that it includes multiple vehicles, both good and evil. Most *Star Wars* sets contain just one LEGO model, but the 7283 Ultimate Space Battle has four vehicles, plus numerous other smaller droids and minifigures, giving it tons of playability. The 7283 Ultimate Space Battle was a Toys R Us Exclusive, so this can be a reason for the specially designed set. Toys R Us often has these special "combination packs" of multiple LEGO models in one specially marked box, so it is not that rare, but they seem to be popular among LEGO fans. Is set has exhibited excellent growth from a retail price of $49.99, appreciating over 500 percent to well over $300. The individual models of the 7283 Ultimate Space Battle are nothing fancy, but as people often say, it's the "sum of the parts," and fans and collectors appreciate this sort of set. LEGO should take note.

$ ▶ **New: $340** ▶ **Used: $120**

Obi-Wan Kenobi: Why do I get the feeling you're going to be the death of me?

Anakin: Don't say that, master. You're the closest thing I have to a father.

The 10178 Motorized Walking AT-AT is the only motorized *Star Wars* LEGO set to date and is probably the best version of an AT-AT done so far.

7662 TRADE FEDERATION MTT

▶ **Year Released: 2007**
▶ **No. of Pieces: 1,330**
▶ **Minifigures: 20**
▶ **Original Retail Price: $99.99**

This set was released in 2007 for $99.99 and came with 1,330 pieces and a whopping twenty one minifigures. The MTT stands for Multi Troop Transport and the 7662 Trade Federation MTT does this very well, creatively storing and transporting an army of droids within its structure. This vehicle has had several LEGO variations since the new Millennium, but the 7662 Trade Federation MTT is by far the biggest and best by a lot, in my opinion. Even with the new 75058 MTT being released, LEGO collectors have still been buying the 7662 Trade Federation MTT, with the prices slowly increasing to almost $400. The 7662 Trade Federation MTT is an illustration of how the quality and design of LEGO sets is the most important factor when evaluating a set's potential on the LEGO secondary market.

The 7662 Trade Federation MTT is much larger and has more minifigures than the newer 75058 MTT.

10178 MOTORIZED WALKING AT-AT

▶ **Year Released: 2007**
▶ **No. of Pieces: 1,137**
▶ **Minifigures: 4**
▶ **Original Retail Price: $129.99**

There has been only one motorized *Star Wars* set and this is it. While people have used the Power Functions sets to add motion to various MOCs and custom *Star Wars* sets, there have not been any retail LEGO *Star Wars* sets produced with a motor. The 10178 Motorized Walking AT-AT does an excellent job of animating and imitating the hulking AT-AT's well-known clunking and screeching stomp. This set was released in 2007 and included 1,137 pieces and four minifigures. The largest and most detailed of all of the AT-ATs released to date, the 10178 Motorized Walking AT-AT has excelled in the LEGO secondary market, tripling in value from the $129.99 retail price to the $450 range. Although there is a new version, the 75054 AT-AT, the 10178 AT-AT is still a better design and with the Power Functions, a lot more fun and playable. There is some talk of an Ultimate Collectors Series AT-AT in the works, but at this writing, it is only rumors. But if there is some truth to that, I think it would be an extremely popular set.

$ ▶ New: $446 ▶ Used: $231

$ ▶ New: $385 ▶ Used: $185

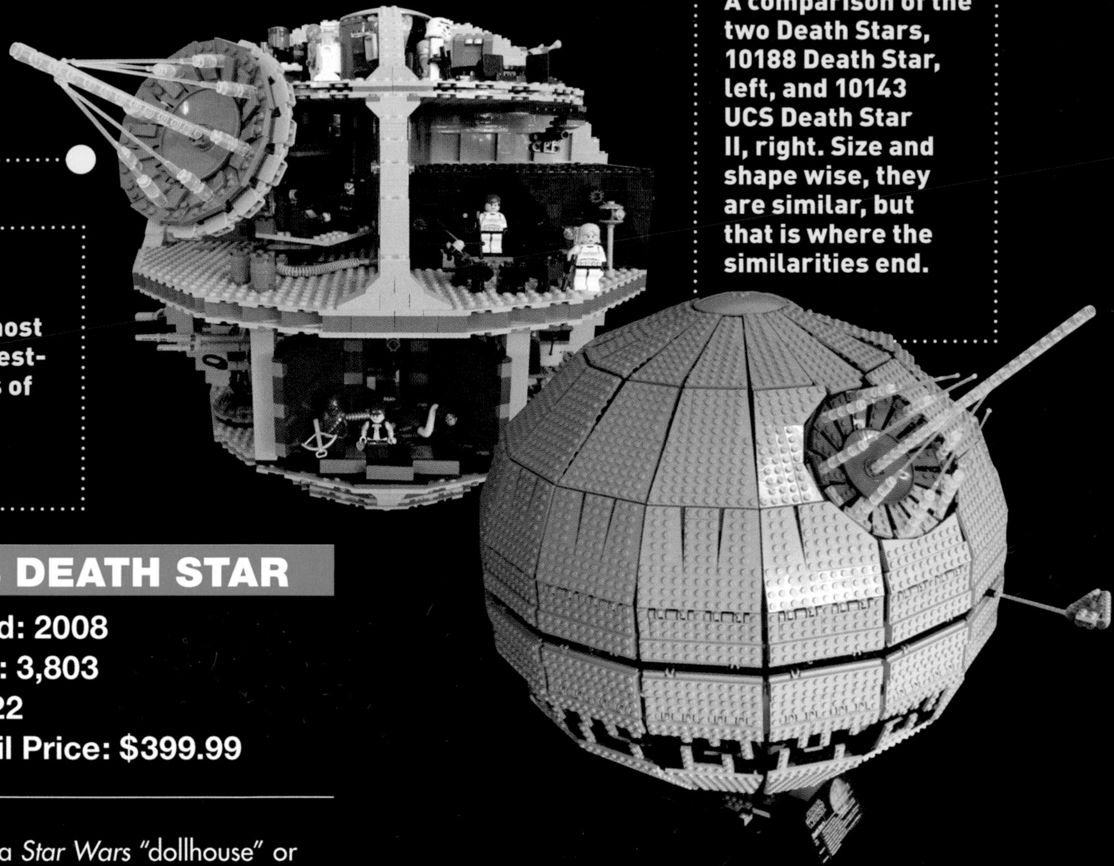

A comparison of the two Death Stars, 10188 Death Star, left, and 10143 UCS Death Star II, right. Size and shape wise, they are similar, but that is where the similarities end.

The *Star Wars* "Dollhouse" has been one of the most popular and longest-selling LEGO sets of all time.

THE 10188 DEATH STAR

▶ Year Released: 2008
▶ No. of Pieces: 3,803
▶ Minifigures: 22
▶ Original Retail Price: $399.99

Sometimes called a *Star Wars* "dollhouse" or "diorama" by fans due to its multiple-room layout and high playability factor, it also has another nickname that collectors and investors like to use: The Live Star.

The 10188 Death Star has been for sale by primary LEGO retailers for a long time, about seven years at this writing. Considering many LEGO sets retire in a two- to three-year time frame, seven years is an amazing production run in the LEGO Universe.

I would imagine that this set is highly popular and sells well in order to stay away from official retirement. There are always discussions on the LEGO forums when this set will retire, but it never does. Honestly, I understand why LEGO keeps it around and why fans love it ... it's a fantastic set and value. Although pricey at $399.99, the set is indeed a value. The 10188 Death Star has almost 4,000 pieces and an unheard of 24 minifigures! People buy this set and "part it out" for more than they bought it for. Regardless of the value, the 10188 is a fun LEGO set and has more playability than almost any set that I know of, making it popular with kids and adult Star Wars fans. Also, it displays well. It's huge! I highly recommend this set to collectors and fans.

$ ▶ New: $490 ▶ Used: $326

The 10188 Death Star has 24 minifigures, the most of any *Star Wars* set. Four are exclusive to it.

7255 GENERAL GRIEVOUS CHASE

▶ **Year Released: 2005**
▶ **No. of Pieces: 111**
▶ **Minifigures: 2**
▶ **Original Retail Price: $19.99**

This set is another example of how exclusive minifigures and maxifigures can help to increase their value on the LEGO secondary market. A smaller, mid-sized set that sold for $19.99 in 2005, the 7255 General Grievous Chase has 111 pieces, but of those pieces, two were exclusive minifigures: Obi-Wan Kenobi and a sought-after General Grievous minifigure, with a special cape. Besides the exclusive minifigures, there is an exclusive maxifigure, the Boga, a large reptilian quadruped used by Obi-Wan

The Boga Varactyl maxifigure is quite unique and sells for more than the original price of this set

Kenobi in his pursuit of General Grievous. The combination of the two exclusive minifigures and the Boga maxifigure has pushed the value of this set to seven times its MSRP, with the Return on Investment at over 600 percent to almost $150. Granted, the set has been retired for a long time, but 600 percent growth is nothing to ignore.

 $ ▶ **New: $144** ▶ **Used: $40**

8039 VENATOR-CLASS REPUBLIC ATTACK CRUISER

▶ **Year Released: 2009**
▶ **No. of Pieces: 1,170**
▶ **Minifigures: 5**
▶ **Original Retail Price: $119.99**

Also known as a Venator-Class Star Destroyer, the 8039 Venator-Class Republic Attack Cruiser is one of my personal favorites in the *Star Wars* Universe. It is the main vehicle the Republic and Galactic Empire used before the development of the Imperial-Class Star Destroyer. The 8039 Venator-Class Republic Attack Cruiser is a 1,170-piece LEGO set with five minifigures that sold for $119.99 in 2009. Current values have reached $300 on the LEGO secondary market, for about a 150 percent Return on Investment.

Not exactly bad growth, but not enough to put it in the top tier of LEGO sets. Unfortunately, this is a regular *Star Wars* set and not an Ultimate Collectors Series set, so it really didn't get the design, details, and size it deserved. Many collectors would love to see a 3,000-piece Venator-Class Republic Attack Cruiser that would be over two feet long ... maybe one day.

$ ▶ **New: $295** ▶ **Used: $151**

Many fans love the 8039 Venator-Class Republic Attack Cruiser and wish that a Ultimate Collector Series version of it was produced.

The Jabba the Hutt maxifigure from the 9516 Jabba's Palace is much more detailed than the earlier version from the 4480 set. It has painted features and is slightly larger.

142

9516 JABBA'S PALACE

▶ **Year Released:** 2012
▶ **No. of Pieces:** 717
▶ **Minifigures:** 9
▶ **Original Retail Price:** $119.99

$ ▶ **New: $149** ▶ **Used: $121**

These two recently retired sets work in tandem. While they can be built and displayed separately, the 9516 Jabba's Palace and 75005 Rancor Pit are meant to be mounted on top of one another to take advantage of all the best features of both sets. Basically, the 9516 Jabba's Palace mounts on top of the 75005 Rancor Pit so that the sliding trap door on the floor of the Palace can open and send a helpless LEGO minifigure to their death below in the Rancor Pit, where the Rancor monster will chew or rip them apart. It's really a creative pair of sets with a ton of playability when combined. What's even better is the fact that both sets have fantastic maxifigures, Jabba the Hutt in the 9516 Jabba's Palace, and Rancor Monster in the 75005 Rancor Pit. The 9516 Jabba's Palace has 717 pieces and nine minifigures and sold for $119.99 in 2012, while the 75005 Rancor Pit has 380 pieces and four minifigures and sold for $59.99 in 2013. The 75005 Rancor Pit just recently disappeared from primary retailers, so prices have not appreciated that much. The 9516 Jabba's Palace has reached $150 on the LEGO secondary market. Future collectors of these sets should acquire both to maximize full profit potential.

The Oola, Bib Fortuna, and Boushh minifigures, from left, are exclusive to the 9516 Jabba's Palace.

75005 RANCOR PIT

▶ Year Released: 2013
▶ No. of Pieces: 380
▶ Minifigures: 4
▶ Original Retail Price: $59.99

$ ▶ New: $47 ▶ Used: $32

The 75005 Rancor Pit fits nicely under the 9516 Jabba's Palace and works in conjunction with that set. Although both sets can stand alone, it is best to pair them up for future resale value.

The AT-OT Walker detaches from the Republic Dropship and carries six Clone Troopers and one Clone Trooper driver.

10195 REPUBLIC DROPSHIPAND AT-OT WALKER

▶ **Year Released: 2009**
▶ **No. of Pieces: 1,758**
▶ **Minifigures: 8**
▶ **Original Retail Price: $249.99**

Large in physical size and extremely playable, the 10195 Republic Dropship and AT-OT Walker is one of the largest non-Ultimate Collectors Series sets. What's neat about it is that it is two completely different vehicles: the Republic Dropship and the All Terrain Open Transport Walker that can work together or be played with separately. At over 1,700 pieces for $249.99, the set was pricey when it was sold at retail. It is a popular "Clone" vehicle and has an entire army of Clone Troopers (eight) included in the set. I don't think many LEGO collectors found value in this unique set, as there hasn't been another similar one made since LEGO began producing *Star Wars* sets, so it is quite possible this set will appreciate to quite high levels. The current value on the LEGO secondary market is close to $500, which is quite a lot, but the Return on Investment is only around 90 percent after being retired for around 3 years and is nothing special. It's quite possible that the 10195 Republic Dropship and AT-OT Walker will find some new investors with the increased interest for the new *Star Wars* movies releasing beginning at the end of 2015.

$ ▶ **New: $470** ▶ **Used: $328**

The side mounting arms of the Republic Dropship have two primary functions: hold the AT-OT Walker in place, and function as a landing gear when no AT-OT Walker is attached.

The Technic subtheme, featured on the next two pages, is a small niche category in the LEGO *Star Wars* Universe. Back at the start of the new millennium, LEGO made a decision to start producing sets that were designed for older fans. The complexity and high detail of LEGO designs increased through many of the themes, including the *Star Wars* theme. LEGO wanted to attract the more advanced builders and fans with the discretionary income to buy these higher-priced sets. Although these Technic sets listed above were not expensive, they were complex and difficult builds, unlike many of the other LEGO sets at the time. They were released from 2000 to 2002 and had retail prices ranging from $19.99 to $49.99. They included many rare and unique pieces, but sometimes these sets are overlooked by traditional LEGO buyers. Too bad really — these are some of the coolest sets ever created, I think. While not the best collectibles, they all have increased in value, some tripling their MSRP. If interested, there are still many good quality used *Star Wars* Technic sets on eBay that can be bought relatively cheap. These sets also make excellent displays.

8000 PIT DROID

▶ **Year Released:** 2000
▶ **No. of Pieces:** 223
▶ **Minifigures:** 0
▶ **Original Retail Price:** $19.99

$ ▶ **New: $42** ▶ **Used: $22**

LEGO designers did a nice job incorporating gold Technic pieces to resemble C-3PO, not the easiest droid to recreate. Growth of this set has been very strong.

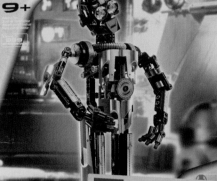

▲ Another accurate replica of a *Star Wars* character, the 8001 Battle Droid suffers from being in one of the most unpopular *Star Wars* movies of all time, *Episode I, The Phantom Menace*. Many sets from that movie just don't perform well.

As with all of the *Star Wars* Technic sets, there is a lot of playability qualities to each, especially the 8008 Stormtrooper, which has a gun that launches LEGO rockets.

8008 STORMTROOPER

▶ Year Released: 2001
▶ No. of Pieces: 361
▶ Minifigures: 0
▶ Original Retail Price: $34.99

$ ▶ New: $57 ▶ Used: $23

8007 C-3PO

- ▶ Year Released: 2001
- ▶ No. of Pieces: 341
- ▶ Minifigures: 0
- ▶ Original Retail Price: $34.99

$ ▶ New: $82 ▶ Used: $33

8001 BATTLE DROID

- ▶ Year Released: 2000
- ▶ No. of Pieces: 363
- ▶ Minifigures: 0
- ▶ Original Retail Price: $29.99

$ ▶ New: $63 ▶ Used: $26

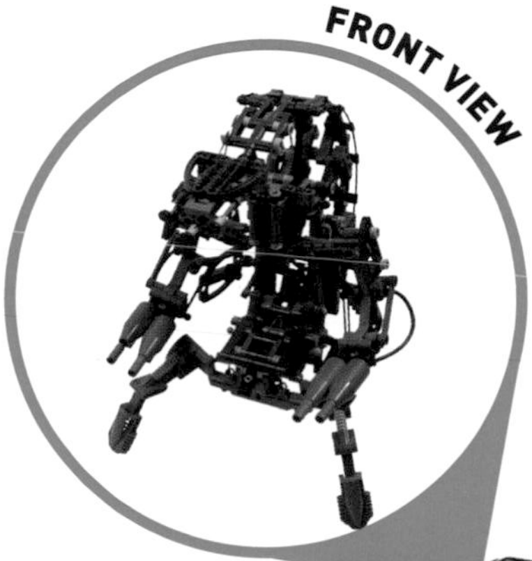

FRONT VIEW

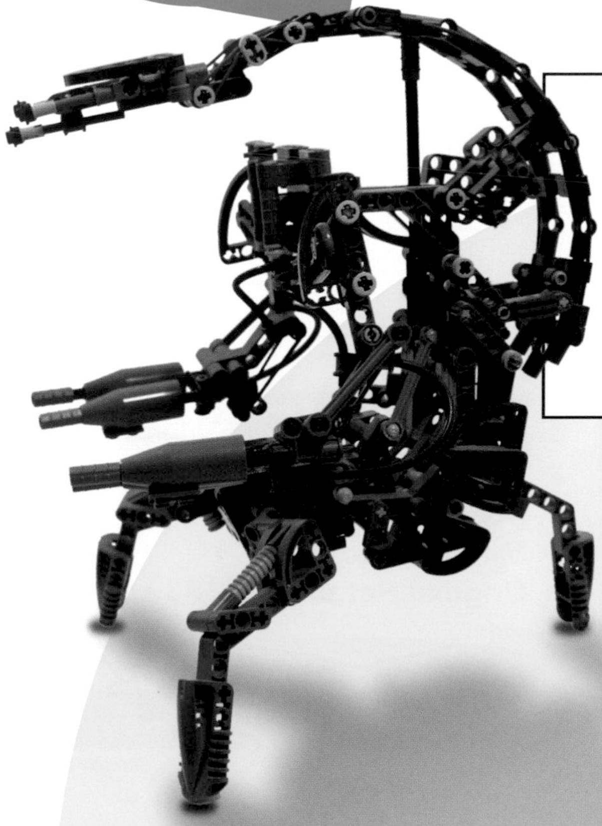

8002 DESTROYER DROID

- ▶ Year Released: 2000
- ▶ No. of Pieces: 558
- ▶ Minifigures: 0
- ▶ Original Retail Price: $49.99

$ ▶ New: $145 ▶ Used: $75

◀ An awesome LEGO Technic set, the 8002 Destroyer Droid has tripled in value from retail and is an accurate recreation of the movie mechanical monster. The 8002 Destroyer Droid actually rolls up into a little ball, then uncurls into its "fighting" position. Very cool.

8011 JANGO FETT

▶ **Year Released:** 2002
▶ **No. of Pieces:** 422
▶ **Minifigures:** 0
▶ **Original Retail Price:** $29.99

$ ▶ **New: $63** ▶ **Used: $30**

Jango Fett, the father of the infamous Boba Fett, has been honored with a set that is another one of my favorite Technic sets. Purple LEGO bricks in non-Friends-themed sets are quite rare and look awesome when paired with bright blue bricks.

8010 DARTH VADER

▶ **Year Released:** 2002
▶ **No. of Pieces:** 391
▶ **Minifigures:** 0
▶ **Original Retail Price:** $39.99

$ ▶ **New: $115** ▶ **Used: $50**

The 8010 Darth Vader is a wonderful set, but surprisingly, growth of these highly collectible and somewhat rare sets has not been strong. This should have easily tripled in value, but Technic sets sometimes scare away collectors due to their build complexity.

While the 4481 Hailfire Droid is not part of the *Star Wars* Technic subtheme, it should be. It's a radical LEGO set, with 10% of its pieces being exclusive to the set. It pairs nicely with the 8002 Destroyer Droid.

4481 HAILFIRE DROID

▶ Year Released: 2003
▶ No. of Pieces: 681
▶ Minifigures: 0
▶ Original Retail Price: $49.99

$ ▶ New: $131 ▶ Used: $66

8009 R2-D2

▶ Year Released: 2002
▶ No. of Pieces: 240
▶ Minifigures: 0
▶ Original Retail Price: $19.99

$ ▶ New: $52 ▶ Used: $23

8012 SUPER BATTLE DROID

▶ Year Released: 2002
▶ No. of Pieces: 379
▶ Minifigures: 0
▶ Original Retail Price: $34.00

$ ▶ New: $52 ▶ Used: $23

This is another cool replica of a movie droid. The blue bricks in combination with the four red blasters on the droid's hands really catch your eye.

▲ The "Bad Boys" of the first six movies: Darth Maul, Emperor Palpatine and Darth Vader. A great deal: Three classic LEGO minifigures and collectible plaques for $4.99.

As has been seen multiple times throughout this price guide, some of the smallest LEGO sets have the highest rates of appreciation. This is the case with these Minifigure Packs from 2000. They were exclusive sets, sold only in the United Kingdom at specific LEGO brick and mortar stores. They are basically three minifigure boxed sets that include little cardboard and plastic dioramas to mount each one of the minifigures, making for very cool little displays. As noted, there are four different sets within this miniset collection, and all are quite valuable on the LEGO secondary market. The 3340 Emperor Palpatine, Darth Maul & Darth Vader Minifig Pack *Star Wars* #1 set has an amazing Return on Investment, growing almost **1,500 percent** from retail. The set sold for $4.99 at retail and now sells for around $80 on LEGO secondary market sites. The 3341 Luke Skywalker, Han Solo, and Boba Fett Minifig Pack *Star Wars* #2 set is not far behind, with almost 1,200 percent in growth to over $60. These are some of the best examples of how rare and unique LEGO sets can explode in growth, regardless of the size and theme.

3340 EMPEROR PALPATINE, DARTH MAUL & DARTH VADER MINIFIG PACK *STAR WARS* #1

▶ Year Released: 2000
▶ No. of Pieces: 32
▶ Minifigures: 3
▶ Original Retail Price: $4.99

$ ▶ New: $79 ▶ Used: $35

3341 LUKE SKYWALKER, HAN SOLO AND BOBA FETT MINIFIG PACK *STAR WARS* #2

▶ Year Released: 2000
▶ No. of Pieces: 22
▶ Minifigures: 3
▶ Original Retail Price: $4.99

$ ▶ New: $63 ▶ Used: $20

3343 2 BATTLE DROIDS AND COMMAND OFFICER MINIFIG PACK *STAR WARS* #4

▶ Year Released: 2000
▶ No. of Pieces: 30
▶ Minifigures: 3
▶ Original Retail Price: $4.99

$ ▶ New: $21 ▶ Used: $11

3342 CHEWBACCA AND 2 BIKER SCOUTS MINIFIG PACK *STAR WARS* #3

▶ Year Released: 2000
▶ No. of Pieces: 22
▶ Minifigures: 3
▶ Original Retail Price: $4.99

$ ▶ New: $37 ▶ Used: $8

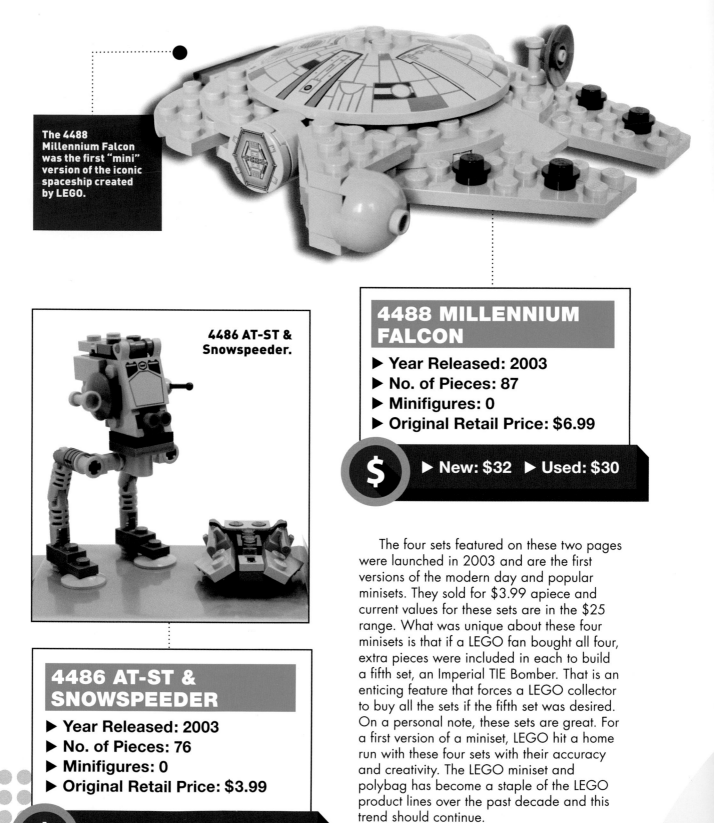

The 4488 Millennium Falcon was the first "mini" version of the iconic spaceship created by LEGO.

4486 AT-ST & Snowspeeder.

4488 MILLENNIUM FALCON

▶ Year Released: 2003
▶ No. of Pieces: 87
▶ Minifigures: 0
▶ Original Retail Price: $6.99

$ ▶ New: $32 ▶ Used: $30

4486 AT-ST & SNOWSPEEDER

▶ Year Released: 2003
▶ No. of Pieces: 76
▶ Minifigures: 0
▶ Original Retail Price: $3.99

$ ▶ New: $19 ▶ Used: $16

The four sets featured on these two pages were launched in 2003 and are the first versions of the modern day and popular minisets. They sold for $3.99 apiece and current values for these sets are in the $25 range. What was unique about these four minisets is that if a LEGO fan bought all four, extra pieces were included in each to build a fifth set, an Imperial TIE Bomber. That is an enticing feature that forces a LEGO collector to buy all the sets if the fifth set was desired. On a personal note, these sets are great. For a first version of a miniset, LEGO hit a home run with these four sets with their accuracy and creativity. The LEGO miniset and polybag has become a staple of the LEGO product lines over the past decade and this trend should continue.

4484 X-Wing Fighter and TIE Advanced.

4484 X-WING FIGHTER & TIE ADVANCED

▶ Year Released: 2003
▶ No. of Pieces: 76
▶ Minifigures: 0
▶ Original Retail Price: $3.99

$ ▶ New: $21 ▶ Used: $12

4487 Jedi Starfighter & Slave I.

4487 JEDI STARFIGHTER & SLAVE I

▶ Year Released: 2003
▶ No. of Pieces: 53
▶ Minifigures: 0
▶ Original Retail Price: $3.99

$ ▶ New: $16 ▶ Used: $10

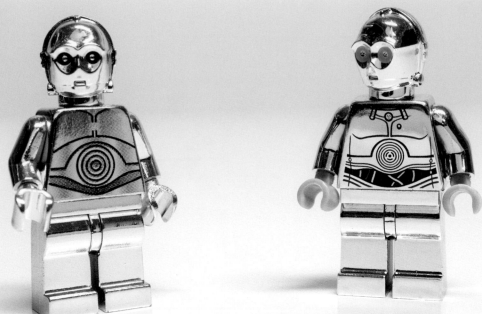

LEFT: **The valuable and scarce 4521221 Gold Chrome-Plated C-3PO.** RIGHT: **A silver C-3PO? TC-14, a protocol droid with feminine programming, is constructed much like C-3PO, except silver. It was a promotional item for 2012's "May the Fourth" celebration.**

4521221 GOLD CHROME-PLATED C-3PO

▶ **Year Released: 2001**
▶ **No. of Pieces: 1**
▶ **Minifigures: 1**
▶ **Original Retail Price: $0**

The 4521221 Gold chrome-plated C-3PO was a promotional item that LEGO released in 2007 in 10,000 random LEGO *Star Wars* sets in honor of the 30th Anniversary of *Star Wars*. The 4521221 is a polybag with a special C-3PO minifigure that has a unique gold chrome coating on it like the movie version. The current values are amazing, hitting the $350 level. One reason for such an increase is the rarity of the item — only 10,000 were produced. Another reason: it's damn cool. There are still plenty of these C-3POs floating around in sealed sets with the 30th Anniversary notations on it. Take a look at some of the more cost effective 2007 *Star Wars* sets still in MISB condition, and you might get lucky and find one of these highly collectible minifigures.

$ ▶ **New: $350** ▶ **Used: $273**

The polybag announces you just uncovered something special.

CHAPTER 24

SUPER HEROES

SUPERMAN BATMAN FLASH WOLVERINE THOR WONDER WOMAN HULK AQUAMAN CAPTAIN AMERICA IRON GREEN LANTERN SPIDERMAN MAN

The lego superheroes sets have exploded in popularity in conjunction with their big-screen counterparts. Minifigures play a major role with any superheroes set, but larger, more dynamic sets designed around vehicles and structures are being released with more frequency.

The LEGO Superheroes licensed theme began in 2011 and found its origins in DC and Marvel comics, and the sets are based on the movies released by the DC Universe and Marvel Cinematic Universe. Each major Universe has their main Superhero characters:

DC Universe: Superman, Batman, Green Lantern, Flash, Wonder Woman, Aquaman.

Marvel Cinematic Universe: Spiderman, Iron Man, Wolverine, Thor, Hulk, Captain America.

For purposes of this book, Batman has his own chapter because of his popularity, but in the world of LEGO, Batman also had his own LEGO theme from 2006 to 2008 and has been recently included in the DC Universe line of the main LEGO Superheroes theme. The DC Universe is involved with the *Man of Steel* and *Dark Knight* movie franchises, while the Marvel Cinematic Universe owns the *Guardians of the Galaxy*, *X-Men*, and *The Avengers* franchises.

Notice the tiny microfigures that inhabit the deck area.

76042 SHIELD HELICARRIER

▶ **Year Released:** 2015
▶ **No. of Pieces:** 2,996
▶ **Minifigures:** 5
▶ **Original Retail Price:** $349.99

This theme is a popular one with fans of all ages, but being that it is relatively new, there really aren't too many retired sets that have appreciated to high values, and the ones that have been released have been for sale for quite awhile. But that is starting to change, as the first wave of retired Superhero sets is starting to appreciate quietly and methodically. That does not mean that these sets will be poor collectible LEGO sets. Quite to the contrary — many of the Superheroes sets have fantastic and highly valuable minifigures that make the sets collectible. There have been a few Superheroes sets that have retired and have appreciated quite well, and they are featured on the next pages.

Many of the larger Superheroes sets are Batman related and featured in that chapter, including 10937 Batman: Arkham Asylum Breakout and 76023 The Tumbler. One current Superheroes set, the 76042 SHIELD Helicarrier, is the largest and quite possibly the most collectible of any of the sets in this theme. The nearly 3,000-piece behemoth is from the *Avengers* franchise and sells for $349 at retail. It will be a popular set after retirement for its size, minifigures and microfigures, coolness, Ultimate Collector Series plaque, and other features.

Unfortunately, there are not a lot of other large Superhero sets besides the three just mentioned. These are all great sets, no doubt, but when compared to the *Star Wars* theme, they pale in comparison. But many of the smaller Superheroes sets are affordable, have tons of playability and "Marvel-ous" minifigures, and will appreciate well after they retire.

$ ▶ **New: $378** ▶ **Used: $289**

The 4529 Iron Man is a "constraction" set and one that flew under most LEGO collectors' radar.

4529 IRON MAN

- ▶ **Year Released: 2012**
- ▶ **No. of Pieces: 44**
- ▶ **Minifigures: 0**
- ▶ **Original Retail Price: $14.99**

The 4529 Iron Man is a rather unique type of set in the LEGO universe. It is in the "Constraction" subtheme of the Marvel Superheroes. A Constraction set is a hybrid and cross between a Technic, Hero Factory, and Marvel Superhero set, resulting in a large LEGO action figure. The Constraction subtheme is found in other themes as well, including The Legends of Chima, but the Superheroes Constraction sets have raised the bar and are by far the most valuable of the subtheme.

This set in particular has fed off the popularity of the recent *Iron Man* movies. The 4529 Iron Man combines LEGO with an action figure, thus creating the playability of an action figure and the assembly qualities of a LEGO set. This set is a close replica to the Iron Man character, and I can see why it has quadrupled in value from its $14.99 MSRP. It is an attractive set with high playability, which is a great combination for a successful LEGO set.

Many of the smaller Superheroes sets will appreciate well after they retire and many are quite affordable, with tons of playability and "Marvel-ous" minifigures, making them cost-effective collectibles. Here are a few Superhero sets of note that have recently retired:

5000022 THE HULK

- ▶ **Year Released: 2012**
- ▶ **No. of Pieces: 4**
- ▶ **Minifigures: 1**
- ▶ **Original Retail Price: $14.99**

The 5000022 The Hulk was a LEGO promotional item given away during May 2012 and is unique in that it is a mini Hulk. Most current Hulk minifigures are, in fact, maxifigures, so this minifigure is rare. To acquire one, you would have to meet a dollar threshold when purchasing sets in a brick and mortar LEGO store or online on LEGO Shop @ Home. Over the past several years, many LEGO collectors have timed their purchases around these VIP promotions because these small promotional polybags and sets can appreciate to moderately high levels for a set that was FREE. The 5000022 Hulk is currently valued at over $30 on the secondary market. A four-piece polybag worth $30? Yes. LEGO collectors know these promotional polybags are limited in production and sometimes rare on the secondary market, so many will only buy sets in or on LEGO locations or sites when there is a worthwhile giveaway that month. Basically, they estimate these limited polybags or promotional sets are worth "X," then subtract it from their purchase total, which is usually around the threshold dollar amount ($75 or $100 typically), then come up with a percentage off the MSRP of the main purchase. It's the game within the game, tricks-of-the-trade mentality that help collectors take advantage of every discount and promotion to make a profit.

$ ▶ New: $72 ▶ Used: $29

$ ▶ New: $31 ▶ Used: $19

LEGO collectors are constantly in pursuit of the next 6866 Wolverine's Chopper Showdown. The set sold at retail for $19.99 and was discounted to even lower levels, yet current values for this set are approaching $80!

6866 WOLVERINE'S CHOPPER SHOWDOWN

▶ **Year Released: 2012**
▶ **No. of Pieces: 199**
▶ **Minifigures: 3**
▶ **Original Retail Price: $19.99**

The old idiom, the best things come in small packages, was written specifically for the 6866 Wolverine's Chopper Showdown. This 199-piece set with a $19.99 MSRP has rocketed to the $70 range in less than a year. What makes this set so special and contributed to its appreciation are the exclusive minifigures of Wolverine, Magneto, and Deadpool.

Besides the minifigures, there is a neat helicopter and motorcycle in the set, which adds some extra pieces and playability. Many collectors consider the extra pieces a bonus.

$ ▶ **New: $70** ▶ **Used: $44**

INVESTING TIP

Marvel and DC Comics Superhero sets are great places to locate exclusive minifigures. Many of the polybags and small sets have valuable minifigures that many collectors will remove from the original sets to resell for more money than what they paid for the LEGO set originally. This is called "parting out" a LEGO set. Parting out has become a multi-million-dollar industry on the LEGO secondary market. As mentioned previously in this book, not only minifigures are parted out, but all the other pieces as well can be resold to other fans and builders. Online sites like www.Bricklink.com have sold tens of millions of dollars of loose LEGO bricks. Bricklink is made up of thousands of smaller mom-and-pop stores selling sets or parts. This is the backbone of the MOC and custom LEGO model portion of the LEGO Universe, and without these fans parting out sets, many awesome custom creations would never come to pass.

CHAPTER 25

TECHNIC

THE DESIGN CREATIVITY OF TECHNIC SETS IS UNPARALLELED IN THE LEGO UNIVERSE. THEY MAY ALSO TAKE THEIR TIME TO APPRECIATE IN VALUE, BUT THERE ARE SOME LARGER SETS THAT HAVE REACHED HIGH LEVELS.

The Technic theme is really an amazing display of LEGO at its best. Sets ranging from motorcycles and helicopters, to dump trucks and racing cars, to almost whatever you can imagine that is a vehicle or machine has been recreated in Technic bricks. All of the sets are functional in some way: doors open, wheels turn, chopper blades spin, cranes lift, and dump truck beds dump.

The design creativity displayed by these sets is unparalleled in the LEGO Universe. Sure, other sets may resemble a *Star Wars* vehicle or *Harry Potter* castle, but do they operate with remote controls like an RC car or truck? Probably not. The sky is the limit with Technic sets.

As a LEGO collectible, some people appreciate the engineering and mechanical component of the theme, while others look at them as aesthetically ugly and incomplete in comparison to other LEGO themes, like the Advanced Models, for instance, that replicate the exterior of many structures and vehicles to a T. It also might be the technical complexity of the sets that either attracts or turns off builders and collectors. Regardless, the Technic theme does have a large population of passionate fans, who produce profitable and collectible sets.

There are quite a few large Technic sets that have reached high values. They are slow and methodical gainers, though, taking their time to appreciate to those lofty levels. What is great about Technic sets is that they are not highly stockpiled by collectors and investors, thus creating a rare set years after they retire. While not all Technic sets are going to appreciate to high levels or growth rates, some do well, but it's not always easy picking out an exceptional set. Many are similar in makeup and functions, so picking out the true collectible Technic set is as much luck as it is skill. For those LEGO collectors who pick correctly, the potential for growth is strong.

The Bulldozer is one impressive piece of LEGO technology.

I still have the tires from the Car Chassis set I owned almost 40 years ago.

853/956 CAR CHASSIS

▶ Year Released: 1977
▶ No. of Pieces: 601
▶ Minifigures: 0
▶ Original Retail Price: $N/A

In various chapters throughout this book, I have mentioned sets that got me personally addicted to the LEGO brick, including the 375/6075 Yellow Castle and 497/928 Galaxy Explorer that I loved as a child in the late 1970s.

Another favorite set is the 853/956 Car Chassis, which is a replica of a basic car frame and mechanicals done in LEGO bricks, and an amazing set for the time period. It had working steering, engine pistons, transmission, adjustable seats, and working suspension. This set contained new pieces created for it in 1977 that looked like gears, axles, pins, beams, large tires, and other irregular-shaped bricks. These new sets were called Technical Sets in 1977, and later changed to Technic in 1984.

$ ▶ New: $169 ▶ Used: $147

8275 MOTORIZED BULLDOZER

▶ Year Released: 2007
▶ No. of Pieces: 1,384
▶ Minifigures: 0
▶ Original Retail Price: $149.99

The 8275 Motorized Bulldozer is at the top of the Technic price chart, currently valued at over $700 on the LEGO secondary market. The 1,384-set sold for $149.99 in 2007 and exhibited over a 400 percent Return on Investment since it retired in 2008. While the growth is not as fast as some other larger sets, it is still quite steady and impressive for a Technic set. The 8275 Motorized Bulldozer comes with Power Functions: four motors and two remote controls that operate the treads and front and rear mechanical blade and ripper. An attractive set, the 8275 Motorized Bulldozer really looks and works like the real thing. There is nothing even close to it in size, style, or complexity on the LEGO secondary market, so that is why this set has appreciated so well.

$ ▶ New: $761 ▶ Used: $327

8288 CRAWLER CRANE

▶ **Year Released: 2006**
▶ **No. of Pieces: 800**
▶ **Minifigures: 0**
▶ **Original Retail Price: $49.99**

The 8288 Crawler Crane is an example of a lower-priced Technic set that has shown explosive growth on the LEGO secondary market — almost 700 percent, in fact. Originally a $49.99 set at retail, the 8288 Crawler Crane has reached the $400 level. It was quite a value at $49.99, with 800 pieces, but it is probably the unique design of the set that has helped stimulate such growth. I can't recall another set similar to this one, with treads and a crane mechanism. While there have been many LEGO cranes, most are with wheels or stationary in nature. Whatever the reason, the 8288 Crawler Crane is another example of a smaller, mid-sized set that can be an excellent choice for collectors.

$ ▶ **New: $400** ▶ **Used: $219**

The Crawler Crane could be one of the best bargains in the history of LEGO sets.

8285 TOW TRUCK

▶ **Year Released: 2006**
▶ **No. of Pieces: 1,877**
▶ **Minifigures: 0**
▶ **Original Retail Price: $119.99**

$ ▶ **New: $704** ▶ **Used: $272**

This is a magnificent LEGO model, if you like trucks. The 8285 Tow Truck is a dead-on replica of a "Big Rig" tow truck, constructed with over 1,800 pieces. The set is an accurate model in appearance and nicely detailed in black with red and bright silver trim. There are plenty of stickers to give the illusion of a high-end paint job. Current value for the 8285 Tow Truck is over $700 on the LEGO secondary market, for almost 500 percent growth from the original $119.99 retail price. While this set does not include any Power Functions, it does have an operational winch and engine with six working cylinders. The 8285 Tow Truck is another slow and steady collectible LEGO set, further illustrating that, if you have the patience, Technic sets can appreciate to high levels.

◀ The Crawler has one of the best looking boxes in LEGO history.

Each 41999 4x4 Crawler Exclusive Edition has a unique license plate number.

41999 4X4 CRAWLER EXCLUSIVE EDITION

▶ **Year Released:** 2013
▶ **No. of Pieces:** 1,585
▶ **Minifigures:** 0
▶ **Original Retail Price:** $199.99

This is an interesting set. It was released for about one month in August 2013 and promoted by LEGO as a "Limited Edition" set with a production run of only 20,000.

It is based on the 9398 4x4 Crawler, but has a different body shell and collector's-type box. It is really an awesome set, with its Power Functions motors and remote controls, that make it operate similarly to an RC car or truck.

What's amazing is that there was such a hype about this set that it sold out in less than a month. Although it was available for a few days a month or two later, it had one of the shortest shelf lives of any LEGO set ever. With all that being said, the growth on the secondary market has been unremarkable. For such a cool and collectible set, it has not appreciated like many experts expected, including myself. It is quite possible that because it is a Technic set, many potential buyers were turned off. My guess is that this will still reach high levels in the future, but like most Technic sets, it will appreciate slowly and methodically.

It is still available for less than $400, so there could be opportunities for new LEGO collectors to buy one at a reasonable cost. With time, interest in this awesome set will only increase.

MORE THAN A TOY

Many top colleges and universities, such as Massachusetts Institute of Technology, use LEGO Technic sets to teach robotics and mechanical engineering, proving these sets are more than just toys and are educational as well.

$ ▶ **New: $338** ▶ **Used: $289**

CHAPTER 26

TRAINS

TOY TRAINS HAVE BEEN COLLECTED BY CHILDREN AND ADULTS SINCE REAL-LIFE TRAINS WERE CREATED CENTURIES AGO. WHAT HAPPENS IF YOU COMBINE TWO ICONIC TOYS LIKE LEGO BRICKS AND TOY TRAINS? YOU GET A HIGHLY POPULAR AND COLLECTIBLE LEGO SET.

Trains is a theme that LEGO excels at, and LEGO bricks do an excellent job of replicating trains and train tracks. LEGO Trains are similar in size to the classic O-gauge electric trains that have been collected by hobbyists for decades. Some fans call LEGO trains L-gauge, in reference to the multitude of train sizes and name classes, such as O, N, HO, and G scale.

LEGO trains had their beginning in 1966, with simple "push" trains. LEGO then developed 4.5-volt battery-operated train models with trains operating off a battery pack and motor. Eventually, LEGO went to a 12- and 9-volt system that incorporated special tracks with metal strips and separate transformers and switches to operate the train models. Fast forward to modern day and LEGO now utilizes simpler and cheaper train track without metal strips, and their new Power Function options and infrared remote controls to animate and light them. The remote controls can operate up to four functions at one time, which gives builders the option to add motion to any LEGO train, whether they included the Power Function options or not.

We will discuss only the LEGO Trains that were released after 2000. The pre-2000 trains, the 4.5- and 12-volt variety, are basic builds, with blocky designs and inaccurate features that are from a train "system." It wasn't until the creation of the 9-volt LEGO trains that more realistic designs were incorporated into this theme. The trains discussed here are more of your standalone, unique sets that can be from various themes and LEGO sources and don't rely on other parts of a system to look complete. Although I refer to a LEGO Train as a 9-volt or Power Function train, most do not include a motor or drive source to propel it. These sources of propulsion could be added later with different LEGO add-on sets and accessory packs. From a collector's viewpoint, any type of current LEGO Trains are popular and solid choices for possible appreciation. There is usually at least one train to choose from on an annual basis in some theme, so a nice collection of display trains can be obtained, if desired. If a person gets bored with looking at a stationary train displayed in an office or den, fear not: It can be converted into a working train with a little ingenuity, time, and some Power Function parts.

10173 HOLIDAY TRAIN

- ▶ **Year Released:** 2000
- ▶ **No. of Pieces:** 965
- ▶ **Minifigures:** 7
- ▶ **Original Retail Price:** $89.99

The 10173 Holiday Train was released in 2006, three years before the first Winter Village set, the 10199 Winter Village Toy Shop, was created. The set itself contains 965 pieces and seven minifigures, not a bad deal for $89.99. The design of the set is somewhat fairy tale based instead of reality based, making it a wonderful complimentary set to the fantasy-like Winter Village sets. The current value on the LEGO secondary market is over $700. It has appreciated almost 700 percent from retail, which is amazing for a simply designed set such as this. Throw in a Santa Claus minifigure, some green bricks and Christmas presents, and watch the magic of collectible Christmas sets take off like a flying reindeer.

$ ▶ **New: $702** ▶ **Used: $438**

10194 EMERALD NIGHT

- ▶ **Year Released:** 2009
- ▶ **No. of Pieces:** 1,085
- ▶ **Minifigures:** 3
- ▶ **Original Retail Price:** $99.99

The 10194 Emerald Night is a beautiful LEGO model. The dark green bricks, with shiny black and gold trim, make for one elegant set. Modeled after a steam locomotive, the 10194 Emerald Night has no major flaws in my eyes. My only issue is that I wish it was bigger, with a few more passenger cars and maybe a matching caboose, which would have been an excellent addition and could have made it one of the all time top LEGO sets. I often thought that LEGO could unify the Trains theme and capitalize on a huge fan base by introducing new trains every year that would easily interchange with one another. All sorts of locomotives and cars could be produced yearly, making a highly collectible theme. Nonetheless, I will take what LEGO dishes out, and the 10194 Emerald Night is a fantastic set from its advanced build to its classy appearance to its stellar growth on the LEGO secondary market.

Current values are quadruple the MSRP of $99.99, with almost a 300 percent Return on Investment, and the strong appreciation should continue.

$ ▶ **New: $384** ▶ **Used: $266**

As with any LEGO Maersk set, the special Maersk "blue" bricks are eye catching and valuable because of their rarity. The 10219 Maersk Train is an attractive recreation of the real life locomotive.

10219 MAERSK TRAIN

▶ **Year Released:** 2011
▶ **No. of Pieces:** 1,237
▶ **Minifigures:** 3
▶ **Original Retail Price:** $99.99

LEGO has long been in a licensing partnership with the Danish shipping giant, The Maersk Group, and many versions of Maersk container ships and trucks have been produced, but it wasn't until 2011 that LEGO got around to producing a Maersk train. With over 1,200 pieces, three minifigures, and a price tag of $119.99, the 10219 Maersk Train was a fair deal and an attractive LEGO Train model. Decked out in the traditional Maersk light blue and gray, the diesel locomotive replica is quite detailed and easy on the eyes. In addition to the locomotive, there are two container train cars and a container truck; Power Functions can be added at a later time. The set had a year-and-a-half production run, which is typical for Maersk LEGO sets. Current value has easily doubled the MSRP and is approaching the $300 level. If you are a LEGO Train collector, then the 10219 Maersk Train is a must have. There is some room to grow as well if it follows the growth patterns of some other LEGO Trains.

$ ▶ **New: $384** ▶ **Used: $266**

◀ **The 10194 Emerald Night might just be one of the most beautiful LEGO sets ever created, in my opinion. With the dark green body, gold trim, and fine details, the train must be seen in person to be appreciated.**

SANTE FE TRAINS

The Sante Fe Train subtheme is a group of sets with similar boxes and styles that were released from 2002 to 2005. Prices ranged from $34.99 to $39.99, and the piece counts were all around 400. Each one of the Sante Fe sets can work with the other sets, especially the 10025 Santa Fe Cars - Set I and 10022 Santa Fe Cars - Set II, which are replicas of passenger cars. One can be converted to a dining car, which gives builders some variety. The two engines, the 10133 Burlington Northern Santa Fe (BNSF) Locomotive and the 10020 Santa Fe Super Chief, are excellent recreations of diesel locomotives. These Santa Fe sets are similar in look, size, and structure to the 10219 Maersk Train and could make a wonderful display if all could be acquired and viewed together. That might not have been a big deal ten years ago when the sets were around $40 each, but now sets like the 10133 Burlington are over $300, for a 700 percent Return on Investment. With the exception of the 10170 TTX Intermodal Double-Stack Car, which has tripled in value from its MSRP of $39.99, for a little over 200 percent Return on Investment, the remaining four Sante Fe sets have appreciated 500 percent or more from retail. Very impressive growth and another example of a low-cost set being an excellent LEGO collectible. Unfortunately, I doubt we will see MSRPs similar to these five sets on newer releases. It seems like these more complex, or "expert," builds are being priced closer to $100 than $40 nowadays. Regardless, the Sante Fe subtheme is a five-set powerhouse, and those lucky enough to own all five have had not only the privilege to build them, but to profit from them.

▼ These Sante Fe cars (Baggage-10025, Passenger-10022) are realistic-looking replicas and great examples of how low-priced, cost-effective sets can be excellent collectibles.

10025 SANTA FE CARS - SET I

▶ **Year Released: 2002**
▶ **No. of Pieces: 326**
▶ **Minifigures: 0**
▶ **Original Retail Price: $34.99**

$ ▶ New: $204 ▶ Used: $182

10022 SANTA FE CARS - SET II

▶ **Year Released: 2002**
▶ **No. of Pieces: 411**
▶ **Minifigures: 0**
▶ **Original Retail Price: $34.99**

$ ▶ New: $273 ▶ Used: $192

BNSF GP-38 Locomotive

LEGO
COLORADO
ages/edades
8+
10133
BNSF GP-38
Locomotive
cont. 407 pcs/pzs
Building Toy
Jouet de Construction
Juguete para Construir
MEXICO

Another attractive LEGO train, the combination of the yellow, orange, and dark green is stunning on the 10133 Burlington Northern Sante Fe Locomotive.

10133 BURLINGTON NORTHERN SANTA FE (BNSF) LOCOMOTIVE

▶ Year Released: 2004
▶ No. of Pieces: 407
▶ Minifigures: 2
▶ Original Retail Price: $39.99

$ ▶ New: $324 ▶ Used: $192

TTX Intermodal Double-Stack Car

LEGO
COLORADO
8+
10170
MEXICO

Santa Fe Super Chief

LEGO
COLORADO
AGES/EDADES
10+
10020
Building Toy
Jouet de Construction
Juguete para Construir
MEXICO
Cont. 436 pcs/pzs
SANTA FE
301
LIMITED EDITION

10170 TTX INTERMODAL DOUBLE-STACK CAR

▶ Year Released: 2005
▶ No. of Pieces: 366
▶ Minifigures: 0
▶ Original Retail Price: $39.99

$ ▶ New: $132 ▶ Used: $94

10020 SANTA FE SUPER CHIEF

▶ Year Released: 2002
▶ No. of Pieces: 435
▶ Minifigures: 2
▶ Original Retail Price: $39.99

$ ▶ New: $265 ▶ Used: $203

CHAPTER 27

VINTAGE

PRE-2000

WHEN IT COMES TO LEGO COLLECTIBLES, OLDER DOESN'T ALWAYS MEAN MORE VALUABLE, AND WHILE NEWER SETS APPRECIATE HIGHER IN VALUE THAN VINTAGE ONES, THERE ARE STILL SOME OLDER SETS THAT CAN REACH LOFTY LEVELS.

When my brother, Jeff, and I started keeping track of LEGO prices, we were amazed by the type of sets that appreciated to the highest levels. You would think that the most valuable sets would be the oldest. While that might be true with coins, stamps, and other collectibles, with LEGO, oldest doesn't always mean the most valuable.

While the main focus of this book is to talk about LEGO sets that were released after 2000, there are many older sets that have grown to substantial values, but why not to the rates of the newer sets? You have to remember, there have been over 10,000 LEGO sets released over the past 50 years, but the majority of sets have been released post 2000, with an ever-increasing amount of sets getting released with each passing year. For example, in 1984, 82 LEGO items were released. Fast forward to 2014, LEGO released 723 to sell to the buying public. That is almost ten times what was released 30 years ago!

One possible reason why older LEGO sets underperform in comparison to their newer

10,000+ LEGO SETS RELEASED OVER THE PAST 50 YEARS

counterparts is that there are so few MISB sets available for sale that you cannot get an accurate price on them. Because there is a lack of sales and examples of what you should pay for such a vintage set, many collectors will shy away from these older sets. On occasion, a rare MISB will come on the market, but might sit there for a long time, waiting for that right buyer to come along who can connect with it on a personal level. Maybe the buyer had that set as a child and wants to relive their childhood building days.

Whatever the reason, some people will pay top dollar for older sets, but it is inconsistent and the lack of sales don't give collectors confidence that if they pay a high price for an item, they can recoup their money later if they want to sell it.

The old and rare LEGO is worth what someone is willing to pay for it, so many rare and old sets never find that right buyer who is willing to risk big money for a 40-year-old set, when newer sets are appreciating to such high levels.

Sails are some of the most difficult things to replace on a set like the 6286 Skull's Eye Schooner. They fade and fall apart with time, so sails in great condition are a must to get top dollar for these types of sets.

6286 SKULL'S EYE SCHOONER

▶ **Year Released: 1993**
▶ **No. of Pieces: 912**
▶ **Minifigures: 9**
▶ **Original Retail Price: $126.99**

$ ▶ **New: $885** ▶ **Used: $286**

Topping the list of pre-2000 LEGO sets in value are two completely different ones: the 912-piece 6286 Skull's Eye Schooner from the Pirates theme, and the 1,757-piece 5571 Giant Truck from the Model Team theme. The Model Team theme was an early version of the Advanced Models theme, basically bigger sets with more detail designed for older fans. Both sets have broken the $800 barrier for over 500 percent Return on Investment.

The 6286 Skull's Eye Schooner is a nicely detailed and sizeable 1990s pirate ship, and the 5571 Giant Truck is a cool replica of a large diesel truck. Both the Pirates and Model Team themes make up 5 of the Top 12 spots on the list. Other popular themes included the varieties of the Castle theme, the old Town/City theme and some Technic sets.

I think a lot of the issues with the older sets relate to the design and build quality. They just don't compare to the post-2000 LEGO sets in size, structure, design, accuracy, minifigure quality, and many other facets. Another reason is that I believe fans and collectors relate more to the newer sets. LEGO collecting and investing is relatively new to the collectibles universe. Investing in LEGO and thinking of them as collectibles really began with the creation of online auction sites like eBay. The growth of eBay coincided with the growth of LEGO and with their improvements in set design. Many new LEGO collectors and investors were not even around 40 years ago to care about older sets, yet they can relate to *Star Wars* or *Harry Potter* sets.

There have been older sets that have appreciated to lofty levels, but many of them are somewhat similar in build and size to sets of modern times. The sets featured here are interesting and make the grade.

5571 GIANT TRUCK

▶ **Year Released: 1996**
▶ **No. of Pieces: 1,757**
▶ **Minifigures: 0**
▶ **Original Retail Price: $138.99**

$ ▶ **New: $880** ▶ **Used: $308**

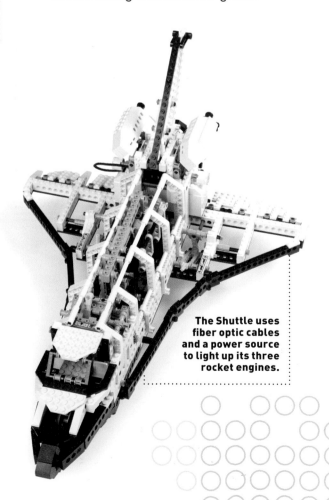

The Shuttle uses fiber optic cables and a power source to light up its three rocket engines.

8480 SPACE SHUTTLE

▶ **Year Released: 1996**
▶ **No. of Pieces: 1,368**
▶ **Minifigures: 0**
▶ **Original Retail Price: $157.99**

Of the Technic sets on the list is one of my favorites, the 8480 Space Shuttle. There are a huge number of fans who think this is the best Technic set ever created. Whether that is true or not can be debated; what is true is that the 8480 Space Shuttle was way ahead of its time. Released in 1996 for $157.99 (odd price?), it has some cool features for the time period, such as fiber optic cables that lit up the engines of the craft and a motor that operated the Canada arm and satellite. Current values for the 1,368-piece Shuttle are over $400, but if more people knew about the coolness of this set, it would probably be even higher.

$ ▶ **New: $424** ▶ **Used: $230**

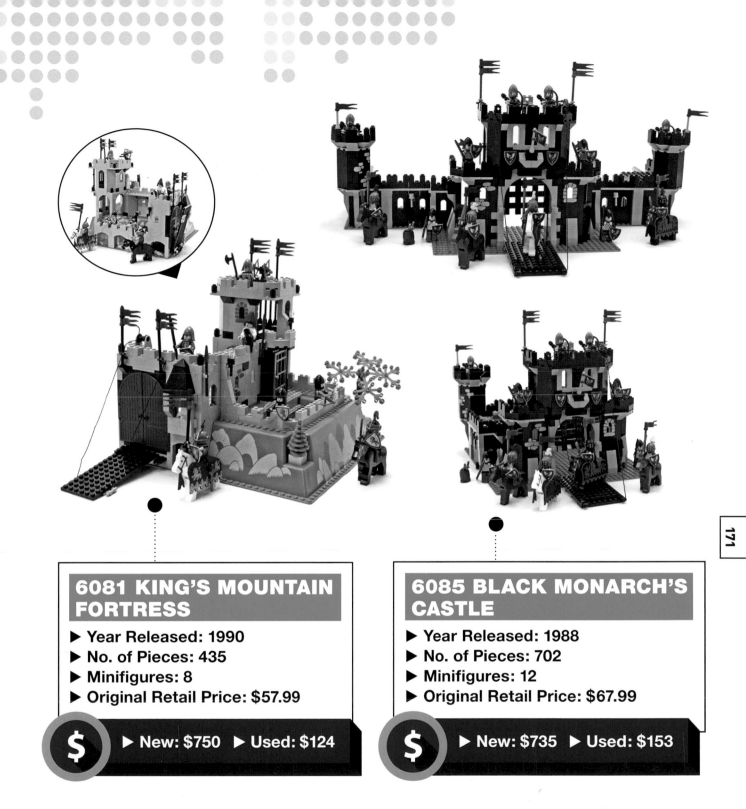

6081 KING'S MOUNTAIN FORTRESS

▶ **Year Released: 1990**
▶ **No. of Pieces: 435**
▶ **Minifigures: 8**
▶ **Original Retail Price: $57.99**

$ ▶ **New: $750** ▶ **Used: $124**

6085 BLACK MONARCH'S CASTLE

▶ **Year Released: 1988**
▶ **No. of Pieces: 702**
▶ **Minifigures: 12**
▶ **Original Retail Price: $67.99**

$ ▶ **New: $735** ▶ **Used: $153**

There is a trio of Castle sets from 1988 to 1992 that appears to have appreciated well together. The 6081 King's Mountain Fortress, the 6085 Black Monarch's Castle, and the 6086 Black Knight's Castle have all hit the $700 level on the LEGO secondary market. The 6081 King's Mountain Fortress, in fact, has appreciated almost 1,200 percent from its retail price of $57.99 to the $750 mark.

Although Castle sets appreciate slowly when compared to others, the 6081 and 6085 are examples of vintage LEGO sets that can reach high values given some time.

These are all great numbers, but remember one thing: these sets have been retired for 25 years, and the Return on Investment over that span is nothing special on a yearly basis. Many newer LEGO sets appreciate much higher annually than these vintage sets do, which goes back to my original point: Newer sets are better for investment purposes. While you might get lucky with some rare MISB vintage sets, the best choices for collectibles were and are produced after the new millennium.

On some of these older Castle sets, the molded base plates are valuable as well. Because the model is designed around the base plate, you cannot part this set out and recreate it without the specialized base plate. They can sell for $25-$50 or more.

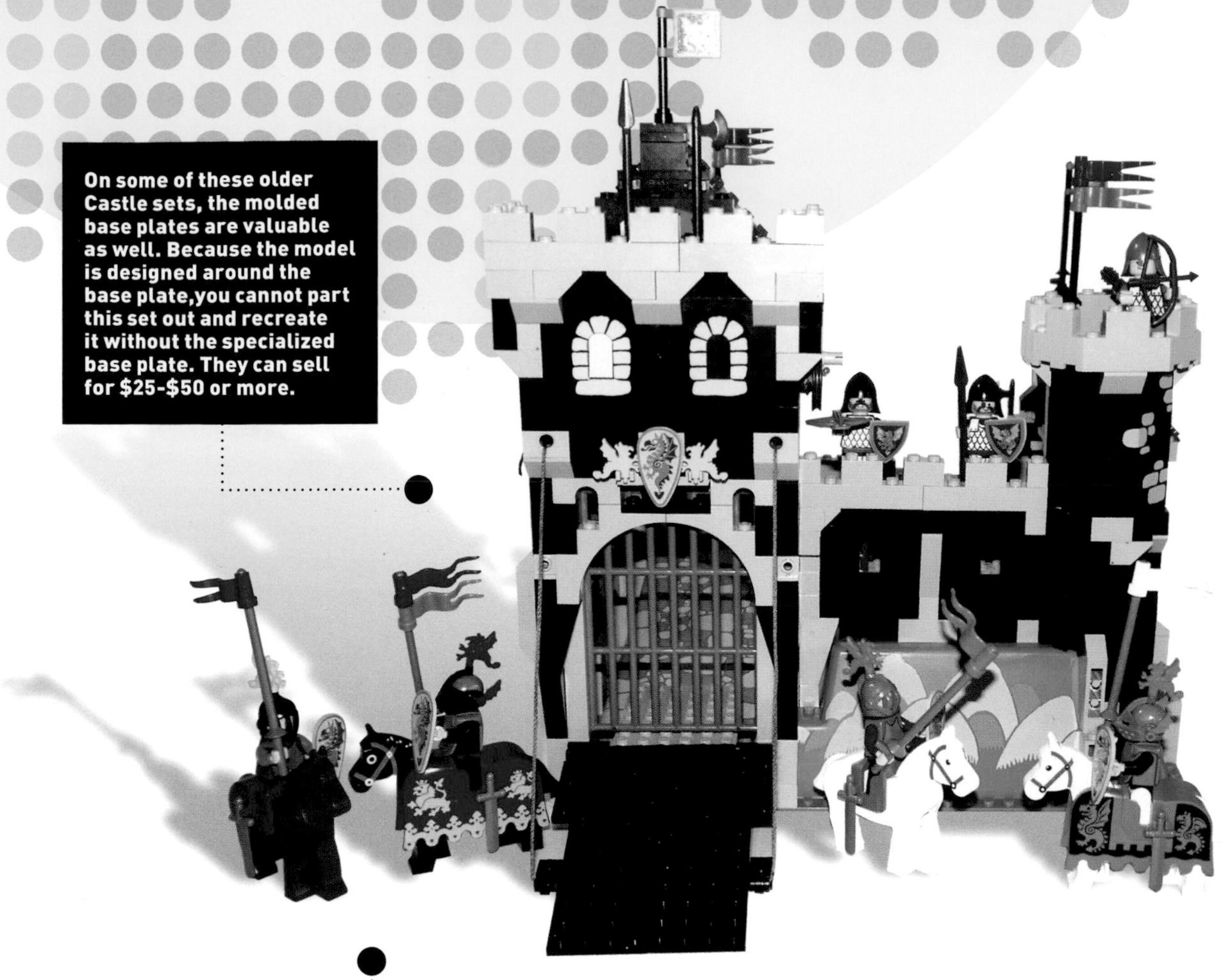

6086 BLACK KNIGHT'S CASTLE

▶ Year Released: 1992
▶ No. of Pieces: 588
▶ Minifigures: 12
▶ Original Retail Price: $84.99

$ ▶ New: $700 ▶ Used: $178

VINTAGE SHIP
A VALUABLE SET

There is one set that we decided to leave out of the regular price guide: the 1650 Maersk Line Container Ship from 1974. It had 220 pieces and was a promotional item released in small quantities. We had one legitimate sale for this set for $1,900, but because there was only one sale, we thought it was prudent not to include it, but it still needs to be noted because it is a perfect example of how every once in awhile, an old and rare MISB LEGO set can sell for huge money. So check your attics!

Even in 1992, the custom Maersk blue was utilized in any Maersk LEGO set. In this case, the entire boat hull is molded in the light blue color. The hull itself is made up of several sections, including the bow, stern, and center sections. I wonder if it floats?

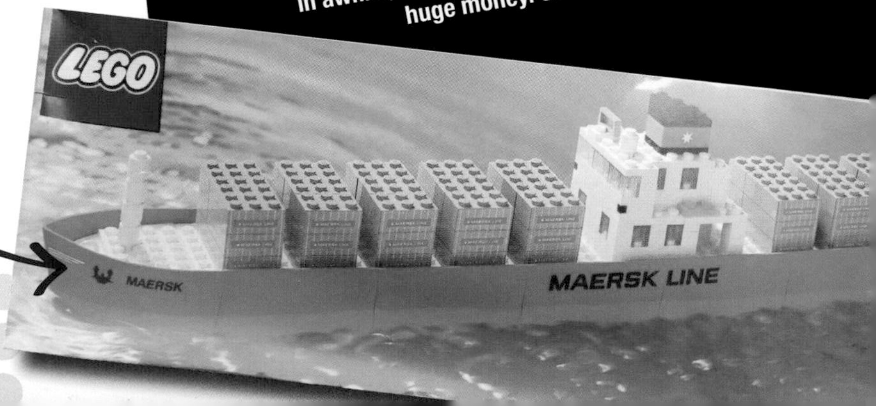

LEGO

MAERSK

MAERSK LINE

CHAPTER 28

MISC ELLANEOUS

——— SETS AND THEMES ———

SOMETIMES THE SMALL THEME OR UNCONVENTIONAL SET CAN BE THE LEGO COLLECTOR'S BEST FRIEND. THERE ARE MANY UNDER-THE-RADAR SETS RELEASED ON AN ANNUAL BASIS THAT MAKE EXCELLENT CHOICES FOR INVESTING AND COLLECTING. MANY OF THESE SMALL THEMES OUTPERFORM THE BIG BOYS OF THE LEGO COLLECTIBLES UNIVERSE, SO NEVER UNDERESTIMATE THE POTENTIAL OF ANY LEGO SET.

As I have mentioned, there have been more than 10,000 LEGO sets created and sold over the past 50 or so years.

With each passing year, LEGO has 600 or more different items for sale on the primary retail markets from retailers including LEGO Shop @ Home, LEGO brick and mortar stores, Target, Amazon, Toys R Us, and Walmart.

That is a huge amount of sets to track and analyze, which is impossible for a single book. But the sets spotlighted in this chapter are some outstanding miscellaneous sets and smaller themes that need to be considered.

The Mobile Command Center probably has more play options than any set I know. It is a tractor trailer and a command base. It also has rocket ships and ATVs. Throw in a jet ski and boat for good measure.

174

8635 MOBILE COMMAND CENTER

▶ Year Released: 2008
▶ No. of Pieces: 1,154
▶ Minifigures: 7
▶ Retail Price: $89.99

$ ▶ New: $230 ▶ Used: $118

8637 VOLCANO BASE

▶ Year Released: 2008
▶ No. of Pieces: 718
▶ Minifigures: 6
▶ Retail Price: $69.99

$ ▶ New: $215 ▶ Used: $152

LEGO Agents Theme

The LEGO Agents theme, originally released in 2008, lasted until 2009 and has since been re-released in 2014 as the "Ultra Agents." While not an exact duplicate of the original Agents theme, the newer versions may have an impact on the older ones. The theme is based on spies and secret agents and their tools, vehicles, and gadgets. The sets are kinda radical and fun, and do well in the LEGO secondary market.

The 8635 Mobile Command Center is a 1,154-piece set that sold for $89.99 at retail; current prices are well over $200. I wonder if the new version, the 70165 Ultra Agents Mission HQ, will have an effect on the older version. Themes like the Agents and Ultra Agents are not *that* collectible, in my opinion, and I can definitely see the values of the older version plateauing, if not falling, over time.

A set like the 718-piece 8637 Volcano Base, which is selling for over $200, might not be as affected by the newer Ultra Agents because there is nothing similar to it at this time.

Overall, this is a theme that is designed for older kids who like special agent and 007 types of toys. As a LEGO collectible, the jury is still out.

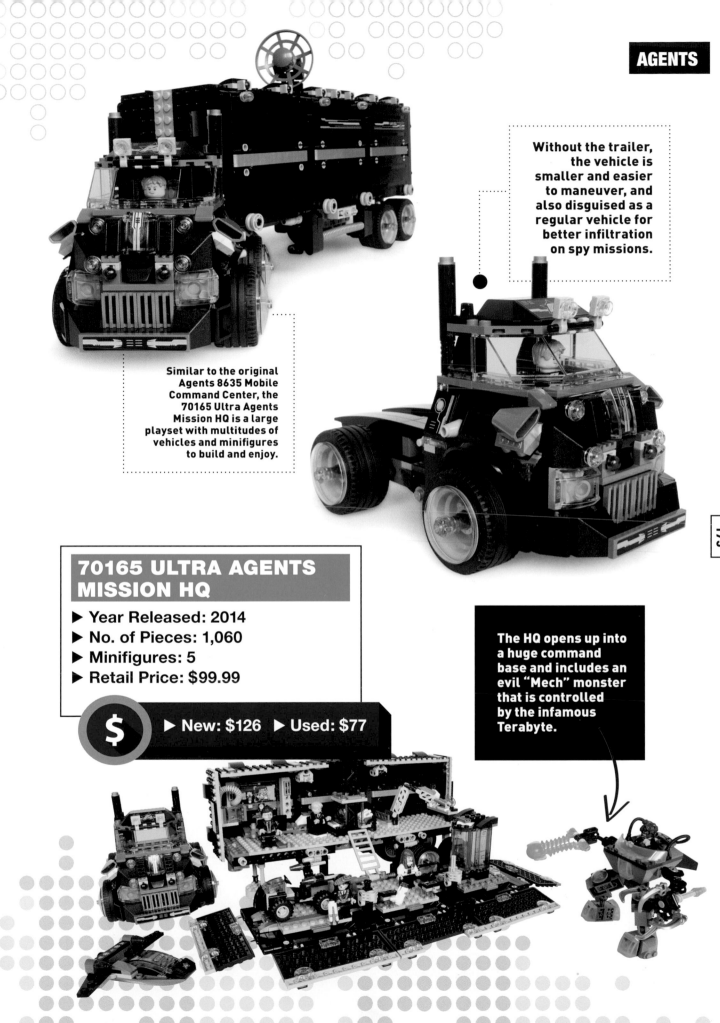

Without the trailer, the vehicle is smaller and easier to maneuver, and also disguised as a regular vehicle for better infiltration on spy missions.

Similar to the original Agents 8635 Mobile Command Center, the 70165 Ultra Agents Mission HQ is a large playset with multitudes of vehicles and minifigures to build and enjoy.

70165 ULTRA AGENTS MISSION HQ

▶ Year Released: 2014
▶ No. of Pieces: 1,060
▶ Minifigures: 5
▶ Retail Price: $99.99

$ ▶ New: $126 ▶ Used: $77

The HQ opens up into a huge command base and includes an evil "Mech" monster that is controlled by the infamous Terabyte.

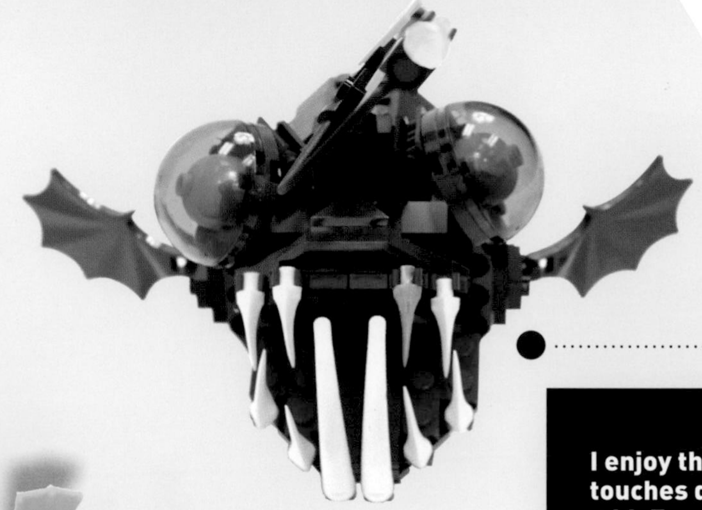

I enjoy the little touches designers add. For this set, notice the small "gold" tooth. This fish must have an expensive dentist.

Bricks are used in a creative fashion to replicate a deep sea terror: space set domes are used for the eyes, bat wings for fins, and minifigure swim fins for the dorsal fin.

7978 ANGLER ATTACK

▶ **Year Released:** 2011
▶ **No. of Pieces:** 200
▶ **Minifigures:** 2
▶ **Retail Price:** $19.99

$ ▶ **New: $38** ▶ **Used: $16**

LEGO Atlantis Theme

The Atlantis theme is my personal LEGO Albatross as a serious collector and investor. I usually consider LEGO themes that have unique and intriguing set designs, creative minifigures, and creepy creatures as sure-fire winners, but the Atlantis theme has disappointed so far. Based on an undersea world and exploration team, the Atlantis theme has nasty and neat undersea monsters and minifigures, with a multitude of man-made machinery that probes the depths of the deep blue sea. Sounds great, but in reality, many of the sets under perform and find little interest from fans. One of the best examples of an Atlantis set with teeth is the 7978 Angler Attack. This 200-piece set has almost doubled in value to $40, and that is saying a lot for an Atlantis set. The 7978 Angler Attack is just a great-looking set in any theme, with its huge eyes and teeth. You have to be careful investing in these sets. Not only does this theme continue to under perform, but the similar Aqua Raiders undersea theme from several years earlier also performed unsatisfactory for the most part. Caution: Undersea LEGO themes could make for underwater investments!

7667 IMPERIAL DROPSHIP BATTLE PACK

▶ **Year Released: 2008**
▶ **No. of Pieces: 81**
▶ **Minifigures: 4**
▶ **Retail Price: $9.99**

$ ▶ **New: $48** ▶ **Used: $28**

7655 CLONE TROOPERS BATTLE PACK

▶ **Year Released: 2007**
▶ **No. of Pieces: 58**
▶ **Minifigures: 4**
▶ **Retail Price: $9.99**

$ ▶ **New: $44** ▶ **Used: $30**

LEGO Battle Packs

While the LEGO Battle Pack is not a theme in itself, it is a set variety that can be found in many other major themes, mainly the Castle and *Star Wars* themes. These Battle Packs contain around 100 pieces on average and 4 to 5 minifigures, which are the key.

These Battle Packs are called "Army Builders" by many LEGO collectors because they enable you to acquire multiple minifigures at a reasonable cost. Many LEGO resellers and people who "part out" sets will sell the minifigures for more than the Battle Pack cost at retail.

An average LEGO minifigure can sell between $3 to $5, and many of these Battle Packs sell for around $12, so you can do the math. In fact, many of these Battle Packs are heavily discounted at some point, sweetening the deal. But these Battle Packs are also proven winners on the secondary LEGO market. Many can appreciate to $40 or more, and the 7655 Clone Troopers Battle Pack is one such example of this.

> **Battle Packs are a LEGO collector's secret weapon. They are cost effective, easy to store, and can appreciate four or five times the retail price.**

The 7667 Imperial Dropship Battle Pack is another $40 set in the aftermarket. There are many other examples of Battle Packs appreciating well, too. These small Battle Packs are fantastic values for the LEGO collectors and resellers out there. Whether you save them as a collectible or break them down to sell separately, they are quality sets.

853373 LEGO KINGDOMS CHESS SET

▶ **Year Released: 2012**
▶ **No. of Pieces: 328**
▶ **Minifigures: 28**
▶ **Retail Price: $49.99**

$ ▶ **New: $102** ▶ **Used: $41**

LEGO Chess Sets

Over the past ten years or so, LEGO has released multiple chess sets that are some of the most unique and playable ever created. They are quite collectible as well.

The 852293 Castle Giant Chess and 853373 LEGO Kingdoms Chess are two excellent examples of these sets. The 852293 Castle Giant Chess set, released in 2008, sold for $199.99 at retail. This is one of my top LEGO sets of all time. It is quite amazing. Value wise, it is a great deal with almost 2,500 pieces and 31 minifigures, 15 of which are exclusive to the set. The packaging is quite possibly the best in the history of LEGO.

The box looks like a large book, with snaps that open up into an inner display of the huge chess board and a clear plastic encased minifigure mounting board. The box itself is made of a soft, antiqued brown plastic (meant to simulate an old leather book) that is embossed with the name of the set on the cover. It really has to be seen in person to appreciate it.

Once the 852293 Castle Giant Chess set is completed, it is literally a work of art. The 31 minifigures, all decked out in various paraphernalia, make an impressive display. Since it is based on a "fantasy castle" theme, there are wizards, trolls, skeletons, dwarves, knights, and princesses all representing important chess pieces. The chess board itself is quite ornate as well, decorated with various castle-like components, all out of LEGO bricks. The finished chess board and pieces is gigantic and could be one of the ultimate display sets for an upscale den or library. The current value of the set on the LEGO secondary market is at $1,000 — five times its retail price. This set was not highly stockpiled and is highly collectible, and maybe one of the best ever. If more people knew about this wonderful set, it would be valued even higher.

The box (if you can call it that!) of the Chess Set is the most unique and beautiful LEGO box ever designed, in my opinion.

852293 CASTLE GIANT CHESS SET

▶ Year Released: 2008
▶ No. of Pieces: 2,481
▶ Minifigures: 31
▶ Retail Price: $199.99

$ ▶ New: $999 ▶ Used: $481

For those of you who were not lucky enough to obtain the 852293 Castle Giant Chess set, there is always the 853373 LEGO Kingdoms Chess set to fall back on. While this set is much smaller and less detailed, it has 28 minifigures, many of which are exclusive. The set is currently retired and sells for a little over $100 on the LEGO secondary market. The set comes with a large plastic molded castle-like base with LEGO pieces attached to the top, creating the classic chess/checker board design. What is great about these sets, especially the 853373, is that they include a large amount of minifigures for the money. The 853373 LEGO Kingdoms Chess set having 28 minifigures for a retail price of $49.99 is a fantastic value. Sometimes sets that have a high minifigure top price ratio are called "army builders," and the 853373 set may be the best example of this.

Overall, the LEGO chess sets, regardless of the theme, are great deals and great fun. They all can be used as a standard chess set, and all offer great value for the money new, and later as a collectible set. A new set, the 40158 Pirates Chess Set, just recently released in Europe. It looks like an 857-piece set with 20 minifigures and is based on the Pirates theme. Keep an eye out for one in the United States. I highly recommend purchasing one, and any other future sets that may be released.

Although not as popular in real life as the Enzo Ferrari, the 8145 Ferrari 599 GTB 1:10 rules in LEGOLAND.

What more can you say about the 8653 Enzo Ferrari 1:10? Gorgeous car ... gorgeous LEGO set! I love those dual exhuasts and Ferrari rims.

8145 FERRARI 599 GTB FIORANO 1:10

▶ Year Released: 2007
▶ No. of Pieces: 1,327
▶ Minifigures: 0
▶ Retail Price: $109.99

$ ▶ New: $533 ▶ Used: $249

8653 ENZO FERRARI 1:10

▶ Year Released: 2005
▶ No. of Pieces: 1,360
▶ Minifigures: 0
▶ Retail Price: $99.99

$ ▶ New: $419 ▶ Used: $153

LEGO Racers Theme

The LEGO Racers theme is self-explanatory: It's all about fast cars and trucks. The theme was introduced, for all intents and purposes, in 2001, and well over 200 different types of car and truck sets have been released since then. These sets come in all sizes, from tiny eight-piece polybags to large Technic sets.

There are subthemes within the Racers, like RC cars, and also licensed sets, such as Ferrari and Lamborghini, which are the most collectible of the theme. One of the coolest sets is the 8653 Enzo Ferrari 1:10. Although the set is based on Technic bricks, it is in the Racers theme. The 8653 Enzo Ferrari 1:10 has 1,360 pieces and sold for $99.99 in 2005. Current prices are well north of $400, for over 300 percent growth since it was released.

The sister set to the 8653 Enzo Ferrari 1:10 is the 8145 Ferrari 599 GTB Fiorano 1:10, released in 2007, with 1,327 pieces. The 8145 Ferrari had a slightly higher MSRP of $109.99 and has a current value of more than $500 on the LEGO secondary market for a MISB set. The 8145 set was a similar Technic set and scale, both in "Ferrari Red" LEGO bricks with special wheel and tires. Both had working steering and engine pistons, along with doors and hoods that opened. Both make awesome displays and are highly playable as well. These are two of my favorite Racers sets.

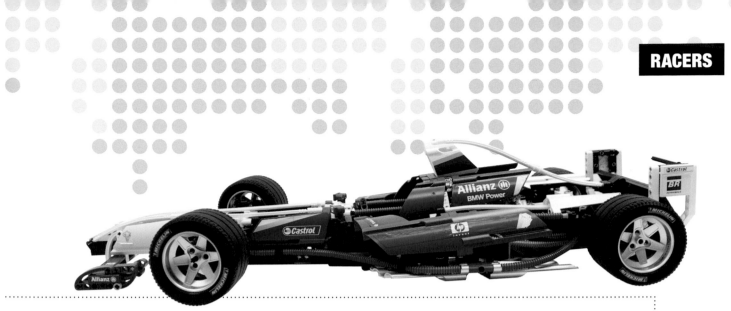

▲ The 8461 Williams F1 Team Racer has some spectacular features, such as a working V10 engine with blue LEGO pistons, working air shocks, and marvelous Michelin tires that really standout and look just like the real deal.

8461 WILLIAMS F1 TEAM RACER

▶ **Year Released: 2002**
▶ **No. of Pieces: 1,484**
▶ **Minifigures: 0**
▶ **Retail Price: $129.99**

$ ▶ **New: $401** ▶ **Used: $273**

My personal favorite and the favorite of many other fans and collectors is the 8461 Williams F1 Team Racer, shown on the next page. This Racer set is the largest of the theme and based on the car from Frank Williams British Formula One racing team. The set is a beautiful rendition of the Formula One race car, in classic blue and white trim, and huge Michelin tires. The vehicle also has working steering and a ten-cylinder engine. The finished model looks like the real deal and is a must have for any Formula One racing fan. Current value for the Racer is just over $400, which is disappointing for such a rare set.

Other interesting sets of the Racers theme is the 8214 Lamborghini Polizia and the 8169 Lamborghini Gallardo LP 560-4. The 8214 Lamborghini Polizia, an Italian police car, is an alternate version of the

8169 Lamborghini Gallardo LP 560-4, which is the standard yellow version of the Lamborghini Gallardo. Both sets are around 800 pieces and were released between 2009 and 2010. The sets sold for $59.99 and current values are about $250 for the 8169 and half that for the 8214. I like both models and they make a great display, if they are put alongside one another.

Overall, the Racers theme has quite a few smaller- to mid-sized sets, but most underperform in comparison to other LEGO themes. Many of these sets are designed for children, with little in the way of collectibility.

Besides the ones that I mention, there are a handful of other Racers sets that could be decent collectibles, but honestly, unless you are a big car fan or another large Racers set is released, I would pass on this theme.

8214 LAMBORGHINI POLIZIA

- ▶ **Year Released: 2010**
- ▶ **No. of Pieces: 801**
- ▶ **Minifigures: 0**
- ▶ **Retail Price: $59.99**

$ ▶ **New: $125** ▶ **Used: $84**

Boy ... those Italian Police sure do ride around in style!

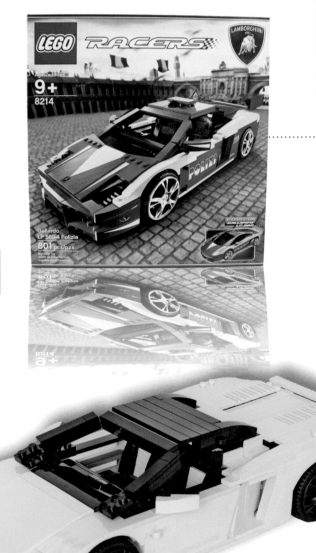

8169 LAMBORGHINI GALLARDO LP 560-4

- ▶ **Year Released: 2009**
- ▶ **No. of Pieces: 741**
- ▶ **Minifigures: 0**
- ▶ **Retail Price: $59.99**

$ ▶ **New: $253** ▶ **Used: $93**

Blacked-out wheels on today's cars are a common option, but not in 2009. The custom wheels of the 8169 Lamborghini were way ahead of their time.

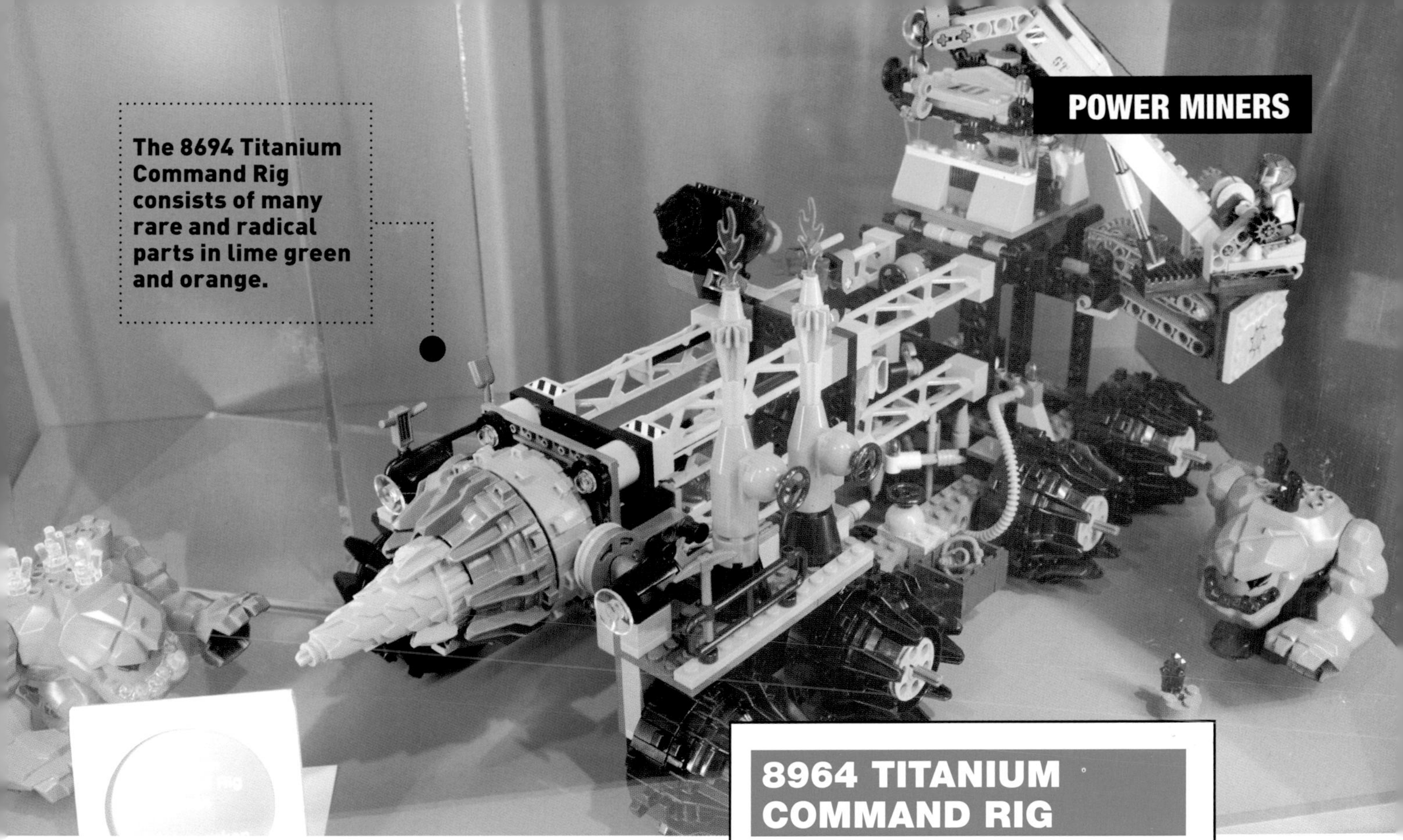

The 8694 Titanium Command Rig consists of many rare and radical parts in lime green and orange.

8964 TITANIUM COMMAND RIG

▶ Year Released: 2009
▶ No. of Pieces: 706
▶ Minifigures: 5
▶ Retail Price: $99.99

$ ▶ New: $198 ▶ Used: $100

A minifigure has a bad run-in with a rock monster from the 8962 Crystal King set.

8962 CRYSTAL KING

▶ Year Released: 209
▶ No. of Pieces: 168
▶ Minifigures: 2
▶ Retail Price: $19.99

$ ▶ New: $79 ▶ Used: $38

LEGO Power Miners Theme

The Power Miners theme is a small one released from 2009 to 2010 and consists of about 20 different-sized sets. This is one of those under-the-radar themes that LEGO collectors ignore, many times to their detriment. The theme as a whole has performed well, outdoing many other popular and licensed themes. Based on subterranean rock drillers, miners, and rock monsters, many of the sets within the theme have appreciated surprisingly well. The 8962 Crystal King has quadrupled in price from its $19.99 MSRP to over $80, while the largest set of the theme, the 706-piece 8964 Titanium Command Rig, has almost doubled its MSRP of $99.99 to reach the $200 level. Many other sets have shown solid gains as well. A theme designed for children, this has found some adult fans in the LEGO secondary market.

n 1999, LEGO worked out a deal with George Lucas to produce the first licensed *Star Wars* sets, and also worked out a deal to produce *Winnie the Pooh* sets. So began The LEGO Group's involvement in some of the major movie and TV franchises of all time. LEGO also worked deals to produce Mickey Mouse, *Harry Potter*, DC and Marvel Superheroes, *Indiana Jones*, *Pirates of the Caribbean*, Ferrari, NBA Basketball, and *Speed Racer*, among others. There are also a few minor licensed themes that are worth discussing. Many of these smaller licensed themes have some quality collectible sets, but the themes usually have shorter production runs and don't appeal to everyone. Many licensed LEGO themes have fans who are passionate about the sets, while others could care less. This translates into a huge guessing game for collectors and investors on deciding whether to purchase a licensed theme as a collectible. Many times, it comes down to personal preference and investors who like a franchise will buy on emotion, rather than common sense and data. Here are some good, and bad, licensed minor LEGO themes.

Disney Princess

This is a relatively new LEGO theme worthy of discussion. The Disney Princess theme is similar to the LEGO Friends theme, with larger and more realistic minifigures and sets targeted toward young girls. Many are smaller- to mid-sized sets, with plenty of pink, aqua, and purple bricks.

The Disney Princess line of sets all have boxes similar to those of the Friends theme.

As the name suggests, the sets are designed around the major Disney Princesses: Ariel, Cinderella, Sleeping Beauty, Jasmine, Rapunzel, and, of course, Elsa. The Disney Princess theme also behaves in a similar way to the Friends theme on the LEGO secondary market. As a long-term collectible, these sets might not be the best option, but short term, supply and inventory shortages can cause them to skyrocket. For example, the 41062 Elsa's Sparkling Ice Castle, due to the popularity of the movie *Frozen*, was in short supply this past holiday season and skyrocketed in price, even though it was still in production. This is commonplace among Friends-like sets to have shortages during the prime shopping seasons and have prices explode on the secondary market. Will the long-term gains be strong as well? Only time will tell.

41062 ELSA'S SPARKLING ICE CASTLE
▶ **Year Released: 2015**
▶ **No. of Pieces: 292**
▶ **Minifigures: 3**
▶ **Retail Price: $39.99**

$ ▶ **New: $63** ▶ **Used: $32**

The three minifigures that come with 41062 Elsa's Sparkling Ice Castle.

The *Frozen* phenomena made Elsa's Sparkling Ice Castle a popular and rare set for a few months, which in turn helped increase its value on the secondary LEGO market.

SpongeBob SquarePants

A small theme of 14 sets spread out from 2006 to 2012, the SpongeBob SquarePants theme does surprisingly well on the LEGO secondary market. The minifigures are quite well done and some of my favorites. While none of the SpongeBob SquarePants sets have hit tremendous levels, many have appreciated from the MSRP retail price. The largest set of the theme, the 579-piece 3827 Adventures in Bikini Bottom, has more than tripled in value from the $39.99 MSRP. Many of the sets have shown similar growth. I guess it's the popularity of the franchise that continually drives sales of these sets, and with the new movie, *The SpongeBob Movie: SpongeBob Out of Water*, the interest in this theme should continue.

3827 ADVENTURES IN BIKINI BOTTOM

▶ **Year Released:** 2006
▶ **No. of Pieces:** 579
▶ **Minifigures:** 3
▶ **Retail Price:** $39.99

$ ▶ **New: $137** ▶ **Used: $50**

Spongebob's house, an orange pineapple, is located at 124 Conch Street. The 3827 Adventures in Bikini Bottom, has a LEGO version of the pineapple, which unfolds and shows the interior components.

The 8679 Tokyo International Circuit box closeup. The Cars theme has been showing signs of improving growth after a slow start after retirement.

Cars

Another smaller licensed theme with a two-year production run of 28 sets, the *Cars* theme has some very creative and accurate sets that resemble the scenes from the movies quite well. Instead of minifigures, the *Cars* theme has cars. Each of the main characters has a replica made of some special pieces and imprinted bricks. The sets appear to exhibit some solid growth patterns overall, and better than many other themes. None of the sets are worth top dollar and probably never will be, but you never know what will happen if another *Cars* movie is released and there is new interest in the theme. The largest sets of the theme, the 8679 Tokyo International Circuit, the 8639 Big Bentley Bust Out, and 8487 Flo's V8 Cafe, would have the best chance of seeing some substantial gains if a new movie is released in 2016-2017, as rumored.

8679 TOKYO INTERNATIONAL CIRCUIT

▶ Year Released: 2011
▶ No. of Pieces: 842
▶ Minifigures: 0
▶ Retail Price: $89.99

$ ▶ New: $97 ▶ Used: $55

8487 FLO'S V8 CAFÉ

▶ Year Released: 2011
▶ No. of Pieces: 517
▶ Minifigures: 0
▶ Retail Price: $59.99

$ ▶ New: $94 ▶ Used: $50

The Cars theme doesn't include minifigures in the traditional sense. They include "minicars," basically tiny LEGO models of the individual characters from the movie.

8639 BIG BENTLEY BUST OUT

▶ Year Released: 2011
▶ No. of Pieces: 743
▶ Minifigures: 0
▶ Retail Price: $69.99

$ ▶ New: $53 ▶ Used: $31

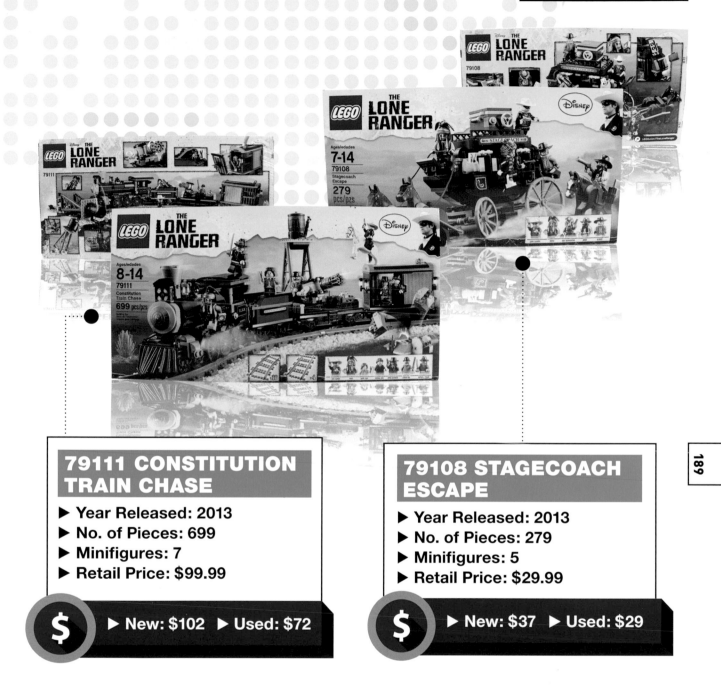

79111 CONSTITUTION TRAIN CHASE

▶ Year Released: 2013
▶ No. of Pieces: 699
▶ Minifigures: 7
▶ Retail Price: $99.99

$ ▶ New: $102 ▶ Used: $72

79108 STAGECOACH ESCAPE

▶ Year Released: 2013
▶ No. of Pieces: 279
▶ Minifigures: 5
▶ Retail Price: $29.99

$ ▶ New: $37 ▶ Used: $29

The Lone Ranger

The Lone Ranger is another Disney-related theme and includes eight sets, which are quite impressive. It is unfortunate *The Lone Ranger* movie did so poorly at the box office because its LEGO sets are excellent. The 79111 Constitution Train Chase and the 79108 Stagecoach Escape are two well done Western-themed sets that will do well, even though the movie bombed. The 79111 Constitution Train Chase is a full train set with 699 pieces and 7 minifigures for $99.99. It was highly discounted, as were many of *The Lone Ranger* sets, thus making it even more of a great choice for investment. The 79108 Stagecoach Escape is an excellent replica of an antique stagecoach and has some great minifigures to "boot." *The Lone Ranger* set designs are all quite varied and excellent choices for LEGO fans who like Westerns or Cowboys/Indians themes. Also, being that this theme only has eight sets, a collector could easily own them all — a rare feat in the LEGO collecting world.

71006 THE SIMPSONS HOUSE

▶ **Year Released:** 2014
▶ **No. of Pieces:** 2,523
▶ **Minifigures:** 6
▶ **Retail Price:** $199.99

$ ▶ New: $193 ▶ Used: $180

The Simpsons House is the largest themed set.

The Simpsons

This is a theme similar to the *Teenage Mutant Ninja Turtles* theme, and either you like the franchise or you don't. That is a possible issue with any licensed themes. If you don't appeal to all the potential LEGO fans out there, you stand to not be as valuable long term as some other LEGO sets and themes that are widely loved. *The Simpsons* theme started out with a release of the sixteen collectible minifigures of all the important characters, from Bart Simpson to Apu Nahasapeemapetilon. LEGO then released the 71006 The Simpsons House in 2014 at a $199.99 retail price. Regardless of whether you like *The Simpsons* or not, you have to strongly consider this as a collectible set. It is unique and well done, and true to the cartoon in every sense of the word. It's a wonderfully detailed set on both the exterior and interior and can make an interesting discussion piece in anyone's office or den. Later in 2015, there is a new Simpsons set coming out, the 71016 Kwik-E-Mart, so interest in this theme should continue.

Toy Story

It is obvious that The LEGO Group and Disney have an outstanding relationship with the multitude of Disney-related LEGO themes that exists, including this one based on the successful movie franchise. The *Toy Story* theme is a slow starter. Many of the sets were some of the poorest performers in recent memory, yet they have slowly started to rebound. In fact, the 7591 Construct-A-Zurg had one of the lowest growth rates of any sets. I don't know why, since I think it's a damn cool set. The sets all have awesome minifigures — some of the best in the LEGO Universe — yet the theme still doesn't attract as many fans as it should. Of the sets in this theme, the smallest (30071 Army Jeep polybag) and the largest (7597 Western Train Chase) seem to show some promise with substantial positive gains. One positive sign is the news that *Toy Story 4* will be released in June of 2017, so maybe now is the time to buy some of these older sets at a reasonable price before the new movie hits theaters.

7591 CONSTRUCT-A-ZURG

▶ **Year Released: 2010**
▶ **No. of Pieces: 118**
▶ **Minifigures: 1**
▶ **Retail Price: $24.99**

$ ▶ **New: $16** ▶ **Used: $10**

7597 WESTERN TRAIN CHASE

▶ **Year Released: 2010**
▶ **No. of Pieces: 584**
▶ **Minifigures: 6**
▶ **Retail Price: $79.99**

$ ▶ **New: $118** ▶ **Used: $76**

30071 ARMY JEEP POLYBAG

▶ **Year Released: 2010**
▶ **No. of Pieces: 37**
▶ **Minifigures: 1**
▶ **Retail Price: $2.99**

$ ▶ **New: $11** ▶ **Used: $5**

The 7597 Western Train Chase set is the largest one in this theme shows some promise with positive gains. With *Toy Story 4* coming out in 2017, the new movie may boost interest.

This rare LEGO submarine offers plenty of fun features such as secret compartments.

79121 TURTLE SUB UNDERSEA CHASE

▶ Year Released: 2014
▶ No. of Pieces: 684
▶ Minifigures: 5
▶ Retail Price: $59.99

$ ▶ New: $52 ▶ Used: $0

79117 TURTLE LAIR INVASION

▶ Year Released: 2014
▶ No. of Pieces: 888
▶ Minifigures: 6
▶ Retail Price: $99.99

$ ▶ New: $77 ▶ Used: $73

The Turtle Lair Invasion is the largest set of the theme and has a cool slide that the Turtles can use for a quick getaway.

Teenage Mutant Ninja Turtles

The Teenage Mutant Ninja Turtles theme has been around since 2013, and many of the sets are still available at retail. These sets are hard to judge as a collectible LEGO theme, as there are many people like myself who never cared for the Teenage Mutant Ninja Turtles and do not really care about the sets. While there are some creative sets like the 79121 Turtle Sub Undersea Chase and 79105 Baxter Robot Rampage, you have to be familiar with Teenage Mutant Ninja Turtles movies and TV shows to appreciate them. If all else fails, buying the largest set of a theme like the 79117 Turtle Lair Invasion usually works as a good collectible LEGO set. There is a huge fanbase of fans, but we will have to wait and see if these sets are worthwhile collectibles.

79105 BAXTER ROBOT RAMPAGE

▶ Year Released: 2013
▶ No. of Pieces: 397
▶ Minifigures: 5
▶ Retail Price: $39.99

$ ▶ New: $40 ▶ Used: $35

Mechs and large robots in any LEGO theme are quite popular and it will be no different with this one.

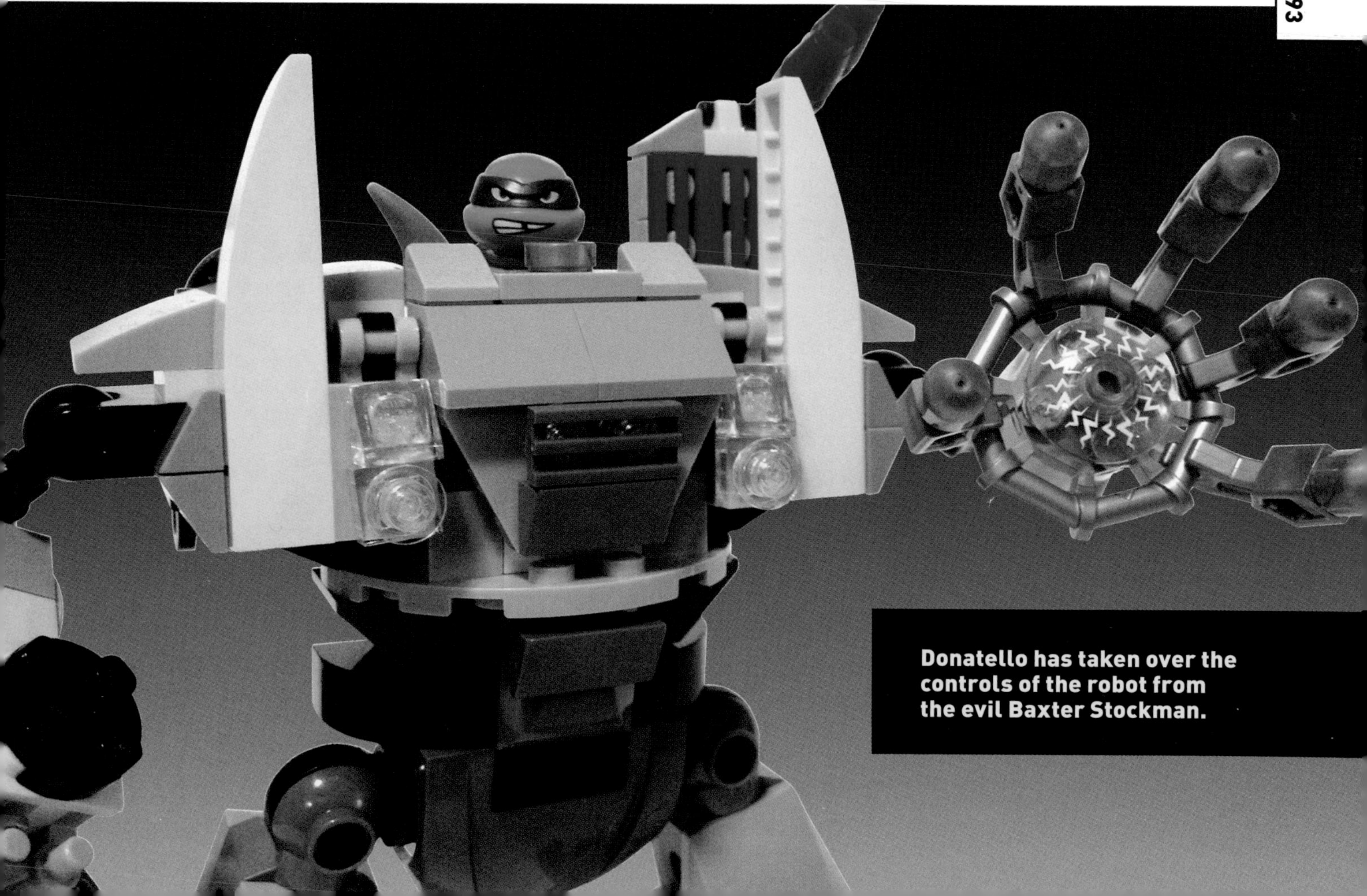

Donatello has taken over the controls of the robot from the evil Baxter Stockman.

Discovery Channel

The Discovery Channel theme consists of six sets that depict some sort of space flight or vehicles. Launched in 2003, these smaller- to mid-sized LEGO sets have appreciated well. The 453-piece 10029 Lunar Lander has appreciated over 700 percent to well over $300 from its original retail price of $39.99. The 7469 Mission to Mars has almost tripled in value to the $90 range.

Overall, these sets are well done and detailed. Their scales are all different from one another, but they still look great displayed together.

In a lot of ways, they remind me of the new Cuusoo sets like the 21104 NASA Mars Science Laboratory Curiosity Rover and 21101 Hayabusa. Realistic NASA and space vehicle sets seem to translate well into LEGO models, so keep an eye on future sets that are of similar designs, as they make excellent collectibles.

10029 LUNAR LANDER

▶ **Year Released: 2003**
▶ **No. of Pieces: 453**
▶ **Minifigures: 2**
▶ **Retail Price: $39.99**

$ ▶ **New: $347** ▶ **Used: $178**

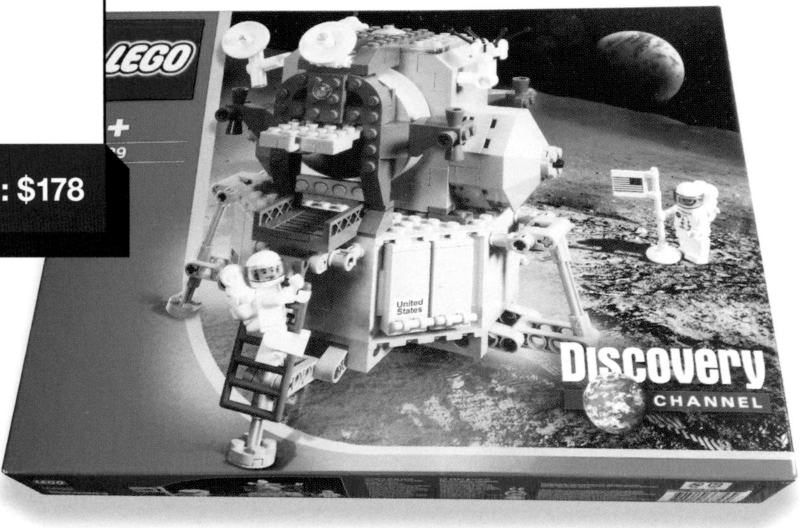

This photo of Mission to Mars is from an awesome LEGO store display. Notice the backdrop and red rocky surface.

7469 MISSION TO MARS

▶ **Year Released: 2003**
▶ **No. of Pieces: 418**
▶ **Minifigures: 0**
▶ **Retail Price: $29.99**

$ ▶ **New: $83** ▶ **Used: $49**

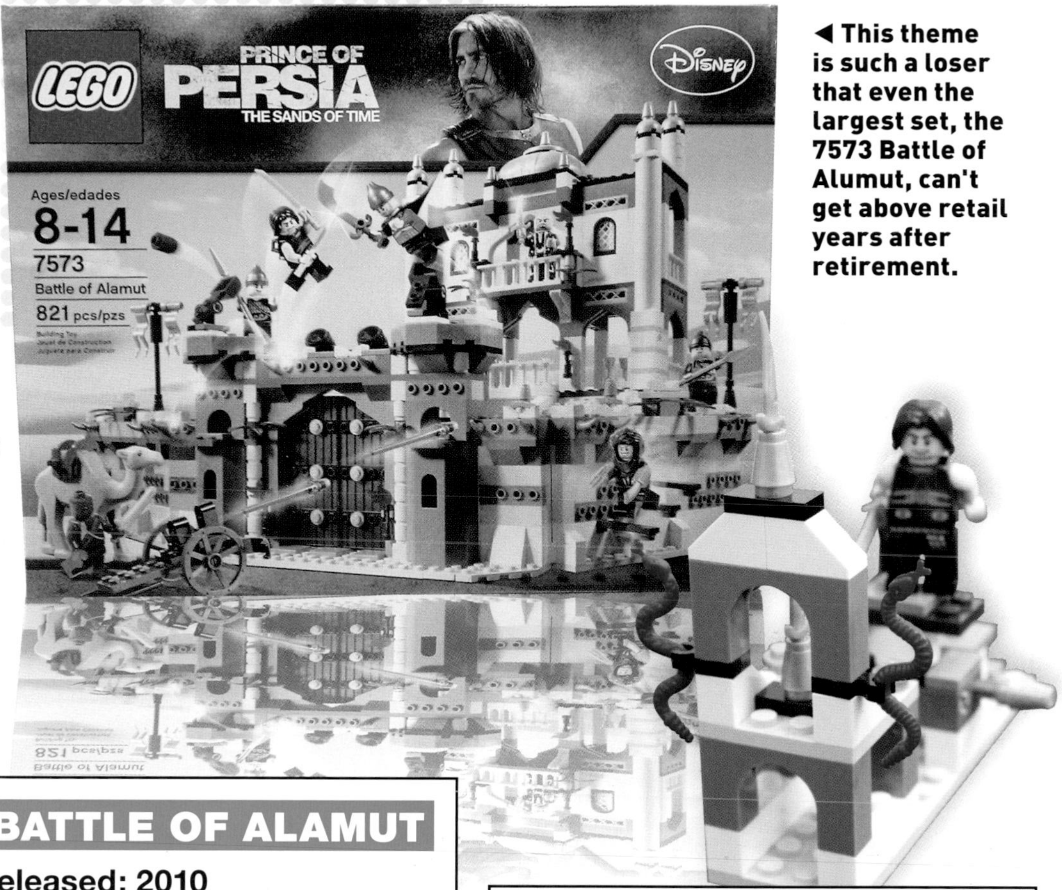

◀ **This theme is such a loser that even the largest set, the 7573 Battle of Alumut, can't get above retail years after retirement.**

7573 BATTLE OF ALAMUT

▶ **Year Released:** 2010
▶ **No. of Pieces:** 821
▶ **Minifigures:** 7
▶ **Retail Price:** $79.99

$ ▶ New: $74 ▶ Used: $51

20017 BRICKMASTER PRINCE OF PERSIA

▶ **Year Released:** 2010
▶ **No. of Pieces:** 49
▶ **Minifigures:** 1
▶ **Retail Price:** $0

$ ▶ New: $9 ▶ Used: $5

Prince of Persia

I would like to announce the WORST LEGO THEME OF ALL TIME: THE PRINCE OF PERSIA. Of all the Disney's *Prince of Persia* sets, only the 20017 BrickMaster Prince of Persia one increased in value — from FREE to $9. Wow. What a horrible theme! Even the largest set, the 821-piece 7573 Battle of Alamut, has not exceeded the $79.99 MSRP after being retired for almost four years. It's the Black Hole of LEGO collecting.

"My name is Dastan...AND I AM A LEGO LOSER!"

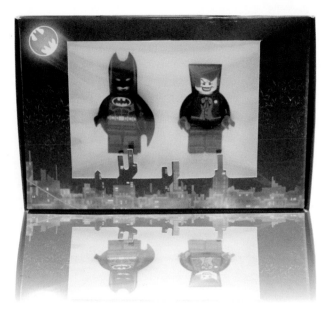

The *Star Wars* Advent Calendar's awesome slip cover looks like a gift box with ribbons.

LEGO Comic Con and Toy Fair Sets

Every year, there are major conventions around the country, Comic Cons, that promote the comic book, TV, and major motion picture industries. There are also large toy fairs and conventions that promote the new toys that are being released that year. These are operated by the major toy manufacturers and help sell their products to retailers. LEGO takes part in many of these events annually and what's great is that they make special and limited edition sets for them. While these events are by special invite in some cases, many do give access to the general public. Comic Con and Toy Fair sets are difficult to obtain at these events because the buying competition has become fierce. If you are lucky enough to attend one of these conventions, then you already know what I am talking about. For those of you who don't, do some research on the internet and look for local conventions. A few of the more popular ones are the San Diego Comic Con, New York City Comic Con, Star Wars Celebration IV-VI, and the New York City Toy Fair. If you are like me, you don't go to any and instead pay top dollar on eBay for these highly collectible and prized sets.

I really enjoy these special sets. They are small, limited, numbered, creative, and valuable. Each convention usually has at least one major special LEGO set that is released, and most sell between $25 to $50. Here are a few of

At the 2010 Comic-Con, LEGO released two small Star Wars sets: The Cube Dude Clone Wars and Cube Dude Bounty Hunter.

In 2013, there were three special LEGO *Star Wars* sets released at three different events: Luke Skywalker's Mini Landspeeder Tin-2012 NYCC; Darth Maul's Mini Sith Infiltrator Tin-2012 SDCC; and Boba Fett's Mini Slave I Tin-2012 Celebration VI CC.

note from the last several years:

At the 2008 San Diego Comic Con, the COMCON003-1:Batman And Joker (SDCC 2008 exclusive) was sold. It was a nice little boxed set of Batman and Joker, and it currently sells for around $200 on the LEGO secondary markets.

In 2010, LEGO released two small sets, the *Star Wars* Cube Dude Clone Wars Edition-2010 SDCC and the *Star Wars* Cube Dude Bounty Hunter Edition-2010 SDCC. Both sets produce five "cube like" characters. They are both selling for around $150 on sites like eBay.

At the 2011 SDCC, the COMCON015-1 *Star Wars* Advent Calendar-2011 SDCC was sold, and it was wrapped in a unique cardboard

"shipping" box. This also sells for around $150 on the secondary market.

In 2013, there were three special sets released at three different events:

- *Star Wars* Luke Skywalker's Mini Landspeeder Tin-2012 NYCC
- *Star Wars* Darth Maul's Mini Sith Infiltrator Tin-2012 SDCC
- *Star Wars* Boba Fett's Mini Slave I Tin-2012 Celebration VI CC

They were each in a collectors "tin" can, which is unique to the LEGO packaging world. The Boba Fett sells for more than $200, while the other two tins sell for around $150 on secondary

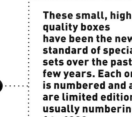

These small, high quality boxes have been the new standard of specialty sets over the past few years. Each one is numbered and all are limited editions, usually numbering 1 to 1000.

LEGO marketplaces. The 2013 versions were the Microscale Bag End-2013 SDCC and the Mini JEK 14 Stealth Starfighter-2013 SDCC. The Micro Bag End is a cute little set. Both sell for around $125 currently. Lastly, there were last year's SDCC sets:

- The Ghost Starship-2014 SDCC
- Batman Classic TV Series Batmobile - 2014 SDCC
- Rocket Raccoon's Warbird-2014 SDCC

These are all awesome sets, especially the Batman one based on the classic Batmobile and characters from the 1960s TV show. The Batman set sells for around $250, while the Rocket Racoon sells for around $200, and the Ghost sells for around $125 in secondary marketplaces.

All in all, these convention sets make the most money for the people who originally buy them, but the secondhand LEGO collectors like myself can see appreciation of these limited sets with time and if you pay a fair price. Never buy these sets right after the event; the prices are too high. If you wait, your patience will be rewarded when the buzz is over.

PRICE GUIDE

Our Price Guide is based on sold auctions from eBay, the largest secondary LEGO marketplace in the world. The data from the eBay completed listings is obtained from the Terapeak Corporation, which purchases this information from eBay, and we at BrickPicker purchase it from Terapeak. We take thousands of these sold listings and aggregate them into our monthly Price Guide. The current Price Guide is based on millions of auctions from the past five years.

For this book, we chose to key on the major LEGO themes and list many of the important sets from those themes. Not all LEGO sets were included because that would be a list of over 10,000 sets. For a complete list and up-to-date prices, please visit our website, www.Brickpicker.com. Remember, the values that we list are approximate ones and are several months old. There are many variations within the set types and it should be used as a *guide*, not as an exact value.

The Price Guide includes the LEGO set name, number, year it was released, number of pieces, number of minifigures (if any), current new and used values in US dollars, the MSRP/retail price, and the Return on Investment percentage from the retail price (ROI%). The prices for new sets are based on MISB sets and the used values are for complete sets (boxes, instructions, all parts).

Please note: Some sets have values listed as $0 because they are either too new to have sold used values on eBay or either too old and rare to have sold new values. Also, some sets might not have a ROI% and that might be because the set was a promotional item with no MSRP and was free.

NUMBER	NAME	YEAR	PIECES	MINIFIGS	NEW	USED	RETAIL	GROWTH%
ADVANCED MODELS								
10024	Red Baron	2002	664	0	374	190.4	49.99	648.15
10124	Wright Flyer	2003	670	0	286.07	168.67	59.99	376.86
10152	Maersk Sealand Container Ship	2004	988	0	218.53	144.2	74.99	191.41
10155	Maersk Container Ship	2010	990	0	257.12	149.33	119.99	114.28
10177	Boeing 787 Dreamliner	2006	1,197	0	544.13	243.47	79.99	580.25
10181	Eiffel Tower	2007	3,428	0	1742.93	681.27	199.99	771.51
10182	Cafe Corner	2007	2,056	3	1671.47	736.19	139.99	1093.99
10184	Town Plan	2008	1,981	8	394.07	255.53	149.99	162.73
10185	Green Grocer	2008	2,352	4	905.38	631.58	149.99	503.63
10187	Volkswagen Beetle	2008	1,626	0	763.93	410.87	119.99	536.66
10189	Taj Mahal	2008	5,922	0	2394.19	965.53	299.99	698.09
10190	Market Street	2007	1,248	3	1539.47	666.13	89.99	1610.71
10196	Grand Carousel	2009	3,263	9	2278	1215.07	249.99	811.24
10197	Fire Brigade	2009	2,231	4	298.33	248.18	149.99	98.90
10211	Grand Emporium	2010	2,182	7	229.74	183.2	149.99	53.17
10213	Shuttle Adventure	2010	1,204	3	229.54	143.13	99.99	129.56

NUMBER	NAME	YEAR	PIECES	MINIFIGS	NEW	USED	RETAIL	GROWTH%
10214	Tower Bridge	2010	4,287	0	244.49	187.24	239.99	1.88
10218	Pet Shop	2011	2,032	4	168.53	132.71	149.99	12.36
10220	Volkswagen T1 Camper Van	2,011	1,332	0	125.01	88.53	119.99	4.18
10224	Town Hall	2012	2,766	8	323.59	205	199.99	61.80
10226	Sopwith Camel	2012	883	0	164.78	70.4	99.99	64.80
10230	Mini Modulars	2012	1,356	0	143.81	105.27	79.99	79.78
10231	Shuttle Expedition	2011	1,230	3	254.58	159.6	99.99	154.61
10232	Palace Cinema	2013	2,196	6	162.28	121.63	149.99	8.19
10234	Sydney Opera House	2013	2,989	0	323.52	256.8	319.99	1.10
10241	Maersk Line Triple-E	2014	1,518	0	188.21	150.5	149.99	25.48
10242	MINI Cooper MK VII	2014	1,077	0	121.46	81.88	99.99	21.47
10243	Parisian Restaurant	2014	2,469	5	151.86	135.13	159.99	-5.08
10244	Fairground Mixer	2014	1,746	12	143.46	119.67	149.99	-4.35
3300001	Brickley	2011	197	0	30.82	24.78	14.99	105.60
3450	Statue of Liberty	2000	2,882	0	2073.93	1054.73	198.99	942.23
3451	Sopwith Camel	2001	574	0	162.4	61.27	49.99	224.86
3723	LEGO Mini-Figure	2000	1,849	0	400.3	237.6	148.99	168.68
3724	LEGO Dragon	2001	1,530	0	476.71	253.73	98.99	381.57

AGENTS

NUMBER	NAME	YEAR	PIECES	MINIFIGS	NEW	USED	RETAIL	GROWTH%
70160	Riverside Raid	2014	88	2	14.09	0	11.99	17.51
70161	Tremor Track Infiltration	2014	241	2	23.75	0	19.99	18.81
70162	Infearno Interception	2014	313	2	44.37	22.67	29.99	47.95
70163	Toxikita's Toxic Meltdown	2014	429	4	44	0	39.99	10.03
70164	Hurricane Heist	2014	589	4	84.93	0	69.99	21.35
70165	Ultra Agents Mission HQ	2014	1,060	5	126	77	99.99	26
8630	Gold Hunt	2008	352	3	60.8	23.67	29.99	102.73
8631	Jetpack Pursuit	2008	88	2	31.87	14.4	9.99	219.02
8632	Swamp Raid	2008	231	2	43.33	23.2	19.99	116.76
8633	Speedboat Rescue	2008	340	3	88.13	27	39.99	120.38
8634	Turbocar Chase	2008	498	3	109.6	62.73	49.99	119.24
8635	Mobile Command Center	2008	1,154	7	230.35	118.2	89.99	155.97
8636	Deep Sea Quest	2008	520	4	46.42	54.2	49.99	-7.14
8637	Volcano Base	2008	718	6	229.53	137.67	69.99	227.95
8967	Gold Tooth's Getaway	2009	68	2	23.79	12.73	9.99	138.14
8968	River Heist	2009	203	3	37.22	18.73	19.99	86.19
8969	4-Wheeling Pursuit	2009	320	2	44.8	34	29.99	49.38
8970	Robo Attack	2009	414	6	89.82	41.33	49.99	79.68
8971	Aerial Defence Unit	2009	733	7	126.41	70.47	79.99	58.03

ARCHITECTURE

NUMBER	NAME	YEAR	PIECES	MINIFIGS	NEW	USED	RETAIL	GROWTH%
21000	Sears Tower	2008	69	0	59.06	30.2	19.99	195.45
21000-2	Willis Tower	2011	69	0	21.96	14.25	19.99	9.85
21001	John Hancock Center	2008	69	0	114.56	60.27	19.99	473.09
21002	Empire State Building	2009	77	0	23.31	16.47	19.99	16.61
21003	Seattle Space Needle	2009	57	0	24.17	17.33	19.99	20.91
21004	Solomon Guggenheim Museum	2009	208	0	77.7	44.93	39.99	94.30
21005	Fallingwater	2009	811	0	118.73	78.28	99.99	18.74
21006	The White House	2010	560	0	52.46	36.29	49.99	4.94
21007	Rockefeller Center	2011	240	0	67.65	32.6	39.99	69.17
21008	Burj Khalifa-Dubai	2011	208	0	53.19	25.07	24.99	112.85
21009	Farnsworth House	2011	546	0	63.58	41.8	59.99	5.98

NUMBER	NAME	YEAR	PIECES	MINIFIGS	NEW	USED	RETAIL	GROWTH%
21010	Robie House	2011	2,276	0	293.51	235.13	199.99	46.76
21011	Brandenburg Gate	2011	363	0	32.88	21.67	34.99	-6.03
21012	Sydney Opera House	2012	270	0	40	26.67	39.99	0.03
21013	Big Ben	2012	346	0	31.21	21.4	29.99	4.07
21014	Villa Savoye	2012	660	0	70.19	40.67	69.99	0.29
21015	The Leaning Tower of Pisa	2012	345	0	43.39	40.25	34.99	24.01
21016	Sungnyemun	2012	325	0	146.48	46	34.99	318.63
21017	Imperial Hotel	2013	1,188	0	97.23	86.67	129.99	-25.20
21018	United Nations Headquarters	2013	597	0	49.62	28.8	49.99	-0.74
21019	The Eiffel Tower	2014	321	0	48.02	25.88	34.99	37.24
21020	Trevi Fountain	2014	731	0	53.63	30.4	49.99	7.28
21021	Marina Bay Sands	2013	602	0	536.87	299.99	49.99	973.95
21050	Architecture Studio	2013	1,211	0	177.42	163.47	149.99	18.29
4000010	LEGO House	2014	250	1	69.58	0	150	-53.61

ATLANTIS								
30040	Octopus	2010	42	0	7.34	5.6	3.99	83.96
30042	Mini Sub	2010	42	1	6.07	1.8	3.99	52.13
7976	Ocean Speeder	2011	54	1	9.47	4.22	4.99	89.78
7977	Seabed Strider	2011	105	2	16.74	9.6	9.99	67.57
7978	Angler Attack	2011	200	2	38.53	16.2	19.99	92.75
7984	Deep Sea Raider	2011	265	2	30.86	17.8	29.99	2.90
7985	City of Atlantis	2011	686	5	95.44	58.67	69.99	36.36
8056	Monster Crab Clash	2010	68	1	13.27	8.07	6.99	89.84
8057	Wreck Raider	2010	64	2	13.15	6.31	9.99	31.63
8058	Guardian of the Deep	2010	144	1	26.61	11.53	14.99	77.52
8059	Seabed Scavenger	2010	119	2	21.87	8.87	14.99	45.90
8060	Typhoon Turbo Sub	2010	197	2	25.94	12.47	24.99	3.80
8061	Gateway of the Squid	2010	354	3	33.79	23.47	39.99	5.50
8072	Sea Jet	2010	23	1	6	3.91	3.99	50.38
8073	Manta Warrior	2010	13	1	8.41	3.43	3.99	110.78
8075	Neptune Carrier	2010	476	4	45.53	25.4	59.99	-24.10
8076	Deep Sea Striker	2010	260	1	19.57	10.8	19.99	-2.10
8077	Atlantis Exploration HQ	2010	473	3	51.73	29.13	49.99	3.48
8078	Portal of Atlantis	2010	1,007	7	78.07	42.8	99.99	-21.92
8079	Shadow Snapper	2010	246	1	26.41	18.16	29.99	1.94
8080	Undersea Explorer	2010	364	1	38.47	22.8	39.99	-3.80

BATMAN								
10937	Batman: Arkham Asylum Breakout	2013	1,619	8	248.33	125	159.99	55.22
30160	Batman Jetski	2012	40	1	19.45	13.3	4.99	289.78
30161	Batmobile	2012	45	0	8.8	5.13	4	120.00
30166	Robin and Redbird Cycle	2013	40	1	15.55	9.99	4.99	211.62
30300	The Batman Tumbler	2014	57	0	8.56	3.6	3.99	114.54
30301	Batwing	2014	45	0	6.38	0	4.99	27.86
4526	Batman	2012	40	0	36.56	13.07	14.99	143.90
4527	The Joker	2012	57	0	20.65	10.92	14.99	37.76
6857	The Dynamic Duo Funhouse Escape	2012	380	5	56.99	36.67	39.99	42.51
6858	Catwoman Catcycle City Chase	2012	89	2	23.45	17.31	12.99	80.52
6860	The Batcave	2012	690	5	74.22	47.73	69.99	6.04

NUMBER	NAME	YEAR	PIECES	MINIFIGS	NEW	USED	RETAIL	GROWTH%
6863	Batwing Battle Over Gotham City	2012	278	3	48.84	31.75	34.99	39.58
6864	The Batmobile and the Two-Face Chase	2012	531	5	86.01	60.13	49.99	72.0
76000	Arctic Batman vs. Mr Freeze: Aquaman on Ice	2013	198	3	34.94	11.56	19.99	74.79
76001	The Bat vs. Bane : Tumbler Chase	2013	367	3	42.87	26.4	39.99	7.20
76010	Batman: The Penguin Face off	2014	136	2	15.55	8.47	12.99	19.71
76011	Batman: Man-Bat Attack	2014	184	3	21.49	27.17	19.99	7.50
76012	Batman: The Riddler Chase	2014	304	3	32.48	32.63	29.99	8.30
76013	Batman: The Joker Steam Roller	2014	486	5	54.58	34.73	49.99	9.18
76023	The Tumbler	2014	1,869	2	269.67	208.87	199.99	34.84
7779	The Batman Dragster: Catwoman Pursuit	2006	92	2	96.13	52.67	9.99	862.26
7780	The Batboat: Hunt for Killer Croc	2006	188	2	200.4	96.33	19.99	902.50
7781	The Batmobile: Two-Face's Escape	2006	386	3	210.07	112.87	29.99	600.47
7782	The Batwing: The Joker's Aerial Assault	2006	523	3	172.69	117.33	49.99	245.45
7783	The Batcave: Penguin and Mr. Freeze's Invasion	2006	1,071	7	554	330.6	89.99	515.62
7784	The Batmobile: Ultimate Collectors' Edition	2006	1,045	0	380.29	211.06	69.99	443.35
7785	Arkham Asylum	2006	860	7	234.67	244.13	79.99	193.3
7786	The Batcopter: The Chase for Scarecrow	2007	293	2	189.32	167.4	29.99	531.28
7787	The Bat-Tank: The Riddler and Bane's Hideout	2007	645	3	208.71	210.07	49.99	317.50
7884	Batman's Buggy: The Escape of Mr. Freeze	2008	76	2	148.53	70.33	9.99	1386.79
7885	Robin's Scuba Jet: Attack of The Penguin	2008	207	2	180.13	73.47	19.99	801.10
7886	The Batcycle: Harley Quinn's Hammer Truck	2008	267	2	199.27	119.53	29.99	564.45
7888	The Tumbler: Joker's Ice Cream Surprise	2008	449	3	487.07	228.13	49.99	874.33

BIONICLE								
10023	Bionicle Master Builder Set	2002	112	0	32.88	15.8	12.99	153.12
10201	Takutanuva	2003	399	0	152.73	102.09	49.99	205.52
10202	Ultimate Dume	2004	564	0	114.73	61.53	49.99	129.51
10203	Voporak	2005	647	0	81.54	40.6	49.99	63.11
10204	Vezon & Kardas	2006	670	0	278.5	145.8	49.99	457.11
1388	Huki	2001	8	0	16.15	10.78	1.99	711.56
1389	Onepu	2001	8	0	21.67	10.53	1.99	988.94
1390	Maku	2001	8	0	13.37	9.82	1.99	571.86
1391	Jala	2001	8	0	15.21	11.05	1.99	664.32
1392	Kongu	2001	8	0	14.33	10.05	1.99	620.10
1393	Matoro	2001	8	0	9.41	10.53	1.99	372.86
1441	Fikou	2003	13	0	9.8	8	0	
4868	Rahaga Gaaki	2005	28	0	11.5	6.29	3.99	188.2
4869	Rahaga Pouks	2005	28	0	12.24	7.24	3.99	206.77
4870	Rahaga Kualus	2005	28	0	15.6	7.69	3.99	290.98
4877	Rahaga Norik	2005	28	0	12.64	8.94	3.99	216.79
4878	Rahaga Bomonga	2005	28	0	7.76	7.38	3.99	94.49

NUMBER	NAME	YEAR	PIECES	MINIFIGS	NEW	USED	RETAIL	GROWTH%
4879	Rahaga Iruini	2005	28	0	9.69	8.4	3.99	142.86
6637	Ultimate Battle Set	2005	5	0	10	12.89	0	
6638	Ultimate Creatures Accessory Set	2006	300	0	100	23.5	19.99	400.25
7116	Tahu	2010	19	0	38.81	16.19	7.99	385.73
7117	Gresh	2010	19	0	19.17	12.06	7.99	139.92
7135	Takanuva	2010	21	0	24.65	12.2	7.99	208.51
7136	Skrall	2010	21	0	15.5	11.93	7.99	93.99
7137	Piraka	2010	15	0	21.35	8.25	7.99	167.21
7138	Rahkshi	2010	18	0	23	11.61	7.99	187.86
8525	Masks	2001	6	0	21.47	11.11	1.99	978.89
8531	Pohatu	2001	49	0	30.13	16.32	6.99	331.04
8532	Onua	2001	30	0	28.2	16.2	6.99	303.43
8533	Gali	2001	35	0	26.27	17.8	6.99	275.82
8534	Tahu	2001	33	0	36.8	19.04	6.99	426.47
8535	Lewa	2001	36	0	38.53	16.79	6.99	451.22
8536	Kopaka	2001	33	0	40.69	17.18	6.99	482.12
8537	Nui-Rama	2001	154	0	32.07	24.44	14.99	113.94
8538	Muaka & Kane-ra	2001	633	0	95.07	59.73	69.99	35.83
8539	Manas	2001	457	0	115.2	79.87	89.99	28.01
8540	Vakama	2001	28	0	18.67	10.05	2.99	524.41
8541	Matau	2001	25	0	20.5	9.84	2.99	585.62
8542	Onewa	2001	29	0	9.75	9.65	2.99	226.09
8543	Nokama	2001	27	0	18.3	9.68	2.99	512.04
8544	Nuju	2001	29	0	20.42	9.46	2.99	582.94
8545	Whenua	2001	28	0	14.47	9.42	2.99	383.95
8548	Nui-Jaga	2001	226	0	40.4	37.65	34.99	15.46
8549	Tarakava	2001	411	0	52.8	46.47	49.99	5.62
8550	Gahlok Va	2002	26	0	23.06	12.33	2.99	671.24
8551	Kohrak Va	2002	28	0	13.07	8.67	2.99	337.12
8552	Lehvak Va	2002	28	0	10.33	8.59	2.99	245.48
8553	Pahrak Va	2002	27	0	9.8	7.19	2.99	227.76
8554	Tahnok Va	2002	27	0	9.93	8.39	2.99	232.11
8555	Nuhvok Va	2002	26	0	14.45	7.29	2.99	383.28
8556	Boxor Vehicle	2002	157	0	37.4	29.67	14.99	149.50
8557	Exo-Toa	2002	378	0	61.53	44.07	34.99	75.85
8558	Cahdok and Gahdok	2002	636	0	93.2	82	59.99	55.36
8560	Pahrak	2002	41	0	20.76	11.81	7.99	159.82
8561	Nuhvok	2002	41	0	20.42	11.19	7.99	155.57
8562	Gahlok	2002	41	0	17.38	13.69	7.99	117.52
8563	Tahnok	2002	41	0	27.25	14.55	7.99	241.05
8564	Lehvak	2002	41	0	22.27	12	7.99	178.72
8565	Kohrak	2002	41	0	25.33	12.9	7.99	217.02
8566	Onua Nuva	2002	41	0	21.33	12.18	7.99	166.96
8567	Lewa Nuva	2002	37	0	22.27	12.89	7.99	178.72
8568	Pohatu Nuva	2002	40	0	18.2	13.69	7.99	127.78
8569	Krana	2002	5	0	14.93	0	1.99	650.25
8570	Gali Nuva	2002	44	0	17	12.56	7.99	112.77
8571	Kopaka Nuva	2002	42	0	20.67	14.8	7.99	158.70
8572	Tahu Nuva	2002	36	0	42.13	16.87	7.99	427.28
8573	Nuhvok-Kal	2003	41	0	23.53	14.61	7.99	194.49
8574	Tahnok-Kal	2003	41	0	19.21	14.63	7.99	140.43

NUMBER	NAME	YEAR	PIECES	MINIFIGS	NEW	USED	RETAIL	GROWTH%
8575	Kohrak-Kal	2003	41	0	28.71	13.67	7.99	259.32
8576	Lehvak-Kal	2003	41	0	34.88	11.42	7.99	336.55
8577	Pahrak-Kal	2003	41	0	20.21	11.06	7.99	152.94
8578	Gahlok-Kal	2003	41	0	18.8	13.67	7.99	135.29
8580	Kraata	2003	3	0	8	7.78	1.99	302.01
8581	Kopeke	2003	25	0	12.37	10.83	3.99	210.03
8582	Matoro	2003	25	0	16.5	9.47	3.99	313.53
8583	Hahli	2003	25	0	18.62	10.47	3.99	366.67
8584	Hewkii	2003	25	0	18	10.28	3.99	351.13
8585	Hafu	2003	25	0	15.91	9.84	3.99	298.75
8586	Macku	2003	25	0	14.38	10.29	3.99	260.40
8587	Rahkshi Panrahk	2003	45	0	18.44	13.27	8.99	105.12
8588	Rahkshi Kurahk	2003	45	1	21.88	12.67	8.99	143.38
8589	Rahkshi Lerahk	2003	45	1	22.93	11.93	8.99	155.06
8590	Rahkshi Guurahk	2003	45	1	21.36	11.44	8.99	137.60
8591	Rahkshi Vorahk	2003	45	1	23.69	11.93	8.99	163.52
8592	Rahkshi Turahk	2003	45	1	21.9	11.31	8.99	143.60
8593	Makuta	2003	199	0	64	42.24	19.99	220.16
8594	Jaller and Gukko	2003	172	0	39.33	28.4	19.99	96.75
8595	Takua and Pewku	2003	221	0	48.13	35.44	19.99	140.77
8596	Takanuva	2003	200	0	91.2	41.18	29.99	204.10
8598	Kanohi Nuva and Krana Pack	2002	5	0	33.9	0	1.99	1,603.52
8599	Krana-Kal	2003	5	0	19.93	0	1.99	901.51
8601	Vakama	2004	48	0	20.63	18.88	7.99	158.20
8602	Nokama	2004	46	0	12.87	11.68	7.99	61.08
8603	Whenua	2004	49	0	21.36	12.94	7.99	167.33
8604	Onewa	2004	44	0	11.07	11.76	7.99	38.55
8605	Matau	2004	46	0	28.29	12.58	7.99	254.07
8606	Nuju	2004	48	0	17.47	15.12	7.99	118.65
8607	Nuhrii	2004	27	0	22.3	18.67	3.99	458.90
8608	Vhisola	2004	27	0	14.17	7.65	3.99	255.14
8609	Tehutti	2004	27	0	12.6	8.56	3.99	215.79
8610	Ahkmou	2004	27	0	14	7.56	3.99	250.88
8611	Orkahm	2004	27	0	7.2	8.13	3.99	80.45
8612	Ehrye	2004	30	0	7	8.88	3.99	75.44
8613	Kanoka Disk Launcher Pack	2004	4	0	6.09	2	1.99	206.03
8614	Nuurakh	2004	32	0	16.06	9.27	8.99	78.64
8615	Bordakh	2004	32	0	17.27	9.81	8.99	92.10
8616	Vorzakh	2004	32	0	17.75	9.56	8.99	97.44
8617	Zadakh	2004	32	0	12.13	10.69	8.99	34.93
8618	Rorzakh	2004	32	0	19.48	10.88	8.99	116.69
8619	Keerakh	2004	32	0	16.82	10.12	8.99	87.10
8621	Turaga Dume and Nivawk	2004	180	0	28.87	22.53	19.99	44.42
8622	Nidhiki	2004	170	0	39	23.19	19.99	95.10
8623	Krekka	2004	214	0	42.93	29.47	19.99	114.76
8624	Race for the Mask of Life	2006	507	8	36.31	7.33	49.99	-27.37
8625	Umbra	2006	179	0	89.75	42.87	24.99	259.14
8626	Irnakk	2006	132	0	110.53	79	24.99	342.30
8685	Toa Kopaka	2008	54	0	21.33	17.87	9.99	113.51
8686	Toa Lewa	2008	52	0	33	20.89	9.99	230.33
8687	Toa Pohatu	2007	68	0	26.67	17.27	9.99	166.97
8688	Toa Gali	2008	60	0	16.53	15.5	12.99	27.25

NUMBER	NAME	YEAR	PIECES	MINIFIGS	NEW	USED	RETAIL	GROWTH%
8689	Toa Tahu	2008	73	0	22.87	18.47	12.99	76.06
8690	Toa Onua	2008	62	0	18.07	15.87	12.99	39.11
8691	Antroz	2008	53	0	26.73	18.53	9.99	167.57
8692	Vamprah	2008	49	0	24.73	16.8	9.99	147.55
8693	Chirox	2008	49	0	25.6	16.83	9.99	156.26
8694	Krika	2008	40	0	17.53	15.38	12.99	34.95
8695	Gorast	2008	51	0	14.27	12	12.99	9.85
8696	Bitil	2008	54	0	15.75	14.07	12.99	21.25
8697	Toa Ignika	2008	140	0	45.4	31.88	19.99	127.11
8698	Vultraz	2008	133	0	27.53	19.67	19.99	37.72
8699	Takanuva	2008	267	0	50.6	40.6	29.99	68.72
8715	Bionicle Exclusive Accessories	2005	401	0	109.93	107.29	19.99	449.92
8719	Zamor Spheres	2006	10	0	9.27	5.5	1.99	365.83
8721	Velika	2006	21	0	13.57	8.41	3.99	240.10
8722	Kazi	2006	25	0	14.91	7.78	3.99	273.68
8723	Piruk	2006	27	0	16.86	9.26	3.99	322.56
8724	Garan	2006	21	0	13.13	8.07	3.99	229.07
8725	Balta	2006	22	0	19.88	8.41	3.99	398.25
8726	Dalu	2006	25	0	13.15	8.87	3.99	229.57
8727	Toa Jaller	2006	46	0	36.8	19.47	9.99	268.37
8728	Toa Hahli	2006	46	0	30.6	17.4	9.99	206.31
8729	Toa Nuparu	2006	54	0	40.93	18.07	9.99	309.71
8730	Toa Hewkii	2006	62	0	21.93	17.47	9.99	119.52
8731	Toa Kongu	2006	46	0	29	18.47	9.99	190.29
8732	Toa Matoro	2006	46	0	26.07	17.19	9.99	160.96
8733	Axonn	2006	196	0	84.2	52.81	19.99	321.21
8734	Brutaka	2006	193	0	94.27	49.79	19.99	371.59
8736	Toa Hordika Vakama	2005	48	0	27.77	13.73	8.99	208.90
8737	Toa Hordika Nokama	2005	48	0	21.56	11.83	8.99	139.82
8738	Toa Hordika Whenua	2005	48	0	13	9.89	8.99	44.61
8739	Toa Hordika Onewa	2005	48	0	14.13	11.42	8.99	57.17
8740	Toa Hordika Matau	2005	48	0	13.19	12.4	8.99	46.72
8741	Toa Hordika Nuju	2005	48	0	12.63	12.53	8.99	40.49
8742	Visorak Vohtarak	2005	48	0	22.59	12.39	8.99	151.28
8743	Visorak Boggarak	2005	48	0	17.26	11.24	8.99	91.99
8744	Visorak Oohnorak	2005	47	0	11.07	12.16	8.99	23.14
8745	Visorak Roporak	2005	48	0	12.47	10.31	8.99	38.71
8746	Visorak Keelerak	2005	48	0	22.87	12.37	8.99	154.39
8747	Visorak Suukorak	2005	48	0	16.47	12.56	8.99	83.20
8748	Rhotuka Spinners	2005	5	0	7.71	0.5	1.99	287.44
8755	Keetongu	2005	203	0	31.87	27.87	19.99	59.43
8756	Sidorak	2005	211	0	35.6	32.27	19.99	78.09
8757	Visorak Battle Ram	2005	176	14	36.73	25.47	29.99	22.47
8758	Tower of Toa	2005	401	14	32	12	49.99	-35.99
8759	Battle of Metru Nui	2005	858	14	66.6	33.6	79.99	6.74
8761	Roodaka	2005	233	0	48.33	36.4	19.99	141.77
8762	Toa Iruini	2005	53	0	31.5	17	0	
8763	Toa Norik	2005	55	0	50.83	20.4	0	
8764	Vezon & Fenrakk	2006	281	0	75.13	49	29.99	150.52
8769	Visorak's Gate	2005	318	14	60.87	30.19	39.99	52.21
8811	Toa Lhikan and Kikanalo	2004	215	0	78.47	44.24	29.99	161.6
8892	Piraka Outpost	2006	211	4	36.59	15.06	29.99	22.01

NUMBER	NAME	YEAR	PIECES	MINIFIGS	NEW	USED	RETAIL	GROWTH%
8893	Lava Chamber Gate	2006	373	8	54.63	39.13	39.99	36.61
8894	Piraka Stronghold	2006	648	12	35.71	29.83	74.99	-52.38
8900	Reidak	2006	41	0	35	19.04	8.99	289.32
8901	Hakann	2006	42	0	37	17.33	8.99	311.57
8902	Vezok	2006	41	0	31.95	16.67	8.99	255.39
8903	Zaktan	2006	41	0	38.13	19.29	8.99	324.14
8904	Avak	2006	41	0	27.33	18.79	8.99	204.00
8905	Thok	2006	42	0	42.13	18.57	8.99	368.63
8910	Toa Kongu	2007	74	0	23.27	19.6	9.99	132.93
8911	Toa Jaller	2007	68	0	21.4	20.13	9.99	114.21
8912	Toa Hewkii	2007	62	0	22.8	18.06	9.99	128.23
8913	Toa Nuparu	2007	59	0	20.33	16.33	9.99	103.50
8914	Toa Hahli	2007	59	0	31.67	17.83	9.99	217.02
8915	Toa Matoro	2007	63	0	29.87	13.06	9.99	199.00
8916	Takadox	2007	62	0	30	15.81	9.99	200.30
8917	Kalmah	2007	53	0	26.11	17	9.99	161.36
8918	Carapar	2007	50	0	23.23	15.75	9.99	132.53
8919	Mantax	2007	58	0	20.42	15.47	9.99	104.40
8920	Ehlek	2007	54	0	23.74	18.73	9.99	137.64
8921	Pridak	2007	47	0	27.71	15.65	9.99	177.38
8922	Gadunka	2007	176	0	45.2	34.44	19.99	126.11
8923	Hydraxon	2007	165	0	63.87	36.4	19.99	219.51
8924	Maxilos and Spinax	2007	256	0	80.93	51.88	29.99	169.86
8925	Barraki Deepsea Patrol	2007	228	4	38.07	19.13	29.99	26.94
8926	Toa Undersea Attack	2007	401	6	34.93	10.29	49.99	-30.13
8927	Toa Terrain Crawler	2007	674	10	99.2	57.67	69.99	41.73
8929	Defilak	2007	37	0	14.35	9.87	4.99	187.58
8930	Dekar	2007	37	0	15.12	11.06	4.99	203.01
8931	Thulox	2007	39	0	13.87	9.38	4.99	177.96
8932	Morak	2007	40	0	12.09	9.75	4.99	142.28
8934	Squid Ammo	2007	7	0	11.07	6.78	1.99	456.28
8935	Nocturn	2007	116	0	62.56	36.75	14.99	317.34
8939	Lesovikk	2007	149	0	52.2	38.47	19.99	161.13
8940	Karzahni	2007	373	0	110.47	79.47	39.99	176.24
8941	Rockoh T3	2008	390	0	45.87	33.69	39.99	14.70
8942	Jetrax T6	2008	422	0	75	39.07	49.99	50.03
8943	Axalara T9	2008	693	0	86.93	58.93	79.99	8.68
8944	Tanma	2008	14	0	25.6	12.4	5.99	327.38
8945	Solek	2008	14	0	13.34	8.73	5.99	122.70
8946	Photok	2008	14	0	20	10.93	5.99	233.89
8947	Radiak	2008	16	0	15.73	9.56	5.99	162.60
8948	Gavla	2008	14	0	10	6.4	5.99	66.94
8949	Kirop	2008	14	0	21.71	10.2	5.99	262.44
8952	Mutran and Vican	2008	90	0	41.62	25.6	14.99	177.65
8953	Makuta Icarax	2008	159	0	78.63	47.2	19.99	293.35
8954	Mazeka	2008	301	0	38.83	17.6	29.99	29.48
8972	Atakus	2009	13	0	15.11	9.67	6.99	116.17
8973	Raanu	2009	14	0	13.81	12.65	6.99	97.57
8974	Tarduk	2009	17	0	14.13	8.33	6.99	102.15
8975	Berix	2009	15	0	17.33	9.13	6.99	147.93
8976	Metus	2009	14	0	12.13	7.75	6.99	73.53
8977	Zesk	2009	16	0	15.94	9.3	6.99	128.04

NUMBER	NAME	YEAR	PIECES	MINIFIGS	NEW	USED	RETAIL	GROWTH%
8978	Skrall	2009	50	0	26.47	19	12.99	103.77
8979	Malum	2009	59	0	23.6	16.88	12.99	81.68
8980	Gresh	2009	55	0	37.07	19.63	12.99	185.37
8981	Tarix	2009	57	0	24.47	16.82	12.99	88.38
8982	Strakk	2009	46	0	27	15.24	12.99	107.85
8983	Vorox	2009	51	0	26	15.79	12.99	100.15
8984	Stronius	2009	55	0	32.53	15.73	12.99	150.42
8985	Ackar	2009	55	0	37.13	17.73	12.99	185.84
8986	Vastus	2009	52	0	26.75	15.22	12.99	105.93
8987	Kiina	2009	43	0	23.08	15.2	12.99	77.68
8988	Gelu	2009	52	0	40.87	16.67	12.99	214.63
8989	Mata Nui	2009	52	0	51.73	31.13	12.99	298.23
8991	Tuma	2009	188	0	54.87	30.6	19.99	174.49
8992	Cendox V1	2009	151	0	26.8	17.4	19.99	34.07
8993	Kaxium V3	2009	251	0	35.19	25.2	29.99	17.34
8994	Baranus V7	2009	263	0	45.69	28.63	39.99	14.25
8995	Thornatus V9	2009	438	0	55.71	29.67	59.99	-7.13
8996	Skopio XV	2009	849	0	158.33	88.67	89.99	75.94
8998	Toa Mata Nui	2009	366	0	185.47	138.6	49.99	271.01

CARS

NUMBER	NAME	YEAR	PIECES	MINIFIGS	NEW	USED	RETAIL	GROWTH%
8200	Radiator Springs Lightning McQueen	2011	35	0	29.16	8.87	6.99	317.17
8201	Classic Mater	2011	52	0	17.86	7.93	6.99	155.51
8206	Tokyo Pit Stop	2011	147	0	22.27	9.07	14.99	48.57
8423	World Grand Prix Racing Rivalry	2011	136	0	28.8	19	14.99	92.13
8424	Mater's Spy Zone	2011	114	0	22.19	8.5	14.99	48.03
8426	Escape at Sea	2011	159	0	29	13.4	15.99	81.36
8484	Ultimate Build Lightning McQueen	2011	242	0	41.85	17.4	29.99	39.55
8486	Mack's Team Truck	2011	374	0	123.33	55.4	39.99	208.40
8487	Flo's V8 Cafe	2011	517	0	93.38	50.6	59.99	55.66
8638	Spy Jet Escape	2011	339	0	50.35	27.6	49.99	0.72
8639	Big Bentley Bust Out	2011	743	0	50.83	30.8	69.99	-27.38
8677	Ultimate Build Mater	2011	288	0	31.38	15.73	29.99	4.63
8678	Ultimate Build Francesco	2011	196	0	27.4	14.87	29.99	-8.64
8679	Tokyo International Circuit (TRU Exclusive)	2011	842	0	97.71	56.42	89.99	8.58
9478	Francesco Bernoulli	2012	49	0	12.11	6.23	6.99	73.25
9479	Ivan Mater	2012	52	0	13	9.29	6.99	85.98
9480	Finn McMissile	2012	52	0	15.17	4.5	6.99	117.02
9481	Jeff Gorvette	2012	54	0	12.83	6.6	6.99	83.55
9483	Agent Mater's Escape	2012	144	0	22.69	7.77	14.99	51.37
9484	Red's Water Rescue	2012	199	0	30.68	9.83	19.99	53.48
9485	Ultimate Race Set	2012	280	0	54.63	17.25	29.99	82.16
9486	Oil Rig Escape	2012	422	0	57.07	32.87	49.99	14.16

CASTLE

NUMBER	NAME	YEAR	PIECES	MINIFIGS	NEW	USED	RETAIL	GROWTH%
10000	Guarded Inn	2001	253	4	156.07	79.2	24.99	524.53
10039	Black Falcon's Fortress	2002	426	6	177.4	101.53	39.99	343.61
10176	King's Castle	2006	869	12	221.53	108.93	99.99	121.55
10193	Medieval Market Village	2009	1601	8	155.7	120.13	99.99	55.72
10223	Kingdoms Joust	2012	1575	9	127.03	94.53	119.99	5.87

NUMBER	NAME	YEAR	PIECES	MINIFIGS	NEW	USED	RETAIL	GROWTH%
1187	Glider	1999	23	1	29.64	6.35	1.99	1,389.45
1269	White Ninja	1999	23	1	14.25	25	2.99	376.59
1463	Treasure Cart	1992	23	1	19.08	10.67	1.99	858.79
1547	Black Knights Boat	1993	58	2	31.17	19.27	3.99	681.20
1596	Ghostly Hideout	1993	37	2	30.89	20.87	3.99	674.19
1597	Castle Value Pack	1993	117	5	155.67	21.2	7.99	1,848.31
1712	Crossbow Cart	1994	23	1	15.17	5	1.99	662.31
1746	Wiz the Wizard	1995	17	1	13.69	9.93	2.99	357.86
1804	Crossbow Boat	1996	21	1	20.8	9.08	1.99	945.23
1906	Majisto's Tower	1994	195	3	75.47	53.47	19.99	277.54
2538	Fire-Cart	1998	20	1	7.59	4.6	1.99	281.41
2539	Flying Machine	1998	21	1	12.2	5.13	1.99	513.07
2540	Catapault Cart	1998	28	1	6.67	4.82	1.99	235.18
30062	Target Practice	2010	29	1	9.7	4.95	3.99	143.11
3017	Ninpo Water Spider	1998	25	1	12.19	14.33	1.99	512.56
3019	Ninpo Big Bat	1998	23	1	13.56	4.31	1.99	581.41
3050	Shanghai Surprise	1999	104	3	40.07	22.87	11.99	234.20
3051	Blaze Attack	1999	145	2	27.4	22.41	14.99	82.79
3052	Ninja Fire Fortress	1999	169	3	85.33	32.6	29.99	184.53
3053	Emperor's Stronghold	1999	331	4	111.4	65.75	39.99	178.57
3346	Three Minifig Pack - Ninja #3	2000	22	3	41.33	43.58	4.99	728.26
3739	Blacksmith Shop	2002	619	2	176.47	102.6	39.99	341.29
4801	Defence Archer	2000	15	1	8	5	1.99	302.01
4805	Ninja Knights	1999	31	5	37.67	17.05	5.99	528.88
4806	Axe Cart	2000	28	1	15.13	8.75	2.99	406.02
4811	Defense Archer	2000	15	1	11.15	4	1.99	460.30
4816	Knights' Catapult	2000	50	2	16.91	11.53	4.99	238.88
4817	Dungeon	2000	38	2	24	7.2	4.99	380.96
4818	Dragon Rider	2000	11	1	21.33	14.2	4.99	327.45
4819	Bulls' Attack Wagon	2000	49	2	23.27	14.89	4.99	366.33
5615	The Knight	2008	21	1	10.42	5.78	3.99	161.15
5618	Troll Warrior	2008	19	1	12.81	5.87	3.99	221.05
5994	Catapult	2005	27	0	5.75	3.82	0.99	480.81
6007	Bat Lord	1997	12	1	15.97	15.65	4.99	220.04
6008	Royal King	1995	10	1	15.87	10.83	2.99	430.77
6009	Black Knight	1992	24	1	26.44	13.87	2.99	784.28
6010	Supply Wagon	1984	35	1	37.88	18.87	2.99	1166.89
6012	Siege Cart	1986	54	2	38.36	13.4	3.99	861.40
6013	Samurai Swordsman	1998	13	1	22.33	9.12	2.99	646.82
6016	Knights' Arsenal	1988	37	1	24	17.33	3.99	501.50
6017	King's Oarsmen	1987	45	2	56.75	16.6	3.99	1322.31
6018	Battle Dragon	1990	56	2	28.33	15.47	4.99	467.74
6020	Magic Shop	1993	47	1	19.47	13.07	4.99	290.18
6021	Jousting Knights	1984	37	2	35.83	21.44	4.99	618.04
6022	Horse Cart	1984	42	2	67.25	26.33	4.99	1247.70
6023	Maiden's Cart	1986	43	2	3.04	5	5.99	-49.25
6024	Bandit Ambush	1996	59	2	31.13	27.18	6.99	345.35
6026	King Leo	2000	21	2	17.8	7.73	4.99	256.71
6027	Bat Lord's Catapult	1997	55	2	20.6	16	6.99	194.71
6029	Treasure Guard	1998	22	1	12.64	4.13	1.99	535.18
6030	Catapult	1984	83	2	70.64	28.73	5.99	1,079.30
6031	Fright Force	1998	30	4	30.6	13.6	5.99	410.85

NUMBER	NAME	YEAR	PIECES	MINIFIGS	NEW	USED	RETAIL	GROWTH%
6032	Catapault Crusher	2000	56	1	9.55	9.13	5.99	59.43
6033	Treasure Transport	1998	54	3	20.47	15.06	5.99	241.74
6034	Black Monarch's Ghost	1990	46	2	48.69	15.8	6.99	596.57
6035	Castle Guard	1988	52	2	88.14	23.6	5.99	1371.45
6036	Skeleton Surprise	1995	74	2	25.65	16.38	7.99	221.03
6037	Witch's Windship	1997	56	1	25.6	19.87	7.99	220.40
6038	Wolfpack Renegades	1992	100	2	49.4	23.53	7.99	518.27
6039	Twin-Arm Launcher	1988	77	2	39.9	20.07	8.99	343.83
6040	Blacksmith Shop	1984	92	2	134.15	36.47	8.99	1,392.21
6042	Dungeon Hunters	1990	110	3	97.08	27.75	12.99	647.34
6043	Dragon Defender	1993	157	2	32.92	18.11	11.99	174.56
6044	King's Carriage	1995	124	4	51.73	35.5	16.99	204.47
6045	Ninja Surprise	1998	112	3	41.6	24	12.99	220.25
6046	Hemlock Stronghold	1996	216	5	102.8	57.2	23.99	328.51
6048	Majisto's Magical Workshop	1993	185	2	51.33	36.47	25.99	97.50
6049	Viking Voyager	1987	99	5	95	41.6	10.99	764.42
6054	Forestmen's Hideout	1988	201	2	183	39.73	17.99	917.23
6056	Dragon Wagon	1993	105	2	41.93	25.53	19.99	109.75
6057	Sea Serpent	1992	126	5	60.73	40.88	16.99	257.45
6059	Knight's Stronghold	1990	224	5	100.33	49.8	21.99	356.25
6060	Knight's Challenge	1989	168	8	287.91	84.87	21.99	1,209.28
6061	Siege Tower	1984	216	4	165.45	63.8	17.99	819.68
6062	Battering Ram	1987	236	6	246	68.8	19.99	1,130.62
6066	Camouflaged Outpost	1988	225	6	346.13	69.87	22.99	1,405.57
6067	Guarded Inn	1986	248	4	289.67	80.47	19.99	1,349.07
6071	Forestmen's Crossing	1990	207	5	269	88	28.99	827.91
6073	Knight's Castle	1984	410	6	332.33	95.13	26.99	1,131.31
6074	Black Falcon's Fortress	1986	435	6	231.2	98.93	34.99	560.76
6075	Wolfpack Tower	1992	236	4	118.6	94.93	29.99	295.47
6075-2	Castle	1981	767	14	233.73	113.8	47.99	387.04
6076	Dark Dragon's Den	1993	214	4	73.4	55.07	42.99	70.74
6077	Knight's Procession	1981	48	6	104.33	33.07	4.99	1,990.78
6077-2	Forestmen's River Fortress	1989	357	6	259.82	101.13	37.99	583.92
6078	Royal Drawbridge	1995	258	5	93.87	49.07	29.99	213.00
6079	Dark Forest Fortress	1996	464	7	248.13	177.2	49.99	396.36
6080	King's Castle	1984	674	12	162.13	151.8	52.99	205.96
6081	King's Mountain Fortress	1990	435	8	699.75	124.13	57.99	1,106.67
6082	Fire Breathing Fortress	1993	397	6	114.85	89.6	63.99	79.48
6083	Knight's Joust	1981	211	6	95.5	65	15.99	497.25
6083-2	Samurai Stronghold	1998	198	3	63.67	42.13	19.99	218.51
6085	Black Monarch's Castle	1988	702	12	671.62	153.33	67.99	887.82
6086	Black Knight's Castle	1992	588	12	431.38	178.33	84.99	407.57
6087	Witch's Magic Manor	1997	250	6	100.73	37.6	43.99	128.98
6088	Robber's Retreat	1998	277	4	77.27	41.67	29.99	157.65
6089	Stone Tower Bridge	1998	409	5	215	58.67	49.99	330.09
6090	Royal Knight's Castle	1995	764	11	281.4	160.4	94.99	196.24
6091	King Leo's Castle	2000	529	8	123.13	111.2	89.99	36.83
6093	Flying Ninja Fortress	1998	694	9	164.07	90.27	89.99	82.32
6094	Guarded Treasure	2000	103	2	25.38	19.73	14.99	69.31
6095	Royal Joust	2000	101	3	42.93	24.53	19.99	114.76
6096	Bull's Attack	2000	313	4	53.73	41.07	49.99	7.48
6097	Night Lord's Castle	1997	601	8	187.33	89.13	79.99	134.19

NUMBER	NAME	YEAR	PIECES	MINIFIGS	NEW	USED	RETAIL	GROWTH%
6098	King Leo's Castle	2000	529	8	126.5	96.8	89.99	40.57
6099	Traitor Transport	1997	140	3	29.2	18.93	19.99	46.07
6103	Castle Mini Figures	1988	42	6	62.4	26	6.99	792.70
6105	Medieval Knights	1993	41	4	33.13	24	6.99	373.96
6918	Blacksmith Attack	2011	104	2	23.55	19.13	9.99	135.74
7009	The Final Joust	2007	62	2	34.44	18.53	7.99	331.04
7029	Skeleton Ship Attack	2007	628	7	237.69	125.6	69.99	239.61
7036	Dwarves' Mine	2007	575	7	167.13	74.87	49.99	234.33
7037	Tower Raid	2008	364	5	72	38.6	29.99	140.08
7038	Troll Assault Wagon	2008	161	4	49.33	31.67	19.99	146.77
7040	Dwarves' Mine Defender	2008	86	3	26.75	19.15	9.99	167.7
70400	Forest Ambush	2013	90	4	10.88	8.5	11.99	-9.26
70401	Gold Getaway	2013	199	3	17.86	15.82	19.99	0.66
70402	The Gatehouse Raid	2013	248	4	28.08	20.27	29.99	-6.37
70403	Dragon Mountain	2013	376	5	45.13	37.6	49.99	-9.72
70404	King's Castle	2013	996	7	95.28	74.33	99.99	-4.71
7041	Troll Battle Wheel	2008	508	6	81.11	40.67	39.99	102.83
7048	Troll Warship	2008	493	9	155.2	105.67	79.99	94.02
7078	King's Battle Chariot	2009	103	4	39.42	23.53	19.99	97.20
7079	Drawbridge Defense	2009	335	7	94.13	53.53	39.99	135.38
7090	Crossbow Attack	2007	54	3	21.23	10.33	5.99	254.42
7091	Knight's Catapult Defense	2007	123	4	19.8	16.73	9.99	98.20
7092	Skeletons' Prison Carriage	2007	193	5	81.93	32.33	19.99	309.85
7093	Skeleton Tower	2007	398	5	105.77	82.67	49.99	111.58
7094	King's Castle Siege	2007	973	10	276.4	151.47	99.99	176.43
7097	Trolls' Mountain Fortress	2009	844	10	155	92.33	99.99	55.02
7187	Escape from Dragon's Prison	2011	185	4	49.07	23.6	19.99	145.47
7188	King's Carriage Ambush	2011	285	4	35.06	25.6	39.99	2.33
7189	Mill Village Raid	2011	663	6	118.21	81.4	69.99	68.90
7946	King's Castle	2010	933	8	178	110.33	99.99	78.02
7947	Prison Tower Rescue	2010	365	5	86.27	50.73	49.99	72.57
7948	Outpost Attack	2010	194	3	54.11	19.53	19.99	170.69
7949	Prison Carriage Rescue	2010	50	3	14	12.47	9.99	40.14
7950	Knight's Showdown	2010	61	2	19.07	10.13	6.99	172.82
7952	Kingdoms Advent Calendar	2010	167	9	66.33	36.57	34.99	89.57
7953	Court Jester	2010	22	1	7.73	3.8	3.99	93.73
7955	Wizard	2010	19	1	10.38	6.8	3.99	160.15

NUMBER	NAME	YEAR	PIECES	MINIFIGS	NEW	USED	RETAIL	GROWTH%
7979	Castle Advent Calendar	2008	176	9	76.38	51	29.99	154.68
850888	Knight Accessory Set	2014	32	4	26.14	0	14.99	74.38
850889	Dragon Accessory Set	2014	42	4	25.2	0	14.99	68.11
852271	Knights Battle Pack	2008	35	5	37.21	8	12.99	186.45
852272	Skeletons Battle Pack	2008	43	5	39.84	15.5	12.99	206.70
852701	Troll Warrior Battle Pack	2009	36	5	37.12	27.34	14.99	147.63
852702	Dwarf Warrior Battle Pack	2009	45	5	50.4	37	14.99	236.22
852921	Kingdoms Battle Pack 1	2010	18	5	43.58	20.58	14.99	190.73
852922	Kingdoms Battle Pack 2	2010	17	5	28.38	13	14.99	89.33
8701	King Jayko	2006	130	0	18.07	9.27	19.99	-9.60
8702	Lord Vladek	2006	112	0	18.31	14.92	19.99	-8.40
8703	Sir Kentis	2006	43	0	21.33	10.87	9.99	113.51
8704	Sir Adric	2006	40	0	11.93	6.2	9.99	19.42
8705	Dracus	2006	38	0	13.87	8.27	9.99	38.84
8706	Karzon	2006	44	0	13.82	9.27	9.99	38.34
8777	Vladek Encounter	2004	42	2	20.5	10.73	8.99	128.03
8778	Border Ambush	2004	177	2	24.67	17.33	19.99	23.41
8779	The Grand Tournament	2004	312	3	33.95	24.73	29.99	13.20
8780	Citadel of Orlan	2004	442	4	69.87	42.87	49.99	39.77
8781	The Castle of Morcia	2004	637	8	130.13	72.87	89.99	44.60
8782	Danju	2004	46	0	15.21	6	7.99	90.36
8783	Jayko	2004	49	0	15.39	6.6	7.99	92.62
8784	Rascus	2004	50	0	12.6	7.33	7.99	57.70
8785	Santis	2004	50	0	14.23	6.27	7.99	78.10
8786	Vladek	2004	52	0	14.47	6.47	7.99	81.10
8791	Sir Danju	2005	42	0	17.64	12.2	8.99	96.22
8792	Sir Jayko	2005	43	0	14.5	9.8	8.99	61.29
8793	Sir Rascus	2005	44	0	22	7	8.99	144.72
8794	Sir Santis	2005	44	0	11.75	4.33	8.99	30.70
8795	Lord Vladek	2005	44	0	9.73	10.27	8.99	8.23
8796	King Mathias	2005	43	0	8.63	5.33	8.99	-4.00
8799	Knights' Castle Wall	2004	178	3	35.3	33.87	19.99	76.59
8800	Vladek's Siege Engine	2004	192	2	32.17	20.2	19.99	60.93
8809	King Mathias	2004	44	0	9.61	5.4	9.99	-3.80
8813	Battle at the Pass	2006	381	11	124.2	68.47	39.99	210.58
8821	Rogue Knight Battleship	2006	152	3	38.87	22.13	19.99	94.45
8822	Gargoyle Bridge	2006	250	3	36.6	30.2	29.99	22.04
8823	Mistlands Tower	2006	431	6	93.87	54.2	49.99	87.78
8873	Fireball Catapult	2005	46	2	19.93	11.27	7.99	149.44
8874	Battle Wagon	2005	129	3	42.87	22.6	19.99	114.46
8875	King's Siege Tower	2005	135	4	45.4	23.33	19.99	127.11
8876	Scorpion Prison Cave	2005	280	5	60.47	39.6	39.99	51.21
8877	Vladek's Dark Fortress	2005	983	9	168.07	112.67	99.99	68.09

CITY

NUMBER	NAME	YEAR	PIECES	MINIFIGS	NEW	USED	RETAIL	GROWTH%
2824	City Advent Calendar	2010	271	6	44.59	18.8	34.99	27.44
30002	Police Boat	2009	30	1	8.35	4.47	2.99	179.26
30010	Fire Chief	2010	31	1	8.2	4.33	2.99	174.25
30012	Microlight	2010	34	1	9.37	5.8	3.99	134.84
30013	Police buggy	2010	34	1	6.87	3.33	3.99	72.18
30014	Police Helicopter	2011	32	1	12.76	4.33	2.99	326.76
30015	Jet Ski	2011	24	2	5.91	9.25	2.99	97.66

NUMBER	NAME	YEAR	PIECES	MINIFIGS	NEW	USED	RETAIL	GROWTH%
30017	Police Boat	2012	35	1	6.5	6.58	3.99	62.91
30018	Police Microlight	2012	32	1	6.24	5.67	3.99	56.39
30150	Racing Car	2012	37	1	6.19	1.72	4.99	24.05
30151	Mining Dozer	2012	32	1	8.28	3.27	3.99	107.52
30152	Mining Quad	2012	40	1	7.95	8.24	4.99	59.32
30221	Fire Car	2013	36	1	7.55	6.5	3.99	89.22
30222	Police Helicopter	2013	33	1	6.14	3.17	3.99	53.88
30225	Coast Guard Seaplane	2013	37	1	5.95	8.63	3.99	49.12
30227	LEGO City Police Watercraft	2014	36	2	6.75	0	4.99	35.27
30228	Police ATV	2014	42	1	7.08	10	2	254.00
30229	Repair Lift	2014	39	1	8.82	2.29	3.49	152.72
3177	Small Car	2010	43	1	18.86	9.67	4.99	277.96
3178	Seaplane	2010	102	1	22.53	12.33	10.99	105.00
3179	Repair Truck	2010	118	1	25.47	14.13	12.99	96.07
3180	Tank Truck	2010	222	1	34.31	22.73	19.99	71.64
3181	Passenger Plane	2010	309	3	118.33	57	39.99	195.90
3182	Airport	2010	703	5	271.58	163.95	99.99	171.61
3221	LEGO City Truck	2010	278	2	93.45	53.16	34.99	167.08
3222	Helicopter and Limousine	2010	267	4	140.71	71.4	29.99	369.19
3365	Space Moon Buggy	2011	37	1	11	8	4.99	120.44
3366	Satellite Launch Pad	2011	165	1	25.92	14.12	19.99	29.66
3367	Space Shuttle	2011	231	1	73.22	34.63	29.99	144.15
3368	Space Centre	2011	494	4	110.42	67.33	69.99	57.77
3648	Police Chase	2011	173	3	28.72	21	24.99	14.93
3658	Police Helicopter	2011	237	3	53.4	31.07	34.99	52.62
3661	Bank & Money Transfer	2011	405	4	66.31	42.87	49.99	32.65
3677	Red Cargo Train	2011	831	4	199.46	178.53	159.99	24.67
40110	Coin Bank	2014	122	1	24.73	0	14.99	64.98
4200	Mining 4x4	2012	102	1	17.32	10.25	11.99	44.45
4201	Loader and Tipper	2012	139	2	26.65	16.47	17.99	48.14
4202	Mining Truck	2012	269	1	43.16	28.07	34.99	23.35
4203	Excavator Transporter	2012	305	2	38.91	25.73	39.99	-2.70
4204	The Mine	2012	748	4	95.62	67.53	99.99	-4.37
4205	Off-Road Command Centre	2012	403	3	88.2	37.87	39.99	120.56
4206-2	Recycling Truck	2012	297	3	31.63	19.27	29.99	5.47
4207	City Garage	2012	933	5	123.98	80.07	119.99	3.33
4208	Fire Truck	2012	243	1	37.05	17.47	19.99	85.34
4209	Fire Plane	2012	522	3	56.06	32.87	59.99	-6.55
4210	Coast Guard Platform	2008	469	4	202.71	84.53	49.99	305.50
4427	Fire ATV	2012	50	1	13.3	5	5.99	122.04
4428	City Advent Calendar	2012	248	7	46	27.53	39.99	15.03
4429	Helicopter Rescue	2012	425	4	65.71	37.53	59.99	9.53
4430	Fire Transporter	2012	522	3	84.79	47.6	49.99	69.61
4431	Ambulance	2012	199	3	41.1	20.93	19.99	105.60
4432	Garbage Truck	2012	208	2	44.14	22.2	19.99	120.81
4433	Dirt Bike Transporter	2012	201	2	33.47	20.4	19.99	67.43
4434	Dump Truck	2012	222	2	28.57	16.33	19.99	42.92
4435	Car and Caravan	2012	218	2	46	25.07	19.99	130.12
4436	Patrol Car	2012	97	2	15.89	10.6	11.99	32.53
4437	Police Pursuit	2012	129	2	16.97	10.53	17.99	-5.67
4438	Robbers' Hideout	2012	317	4	94.27	42.33	39.99	135.73
4439	Heavy-Lift Helicopter	2012	393	3	54.18	33.4	49.99	8.38

NUMBER	NAME	YEAR	PIECES	MINIFIGS	NEW	USED	RETAIL	GROWTH%
4440	Forest Police Station	2012	633	5	87.55	59.87	79.99	9.45
4441	Police Dog Van	2012	313	2	52.56	25.27	34.99	50.21
4641	Speed Boat	2011	34	1	12.21	7.13	4.99	144.69
4642	Fishing Boat	2011	64	2	45.95	21.07	19.99	129.86
4643	Power Boat Transporter	2011	254	2	66.47	30.6	39.99	66.22
4644	Marina	2011	294	5	54.92	31.6	49.99	9.86
4645	Harbour	2011	551	4	122.18	74.2	89.99	35.77
4936	Doc & Patient	2007	18	2	13.18	6.76	2.99	340.80
5000281	Chase McCain	2012	4	1	8.44	4.56	1	744.00
5610	Builder	2008	23	1	13	6.27	3.99	225.81
5611	Public Works	2008	31	1	7.78	5.1	3.99	94.99
5612	Police Officer	2008	21	1	8.18	5.2	3.99	105.01
5613	Firefighter	2008	25	1	8.94	5.24	3.99	124.06
5620	Street Cleaner	2008	22	1	10.61	6	3.99	165.91
5621	Coast Guard Kayak	2008	21	1	10.89	5.53	3.99	172.93
60000	Fire Motorcycle	2013	40	1	11.32	6.19	6.99	61.95
60001	Fire Chief Car	2013	80	2	16.71	11.75	11.99	39.37
60002	Fire Truck	2013	208	2	20.88	16.27	19.99	4.45
60003	Fire Emergency	2013	300	3	29.9	22.94	39.99	-25.23
60004	Fire Station	2013	752	5	101.47	62.73	99.99	1.48
60005	Fire Boat	2013	222	4	40.35	17.6	29.99	34.54
60006	Police ATV	2013	51	2	11.84	6	6.99	69.38
60007	High Speed Chase	2013	283	3	31.88	19.65	29.99	6.30
60008	Museum Break-in	2013	563	6	49.26	35.47	69.99	-29.62
60009	Helicopter Arrest	2013	352	5	54.38	38.83	49.99	8.78
60010	Fire Helicopter	2013	232	2	50.05	28.4	39.99	25.16
60011	Surfer Rescue	2013	32	2	7.22	7.65	6.99	3.29
60012	4x4 & Diving Boat	2013	128	2	26.17	18.33	19.99	30.92
60013	Coast Guard Helicopter	2013	230	4	33.92	25.27	39.99	5.18
60014	Coast Guard Patrol	2013	449	6	61.92	54.29	79.99	-22.59
60015	Coast Guard Plane	2013	279	3	67.71	32.6	44.99	50.50
60016	Tanker Truck	2013	191	1	25.84	17.27	19.99	29.26
60017	Flatbed Truck	2013	212	2	19.55	15.6	19.99	-2.20
60018	Cement Mixer	2013	221	2	24.72	11.87	19.99	23.66
60019	Stunt Plane	2013	140	2	24.33	17.11	19.99	21.71
60020	Cargo Truck	2013	321	3	33.4	22.67	39.99	6.48
60021	Cargo Heliplane	2013	393	3	44.48	32.73	44.99	.13
60022	Cargo Terminal	2013	658	5	102.25	66	99.99	2.26
60023	LEGO City Starter Set	2013	272	5	42.33	40	29.99	41.15
60024	City Advent Calendar	2013	244	8	46.53	27.37	29.99	55.15
60025	Grand Prix Truck	2013	315	3	45.95	19.07	29.99	53.22
60026	Town Square	2013	914	8	121.89	72.59	119.99	1.58
60027	Monster Truck Transporter	2013	299	3	35	23.5	29.99	16.71
60032	Arctic Snowmobile	2014	44	1	10.8	5.88	6.99	54.51
60033	Arctic Ice Crawler	2014	113	1	22.73	0	14.99	51.63
60034	Arctic Helicrane	2014	262	2	43.73	24.6	39.99	9.35
60035	Arctic Outpost	2014	374	3	56.5	21.08	49.99	13.02
60036	Arctic Base Camp	2014	733	7	82.14	71.45	89.99	-8.72
60041	Crook Pursuit	2014	38	2	9	6.93	6.99	28.76
60042	High Speed Police Chase	2014	110	3	22.29	16.5	19.99	11.51
60043	Prisoner Transporter	2014	196	3	26.07	11.69	24.99	4.32
60044	Mobile Police Unit	2014	375	3	44.29	32.27	44.99	.56

NUMBER	NAME	YEAR	PIECES	MINIFIGS	NEW	USED	RETAIL	GROWTH%
60045	Police Patrol	2014	408	3	43.46	34	44.99	-3.40
60046	Helicopter Surveillance	2014	528	5	49.3	40.25	74.99	-34.26
60047	Police Station	2014	854	7	88.47	59.66	99.99	1.52
60048	Police Dog Unit	2014	249	4	46.72	11.73	29.99	55.79
60049	Helicopter Transporter	2014	382	4	52.84	31	44.99	17.45
60050	Train Station	2014	423	5	99.52	55.5	64.99	53.13
60051	High-Speed Passenger Train	2014	610	3	143.65	102.5	149.99	-4.23
60052	Cargo Train	2014	888	4	176.41	180	199.99	1.79
60053	Race Car	2014	100	1	13.1	8.6	9.99	31.13
60054	Light Repair Truck	2014	95	1	11.29	0	9.99	13.01
60055	Monster Truck	2014	78	1	12.9	4.81	9.99	29.13
60056	Tow Truck	2014	227	1	21.48	14.01	19.99	7.45
60057	Camper Van	2014	195	2	21.1	16.54	19.99	5.55
60058	SUV with Watercraft	2014	219	2	20.44	13.5	19.99	2.25
60059	Logging Truck	2014	228	2	22.34	16.4	19.99	11.76
60060	Auto Transporter	2014	350	2	31.36	18.09	29.99	4.57
60061	Airport Fire Truck	2014	326	2	39.86	15.21	29.99	32.91
60062	Arctic Ice Breaker	2014	717	7	176.28	90.24	99.99	76.30
60063	City Advent Calendar	2014	218	7	48.57	9.52	29.99	61.95
60064	Arctic Supply Plane	2014	374	3	68.46	35	49.99	36.95
7206	Fire Helicopter	2010	342	3	55.25	29.8	39.99	38.16
7207	Fire Boat	2010	306	4	131	51.33	49.99	162.05
7208	Fire Station	2010	662	4	108.06	54.33	79.99	35.09
7213	Off-Road Fire Truck & Fireboat	2010	388	3	56.43	30.2	39.99	41.11
7235	Police Motorcycle	2005	28	1	10.65	13.67	3.99	166.92
7236	Police Car	2005	59	1	19	9.2	4.99	280.76
7237	Police Station	2005	586	5	149.67	84.2	69.99	113.84
7238	Fire Helicopter	2005	75	1	19.07	14.67	9.99	90.89
7239	Fire Truck	2005	214	2	47.63	22.73	19.99	138.27
7240	Fire Station	2005	260	3	77.4	34.8	29.99	158.09
7241	Fire Car	2005	46	1	14.45	7.07	2.99	383.28
7242	Street Sweeper	2005	63	1	39.67	18.33	4.99	694.99
7243	Construction Site	2005	298	3	128.8	58.33	39.99	222.08
7244	Speedboat	2005	107	2	47.8	35.07	29.99	59.39
7245	Prisoner Transport	2005	98	2	30	17.27	9.99	200.30
7246	Mini Digger	2005	36	1	15.53	8.27	2.99	419.40
7248	Digger	2005	127	1	60.87	31.47	19.99	204.50
7249	XXL Mobile Crane	2005	524	2	188.93	91.93	49.99	277.94
7279	Police Minifigure Collection	2011	57	4	16.25	14.33	9.99	62.66
7280	Straight & Crossroad Plates	2005	2	0	21	11.11	14.99	40.09
7281	T-Junction & Curved Road Plates	2005	2	0	16.7	11	14.99	11.41
7285	Police Dog Unit	2011	96	1	33.47	15.8	12.99	157.66
7286	Prisoner Transport	2011	173	2	23.47	16.4	19.99	17.41
7287	Police Boat	2011	172	3	90.93	56.27	39.99	127.38
7288	Mobile Police Unit	2011	408	3	57	30.87	44.99	26.69
7324	City Advent Calendar	2005	203	9	42.6	16.4	14.99	184.19
7344	Dump Truck	2005	187	1	82.29	40.6	29.99	174.39
7498	Police Station	2011	783	6	136.82	84.42	99.99	36.83
7499	Flexible and Straight Tracks	2011	24	0	24.21	21	19.99	21.11
7553	Advent Calendar	2011	232	6	42.06	24.6	34.99	20.21
7566	Farmer	2010	16	1	9.61	3.95	3.99	140.85
7567	Traveller	2010	21	1	12.93	6.18	5	158.60

NUMBER	NAME	YEAR	PIECES	MINIFIGS	NEW	USED	RETAIL	GROWTH%
7630	Front-End Loader	2009	108	1	37.53	27.2	12.99	188.91
7631	Dump Truck	2009	189	1	39.67	22.4	19.99	98.45
7632	Crawler Crane	2009	481	2	149.6	78.53	64.99	130.19
7633	Construction Site	2009	898	5	243	136.47	99.99	143.02
7634	Tractor	2009	78	1	45.22	24.47	12.99	248.11
7635	4WD with Horse Trailer	2009	176	2	48.94	26.2	22.99	112.88
7636	Combine Harvester	2009	360	1	199.13	83.07	44.99	342.61
7637	Farm	2009	609	3	198.2	112	89.99	120.25
7638	Tow Truck	2009	129	1	38.67	17.13	12.99	197.69
7639	Camper	2009	165	2	37.24	16.6	16.99	119.19
7641	City Corner	2009	483	5	110.4	55.6	59.99	84.03
7642	Garage	2009	953	4	198.6	120.53	99.99	98.62
7684	Pig Farm & Tractor	2010	256	2	104.29	50.13	34.99	198.06
7685	Dozer	2009	352	1	92.83	51.33	39.99	132.13
7686	Helicopter Transporter	2009	377	3	76.59	35	39.99	91.52
7687	City Advent Calendar	2009	257	8	47.27	16.6	29.99	57.62
7696	Commuter Jet	2011	108	2	36.54	20	0	
7723	Police Pontoon Plane	2008	215	1	82.67	33.93	39.99	106.73
7724	City Advent Calendar	2008	196	10	42.67	22.83	29.99	42.28
7726	Coast Guard Truck with Speed Boat	2008	361	2	74.73	44	39.99	86.87
7731	Mail Van	2008	66	1	35.73	17.33	7.99	347.18
7732	Air Mail	2008	88	1	40.71	29.67	14.99	171.58
7733	Truck & Forklift	2008	343	2	118.47	50.27	24.99	374.07
7734	Cargo Plane	2008	463	3	207.13	74.6	39.99	417.9
7736	Coast Guard Quad Bike	2008	33	1	12.21	10.6	4.99	144.69
7737	Coast Guard 4WD & Jet Scooter	2008	130	1	27.81	15.33	9.99	178.38
7738	Coast Guard Helicopter & Life Raft	2008	445	4	81.33	41.6	39.99	103.38
7739	Coast Guard Patrol Boat & Tower	2008	444	4	184.53	68.07	59.99	207.60
7741	Police Helicopter	2008	94	1	21.12	9.47	9.99	111.41
7743	Police Command Centre	2008	524	4	92.73	38.8	44.99	106.11
7744	Police Headquarters	2008	953	7	211.56	81	89.99	135.09
7746	Single-Drum Roller	2009	208	2	40.13	24.6	29.99	33.81
7747	Wind Turbine Transport	2009	444	2	88.84	68.2	59.99	48.09
7848	Toys R Us City Truck	2010	356	3	57.29	38.87	49.99	14.60
7890	Ambulance	2006	118	1	30.33	21.47	7.99	279.60
7891	Airport Fire Truck	2006	148	1	39.73	22.8	14.99	165.04
7892	Hospital	2006	382	4	206	78.93	49.99	312.08
7893	Passenger Plane	2006	401	4	271.87	119.5	39.99	579.84
7894	Airport	2006	700	5	285	161.8	79.99	256.29
7895	Switching Tracks	2006	8	0	23.89	18.88	15.99	49.41
7896	Straight and Curved Rails	2006	16	0	45	31.5	15.99	181.43
7898	Cargo Train Deluxe	2006	856	5	352.47	212.47	149.99	135.00
7899	Police Boat	2006	199	3	95.5	47.67	24.99	282.15
7900	Heavy Loader	2006	347	1	97.35	83.87	24.99	289.56
7901	Airplane Mechanic	2006	26	1	24.46	14.25	3.99	513.03
7902	Doctor's Car	2006	66	1	19.73	13.27	5.99	229.38
7903	Rescue Helicopter	2006	249	3	36.07	20.73	19.99	80.44
7904	City Advent Calendar	2006	257	9	10.95	15.25	19.99	-45.22
7905	Building Crane	2006	721	3	349.2	194.67	69.99	398.93
7906	Fireboat	2007	187	3	103.22	37.47	34.99	195.00
7907	City Advent Calendar	2007	232	8	44.39	22.8	24.99	77.63

NUMBER	NAME	YEAR	PIECES	MINIFIGS	NEW	USED	RETAIL	GROWTH%
7936	Level Crossing	2010	142	1	135.56	75.47	19.99	578.14
7937	Train Station	2010	361	4	64.82	43.47	49.99	29.67
7938	Passenger Train	2010	669	3	176.48	122	129.99	35.76
7939	Cargo Train	2010	839	4	207.41	152	179.99	15.23
7942	Off-Road Fire Rescue	2007	131	1	18.96	11	9.99	89.79
7944	Fire Hovercraft	2007	274	3	99.73	39.07	29.99	232.54
7945	Fire Station	2007	600	4	124.73	66.4	59.99	107.92
7990	Cement Mixer	2007	213	1	54.79	24.73	14.99	265.51
7991	Recycle Truck	2007	206	1	44.93	25.93	14.99	199.73
7992	Container Stacker	2007	218	1	48.71	32.27	19.99	143.67
7993	Service Station	2007	402	3	168.8	62.73	39.99	322.11
7994	LEGO City Harbour	2007	659	5	292.87	166.53	89.99	225.45
7996	Train Rail Crossing	2007	4	0	136.2	140.8	24.99	445.02
7997	Train Station	2007	387	5	165.05	79.33	44.99	266.86
7998	Heavy Hauler	2007	332	1	94.2	46.53	34.99	169.22
8398	BBQ Stand	2009	22	1	12.6	8.2	3.99	215.79
8401	City Mini-Figure Collection	2009	60	4	7.97	10.47	9.99	-20.22
8402	Sports Car	2009	68	1	18.72	10.87	9.99	87.39
8403	City House	2010	383	3	81.88	53.4	39.99	104.75
8404	Public Transport	2010	864	6	177.05	109.33	99.99	77.07
850932	Polar Accessory Set	2014	42	2	32.35	0	14.99	115.81
853378	LEGO City Accessory Pack	2012	43	4	19.22	0	14.99	28.22
8866	Train Motor	2009	7	0	17.03	13.71	10.99	54.96
8867	Flexible Train Track	2009	64	0	31.95	21.08	24.99	27.85

CREATOR

NUMBER	NAME	YEAR	PIECES	MINIFIGS	NEW	USED	RETAIL	GROWTH%
30008	Snowman	2009	44	0	13.74	7.2	3.99	244.36
30009	Christmas Tree	2009	51	0	7.83	5.4	3.99	96.24
30023	Lighthouse	2011	25	0	12.24	7.07	2.99	309.36
30025	Clown Fish	2011	59	0	8.79	5.92	3.99	120.30
30028	Wreath	2011	50	0	12.19	4.09	4.99	144.2
30181	Helicopter	2012	53	0	8.14	3	3.5	132.57
30185	Little Eagle	2013	48	0	16.54	4.83	14	18.14
30186	Christmas Tree	2013	51	0	9.41	5	3.99	135.84
30187	Fast Car	2014	56	0	6.49	3.18	3.29	97.26
30197	Snowman	2014	0	0	8.1	0	3.99	103.01
31000	Mini Speeder	2013	65	0	13.26	5.75	6.99	89.70
31001	Mini Skyflyer	2013	62	0	13.23	7.63	6.99	89.27
31002	Super Racer	2013	121	0	19.9	5.68	14.99	32.76
31003	Red Rotors	2013	145	0	23.9	8.45	14.99	59.4
31004	Fierce Flyer	2013	166	0	19.94	8.88	14.99	33.02
31005	Construction Hauler	2013	256	0	24.14	18.2	17.99	34.19
31006	Highway Speedster	2013	286	0	29.27	14.2	24.99	17.13
31007	Power Mech	2013	223	0	23.93	15.73	19.99	19.71
31008	Thunder Wings	2013	235	0	29.72	15.6	19.99	48.67
31009	Small Cottage	2013	271	1	30.38	20.29	24.99	21.5
31010	Tree House	2013	356	1	34.72	35.38	29.99	15.77
31011	Aviation Adventures	2013	618	0	50.06	48.33	59.99	6.55
31012	Family House	2013	756	2	72.45	54.58	69.99	3.51
31013	Red Thunder	2014	66	0	11.93	0	4.99	139.08
31014	Power Digger	2014	64	0	8.67	0	4.99	73.75
31015	Emerald Express	2014	56	0	9.83	2.27	4.99	96.99

NUMBER	NAME	YEAR	PIECES	MINIFIGS	NEW	USED	RETAIL	GROWTH%
31017	Sunset Speeder	2014	119	0	15.59	8.37	12.99	20.02
31018	Highway Cruiser	2014	129	0	18.04	0	12.99	38.88
31019	Forest Animals	2014	272	0	31.39	0	19.99	57.03
31020	Twinblade Adventures	2014	216	0	23.55	0	17.99	30.91
31021	Furry Creatures	2014	285	0	29.27	0	19.99	46.42
31022	Turbo Quad	2014	186	0	27	0	24.99	8.04
31023	Yellow Racers	2014	328	0	28.59	15	29.99	-4.67
31024	Roaring Power	2014	374	0	26.86	17	29.99	0.44
31025	Mountain Hut	2014	550	1	42.82	26.57	39.99	7.08
31026	Bike Shop & Cafe	2014	1,023	3	75.13	59.38	89.99	6.51
40025	New York Taxi	2012	44	0	14.76	12.5	4.99	195.79
40026	Statue Of Liberty	2012	39	0	10	6	4.99	100.40
40108	Balloon Cart	2014	66	2	15.53	7.87	4.99	211.22
4019	Aeroplane	2001	17	0	2.81	1.4	1.99	41.21
4023	Fun and Adventure	2003	55	1	10.13	0	3.99	153.88
4024	Advent Calendar	2003	24	0	35.77	25.11	14.99	138.63
4026	Create Your Dreams	2003	100	0	9.59	5	3.99	140.35
4027	Build and Imagine	2003	100	0	7.8	1	3.99	95.49
4105	Creator Bucket	2002	500	0	22.17	11.33	9.99	121.92
4107	Build Your Dreams	2002	1,000	0	31.11	19.6	19.99	55.63
4116	Animal Adventures Bucket	2001	209	2	10.73	8.67	9.99	7.41
4120	Fun and Cool Transportation	2001	606	2	23.13	21.18	19.99	15.71
4121	All Kinds of Animals	2001	171	2	41.5	18.64	19.99	107.60
4400	Build With Bricks	2003	705	0	38.07	16	19.99	90.45
4408	Animals	2004	202	0	21.22	12.5	9.99	112.41
4415	Auto Pod	2006	56	0	24.21	6.88	3.49	593.70
4416	Robo Pod	2006	65	0	11.74	5.11	3.99	194.24
4417	Aero Pod	2006	60	0	6.5	3.63	3.99	62.91
4418	Dino Pod	2006	55	0	12.58	6.71	3.99	215.29
4496-2	50th Anniversary Tub	2005	1,000	0	46.5	17	19.99	132.62
4837	Mini Trains	2008	73	0	18.73	14.8	4.99	275.35
4838	Mini Vehicles	2008	79	0	17.67	7.33	4.99	254.11
4891	Highway Haulers	2006	209	0	32.4	17.27	9.99	224.32
4892	Prehistoric Power	2006	380	0	99.93	50.93	19.99	399.90
4893	Revvin' Riders	2006	360	0	34.47	22.67	19.99	72.44
4894	Mythical Creatures	2006	588	0	114.19	55.4	29.99	280.76
4895	Motion Power	2006	611	0	61.27	42.47	49.99	22.56
4896	Roaring Roadsters	2006	931	0	136.13	69.73	59.99	126.92
4915	Mini Construction	2007	68	0	17.73	10.53	4.99	255.31
4916	Mini Animals	2007	77	0	11.07	7.27	4.99	121.84
4917	Mini Robots	2007	77	0	13.67	6.4	4.99	173.95
4918	Mini Flyers	2007	78	0	11.4	6.53	4.99	128.46
4924	Advent Calendar	2004	335	0	35.53	20.47	14.99	137.02
4939	Cool Cars	2007	206	0	36.13	16.87	9.99	261.66
4953	Fast Flyers	2007	312	0	66.27	32.8	19.99	231.52
4954	Model Town House	2007	1,174	0	318.47	209.2	69.99	355.02
4955	Big Rig	2007	550	0	102.67	45.93	29.99	242.35
4956	House	2007	731	0	178.6	86.93	49.99	257.27
4957	Ferris Wheel	2007	1,063	0	357.87	184.6	69.99	411.3
4958	Monster Dino	2007	792	0	220	143.67	89.99	144.47
4993	Cool Convertible	2008	648	0	87.88	47.13	44.99	95.33
4994	Fierce Creatures	2008	193	0	44.33	21.4	12.99	241.26

NUMBER	NAME	YEAR	PIECES	MINIFIGS	NEW	USED	RETAIL	GROWTH%
4995	Cargo Copter	2008	272	0	34.13	17.33	19.99	70.74
4996	Beach House	2008	522	0	99.06	45.7	34.99	183.11
4997	Transport Ferry	2008	1279	0	192.13	97.07	69.99	174.51
4998	Stegosaurus	2008	731	0	106.33	59.67	44.99	136.34
5761	Mini Digger	2011	56	0	10.27	5.47	5.99	71.45
5762	Mini Plane	2011	52	0	12.44	7	5.99	107.68
5763	Dune Hopper	2011	137	0	18.44	9.47	12.99	41.96
5764	Rescue Robot	2011	149	0	38.94	17.2	16.99	129.19
5765	Transport Truck	2011	276	0	39.2	16.47	19.99	96.10
5766	Log Cabin	2011	355	1	40.88	26.33	29.99	36.31
5767	Cool Cruiser	2011	621	0	45.91	23.47	39.99	14.80
5770	Lighthouse Island	2011	442	1	85.97	49.53	39.99	114.98
5771	Hillside House	2011	714	1	105.44	72	69.99	50.65
5864	Mini Helicopter	2010	52	0	11.33	8.2	5.99	89.15
5865	Mini Dumper	2010	60	0	12.35	5.87	5.99	106.18
5866	Rotor Rescue	2010	149	0	24.2	12.6	12.99	86.30
5867	Super Speedster	2010	278	0	47.82	28.87	19.99	139.22
5868	Ferocious Creatures	2010	416	0	55.8	31.6	29.99	86.06
5891	Apple Tree House	2010	539	0	66.76	45.22	44.99	48.39
5892	Sonic Boom	2010	539	0	108.68	53.93	59.99	81.16
5893	Off-Road Power	2010	1,061	0	106.92	61.13	89.99	18.81
6162	Building Fun with LEGO	2007	286	0	28.53	16.2	9.99	185.59
6163	A World of LEGO Mosaic	2007	598	0	51.93	23.27	19.99	159.78
66208	Mr. Magorium's Wonder Emporium	2007	324	0	39.13	8.5	19.99	95.75
6741	Mini Jet	2009	63	0	10.37	6	5.99	73.12
6742	Mini Off-Roader	2009	64	0	9.79	7.4	5.99	63.44
6743	Street Speeder	2009	165	0	23.29	11.47	12.99	79.29
6745	Propeller Power	2009	247	0	35.93	18.13	19.99	79.74
6747	Race Rider	2009	266	0	35.73	12.53	19.99	78.74
6751	Fiery Legend	2009	479	0	77.18	47.29	39.99	93.00
6752	Fire Rescue	2009	771	0	74.43	47.53	49.99	48.89
6753	Highway Transport	2009	1,294	0	167.5	103.4	89.99	86.13
6754	Family Home	2009	976	0	136.47	85.13	59.99	127.49
6910	Mini Sports Car	2012	70	0	14.82	4.73	5.99	147.41
6911	Mini Fire Truck	2012	69	0	18.46	6.4	5.99	208.18
6912	Super Soarer	2012	130	0	21.27	7.4	14.99	41.89
6913	Blue Roadster	2012	152	0	22.76	8.93	14.99	51.83
6914	Prehistoric Hunters	2012	191	0	49.17	11.4	17.99	173.32
7291	Street Rebel	2012	196	0	22.27	11.15	19.99	11.41
7292	Propeller Adventures	2012	241	0	32.25	15.07	19.99	61.33
7345	Transport Chopper	2012	383	0	42.94	20.27	34.99	22.72
7346	Seaside House	2012	415	1	49.04	32.4	49.99	.90
7347	Highway Pickup	2012	805	0	71.05	39.53	79.99	1.18
7831	Creator Bucket	2002	200	0	16.5	8.5	4.99	230.66
7876	Cement Truck	2007	44	0	7.56	9.73	3.99	89.47

DINO

NUMBER	NAME	YEAR	PIECES	MINIFIGS	NEW	USED	RETAIL	GROWTH%
5882	Ambush Attack	2012	80	1	45.24	15.56	11.99	277.31
5883	Tower Takedown	2012	136	1	51.32	25.81	19.99	156.73
5884	Raptor Chase	2012	259	2	68.31	35.8	29.99	127.78
5885	Triceratops Trapper	2012	271	2	78.64	40.53	49.99	57.31

NUMBER	NAME	YEAR	PIECES	MINIFIGS	NEW	USED	RETAIL	GROWTH%
5886	T-Rex Hunter	2012	480	2	144.27	75.05	69.99	106.13
5887	Dino Defense HQ	2012	793	4	291.46	179.53	99.99	191.49
5888	Ocean Interceptor	2012	222	2	81.82	20.27	34.99	133.84

DISCOVERY								
10029	Lunar Lander	2003	453	2	355.13	168.6	39.99	788.05
7467	International Space Station	2003	162	0	139	53.53	14.99	827.28
7468	Saturn V Moon Mission	2003	178	0	191.4	71.27	19.99	857.48
7469	Mission To Mars	2003	418	0	79.87	48.8	29.99	166.32
7470	Space Shuttle Discovery-STS-31	2003	828	0	175.33	76.33	49.99	250.73
7471	Mars Exploration Rover	2003	870	0	177.93	97.4	89.99	97.72

DISNEY PRINCESS

NUMBER	NAME	YEAR	PIECES	MINIFIGS	NEW	USED	RETAIL	GROWTH%
30116	Rapunzel at the Marketplace	2014	37	1	7.57	0	4.99	51.70
41050	Ariel's Amazing Treasures	2014	77	1	18.33	0	12.99	41.11
41051	Merida's Highland Games	2014	145	1	24.31	12.5	19.99	21.61
41052	Ariel's Magical Kiss	2014	250	2	29.76	22.4	29.99	-0.77
41053	Cinderella's Dream Carriage	2014	274	1	32.13	21.4	29.99	7.14
41054	Rapunzel's Creativity Tower	2014	299	2	41.85	39	39.99	4.65
41055	Cinderella's Romantic Castle	2014	646	2	70.33	43	69.99	0.49

FACTORY								
10183	Hobby Trains	2007	1,080	0	274.79	185.33	99.99	174.82
10191	Star Justice	2008	895	8	76.73	75	99.99	-23.26
10192	Space Skulls	2008	956	4	51.77	21.07	99.99	-48.22
10200	Custom Car Garage	2008	893	4	84.87	58.73	69.99	21.26
5524	Airport	2005	607	0	51.53	33.9	39.99	28.86
5525	Amusement Park	2005	1,344	0	68.4	28.43	69.99	-2.27
5526	Skyline	2005	2,747	0	437.27	188.2	129.99	236.39

FRIENDS								
30101	Skateboarder	2012	28	1	11.76	6.33	4.99	135.67
30102	Desk	2012	26	1	6.23	7.67	3.97	56.93
30103	Car	2012	32	1	11.26	8	3.97	183.63
30105	Mailbox	2012	41	1	7.61	7.17	3.99	90.73
30106	Ice Cream Stand	2013	34	1	7.13	4.27	4.99	42.89
30107	Birthday Party	2013	39	1	7.53	4.33	4.99	50.90
30108	Summer Picnic	2013	33	1	6.39	4.33	4.99	28.06

NUMBER	NAME	YEAR	PIECES	MINIFIGS	NEW	USED	RETAIL	GROWTH%
30112	Flower Stand	2014	33	1	10.06	4	4.99	101.60
30113	Stephanie's Bakery Stand	2014	28	1	6.91	0	5.59	23.61
30115	Jungle Boat	2014	31	1	7.53	0	4.99	50.90
3061	City Park Cafe	2012	222	2	48.98	28.22	34.99	39.98
3063	Heartlake Flying Club	2012	195	1	33.94	4.71	19.99	69.78
3065	Olivia's Tree House	2012	191	1	48.24	27.13	19.99	141.32
3183	Stephanie's Cool Convertible	2012	130	1	39.26	15.13	14.99	161.91
3184	Adventure Camper	2012	309	2	55.58	32.6	34.99	58.85
3185	Summer Riding Camp	2012	1,112	4	172.63	94.53	99.99	72.65
3186	Emma's Horse Trailer	2012	233	1	45.58	25.07	24.99	82.39
3187	Butterfly Beauty Shop	2012	221	2	104.44	41.8	24.99	317.93
3188	Heartlake Vet	2012	343	2	109.65	44.8	44.99	143.72
3189	Heartlake Stables	2012	401	2	86.22	50.73	49.99	72.47
3315	Olivia's House	2012	695	3	70.92	46	74.99	-5.43
3316	Friends Advent Calendar	2012	193	2	52.9	46.43	29.99	76.39
3930	Stephanie's Outdoor Bakery	2012	45	1	11.27	7.27	6.99	61.23
3931	Emma's Splash Pool	2012	43	1	15.85	9	5.99	164.61
3932	Andrea's Stage	2012	87	1	23.38	11.6	9.99	134.03
3933	Olivia's Invention Workshop	2012	81	1	35.13	14.2	9.99	251.65
3934	Mia's Puppy House	2012	64	1	30.89	12.73	9.99	209.21
3935	Stephanie's Pet Patrol	2012	73	1	22.81	10.07	9.99	128.33
3936	Emma's Fashion Design Studio	2012	79	1	35.8	16.4	9.99	258.36
3937	Olivia's Speedboat	2012	65	1	19.75	4.47	9.99	97.70
3938	Andrea's Bunny House	2012	62	1	17.12	2.91	9.99	71.37
3939	Mia's Bedroom	2012	85	1	21.56	10.6	9.99	115.82
3942	Heartlake Dog Show	2012	183	1	69.31	28.4	19.99	246.72
41000	Water Scooter Fun	2012	28	1	8.86	5.75	6.99	26.75
41001	Mia's Magic Tricks	2012	90	1	12.62	8.33	9.99	26.33
41002	Emma's Karate Class	2012	93	1	14.67	18.8	9.99	46.85
41003	Olivia's Newborn Foal	2012	70	1	16.88	7.59	9.99	68.97
41004	Rehearsal Stage	2012	198	1	20.37	15	19.99	1.90
41005	Heartlake High	2013	487	3	82.09	45.25	49.99	64.21
41006	Downtown Bakery	2013	253	2	46.91	0	29.99	56.42
41007	Heartlake Pet Salon	2013	242	2	35.17	22.6	29.99	17.27
41008	Heartlake City Pool	2013	423	2	45.35	27.87	39.99	13.40
41009	Andrea's Bedroom	2013	75	1	15.76	9.5	9.99	57.76
41010	Olivia's Beach Buggy	2013	94	1	12.36	9	9.99	23.72
41013	Emma's Sports Car	2013	159	1	23.4	9.33	14.99	56.10
41015	Dolphin Cruiser	2013	612	3	63.37	54.87	69.99	-9.46
41016	Advent Calendar	2013	213	2	44.72	0	29.99	49.12
41017	Squirrel's Tree House	2013	41	0	13.41	5.58	4.99	168.74
41023	Fawn's Forest	2013	35	0	21.2	0	4.99	324.85
41024	Parrot's Perch	2013	32	0	7.04	0	4.99	41.08
41025	Puppy's Playhouse	2013	39	0	8.57	0	4.99	71.74
41026	Sunshine Harvest	2014	233	1	21.32	17.33	19.99	6.65
41027	Mia's Lemonade Stand	2014	112	1	16.42	7	9.99	64.36
41028	Emma's Lifeguard Post	2014	78	1	13.76	0	9.99	37.74
41029	Stephanie's New Born Lamb	2014	78	1	14.31	0	9.99	43.24
41030	Olivia's Ice Cream Bike	2014	98	1	12.48	4	9.99	24.92
41031	Andrea's Mountain Hut	2014	119	1	13.77	0	9.99	37.84
41032	First Aid Jungle Bike	2014	156	1	19.13	10.5	14.99	27.62
41033	Jungle Falls Rescue	2014	183	1	25.76	17.6	19.99	28.86

NUMBER	NAME	YEAR	PIECES	MINIFIGS	NEW	USED	RETAIL	GROWTH%
41034	Summer Caravan	2014	297	2	32.28	0	29.99	7.64
41035	Heartlake Juice Bar	2014	277	2	34.5	25.5	29.99	15.04
41036	Jungle Bridge Rescue	2014	365	2	32.53	18	29.99	8.47
41037	Stephanie's Beach House	2014	369	2	35.4	31.63	39.99	1.48
41038	Jungle Rescue Base	2014	473	2	57.88	39.67	59.99	-3.52
41039	Sunshine Ranch	2014	721	2	62.67	48.78	69.99	0.46
41040	Friends Advent Calendar	2014	228	2	36.33	0	29.99	21.14
41041	Turtle's Little Paradise	2014	43	0	6.12	0	3.99	53.38
41042	Tiger's Beautiful Temple	2014	42	0	7.05	0	3.99	76.69
41043	Penguin's Playground	2014	46	0	7.82	0	3.99	95.99
41044	Macaw's Fountain	2014	39	0	15	0	3.99	275.94
41045	Orangutan's Banana Tree	2014	37	0	5.94	0	3.99	48.87
41046	Brown Bear's River	2014	37	0	7.38	0	3.99	84.96
41047	Seal's Little Rock	2014	37	0	25	0	3.99	526.57
41049	Panda's Bamboo	2014	47	0	3.6	0	3.99	-9.77
41056	Heartlake News Van	2014	278	2	39.8	19	24.99	59.26
41057	Heartlake Horse Show	2014	355	2	55.05	0	39.99	37.66
41058	Heartlake Shopping Mall	2014	1,120	4	104.78	80	109.99	-4.74
41059	Jungle Tree House	2014	320	1	41.08	25	29.99	36.98
5000245	Stephanie	2012	5	1	5.4	0	4.99	8.22
850581	Brick Calendar	2013	140	0	25.71	0	14.99	71.51
850967	Jungle Accessory Set	2014	0	1	24.08	0	14.99	60.64
853393	LEGO Friends Picture Frame	2012	49	0	14.9	27	14.99	-0.60

HARRY POTTER

NUMBER	NAME	YEAR	PIECES	MINIFIGS	NEW	USED	RETAIL	GROWTH%
10132	Motorized Hogwarts Express	2004	708	4	434.53	335.47	119.99	262.14
10217	Diagon Alley	2011	2,025	12	314.76	242.16	149.99	109.85
30110	Trolley	2011	17	1	16.06	7.16	4.99	221.84
30111	The Lab	2011	34	1	7.43	6.93	3.99	86.22
40028	Mini Hogwarts Express	2011	64	0	9.08	8.29	3.99	127.57
4701	Sorting Hat	2001	48	1	51.58	24.19	6.99	637.91
4702	The Final Challenge	2001	60	2	47.44	28.44	9.99	374.87
4704	The Room of the Winged Keys	2001	175	3	71.38	38.2	19.99	257.08
4705	Snape's Class	2001	163	3	62.93	41.63	19.99	214.81
4706	Forbidden Corridor	2001	238	3	96.93	65.18	29.99	223.21
4707	Hagrid's Hut	2001	299	2	92.13	51.73	29.99	207.20
4708	Hogwarts Express	2001	410	3	204.27	99.57	49.99	308.62
4709	Hogwarts Castle	2001	682	9	258.07	187.31	89.99	186.78
4711	Flying Lesson	2002	23	2	26.4	15.07	3.99	561.65
4712	Troll on the Loose	2002	71	2	41.27	25.8	9.99	313.11
4714	Gringott's Bank	2002	250	4	92.53	45.81	29.99	208.54
4719	Quality Quidditch Supplies	2003	120	1	46.8	29.73	9.99	368.47
4720	Knockturn Alley	2003	209	2	97.33	59.13	19.99	386.89
4721	Hogwarts Classrooms	2001	73	1	50.8	31	9.99	408.51
4722	Gryffindor House	2001	68	1	51.75	22.87	9.99	418.02
4723	Diagon Alley Shops	2001	80	1	57.4	34.19	9.99	474.57
4726	Quidditch Practice	2002	128	3	51.53	33.27	12.99	296.69
4727	Aragog in the Dark Forest	2002	178	2	41.89	28.16	19.99	109.55
4728	Escape from Privet Drive	2002	278	3	112.33	67.56	29.99	274.56
4729	Dumbledore's Office	2002	446	3	162.67	88.72	49.99	225.41
4730	The Chamber of Secrets	2002	591	5	223.13	127.52	69.99	218.80
4731	Dobby's Release	2002	70	2	28.6	21.2	6.99	309.16

NUMBER	NAME	YEAR	PIECES	MINIFIGS	NEW	USED	RETAIL	GROWTH%
4733	The Dueling Club	2002	129	4	54.72	33.94	19.99	173.74
4735	Slytherin	2002	90	3	55.67	31.11	9.99	457.26
4736	Freeing Dobby	2010	73	3	27.23	18.84	10.99	147.77
4737	Quidditch Match	2010	153	5	90.37	53.47	19.99	352.08
4738	Hagrid's Hut	2010	442	4	127.87	78.12	39.99	219.75
4750	Draco's Encounter with Buckbeak	2004	36	1	47.27	32.17	7.99	491.61
4751	Harry and the Marauder's Map	2004	109	3	43.87	29.4	9.99	339.14
4752	Professor Lupin's Classroom	2004	156	3	75.67	56.4	19.99	278.54
4753	Sirius Black's Escape	2004	188	3	101.47	59.93	19.99	407.60
4754	Hagrid's Hut	2004	302	2	90.27	59.73	29.99	201.00
4755	Knight Bus	2004	243	2	66.73	47.53	29.99	122.51
4756	Shrieking Shack	2004	444	4	273.6	170.27	49.99	447.31
4757	Hogwarts Castle	2004	944	9	325	206.8	89.99	261.15
4758	Hogwarts Express	2004	389	4	184.67	95.06	39.99	361.79
4762	Rescue from the Merpeople	2005	175	5	158.47	118.21	19.99	692.75
4766	Graveyard Duel	2005	548	8	285.6	141.86	29.99	852.32
4767	Harry and the Hungarian Horntail	2005	265	3	278.33	185.53	29.99	828.08
4768	The Durmstrang Ship	2005	550	2	220.81	120	49.99	341.71
4840	The Burrow	2010	568	6	198.64	130.77	59.99	231.12
4841	Hogwarts Express	2010	646	5	254.61	162.38	79.99	218.30
4842	Hogwarts Castle	2010	1,290	11	378.21	275.93	129.99	190.95
4865	The Forbidden Forest	2011	64	4	45.2	26.13	11.99	276.98
4866	Knight Bus	2011	281	3	79.75	53.09	34.99	127.92
4867	Battle For Hogwarts	2011	466	7	176.36	107.78	49.99	252.79
5378	Hogwarts Castle	2007	943	9	196.96	304.73	89.99	118.87

HERO FACTORY

NUMBER	NAME	YEAR	PIECES	MINIFIGS	NEW	USED	RETAIL	GROWTH%
2063	Stormer 2.0	2011	31	0	35.5	25.47	7.99	344.31
2065	Furno 2.0	2011	30	0	14.47	13.8	7.99	81.10
2067	Evo 2.0	2011	31	0	14	21.53	7.99	75.22
2068	Nex 2.0	2011	31	0	30.06	17.93	7.99	276.22
2141	Surge 2.0	2011	30	0	29.88	26.27	7.99	273.97
2142	Breez 2.0	2011	29	0	16.5	7.67	7.99	106.51
2143	Rocka 3.0	2011	30	0	13.85	12.38	7.99	73.34
2144	Nex 3.0	2011	29	0	12.68	10.07	7.99	58.70
2145	Stormer 3.0	2011	31	0	22.5	12.6	7.99	181.60
2183	Stringer 3.0	2011	30	0	16.85	12.31	7.99	110.89
2191	Furno 3.0	2011	28	0	32.15	17.07	7.99	302.38
2192	Drilldozer	2011	61	0	40.5	20.27	12.99	211.78
2193	Jetbug	2011	63	0	25.38	17.33	12.99	95.38
2194	Nitroblast	2011	57	0	29	14.94	12.99	123.25
2231	Waspix	2011	48	0	28.47	15.73	12.99	119.17
2232	Raw-Jaw	2011	52	0	32.53	16.6	12.99	150.42
2233	Fangz	2011	55	0	32.27	18.13	12.99	148.42
2235	Fire Lord	2011	125	0	74.83	39.53	19.99	274.34
2236	Scorpio	2011	104	0	41.38	19.67	24.99	65.59
2282	Rocka XL	2011	174	0	65.88	42.38	24.99	163.63
2283	Witch Doctor	2011	331	0	115	59.33	29.99	283.46
44000	FURNO XL	2013	103	0	23.23	12.75	19.99	16.21
44001	PYROX	2013	50	0	20.62	12.15	12.99	58.74
44002	ROCKA	2013	43	0	18.98	9.33	9.99	89.99

NUMBER	NAME	YEAR	PIECES	MINIFIGS	NEW	USED	RETAIL	GROWTH%
44003	SCAROX	2013	46	0	14.67	5	9.99	46.85
44004	BULK	2013	50	0	18.75	9.5	9.99	87.69
44005	BRUIZER	2013	62	0	13.47	8.67	12.99	3.70
44006	BREEZ	2013	49	0	15.13	8.5	9.99	51.45
44007	OGRUM	2013	59	0	12.68	0	12.99	-2.39
44008	SURGE	2013	66	0	27.04	0	12.99	108.16
44009	DRAGON BOLT	2013	149	0	39	16	19.99	95.10
44010	STORMER	2013	69	0	23.87	0	12.99	83.76
44011	FROST BEAST	2013	60	0	22.08	9	12.99	69.98
44012	EVO	2013	51	0	18.97	0	9.99	89.89
44013	AQUAGON	2013	41	0	15.81	7	9.99	58.26
44014	JET ROCKA	2013	290	0	29.85	17.8	34.99	4.69
44015	EVO Walker	2014	51	0	13.05	0	9.99	30.63
44016	JAW Beast vs. STORMER	2014	49	0	15.3	0	9.99	53.15
44017	STORMER Freeze Machine	2014	88	0	23.06	54	14.99	53.8
44018	FURNO Jet Machine	2014	79	0	21.76	0	14.99	45.16
44019	ROCKA Stealth Machine	2014	89	0	19.89	0	14.99	32.69
44020	FLYER Beast vs. BREEZ	2014	91	0	18.56	6.41	14.99	23.82
44021	SPLITTER Beast vs. FURNO & EVO	2014	108	0	22.45	0	19.99	12.31
44022	EVO XL Machine	2014	193	0	26.06	0	24.99	4.28
44023	ROCKA Crawler	2014	49	0	19.85	0	9.00	98.70
44024	TUNNELER Beast vs. SURGE	2014	59	0	21.57	0	9.99	115.92
44026	CRYSTAL Beast vs. BULK	2014	83	0	25.56	0	14.99	70.51
44028	SURGE & ROCKA Combat Machine	2014	188	0	36.21	13.5	24.99	44.90
44029	"Queen Beast vs. Furno, Evo and Stormer"	2014	217	4	51.2	0	34.99	46.33
6200	Double Pack	2012	45	0	23.37	12.6	8.99	159.96
6200-2	Evo	2012	36	0	16.1	8.92	8.99	79.09
6201	Toxic Reapa	2012	42	0	24.7	11.5	8.99	174.75
6202	Rocka	2012	55	0	41.53	12.93	12.99	219.71
6203	Black Phantom	2012	124	0	116	52.47	19.99	480.29
6216	Jawblade	2012	45	0	41.07	15.47	8.99	356.84
6217	Surge	2012	39	0	31.93	13.44	8.99	255.17
6218	Splitface	2012	50	0	40.53	6.56	12.99	212.01
6221	Nex	2012	39	0	16.58	9.92	8.99	84.43
6222	Core Hunter	2012	51	0	29.36	15.2	12.99	126.02
6223	Bulk	2012	61	0	15.65	12.8	12.99	20.48
6227	Breez	2012	55	0	16.14	11.3	12.99	24.25
6228	Thornraxx	2012	44	0	18.85	10.33	8.99	109.68
6229	XT4	2012	39	0	18.5	8.39	8.99	105.78
6230	Stormer XL	2012	89	0	33.53	18.53	24.99	34.17
6231	Speeda Demon	2012	192	0	39.94	23.33	34.99	14.15
6282	Stringer	2012	42	0	24.58	10	8.99	173.41
6283	Voltix	2012	61	0	18	5.8	12.99	38.57
6293	Furno	2012	56	0	45.93	16.4	12.99	253.58
7145	Von Nebula	2010	156	0	21.15	56.4	19.99	5.80
7147	XPlode	2010	45	0	20.76	11.8	12.99	59.82
7148	Meltdown	2010	50	0	35.14	17.87	12.99	170.52
7156	Corroder	2010	40	0	29.33	15.2	12.99	125.7
7157	Thunder	2010	47	0	36.38	16.63	12.99	180.06

223

NUMBER	NAME	YEAR	PIECES	MINIFIGS	NEW	USED	RETAIL	GROWTH%
7158	Furno Bike	2010	165	0	58.29	39.6	29.99	94.36
7160	Drop Ship	2010	390	0	59.63	23.53	49.99	19.28
7162	Rotor	2010	145	0	56.4	33.13	19.99	182.14
7164	Preston Stormer	2010	17	0	20.63	18.87	7.99	158.20
7165	Natalie Breez	2010	19	0	16.58	13.4	7.99	107.51
7167	William Furno	2010	19	0	16.69	18.87	7.99	108.89
7168	Duncan Bulk	2010	17	0	32.5	15.6	7.99	306.76
7169	Mark Surge	2010	19	0	19.2	15.88	7.99	140.30
7170	Jim Stringer	2010	17	0	25.87	17.13	7.99	223.78
7179	Duncan Bulk and Vapour	2010	89	0	63.35	38.27	24.99	153.50

IDEAS

NUMBER	NAME	YEAR	PIECES	MINIFIGS	NEW	USED	RETAIL	GROWTH%
21100	Shinkai 6500 Submarine	2010	412	0	408.5	199.17	49.99	717.16
21101	Hayabusa	2012	369	1	109.33	60.75	49.99	118.70
21102	Minecraft Micro World	2012	480	0	46	25	34.99	31
21103	The DeLorean Time Machine	2013	401	2	45.55	32.13	34.99	30.18
21104	NASA Mars Science Laboratory Curiosity Rover	2014	295	0	99	67	29.99	230
21108	Ghostbusters ECTO	2014	508	4	50.89	41.8	49.99	1.80
21109	Exo-Suit	2014	321	2	42.06	43.13	34.99	20.21
21110	Research Institute	2014	165	3	51.04	0	19.99	155.33

INDIANA JONES

NUMBER	NAME	YEAR	PIECES	MINIFIGS	NEW	USED	RETAIL	GROWTH%
7195	Ambush In Cairo	2009	79	4	50	30.53	10.99	354.96
7196	Chauchilla Cemetery Battle	2009	187	5	81.82	47.07	19.99	309.30
7197	Venice Canal Chase	2009	420	4	63.36	46.87	39.99	58.44
7198	Fighter Plane Attack	2009	384	3	95.8	57.93	49.99	91.64
7199	The Temple of Doom	2009	652	6	227	157.8	89.99	152.2
7620	Indiana Jones Motorcycle Chase	2008	79	3	55.81	31	9.99	458.66
7621	Indiana Jones and the Lost Tomb	2008	277	3	97.42	49.63	19.99	387.34
7622	Race for the Stolen Treasure	2008	272	4	139.47	68.4	29.99	365.06
7623	Temple Escape	2008	554	6	200.69	121.87	59.99	234.54
7624	Jungle Duel	2008	90	3	53.33	34.73	9.99	433.83
7625	River Chase	2008	234	4	79.87	39.4	19.99	299.55
7626	Jungle Cutter	2008	511	4	82.61	40.2	39.99	106.58
7627	Temple of the Crystal Skull	2008	929	10	149.86	91.33	79.99	87.35
7628	Peril in Peru	2008	625	6	124.79	69.27	49.99	149.63
7682	Shanghai Chase	2009	244	5	94.07	49.47	29.99	213.67
7683	Fight on the Flying Wing	2009	376	4	154.5	76.27	39.99	286.35

LEGENDS OF CHIMA

NUMBER	NAME	YEAR	PIECES	MINIFIGS	NEW	USED	RETAIL	GROWTH%
30250	Ewar's Acro Fighter	2013	33	1	13.27	6.22	3.99	232.58
30251	Winzar's Pack Patrol	2013	38	1	5	4.27	3.99	25.31
30252	Crug's Swamp Jet	2013	23	1	7.24	5	4.99	45.09
30253	Leonidas' Jungle Dragster	2013	30	1	7.72	2.33	3.99	93.48
30254	Razcal's Double-Crosser	2013	36	1	7.61	4.06	3.97	91.69
30264	Frax's Phoenix Flyer	2014	0	1	6	0	3.99	50.38
30265	Worriz Fire Bike	2014	0	1	4.46	1.95	4.69	-4.90
70000	Razcal's Glider	2013	109	1	18.09	11.41	11.99	50.88
70001	Crawley's Claw Ripper	2013	139	2	25.46	10.4	14.99	69.85
70002	Lennox' Lion Attack	2013	230	2	37.26	15.53	24.99	49.10

NUMBER	NAME	YEAR	PIECES	MINIFIGS	NEW	USED	RETAIL	GROWTH%
70003	Eris' Eagle Interceptor	2013	348	3	35.17	23.78	34.99	0.51
70004	Wakz' Pack Tracker	2013	297	3	24.55	18.87	29.99	8.14
70005	Laval's Royal Fighter	2013	417	3	36.14	21.13	39.99	-9.63
70006	Cragger's Command Ship	2013	609	6	61.94	44	79.99	-22.57
70007	Eglor's Twin Bike	2013	223	2	39.91	30.33	24.99	59.70
70008	Gorzan's Gorilla Striker	2013	505	4	43.63	29.22	49.99	2.72
70009	Worriz' Combat Lair	2013	664	6	41.97	21.35	69.99	-40.03
70010	The Lion CHI Temple	2013	1,258	7	144.53	94.8	119.99	20.45
70011	Eagles' Castle	2013	369	3	34.08	0	39.99	4.78
70012	Razar's CHI Raider	2013	412	3	56.59	27.92	39.99	41.51
70013	Equila's Ultra Striker	2013	339	3	58.03	22.89	39.99	45.11
70014	The Croc Swamp Hideout	2013	647	5	69.53	49.33	69.99	-0.66
70100	Ring of Fire	2013	83	1	18.58	3.5	14.99	23.95
70101	Target Practice	2013	101	1	15.44	6.25	14.99	3.00
70102	CHI Waterfall	2013	106	1	20.62	0	14.99	37.56
70103	Boulder Bowling	2013	93	1	15.74	13	14.99	5.00
70104	Jungle Gates	2013	81	1	11.35	0	14.99	-24.28
70105	Nest Dive	2013	97	1	18.42	0	14.99	22.88
70106	Ice Tower	2013	101	1	12.25	0	14.99	8.28
70107	Skunk Attack	2013	97	1	13.06	10.8	14.99	2.88
70108	Royal Roost	2013	105	1	18.96	0	14.99	26.48
70109	Whirling Vines	2013	77	1	23.35	0	14.99	55.77
70110	Tower Target	2013	92	1	12.11	0	14.99	9.21
70111	Swamp Jump	2013	91	1	27.65	0	14.99	84.46
70113	CHI Battles	2013	93	2	14.91	7.09	19.99	-25.41
70114	Sky Joust	2013	117	2	22.7	0	19.99	13.56
70115	Ultimate Speedor Tournament	2013	246	0	29.5	20.44	29.99	.63
70123	Lion Legend Beast	2014	120	0	11.21	9	9.99	12.21
70124	Eagle Legend Beast	2014	104	1	16.89	0	9.99	69.07
70125	Gorilla Legend Beast	2014	106	1	13.84	0	9.99	38.54
70126	Crocodile Legend Beast	2014	122	1	10.42	4	9.99	4.30
70127	Wolf Legend Beast	2014	110	1	15.6	6.77	9.99	56.16
70128	Braptor's Wing Striker	2014	146	2	24.91	0	14.99	66.18
70129	Lavertus' Twin Blade	2014	183	2	20.3	12.5	19.99	1.55
70130	Sparratus' Spider Stalker	2014	292	2	37.6	0	24.99	50.46
70131	Rogon's Rock Flinger	2014	257	3	47.92	0	29.99	59.79
70132	Scorm's Scorpion Stinger	2014	434	3	65.61	0	39.99	64.07
70133	Spinlyn's Cavern	2014	407	3	69.05	0	39.99	72.67
70134	Lavertus' Outland Base	2014	684	4	52.69	40.5	59.99	2.17
70135	Cragger's Fire Striker	2014	380	3	78.15	35.5	39.99	95.42
70137	Bat Strike	2014	101	1	19.23	0	12.99	48.04
70140	Stinger Duel	2014	93	2	20.5	0	19.99	2.55
70141	Vardy's Ice Vulture Glider	2014	217	2	32.45	20	19.99	62.33
70142	Eris' Fire Eagle Flyer	2014	330	3	47.78	0	29.99	59.32
70143	Sir Fangar's Sabre-Tooth Walker	2014	415	3	65.61	0	39.99	64.07
70144	Laval's Fire Lion	2014	450	3	64.67	0	49.99	29.37
70145	Maula's Ice Mammoth Stomper	2014	604	6	129.78	0	89.99	44.22
70146	Flying Phoenix Fire Temple	2014	1,301	7	108	86	119.99	-12
70147	Sir Fangar's Ice Fortress	2014	0	5	109.32	65	69.99	56.19
70150	Flaming Claws	2014	74	1	20.8	0	12.99	60.12
70151	Frozen Spikes	2014	77	1	22.3	0	12.99	71.67
70155	Inferno Pit	2014	74	1	21.14	0	12.99	62.74

NUMBER	NAME	YEAR	PIECES	MINIFIGS	NEW	USED	RETAIL	GROWTH%
70156	Fire vs. Ice	2014	102	2	13.22	0	19.99	-33.87
70200	CHI Laval	2013	55	0	22.46	0	14.99	49.83
70201	CHI Eris	2013	67	0	22.5	0	14.99	50.10
70202	CHI Gorzan	2013	59	0	20.62	0	14.99	37.56
70203	CHI Cragger	2013	65	0	13.64	0	14.99	-9.01
70204	CHI Worriz	2013	55	0	13.26	0	14.99	1.54
70205	CHI Razar	2013	68	0	17.5	0	14.99	16.74
70206	CHI Laval	2014	49	0	25	0	14.99	66.78
70208	Panther - Prel	2014	59	0	24	0	14.99	60.11
70209	CHI Mungus	2014	64	0	25	10	14.99	66.78
70210	CHI Vardy	2014	68	0	14	0	14.99	-6.60
70211	CHI Fluminox	2014	91	0	36	0	19.99	80.09
70212	CHI Sir Fangar	2014	97	0	29	0	19.99	45.07

LONE RANGER

NUMBER	NAME	YEAR	PIECES	MINIFIGS	NEW	USED	RETAIL	GROWTH%
30260	Lone Ranger's Pump Car	2013	24	1	12.47	10.67	3.99	212.53
30261	Tonto's Campfire	2013	20	1	6.98	7.5	4.99	39.88
79106	Cavalry Builder Set	2013	69	4	21.13	13	12.99	62.66
79107	Comanche Camp	2013	161	3	24.75	17.13	19.99	23.81
79108	Stagecoach Escape	2013	279	5	36.71	29.47	29.99	22.41
79109	Colby City Showdown	2013	587	5	48.27	32.73	49.99	-3.44
79110	Silver Mine Shootout	2013	644	5	51.83	45.33	69.99	-25.95
79111	Constitution Train Chase	2013	699	7	101.98	72.6	99.99	1.99

LORD OF THE RINGS

NUMBER	NAME	YEAR	PIECES	MINIFIGS	NEW	USED	RETAIL	GROWTH%
10237	Tower of Orthanc	2013	2,359	5	237.19	182.93	199.99	18.60
30210	Frodo w/cooking corner	2012	33	1	8.74	6.38	3.99	119.05
30211	Uruk-Hai w/Ballista	2012	21	1	10.5	6.31	4	162.50
30212	Mirkwood Elf Guard	2012	27	1	22.6	12.41	4.99	352.91
30213	Gandalf at Dol Guldur	2012	31	1	8.05	4.12	4.99	61.32
30216	Lake-town Guard	2013	31	1	9.51	6	4.99	90.58
79000	Riddles for the Ring	2012	105	2	14.47	8.2	9.99	44.84
79001	Escape from Mirkwood Spiders	2012	298	4	30.86	19.4	29.99	2.90
79002	Attack of the Wargs	2012	400	5	42.21	31.6	49.99	5.56
79003	An Unexpected Gathering	2012	652	6	66.87	47.8	69.99	-4.46
79004	Barrel Escape	2012	334	5	38.99	27.73	39.99	-2.50
79005	The Wizard Battle	2013	113	2	16.86	12.27	12.99	29.79
79006	The Council of Elrond	2013	243	4	24.98	15.67	29.99	6.71
79007	Battle at the Black Gate	2013	656	6	38.2	37.07	59.99	-36.32
79008	Pirate Ship Ambush	2013	756	9	77.18	59.4	99.99	-22.81
79010	The Goblin King Battle	2012	841	8	71.01	58.27	99.99	-28.98
79011	Dol Guldur Ambush	2013	217	3	16.95	18.08	19.99	5.21
79012	Mirkwood Elf Army	2013	276	6	46.5	30.29	29.99	55.05
79013	Lake Town Chase	2013	470	5	50.94	45	49.99	1.90
79014	Dol Guldur Battle	2013	797	6	37.58	52	69.99	-46.31
79015	Witch-King Battle	2014	101	3	23.2	0	14.99	54.77
79016	Attack on Lake-town	2014	313	5	48.58	0	29.99	61.99
79017	The Battle of Five Armies	2014	472	7	69.38	0	59.99	15.65
79018	The Lonely Mountain	2014	866	5	128	107	129.99	0
9469	Gandalf Arrives	2012	83	2	19.49	11.33	12.99	50.04
9470	Shelob Attacks	2012	227	3	35.49	21.87	19.99	77.54
9471	Uruk-Hai Army	2012	257	6	44.82	32.47	29.99	49.45

NUMBER	NAME	YEAR	PIECES	MINIFIGS	NEW	USED	RETAIL	GROWTH%
9472	Attack On Weathertop	2012	430	5	58.03	38.2	59.99	-3.27
9473	The Mines of Moria	2012	776	9	74.47	60.73	79.99	-6.90
9474	The Battle Of Helm's Deep	2012	1,368	8	167.77	135.8	129.99	29.06
9476	The Orc Forge	2012	366	4	59.38	41.13	39.99	48.49
COMCON 033	Micro Scale Bag End	2013	130	1	89.8	41	39.99	124.56

MINECRAFT

NUMBER	NAME	YEAR	PIECES	MINIFIGS	NEW	USED	RETAIL	GROWTH%
21105	Minecraft Micro World: The Village	2013	466	0	51.11	29.4	34.99	46.07
21106	Minecraft Micro World: The Nether	2013	469	0	45.54	30.55	34.99	30.15
21107	Microworld: The End	2014	440	0	39.12	0	34.99	11.80
21113	The Cave	2014	249	2	43.88	15	19.99	119.51
21114	The Farm	2014	262	2	52.28	0	29.99	74.32
21115	The First Night	2014	408	2	56.24	0	39.99	40.64
21116	Crafting Box	2014	518	0	84.84	70	49.99	69.71
21117	The Ender Dragon	2014	634	0	81.87	53	69.99	16.97
21118	The Mine	2014	922	0	155.71	0	109.99	41.57

MISCELLANEOUS

NUMBER	NAME	YEAR	PIECES	MINIFIGS	NEW	USED	RETAIL	GROWTH%
21200	Life of George	2011	146	0	17.88	17.5	29.99	-40.38
21201	Life Of George	2012	146	0	18.44	11.67	29.99	-38.51
3300014	2012 Christmas Set	2012	109	4	36.26	27.07	14.99	141.89
40032	Witch	2012	71	0	11.27	0	4.99	125.85
40033	Turkey	2012	52	0	9.65	6	4.99	93.39
40034	Christmas Train	2012	82	0	39.12	11.73	4.99	683.97
40035	Rocking Horse	2012	49	0	10.03	8	4.99	101.00
40077	Geoffrey	2013	90	0	6.92	4.38	4.99	38.68
40118	Buildable Brick Box 2x2	2014	203	1	31.56	0	16.99	85.76
40180	Bricktober Theater	2014	164	0	21.58	0	19.99	7.95
40181	Bricktober Pizza Place	2014	0	0	24.64	26.31	19.99	23.26
40182	Bricktober Fire Station	2014	0	0	22.52	15	19.99	12.66
40183	Bricktober Town Hall	2014	0	0	22.86	19.95	19.99	14.36
41011	Stephanie's Soccer Practice	2012	80	1	11.59	8.67	9.99	16.02
41018	Cat's Playground	2012	31	0	8.57	5.93	4.99	71.74
41019	Turtle's Little Oasis	2013	33	0	9	5.86	4.99	80.36
41020	Hedgehog's Hideaway	2013	34	0	10.11	7.67	4.99	102.61
41021	Poodle's Little Palace	2013	46	0	6.19	0	4.99	24.05
41022	Bunny's Hutch	2013	37	0	6.31	3.33	4.99	26.45
5000437	Vintage Minifig Collection Vol. 1 (TRU edition)	2012	21	5	25.7	0	19.99	28.56
55001	Universe Rocket	2010	55	0	13.06	6	9.99	30.73
66373	Fun Favor Pack	2010	304	0	39	17.63	19.99	95.10
850425	Desk Business Card Holder	2012	150	2	23.75	0	14.99	58.44
850426	Pencil Holder	2012	155	1	22.39	0	14.99	49.37
850702	Classic Picture Frame	2013	55	0	21.58	0	14.99	43.96
850935	Classic Minifigure Graduation Set	2014	30	1	16	0	7.99	100.25
853195	Brick Calendar	2011	120	2	34.37	10.42	14.99	129.29
853340	Minifigure Wedding Favour Set	2011	24	2	13.78	13	7.99	72.47

NUMBER	NAME	YEAR	PIECES	MINIFIGS	NEW	USED	RETAIL	GROWTH%
MODEL TEAM								
5571	Giant Truck	1996	1,757	0	655.73	308.6	138.99	371.78
MONSTER FIGHTERS								
10228	Haunted House	2012	2,064	6	304.13	235.07	179.99	68.97
30200	Zombie Chauffeur Coffin Car	2012	32	1	13.12	11.23	3.5	274.86
30201	Ghost	2012	33	1	25.89	8.27	3.5	639.71
40076	Zombie Car	2012	60	1	22.68	18.53	3.99	468.42
5000644	Monster Fighters promo pack	2012	12	0	22.24	14	3.99	457.39
9461	The Swamp Creature	2012	70	2	14.24	6	6.99	103.72
9462	The Mummy	2012	90	2	18.89	11.27	11.99	57.55
9463	The Werewolf	2012	243	2	26.28	14.33	19.99	31.47
9464	The Vampyre Hearse	2012	314	3	37.78	24.53	34.99	7.97
9465	The Zombies	2012	447	4	179.63	134.93	39.99	349.19
9466	The Crazy Scientist & His Monster	2012	430	4	57.87	36	49.99	15.76
9467	The Ghost Train	2012	741	5	96.94	61.93	79.99	21.19
9468	Vampyre Castle	2012	949	7	137.55	99.33	99.99	37.56
NINJAGO								
2111	Kai	2011	19	1	12.65	9.5	9.99	26.63
2112	Cole	2011	19	1	18.87	21	9.99	88.89
2113	Zane	2011	19	1	20.47	14	9.99	104.90
2114	Chopov	2011	20	1	13.67	9.25	9.99	36.84
2115	Bonezai	2011	21	1	13.42	7.65	9.99	34.33
2116	Krazi	2011	22	1	14.25	11.38	9.99	42.64
2170	Cole DX	2011	21	1	12.36	9.72	9.99	23.72
2171	Zane DX	2011	22	1	13.75	10.53	9.99	37.64
2172	Nya	2011	21	1	18.84	15.79	9.99	88.59
2173	Nuckal	2011	26	1	18.08	5.88	9.99	80.98
2174	Kruncha	2011	24	1	12.08	6.19	9.99	20.92
2175	Wyplash	2011	23	1	9.22	7.8	9.99	-7.71
2254	Mountain Shrine	2011	169	2	40	35.21	19.99	100.10
2255	Sensei Wu	2011	20	1	14.88	12.81	9.99	48.95
2256	Lord Garmadon	2011	23	1	19.29	12.82	9.99	93.09
2257	Spinjitzu Starter Set	2011	57	2	20.63	17.44	19.99	3.20
2258	Ninja Ambush	2011	71	2	20.78	15.2	6.99	197.28
2259	Skull Motorbike	2011	157	2	42.28	18.87	14.99	182.05
2260	Ice Dragon Attack	2011	158	2	95.57	41.67	19.99	378.09
2263	Turbo Shredder	2011	223	3	50.4	34.29	29.99	68.06
2504	Spinjitzu Dojo	2011	373	3	79.89	47.27	49.99	59.81
2505	Garmadon's Dark Fortress	2011	518	6	179.4	92.27	69.99	156.32
2506	Skull Truck	2011	515	4	70.44	54.56	59.99	17.42
2507	Fire Temple	2011	1,180	8	184.15	144.13	119.99	53.47
2508	Blacksmith Shop	2011	189	2	62.44	25.87	19.99	212.36
2509	Earth Dragon Defence	2011	227	2	127.71	58.13	34.99	264.99
2516	Ninja Training Outpost	2011	45	1	14	8.6	4.99	180.56
2518	Nuckal's ATV	2011	174	2	27.19	25.47	24.99	8.80
2519	Skeleton Bowling	2011	371	1	29.95	30.77	29.99	-0.13
2520	Ninja Battle Arena	2011	463	2	50.93	36.72	49.99	1.88
2521	Lightning Dragon Battle	2011	645	4	193.93	110.87	79.99	142.44
2856134	Ninjago Card Shrine	2011	98	0	8.27	4.5	6.99	18.31
30080	Ninja Glider	2011	26	1	8.62	5.5	3.47	148.41

NUMBER	NAME	YEAR	PIECES	MINIFIGS	NEW	USED	RETAIL	GROWTH%
30082	Ninja Training	2011	34	1	8.64	6.71	3.47	148.99
30083	Dragon Fight	2011	31	1	13.59	5.91	3.49	289.40
5002144	Dareth vs. Nindroid	2014	10	2	9.96	0	4.99	99.60
70500	Kai's Fire Mech	2013	102	2	14.5	12.27	9.99	45.15
70501	Warrior Bike	2013	210	2	32.86	15.13	19.99	64.38
70502	Cole's Earth Driller	2013	171	2	27.27	14.4	19.99	36.42
70503	The Golden Dragon	2013	252	3	31.39	25.93	29.99	4.67
70504	Garmatron	2013	328	3	30.76	24	39.99	-23.08
70505	Temple of Light	2013	565	5	74.69	39.47	69.99	6.72
70720	Hover Hunter	2014	79	2	18	0	11.99	50.13
70721	Kai Fighter	2014	196	2	31.33	15.13	19.99	56.73
70722	OverBorg Attack	2014	207	2	24.76	17.33	19.99	23.86
70723	Thunder Raider	2014	334	3	60.17	17.8	29.99	100.63
70724	NinjaCopter	2014	516	4	43.57	0	59.99	-27.37
70725	Nindroid MechDragon	2014	691	5	55.22	0	89.99	-38.64
70726	Destructoid	2014	253	3	42.19	0	34.99	20.58
70727	X Ninja Charger	2014	426	3	45.51	0	39.99	13.80
70728	Battle for Ninjago City	2014	1,223	8	102.02	81	119.99	4.98
850445	Ninjago Character Card Shrine	2012	88	1	17.1	0	14.99	14.08
850632	Samurai Accessory Set	2013	36	4	26.39	0	14.99	76.05
853111	Exclusive Weapon Training Set	2011	26	1	30	9	14.99	100.13
9440	Venomari Shrine	2012	86	1	15.42	10.56	6.99	120.60
9441	Kai's Blade Cycle	2012	188	2	36.02	19.93	14.99	140.29
9442	Jay's Storm Fighter	2012	242	2	38.97	23.2	24.99	55.94
9443	Rattlecopter	2012	327	3	32.56	22.07	29.99	8.57
9444	Cole's Tread Assault	2012	286	2	90.83	34.27	39.99	127.13
9445	Fangpyre Truck Ambush	2012	452	4	80.18	40.8	49.99	60.39
9446	Destiny's Bounty	2012	680	6	138.94	84.33	79.99	73.70
9447	Lasha's Bite Cycle	2012	250	2	34.96	15.93	24.99	39.90
9448	Samurai Mech	2012	452	3	42.84	25.47	39.99	7.13
9449	Ultra Sonic Raider	2012	622	6	65.7	42.53	79.99	7.86
9450	Epic Dragon Battle	2012	915	7	103.87	56.13	119.99	3.43
9455	Fangpyre Mech	2012	255	2	38.61	18.8	24.99	54.50
9456	Spinner Battle Arena	2012	418	2	87.82	31.94	39.99	119.60
9457	Fangpyre Wrecking Ball	2012	415	3	68.18	42.53	49.99	36.39
9551	Kendo Cole	2012	28	1	9.34	9.42	4.99	87.17
9552	Lloyd Garmadon	2012	21	1	13.13	4.43	4.99	163.13
9553	Jay ZX	2012	28	1	10.16	5.24	4.99	103.61

NUMBER	NAME	YEAR	PIECES	MINIFIGS	NEW	USED	RETAIL	GROWTH%
9554	Zane ZX	2012	37	1	10.5	8.9	4.99	110.42
9555	Mezmo	2012	32	1	17.81	8.17	4.99	256.91
9556	Bytar	2012	25	1	10.32	5.29	4.99	106.81
9557	Lizaru	2012	25	1	8.84	6	4.99	77.15
9558	Training Set	2012	219	1	28.13	15.47	19.99	40.72
9561	Kai ZX	2012	21	1	22.17	17.75	9.99	121.92
9562	Lasha	2012	21	1	20.2	10.5	9.99	102.20
9563	Kendo Zane	2012	22	1	16.29	7.5	9.99	63.06
9564	Snappa	2012	20	1	15.48	6	9.99	54.95
9566	Samurai X	2012	23	1	21.77	20	9.99	117.92
9567	Fang-Suei	2012	19	1	18.39	16	9.99	84.08
9569	Spitta	2012	20	1	11.27	8.26	9.99	12.81
9570	NRG Jay	2012	20	1	33.41	20.87	9.99	234.43
9571	Fangdam	2012	20	1	22.39	10	9.99	124.12
9572	NRG Cole	2012	20	1	18.08	12.31	9.99	80.98
9573	Slithraa	2012	20	1	13.17	9.74	9.99	31.83
9574	Lloyd ZX	2012	23	1	27.65	24.55	9.99	176.78
9579	Starter Set	2012	62	2	34.81	27.89	19.99	74.14
9590	NRG Zane	2012	23	1	23.5	11.1	9.99	135.24
9591	Weapon Pack	2012	73	2	30.38	22.37	19.99	51.98

PIRATES

NUMBER	NAME	YEAR	PIECES	MINIFIGS	NEW	USED	RETAIL	GROWTH%
10040	Black Seas Barracuda	2002	906	8	436.6	177.6	89.99	385.17
10210	Imperial Flagship	2010	1,664	9	522.5	400.67	179.99	190.29
1747	Treasure Surprise	1996	22	1	5.14	7.33	1.99	158.29
1788	Treasure Chest	1995	159	4	167.13	36.27	21.99	660.03
1802	Tidy Treasure	1996	22	1	10.6	9.83	1.99	432.66
6204	Buccaneers	1997	36	5	39.75	15.2	5.99	563.61
6232	Skeleton Crew	1996	28	2	14.33	7.73	2.99	379.26
6234	Renegade's Raft	1991	38	1	18.71	11.29	2.99	525.75
6235	Buried Treasure	1989	20	1	18.87	6.67	2.99	531.10
6236	King Kahuka	1994	45	1	15.8	13.6	3.99	295.99
6237	Pirates Plunder	1992	21	2	24.54	11.13	2.99	720.74
6239	Cannon Battle	2009	45	2	13.63	10.67	5.99	127.55
6240	Kraken Attackin'	2009	78	2	25.06	15.73	9.99	150.85
6241	Loot Island	2009	142	3	61	28.8	19.99	205.15
6242	Soldiers' Fort	2009	367	6	142.82	77.93	49.99	185.70
6243	Brickbeard's Bounty	2009	592	8	281	175.13	84.99	230.63
6244	Armada Sentry	1996	71	1	29.89	22.73	8.99	232.48
6245	Harbor Sentry	1989	25	1	37.87	14.06	3.99	849.12
6246	Crocodile Cage	1994	59	2	25.2	17.13	6.99	260.52
6247	Bounty Boat	1992	36	3	27.6	17.07	4.99	453.11
6248	Volcano Island	1996	119	2	39.2	21.87	11.99	226.94
6249	Pirates Ambush	1997	156	3	61.67	34.6	21.99	180.45
6250	Cross Bone Clipper	1997	154	3	186.4	81.67	32.99	465.02
6251	Pirate Mini Figures	1989	33	5	89.5	16.86	6.99	1180.40
6252	Sea Mates	1993	32	4	39.73	21.14	6.99	468.38
6253	Shipwreck Hideout	2009	310	6	88.76	46.6	39.99	121.96
6254	Rocky Reef	1995	103	3	35.27	18.4	14.99	135.29
6256	Islander Catamaran	1994	63	2	48.53	21.53	11.99	304.75
6257	Castaway's Raft	1989	54	3	48.42	17.8	8.99	438.60
6258	Smuggler's Shanty	1992	70	3	37.27	17.67	8.99	314.57

NUMBER	NAME	YEAR	PIECES	MINIFIGS	NEW	USED	RETAIL	GROWTH%
6259	Broadside's Brig	1991	68	3	52.71	24.53	8.99	486.32
6260	Shipwreck Island	1989	71	2	80.67	24.2	11.99	572.81
6261	Raft Raiders	1992	81	3	36	22.67	12.99	177.14
6262	King Kahuka's Throne	1994	146	5	40.33	26.73	20.99	92.14
6263	Imperial Outpost	1995	216	4	85.13	48.87	27.99	204.14
6264	Forbidden Cove	1994	214	4	61.4	42.33	29.99	104.73
6265	Sabre Island	1989	96	3	134.93	30.07	15.99	743.84
6266	Cannon Cove	1993	106	3	61.13	24.81	17.99	239.80
6267	Lagoon Lock-Up	1991	193	5	90.67	49.2	28.99	212.76
6268	Renegade Runner	1993	178	4	185.4	72.93	39.99	363.62
6270	Forbidden Island	1989	182	4	192.8	57.07	37.99	407.50
6271	Imperial Flagship	1992	317	4	270.92	122.8	49.99	441.95
6273	Rock Island Refuge	1991	381	7	166.82	102.87	65.99	152.80
6274	Caribbean Clipper	1989	378	4	387.55	122.9	53.99	617.82
6276	Eldorado Fortress	1989	506	8	114.36	150.6	65.99	73.30
6277	Imperial Trading Post	1992	608	9	633.71	198.13	84.99	645.63
6278	Enchanted Island	1994	428	7	151.6	115.27	65.99	129.73
6279	Skull Island	1995	378	6	152	62.33	52.99	186.85
6280	Armada Flagship	1996	284	3	154.47	139.88	49.99	209.00
6281	Pirates Perilous Pitfall	1997	395	6	228.87	167.93	72.99	213.56
6285	Black Seas Barracuda	1989	909	8	412	214	109.99	274.58
6286	Skull's Eye Schooner	1993	912	9	669.4	286.67	126.99	427.13
6289	Red Beard Runner	1996	703	7	245.47	128.67	98.99	147.97
6290	Red Beard Runner	2001	698	7	236.6	144.07	99.99	136.62
6291	Armada Flagship	2001	280	3	147.13	97.73	49.99	194.32
6292	Enchanted Island	2001	419	7	196.17	68.81	69.99	180.28
6296	Shipwreck Island	1996	216	4	87.67	49.8	29.99	192.33
6299	Pirates Advent Calendar	2009	148	8	68.47	50.5	39.99	71.22
8396	Soldier's Arsenal	2009	17	1	9.94	5.73	3.99	149.12
8397	Pirate Survival	2009	16	1	10.13	5.15	3.99	153.88
850839	Classic Pirate Set	2013	39	4	19.28	0	14.99	28.62
852747	Pirates Battle Pack	2009	37	4	23.2	15	14.99	54.77

PIRATES OF THE CARIBBEAN

NUMBER	NAME	YEAR	PIECES	MINIFIGS	NEW	USED	RETAIL	GROWTH%
30130	Mini Black Pearl	2011	50	0	18.47	12.67	3.99	362.91
30131	Jack Sparrow's Boat	2011	22	1	21.3	7.44	3.99	433.83
30132	Captain Jack Sparrow	2011	4	1	9.88	6.6	2.99	230.43
30133	Jack Sparrow	2011	4	1	12.13	0	3.99	204.01
4181	Isla De La Muerta	2011	152	4	44.16	23.19	19.99	120.91
4182	The Cannibal Escape	2011	279	4	39.62	21.13	29.99	32.11
4183	The Mill	2011	365	4	45.1	31.6	39.99	12.78
4184	Black Pearl	2011	804	6	252.87	202.26	99.99	152.90
4191	The Captain's Cabin	2011	95	3	18.91	12.73	11.99	57.71
4192	Fountain of Youth	2011	125	3	43.82	24.4	19.99	119.21
4193	The London Escape	2011	462	5	49.38	42.33	49.99	.22
4194	Whitecap Bay	2011	746	6	78.72	53.13	79.99	.59
4195	Queen Anne's Revenge	2011	1,097	7	286.04	204.83	119.99	138.3
853219	Pirates of Caribbean Battle Pack	2011	30	5	19.26	0	14.99	28.49

POWER MINERS

NUMBER	NAME	YEAR	PIECES	MINIFIGS	NEW	USED	RETAIL	GROWTH%
8188	Fire Blaster	2010	67	2	35.4	22	9.99	254.35
8189	Magma Mech	2010	183	2	30.9	18.27	19.99	54.58

NUMBER	NAME	YEAR	PIECES	MINIFIGS	NEW	USED	RETAIL	GROWTH%
8190	Claw Catcher	2010	259	2	53.31	31.2	34.99	52.36
8191	Lavatraz	2010	381	4	78.19	60.8	49.99	56.41
8707	Boulder Blaster	2009	293	2	71.93	33.4	26.99	166.51
8708	Cave Crusher	2009	259	3	111.13	57.4	49.99	122.30
8709	Underground Mining Station	2009	637	4	161.2	83.93	79.99	101.53
8956	Stone Chopper	2009	31	2	24.06	11.93	5.99	301.67
8957	Mine Mech	2009	67	2	31.4	15	7.99	292.99
8958	Granite Grinder	2009	94	2	35.68	20.13	9.99	257.16
8959	Claw Digger	2009	197	2	61.5	25.6	19.99	207.65
8960	Thunder Driller	2009	235	3	103.33	37.8	29.99	244.55
8961	Crystal Sweeper	2009	474	4	210.2	76.8	69.99	200.33
8962	Crystal King	2009	168	2	73.07	38.33	19.99	265.53
8963	Rock Wrecker	2009	225	2	61.33	30.8	34.99	75.28
8964	Titanium Command Rig	2009	706	5	198.64	100.33	99.99	98.66

PRINCE OF PERSIA

NUMBER	NAME	YEAR	PIECES	MINIFIGS	NEW	USED	RETAIL	GROWTH%
20017	BrickMaster - Prince of Persia	2010	49	1	8.39	5.27	3.99	110.28
7569	Desert Attack	2010	67	4	10.46	9.06	10.99	-4.82
7570	The Ostrich Race	2010	169	3	19.7	10.67	19.99	.45
7571	The Fight for the Dagger	2010	258	4	28.44	16	29.99	-5.17
7572	Quest Against Time	2010	506	4	35.78	21.53	49.99	-28.43
7573	Battle of Alamut	2010	821	7	72.88	51.4	79.99	-8.89

RACERS

NUMBER	NAME	YEAR	PIECES	MINIFIGS	NEW	USED	RETAIL	GROWTH%
8145	Ferrari 599 GTB Fiorano 1:10	2007	1,327	0	574.93	244.6	109.99	422.71
8169	Lamborghini Gallardo LP 560-4	2009	741	0	253.94	93.2	39.99	535.01
8214	Lamborghini Polizia	2010	801	0	87.19	59.99	109.80	
8353	Slammer Rhino	2003	220	0	12.58	10.63	19.99	-37.07
8354	Exo Force Bike	2003	101	0	9.5	10	9.99	-4.90
8356	Jungle Monster	2003	116	1	17.2	8.6	14.99	14.74
8357	Zonic Strike	2003	107	1	16	6.71	14.99	6.74
8371	Extreme Power Bike	2003	98	0	10.83	5.77	9.99	8.41
8461	Williams F1 Team Racer	2002	1,484	0	399.93	273.73	129.99	207.66
8653	Enzo Ferrari 1:10	2005	1,360	0	437.47	153.47	99.99	337.51
8674	Ferrari F1 Racer 1:8	2006	1,246	0	527.27	217.8	139.99	276.65

SEASONAL

NUMBER	NAME	YEAR	PIECES	MINIFIGS	NEW	USED	RETAIL	GROWTH%
10106	LEGO Snowflake	2006	105	0	21.09	16.5	7.99	163.95
10199	Winter Toy Shop	2009	815	7	230.52	171.59	59.99	284.26
10216	Winter Village Bakery	2010	687	7	161.43	128.2	54.99	193.56
10222	Winter Village Post Office	2011	822	7	215.68	158.87	69.99	208.16
10229	Winter Village Cottage	2012	1,490	8	191.53	148.67	99.99	91.55
10235	Winter Village Market	2013	1,261	9	139.41	66.28	99.99	39.42
10245	Santa's Workshop	2014	883	6	108	48	69.99	54
3300002	2011 Holiday Set 2 of 2	2011	117	1	22.35	8.5	3.99	460.15
3300020	2011 Holiday Set 1 of 2	2011	98	1	14.78	14.75	3.99	270.43
40000	Cool Santa Set	2009	152	0	23.41	13.33	9.99	134.33
40001	Santa Claus	2009	42	0	12.27	5	4.99	145.89
40002	Xmas Tree	2009	61	0	6.86	6	4.99	37.47
40003	Snowman	2009	44	0	9.05	6.67	4.99	81.36
40004	Heart	2010	26	0	15	4.21	4.99	200.60
40005	Bunny	2010	81	0	18.81	5.79	9.99	88.29

NUMBER	NAME	YEAR	PIECES	MINIFIGS	NEW	USED	RETAIL	GROWTH%
40008	Snowman Building Set	2010	64	0	10.23	0	4.99	105.01
40009	Holiday Building Set	2010	85	0	11	8.14	4.99	120.44
40010	Santa with Sleigh Building Set	2010	71	0	14.82	10.8	4.99	196.99
40011	Thanksgiving Turkey	2010	53	0	10.91	3.75	4.99	118.64
40012	Halloween Pumpkin	2010	18	0	5.39	6.75	1.99	170.85
40013	Halloween Ghost	2010	18	0	5.75	2.75	1.99	188.94
40014	Halloween Bat	2010	25	0	6.04	0	1.99	203.52
40015	Heart Book	2011	51	0	13.12	10.17	4.99	162.93
40016	Valentine Letter Set	2011	41	0	12.47	8.4	4.99	149.90
40017	Easter Basket	2011	86	0	23.73	10	4.99	375.55
40018	Easter Bunny	2011	95	0	12	4.5	4.99	140.48
40019	Brickley The Sea Serpent	2011	59	0	8.36	5.45	3.99	109.52
40020	Halloween Set	2011	71	0	15.62	7.95	4.99	213.03
40021	Spider Set	2011	54	0	6.46	2.33	4.99	29.46
40022	Mini Santa Set	2011	72	0	11.8	0	4.99	136.47
40023	Holiday Stocking	2011	76	0	9.32	9.8	3.99	133.58
40024	Christmas Tree	2011	77	0	12.24	9.95	3.99	206.77
40029	Valentine's Day Box	2012	51	0	19.75	10.64	4.99	295.79
40030	Duck with Ducklings	2012	51	0	16.82	6	4.99	237.07
40031	Bunny and Chick	2012	52	0	11.22	6.56	4.99	124.85
40048	Birthday Cake	2012	24	0	12.73	7.85	3.99	219.05
40051	Valentine's Day Heart Box	2013	54	0	13.82	6.88	4.99	176.95
40052	Springtime Scene	2013	88	2	11.41	8.5	7.99	42.80
40053	Easter Bunny with Basket	2013	96	0	18.47	0	4.99	270.14
40054	Summer Scene	2013	40	1	16.35	8.44	4.99	227.66
40055	Halloween Pumpkin	2013	52	0	8.19	7.5	4.99	64.13
40056	Thanksgiving Feast	2013	46	2	17.55	0	7.99	119.65
40057	Fall Scene	2013	72	3	15.76	0	7.99	97.25
40058	Decorating the Tree	2013	110	2	12.09	12.99	7.99	51.31
40059	Santa Sleigh	2013	77	2	22.88	13	7.99	186.36
40085	Teddy Bear	2014	127	0	16.91	0	9.99	69.27
40086	Easter Bunny	2014	106	0	15.8	9.45	9.99	58.16
40090	Halloween Bat	2014	156	0	14.83	0	9.99	48.45
40091	Turkey	2014	125	0	17.69	0	9.99	77.08
40092	Reindeer	2014	139	0	18.61	0	9.99	86.29
40093	Snowman	2014	140	0	19.08	0	9.99	90.99
40106	Elves' Workshop	2014	107	2	27.52	18.72	3.99	589.72
40107	Ice Skating	2014	129	2	20.94	0	3.99	424.81
5002813	Christmas Train Ornament	2014	26	0	16.77	0	3.99	320.30
850843	Christmas Bauble - Dinosaur	2013	25	0	9.76	0	7.99	22.15
850849	Christmas Bauble - Friends puppy	2013	29	0	13.61	0	7.99	70.34
850936	Halloween Set	2014	11	0	14.63	0	7.99	83.10
850939	Santa Set	2014	27	0	12.54	0	7.99	56.95
850949	{holiday bauble}	2014	45	0	13	0	7.99	62.70
850950	{holiday bauble}	2014	34	0	14.4	0	7.99	80.23
853345	Gold Ornament	2011	40	0	17.45	0	7.99	118.40

SPACE

NUMBER	NAME	YEAR	PIECES	MINIFIGS	NEW	USED	RETAIL	GROWTH%
30230	Mini Mech	2013	28	1	5.91	4.86	3.99	48.12
30231	Space Insectoid	2013	27	1	7.97	0	3.49	128.37
5616	Mini-Robot	2008	24	2	12.63	7.7	3.99	216.54

NUMBER	NAME	YEAR	PIECES	MINIFIGS	NEW	USED	RETAIL	GROWTH%
5619	Crystal Hawk	2008	26	1	20	10.8	3.99	401.25
5969	Squidman Escape	2009	42	2	10.11	7.47	5.99	68.78
5970	Freeze Ray Frenzy	2009	80	2	19.4	10.4	9.99	94.19
5971	Gold Heist	2009	205	2	21.07	18.6	19.99	5.40
5972	Space Truck Getaway	2009	282	2	31.06	23.87	29.99	3.57
5973	Hyperspeed Pursuit	2009	456	3	62.73	30.93	49.99	25.49
5974	Galactic Enforcer	2009	825	7	94.66	59.4	99.99	-5.33
5979	Max Security Transport	2009	330	3	81.29	38.53	39.99	103.28
5980	Squidman's Pitstop	2009	389	4	39.88	42.47	49.99	-20.22
5981	Raid VPR	2010	69	2	22.21	11.13	9.99	122.32
5982	Smash 'n' Grab	2010	188	2	22.82	14.53	19.99	14.16
5983	Undercover Cruiser	2010	317	2	34.82	19.93	29.99	16.11
5984	Lunar Limo	2010	391	3	47.06	22	39.99	17.68
5985	Space Police Central	2010	631	4	118.38	62.53	79.99	47.99
7049	Alien Striker	2011	42	2	10.14	6.67	4.99	103.21
7050	Alien Defender	2011	105	2	14.35	12.5	9.99	43.64
7051	Tripod Invader	2011	166	2	21.27	13.8	19.99	6.40
7052	UFO Abduction	2011	211	3	29.78	16.6	29.99	-0.70
7065	Alien Mothership	2011	416	2	40.77	23.87	59.99	-32.04
7066	Earth Defence HQ	2011	879	5	83.86	56	89.99	-6.81
7067	Jet-Copter Encounter	2011	375	3	32	21.27	39.99	9.98
70700	Space Swarmer	2013	86	2	15.1	8.06	11.99	25.94
70701	Swarm Interceptor	2013	218	2	21.82	10.67	19.99	9.15
70702	Warp Stinger	2013	310	3	26.1	22.5	29.99	2.97
70703	Star Slicer	2013	311	3	30.23	32.88	39.99	-24.41
70704	Vermin Vaporizer	2013	506	3	48.07	36.31	59.99	9.87
70705	Bug Obliterator	2013	711	4	55.1	37.8	79.99	-31.12
70706	Crater Creeper	2013	171	0	15.82	14	19.99	-20.86
70707	CLS-89 Eradicator Mech	2013	440	2	39.21	52.67	39.99	.95
70708	Hive Crawler	2013	560	3	39.16	47.64	69.99	-44.05
70709	Galactic Titan	2013	1,012	5	85.96	76	99.99	4.03
7300	Double Hover	2001	21	1	7.2	6.29	2.99	140.80
7301	Rover	2001	28	1	13	3.93	2.99	334.78
7302	Worker Robot	2001	30	1	13	2.93	2.99	334.78
7310	Mono Jet	2001	33	1	5.07	4.53	3.99	27.07
7311	Red Planet Cruiser	2001	73	1	13.06	9.07	6.99	86.84
7312	T-3 Trike	2001	99	1	21.3	10.6	9.99	113.21
7313	Red Planet Protector	2001	194	1	23.33	15.27	19.99	16.71
7314	Recon Mech RP	2001	194	1	26.2	17.93	19.99	31.07
7315	Solar Explorer	2001	242	3	35.67	27.47	34.99	1.94
7316	Excavation Searcher	2001	471	3	30.71	17.56	49.99	-38.57
7317	Aero Tube Hanger	2001	706	5	102.07	48.6	89.99	13.42
7644	MX-81 Hypersonic Operations Aircraft	2008	795	5	173.07	88	79.99	116.36
7645	MT-61 Crystal Reaper	2008	600	6	124.4	58.07	49.99	148.85
7646	ETX Alien Infiltraitor	2008	333	4	64.75	37.8	29.99	115.91
7647	MX-41 Switch Fighter	2008	235	2	68.27	29	19.99	241.52
7648	MT-21 Mobile Mining Unit	2008	130	2	34.93	24.07	9.99	249.65
7649	MT-201 Ultra-Drill Walker	2008	759	3	115.26	73.07	69.99	64.68
7690	MB-01 Eagle Command Base	2007	760	8	206.87	94.87	89.99	129.88
7691	ETX Alien Mothership Assault	2007	434	7	118.5	63.4	49.99	137.05
7692	MX-71 Recon Dropship	2007	435	6	75.67	39.93	39.99	89.22

NUMBER	NAME	YEAR	PIECES	MINIFIGS	NEW	USED	RETAIL	GROWTH%
7693	ETX Alien Strike	2007	246	3	52.6	24	19.99	163.13
7694	MT-31 Trike	2007	95	2	34.19	18.6	9.99	242.24
7695	MX1 Astro Fighter	2007	57	2	17.8	9.67	4.99	256.71
7697	MT-51 Claw-Tank Ambush	2007	374	3	55.41	30.73	29.99	84.76
7699	MT01 Armoured Drilling Unit	2007	635	5	104.07	62.13	79.99	30.10
8399	K-9 Bot	2009	22	1	14.5	4.64	3.99	263.41
8400	Space Speeder	2009	14	1	8.4	7.91	3.99	110.53
853301	Alien Conquest Battle Pack	2011	31	5	15.09	3.33	14.99	0.67

SPIDER-MAN

NUMBER	NAME	YEAR	PIECES	MINIFIGS	NEW	USED	RETAIL	GROWTH%
4850	Spider-Man's First Chase	2003	191	3	86.5	41.27	19.99	332.72
4851	Spider-Man and Green Goblin, The Origins	2003	218	6	180.63	73.67	29.99	502.30
4852	Spider-Man vs. Green Goblin, The Final Showdown	2003	360	4	177.75	93.67	49.99	255.57
4853	Spider-Man's Street Chase	2004	73	3	50.19	27.87	9.99	402.40
4854	Doc Ock's Bank Robbery	2004	174	5	73.5	39.53	19.99	267.68
4855	Spider-Man's Train Rescue	2004	299	4	84.39	83	29.99	181.39
4856	Doc Ock's Hideout	2004	486	5	14.89	93.93	49.99	-70.21
4857	Doc Ock's Fusion Lab	2004	237	4	87.47	47.47	19.99	337.57

SPONGEBOB SQUAREPANTS

NUMBER	NAME	YEAR	PIECES	MINIFIGS	NEW	USED	RETAIL	GROWTH%
3815	Heroic Heroes of the Deep	2011	95	3	29.25	16.73	14.99	95.13
3816	Glove World	2011	169	4	30.85	18.07	19.99	54.33
3817	The Flying Dutchman	2012	241	3	32.17	18.44	24.99	28.73
3818	Bikini Bottom Undersea Party	2012	471	4	87.55	47.13	49.99	75.14
3825	Krusty Krab	2006	295	3	63.48	50.07	19.99	217.56
3826	Build-A-Bob	2006	445	1	171.53	48.05	29.99	471.96
3827	Adventures in Bikini Bottom	2006	579	3	131.4	50.07	39.99	228.58
3830	The Bikini Bottom Express	2008	210	3	92.6	41.8	19.99	363.23
3831	Rocket Ride	2008	279	3	135.93	55.47	29.99	353.25
3832	The Emergency Room	2008	236	3	110.19	60.13	29.99	267.42
3833	Krusty Krab Adventures	2009	209	3	50.75	30.52	19.99	153.88
3834	Good Neighbours at Bikini Bottom	2009	425	3	66.45	36.61	39.99	66.17
4981	Chum Bucket	2007	337	1	49.5	56.87	34.99	41.47
4982	Mrs. Puff's Boating School	2007	393	3	97.56	54.33	49.99	95.16

STAR WARS

NUMBER	NAME	YEAR	PIECES	MINIFIGS	NEW	USED	RETAIL	GROWTH%
10018	Darth Maul	2001	1,868	0	795.93	454.87	149.99	430.66
10019	Rebel Blockade Runner	2001	1747	0	1232.6	589.2	199.99	516.33
10026	Special Edition Naboo Starfighter	2002	187	0	401.67	159.31	39.99	904.43
10030	Imperial Star Destroyer	2002	3,096	0	1527	783.38	298.99	410.72
10123	Cloud City	2003	705	7	975.4	566.47	99.99	875.50
10129	Rebel Snowspeeder	2003	1,455	0	1084.67	593.13	129.99	734.43
10131	TIE Fighter Collection	2004	682	3	219.13	120.07	69.99	213.09
10134	Y-wing Attack Starfighter	2004	1,473	1	842.53	465.53	119.99	602.17
10143	Death Star II	2005	3,441	0	1,481.4	767	298.99	395.47
10144	Sandcrawler	2005	1,669	8	268.73	177.13	139.99	91.6
10174	Imperial AT-ST	2006	1,068	0	291.94	160.47	79.99	264.97
10175	Vader's TIE Advanced	2006	1,212	0	523.8	262.53	99.99	423.85
10178	Motorized Walking AT-AT	2007	1,137	4	446.33	231.4	129.99	243.36

NUMBER	NAME	YEAR	PIECES	MINIFIGS	NEW	USED	RETAIL	GROWTH%
10179	Ultimate Collector's Millennium Falcon	2007	5,195	5	3,450.65	2,064.75	499.99	590.14
10186	General Grievous	2008	1,085	0	189.87	91.47	89.99	110.99
10188	Death Star	2008	3,803	22	490.38	326.03	399.99	22.60
10195	Republic Dropship with AT-OT Walker	2009	1,758	8	470.56	328.07	249.99	88.23
10198	Tantive IV	2009	1,408	5	255.37	179.33	149.99	70.26
10212	Imperial Shuttle	2010	2,503	5	453.96	333.53	259.99	74.61
10215	Obi-Wan's Jedi Starfighter	2010	676	4	113.32	77.33	99.99	13.33
10221	Super Star Destroyer	2011	3,152	5	648.3	511.73	399.99	62.08
10225	R2-D2	2012	2,127	1	254.4	179.73	179.99	41.34
10227	B-Wing Starfighter	2012	1,487	0	209.3	155.13	199.99	4.66
10236	Ewok Village	2013	1,990	16	244.31	212.73	249.99	-2.27
10240	Red Five X-wing Starfighter	2013	1,558	1	213.42	157.2	199.99	6.72
20006	Clone Turbo Tank	2008	64	0	75.87	23.73	0	
20007	Republic Attack Cruiser	2009	84	0	34.9	22.31	3.99	774.69
20009	AT-TE Walker	2009	94	0	22.1	11	3.99	453.88
20010	Republic Gunship	2009	99	0	27.18	13.47	3.99	581.20
20016	BrickMaster Imperial Shuttle	2010	70	0	16.59	10.07	3.99	315.79
20018	BrickMaster AT-AT Walker	2010	88	0	28.01	12.81	3.99	602.01
20019	Slave I	2011	76	0	10.2	9.61	3.99	155.64
20021	Bounty Hunter Assault Gunship	2011	81	0	11.89	0	3.99	197.99
2856197	Shadow ARF Trooper	2011	5	1	37.07	0	3.99	829.07
30004	Battle Droid on STAP	2009	28	1	8.43	4.8	3.99	111.28
30005	Imperial Speeder Bike	2009	30	1	10.04	5.53	3.99	151.63
30006	Clone Walker	2009	30	1	18.7	7.2	3.99	368.67
30050	Republic Attack Shuttle	2010	54	0	9.56	6.74	3.99	139.60
30051	X-wing Fighter	2010	67	0	13.73	8.6	3.99	244.11
30052	AAT	2011	46	0	9	5.76	3.99	125.56
30053	Venator Class Republic Attack Cruiser	2011	41	0	6.7	5.31	3.99	67.92
30054	AT-ST	2011	46	0	8.92	4.95	3.99	123.56
30055	Droid Fighter	2011	45	0	9.41	2.08	2.99	214.72
30056	Star Destroyer	2012	38	0	7.44	4.05	3.99	86.47
30057	Anakin's Pod Racer	2012	38	0	6.53	4.4	4.99	30.86
30058	STAP	2012	24	1	9.25	6.23	3.99	131.83
30059	MTT	2012	51	0	5.66	3.17	3.97	42.57
30240	Z-95 Headhunter	2013	54	0	7.22	5.43	4.99	44.69
30241	Mandalorian Fighter	2013	49	0	6.36	6.13	4.99	27.45
30242	Republic Frigate	2013	54	0	8.96	7	4.99	79.56
30243	Umbaran MHC	2013	49	0	5.7	0	3.99	42.86
30244	Anakin's Jedi Intercepter	2014	45	0	7.59	0	4.49	69.04
30246	Imperial Shuttle	2014	57	0	5.9	8.57	3.99	47.87
3219	Mini TIE Fighter	2002	12	0	6.84	4.95	2.99	128.76
3340	Emperor Palpatine, Darth Maul, Darth Vader Minifig Pack-Star Wars #1	2000	32	3	79.6	31.53	4.99	1,495.1
3341	Luke Skywalker, Han Solo, Boba Fett Minifig Pack-Star Wars #2	2000	22	3	62.13	21.53	4.99	1,145.09
3342	Chewbacca, 2 Biker Scouts Minifig Pack-Star Wars #3	2000	22	3	35.33	9.27	4.99	608.02
3343	2 Battle Droids, Command Officer Minifig Pack-Star Wars #4	2000	30	3	21.56	12	4.99	332.06

NUMBER	NAME	YEAR	PIECES	MINIFIGS	NEW	USED	RETAIL	GROWTH%
4475	Jabba's Message	2003	46	3	42.47	34.73	6.99	507.58
4476	Jabba's Prize	2003	40	2	35.87	22.53	6.99	413.16
4477	T6 Skyhopper	2003	98	1	36.53	16.93	14.99	143.70
4478	Geonosian Fighter	2003	170	4	66.73	28.27	19.99	233.82
4479	TIE Bomber	2003	230	1	129.27	45.6	29.99	331.04
4480	Jabba's Palace	2003	231	4	139.5	83.33	29.99	365.16
4481	Hailfire Droid	2003	681	0	131.87	66.33	49.99	163.79
4482	AT-TE	2003	658	4	241.8	89.93	69.99	245.48
4483	AT-AT	2003	1,068	4	268.2	141.67	99.99	168.23
4484	X-Wing Fighter & TIE Advanced	2003	76	0	21.67	12.88	3.99	443.11
4485	Sebulba's Podracer & Anakin's Podracer	2003	72	0	14.23	10.82	3.99	256.64
4486	AT-ST & Snowspeeder	2003	76	0	20	15.24	3.99	401.25
4487	Jedi Starfighter & Slave I	2003	53	0	15	10.07	3.99	275.94
4488	Millennium Falcon	2003	87	0	32.44	30.53	6.99	364.09
4489	AT-AT	2003	98	0	25.95	22.33	6.99	271.24
4490	Republic Gunship	2003	102	0	21.2	15	6.99	203.29
4491	MTT	2003	99	0	14.6	10.8	6.99	108.87
4492	Star Destroyer	2004	87	0	19.56	11.67	6.99	179.83
4493	Sith Infiltrator	2004	55	0	16	8.87	6.99	128.90
4494	Imperial Shuttle	2004	82	0	17.38	14.38	6.99	148.64
4495	AT-TE	2004	63	0	25	13.69	6.99	257.65
4500	Rebel Snowspeeder	2004	214	3	51.07	22.6	19.99	155.48
4501	Mos Eisley Cantina	2004	193	5	137.67	88.07	29.99	359.05
4502	X-wing Fighter	2004	563	2	166.53	78.87	49.99	233.13
4504	Millennium Falcon	2004	985	5	212.69	94.77	99.99	112.71
4521221	Gold chrome plated C-3PO	2007	1	1	354.06	273.94	3.99	8,773.68
5000062	Darth Maul	2012	7	1	21.72	14.56	3.99	444.36
5000063	TC4	2012	3	1	25.68	20	3.99	543.61
5001621	Han Solo (Hoth)	2013	5	1	11.18	11.75	3.99	180.20
5001709	Clone Trooper Lieutenant	2013	5	1	10.15	14	3.99	154.39
5002122	TC-4	2014	3	1	24	0	3.99	501.50
5002123	Darth Revan	2014	7	1	28.46	22	3.99	613.28
6205	V-wing Fighter	2006	118	1	22.53	16.07	9.99	125.53
6206	TIE Interceptor	2006	212	1	62.6	29.81	19.99	213.16
6207	A-wing Fighter	2006	194	2	30.73	18.2	15.99	92.18
6208	B-wing Fighter	2006	435	2	126.87	43.73	34.99	262.59
6209	Slave I	2006	537	4	139.33	69.2	49.99	178.72
6210	Jabba's Sail Barge	2006	781	8	204.27	113	74.99	172.40
6211	Imperial Star Destroyer	2006	1,367	9	252.46	148.6	99.99	152.49
6212	X-wing Fighter	2006	437	6	66.16	45.11	49.99	32.35
65081	R2-D2 / C-3PO Droid Collectors Set	2002	581	0	129.07	71.36	39.99	222.76
66512	Rebels Co-Pack	2014	1,163	0	111.58	50	109.99	1.45
6963	X-wing Fighter	2004	41	0	14.92	18.46	4.99	199.00
6964	Boba Fett's Slave I	2004	25	0	19.18	16.55	4.99	284.37
6965	TIE Interceptor	2004	32	0	15.09	8.8	4.99	202.40
6966	Jedi Starfighter	2005	38	0	8.11	6.19	4.99	62.53
6967	ARC Fighter	2005	42	0	16.33	10.87	4.99	227.25
7101	Lightsaber Duel	1999	52	2	33.38	17.8	5.99	457.26
7103	Jedi Duel	2002	82	2	41.6	20.83	9.99	316.42
7104	Desert Skiff	2000	55	2	23.67	15	5.99	295.16

NUMBER	NAME	YEAR	PIECES	MINIFIGS	NEW	USED	RETAIL	GROWTH%
7106	Droid Escape	2001	45	2	26.2	18.75	5.99	337.40
7110	Landspeeder	1999	49	2	31.8	17.67	5.99	430.88
7111	Droid Fighter	1999	62	0	18.2	10	5.99	203.84
7113	Tusken Raider Encounter	2002	93	3	40.47	23.13	9.99	305.11
7115	Gungan Patrol	2000	77	2	31.87	26	9.99	219.02
7119	Twin-Pod Cloud Car	2002	118	1	29.31	15.07	9.99	193.39
7121	Naboo Swamp	1999	82	4	29.6	18.95	9.99	196.30
7124	Flash Speeder	2000	106	1	30.27	17.83	9.99	203.00
7126	Battle Droid Carrier	2001	133	7	68.93	30.35	9.99	589.99
7127	Imperial AT-ST	2001	107	1	43.33	23.67	9.99	333.73
7128	Speeder Bikes	1999	93	3	37	18.07	9.99	270.37
7130	Snowspeeder	1999	215	3	56.33	25.41	19.99	181.79
7131	Anakin's Podracer	1999	136	2	36.27	19.19	14.99	141.96
7133	Bounty Hunter Pursuit	2002	259	3	112.73	44.8	29.99	275.89
7134	A-wing Fighter	2000	125	2	32.53	16.81	14.99	117.01
7139	Ewok Attack	2002	121	4	43.6	22.4	12.99	235.64
7140	X-wing Fighter	1999	266	4	86.6	34.22	29.99	188.76
7141	Naboo Fighter	1999	179	4	37.4	20.87	19.99	87.09
7142	X-wing Fighter	2002	267	4	87.07	29	29.99	190.33
7143	Jedi Starfighter	2002	139	1	53.07	24.27	19.99	165.48
7144	Slave I	2000	166	1	88.27	33.94	19.99	341.57
7146	TIE Fighter	2001	171	2	53.87	35.8	19.99	169.48
7150	TIE Fighter & Y-wing	1999	409	3	80.93	47.6	49.99	61.89
7151	Sith Infiltrator	1999	244	1	45.2	21.6	29.99	50.72
7152	TIE Fighter & Y-wing	2002	410	3	38.55	17.53	49.99	-22.88
7153	Jango Fett's Slave I	2002	360	2	213	107.19	49.99	326.09
7155	Trade Federation AAT	2000	158	2	112.07	38	19.99	460.63
7159	Star Wars Bucket	2000	292	3	94.87	44.2	24.99	279.63
7161	Gungan Sub	1999	379	3	71.07	34.67	49.99	42.17
7163	Republic Gunship	2002	693	8	174.13	115.8	89.99	93.50
7166	Imperial Shuttle	2001	238	4	123.13	50.47	34.99	251.90
7171	Mos Espa Podrace	1999	896	7	115.93	56.27	89.99	28.83
7180	B-wing at Rebel Control Center	2000	338	3	61.93	25.8	29.99	106.50
7181	TIE Interceptor	2000	703	0	697.8	179.53	99.99	597.87
7184	Trade Federation MTT	2000	470	7	130.6	72.13	49.99	161.25
7186	Watto's Junkyard	2001	443	2	168.13	67.5	49.99	236.33
7190	Millennium Falcon	2000	663	6	282.2	104.87	99.99	182.23
7191	X-wing Fighter	2000	1,300	1	923.33	305.13	149.99	515.59
7194	Yoda	2002	1,075	0	451.27	199.53	99.99	351.32
7200	Final Duel I	2002	31	2	49.57	24	6.99	609.16
7201	Final Duel II	2002	26	3	20.44	15.47	6.99	192.42
7203	Jedi Defense I	2002	111	1	35.13	18.19	6.99	402.58
7204	Jedi Defense II	2002	53	3	22.07	16	6.99	215.74
7250	Clone Scout Walker	2005	108	1	42.2	18.18	9.99	322.42
7251	Darth Vader Transformation	2005	53	2	62.4	34.67	6.99	792.70
7252	Droid Tri-Fighter	2005	148	1	30.67	15.4	14.99	104.60
7255	General Grievous Chase	2005	111	2	144.13	40.07	19.99	621.01
7256	Jedi Starfighter and Vulture Droid	2005	202	1	70	25.53	19.99	250.18
7257	Ultimate Lightsaber Duel	2005	282	2	202	92.93	29.99	573.56
7258	Wookiee Attack	2005	366	4	133.27	52.2	29.99	344.38
7259	ARC70 Fighter	2005	396	4	74.87	36.27	39.99	87.22

NUMBER	NAME	YEAR	PIECES	MINIFIGS	NEW	USED	RETAIL	GROWTH%
7260	Wookiee Catamaran	2005	376	6	156.6	71.13	49.99	213.26
7261	Clone Turbo Tank	2005	801	8	240.67	138.2	89.99	167.44
7261-2	Clone Turbo Tank (non-light-up)	2006	801	8	21	12.55	89.99	-76.66
7262	TIE Fighter and Y-Wing	2004	412	3	83.6	44.8	49.99	67.23
7263	TIE Fighter	2005	159	2	69.93	33.47	19.99	249.82
7264	Imperial Inspection	2005	367	10	228.67	151.33	49.99	357.43
7283	Ultimate Space Battle	2005	567	2	307.07	121.67	49.99	514.26
75000	Clone Troopers vs. Droidekas	2013	124	4	13.1	9.59	12.99	0.85
75001	Republic Troopers vs. Sith Troopers	2013	63	4	16.5	9.83	12.99	27.02
75002	AT-RT	2013	222	4	19.16	14.47	19.99	-4.15
75003	A-wing Starfighter	2013	177	3	27.63	16.56	24.99	10.56
75004	Z-95 Headhunter	2013	373	3	34.32	26.6	49.99	-31.35
75005	Rancor Pit	2013	380	4	40.63	32.53	59.99	-32.27
75006	Jedi Starfigher & Kamino	2013	61	1	12.74	8.3	9.99	27.53
75007	Republic Assault Ship & Coruscant	2013	74	1	16.27	11.95	9.99	62.86
75008	TIE Bomber & Asteroid Field	2013	60	1	13.06	2	9.99	30.73
75009	Snowspeeder & Hoth	2013	69	1	35.17	28	9.99	252.05
75010	B-wing Starfighter & Endor	2013	83	1	24.39	0	9.99	144.14
75011	Tantive IV & Alderaan	2013	102	1	25.42	25	9.99	154.45
75012	BARC Speeder with Sidecar	2013	226	4	34.88	16	24.99	39.58
75013	Umbaran MHC (Mobile Heavy Cannon)	2013	493	4	27.19	30.93	49.99	-45.61
75014	Battle of Hoth	2013	426	6	75.72	46.53	49.99	51.47
75015	Corporate Alliance Tank Droid	2013	271	3	18.64	11.2	19.99	-6.75
75016	Homing Spider Droid	2013	295	4	25.97	17	29.99	3.40
75017	Duel on Geonosis	2013	391	4	35.94	24.27	39.99	0.13
75018	JEK4's Stealth Starfighter	2013	550	4	57.76	26.93	69.99	7.47
75019	AT-TE	2013	794	5	67.77	54.63	89.99	-24.69
75020	Jabba's Sail Barge	2013	850	6	76.45	60.67	119.99	-36.29
75021	Republic Gunship	2013	1,175	7	95.2	79.2	119.99	-20.66
75022	Mandalorian Speeder	2013	211	3	27.34	15.87	24.99	9.40
75023	Star Wars Advent Calendar	2013	254	9	66.81	0	39.99	67.07
75024	HH-87 Starhopper	2013	362	3	30.88	9.27	39.99	-22.78
75025	Jedi Defender-Class Cruiser	2013	927	4	80.52	49	89.99	0.52
75028	Clone Turbo Tank	2014	96	1	11.85	8.63	9.99	18.62
75029	AAT	2014	95	1	12.85	8.67	9.99	28.63
75030	Millennium Falcon	2014	94	1	14.87	9	9.99	48.85
75031	TIE Interceptor	2014	92	1	15	6.77	9.99	50.15
75032	X-Wing Fighter	2014	97	1	14.84	6.91	9.99	48.55
75033	Star Destroyer	2014	97	1	11	10	9.99	10.11
75034	Death Star Troopers	2014	100	4	32.18	19.5	12.99	147.73
75035	Kashyyyk Troopers	2014	99	4	26.07	11	12.99	100.69
75036	Utapau Troopers	2014	83	4	19.1	15.4	12.99	47.04
75037	Battle on Saleucami	2014	178	5	30.35	19.67	14.99	102.47
75038	Jedi Interceptor	2014	223	2	40.72	19.22	24.99	62.95
75039	V-Wing Starfighter	2014	201	2	23.18	20.19	24.99	-7.24
75040	General Grievousí Wheel Bike	2014	261	2	42.4	15.77	24.99	69.67
75041	Vulture Droid	2014	205	3	30.5	19.57	24.99	22.05
75042	Droid Gunship	2014	439	4	60.6	35.66	49.99	21.22
75043	AT-AP	2014	717	5	49.12	35.87	59.99	8.12
75044	Droid Tri-Fighter	2014	262	4	31.65	0	29.99	5.54

NUMBER	NAME	YEAR	PIECES	MINIFIGS	NEW	USED	RETAIL	GROWTH%
75045	Republic AV-7 Anti-Vehicle Cannon	2014	434	4	54.68	27.56	39.99	36.73
75046	Coruscant Police Gunship	2014	481	4	90.06	44.95	49.99	80.16
75048	Phantom	2014	234	2	25.08	18.72	29.99	6.37
75049	Snowspeeder	2014	279	3	32.27	32	29.99	7.60
75050	B-Wing	2014	448	3	38.43	44.44	49.99	-23.12
75051	Jedi Scout Fighter	2014	490	4	50.57	43.75	59.99	5.70
75052	Mos Eisley Cantina	2014	616	8	62.45	53.77	69.99	0.77
75053	The Ghost	2014	929	4	70.58	87.67	89.99	-21.57
75054	AT-AT	2014	1,137	5	98.59	85.63	99.99	.40
75055	Imperial Star Destroyer	2014	1,359	6	106.23	95.89	129.99	8.28
75056	Advent Calendar	2014	274	9	55.28	177	39.99	4
75058	MTT	2014	0	12	88.55	64.67	89.99	.60
75059	Sandcrawler	2014	3,296	7	303	250	299.99	1
75060	UCS Slave I	2014	1,996	4	208	0	199.99	48.95
7654	Droids Battle Pack	2007	102	7	31.88	21.53	9.99	219.12
7655	Clone Troopers Battle Pack	2007	58	4	44.37	30.73	9.99	344.14
7656	General Grievous Starfighter	2007	232	1	47.87	29.4	19.99	139.47
7657	AT-ST	2007	244	1	92.08	42.11	19.99	360.63
7658	Y-wing Fighter	2007	454	2	58.23	38.24	39.99	45.61
7659	Imperial Landing Craft	2007	471	5	81.2	43.27	49.99	62.43
7660	Naboo N Starfighter with Vulture Droid	2007	280	3	48.89	24.87	29.99	63.02
7661	Jedi Starfighter with Hyperdrive Booster Ring	2007	575	2	117.21	51.61	49.99	134.47
7662	Trade Federation MTT	2007	1,330	20	385.67	185.61	99.99	285.71
7663	Sith Infiltrator	2007	310	1	52.67	26.6	29.99	75.63
7664	TIE Crawler	2007	548	2	67	44.2	49.99	34.03
7665	Republic Cruiser	2007	919	5	187.2	93.2	89.99	108.02
7666	Hoth Rebel Base	2007	548	7	144.11	81.27	49.99	188.28
7667	Imperial Dropship	2008	81	4	47.59	27.52	9.99	376.38
7668	Rebel Scout Speeder	2008	82	4	29.76	19.2	9.99	197.90
7669	Anakin's Jedi Starfighter	2008	153	2	62.18	21.94	19.99	211.06
7670	Hailfire Droid & Spider Droid	2008	249	4	71.19	28.73	20	255.95
7671	AT-AP Walker	2008	392	2	94.27	37.13	39.99	135.73
7672	Rogue Shadow	2008	482	3	162.8	78.47	49.99	225.67
7673	MagnaGuard Starfighter	2008	431	2	62.4	39.67	44.99	38.70
7674	V9 Torrent	2008	471	1	71.57	39.47	54.99	30.15
7675	AT-TE Walker	2008	798	6	151.8	61.2	89.99	68.69
7676	Republic Attack Gunship	2008	1,034	5	201.12	74.63	119.99	67.61
7678	Droid Gunship	2008	329	3	83.2	30.73	29.99	177.43
7679	Republic Fighter Tank	2008	592	2	129.05	57.87	49.99	158.15
7680	The Twilight	2008	882	4	106	58.33	99.99	6.01
7681	Separatist Spider Droid	2008	206	5	66.88	40.6	29.99	123.01
7748	Corporate Alliance Tank Droid	2009	216	4	27.63	17.67	24.99	10.56
7749	Echo Base	2009	155	5	35.47	26.59	24.99	41.94
7751	Ahsoka's Starfighter and Droids	2009	291	2	135.94	63.27	39.99	239.93
7752	Count Dooku's Solar Sailer	2009	385	4	60.38	38.47	54.99	9.80
7753	Pirate Tank	2009	372	3	45.81	30.73	39.99	14.55
7754	Home One Mon Calimari Star Cruiser	2009	789	6	76.2	55.07	109.99	-30.72
7778	Midi-scale Millennium Falcon	2009	356	0	75.13	38.53	39.99	87.87
7868	Mace Windu's Jedi Starfighter	2011	313	5	55.56	40.67	39.99	38.93

NUMBER	NAME	YEAR	PIECES	MINIFIGS	NEW	USED	RETAIL	GROWTH%
7869	Battle for Geonosis	2011	331	5	64.98	36	39.99	62.49
7877	Naboo Starfighter	2011	318	5	56.75	30.27	49.99	13.52
7879	Hoth Echo Base	2011	773	8	124.89	82.47	89.99	38.78
7913	Clone Trooper Battle Pack	2011	85	4	22.98	12.84	12.99	76.91
7914	Mandalorian Battle Pack	2011	68	4	19.65	15.39	11.99	63.89
7915	Imperial V-wing Starfighter	2011	139	2	21.75	18.4	19.99	8.80
7929	The Battle of Naboo	2011	241	12	43.06	26.47	24.99	72.31
7930	Bounty Hunter Assault Gunship	2011	389	4	46.14	32.53	49.99	-7.70
7931	T-6 Jedi Shuttle	2011	389	4	48.88	33	59.99	8.52
7956	Ewok Attack	2011	166	3	40.17	25	24.99	60.74
7957	Sith Nightspeeder	2011	214	3	31.26	21.8	24.99	25.09
7958	Star Wars Advent Calendar	2011	266	8	46.63	24.6	39.99	16.60
7959	Geonosian Starfighter	2011	155	3	28	13.67	29.99	-6.64
7961	Darth Maul's Sith Infiltrator	2011	479	4	66.81	48	69.99	-4.54
7962	Anakin's & Sebulba's Podracers	2011	810	5	77.36	51.13	89.99	4.03
7964	Republic Frigate	2011	1,022	5	159.33	89.83	119.99	32.79
7965	Millennium Falcon	2011	1,254	6	156.12	105.89	139.99	11.52
8000	Pit Droid	2000	223	0	42.67	22.73	19.99	113.46
8001	Battle Droid	2000	363	0	62.73	26.93	29.99	109.17
8002	Destroyer Droid	2000	558	0	142.53	75	49.99	185.12
8007	C-3PO	2001	341	0	82.73	33	34.99	136.44
8008	Stormtrooper	2001	361	0	57.93	23.4	34.99	65.56
8009	R2-D2	2002	240	0	52.2	23.13	19.99	161.13
8010	Darth Vader	2002	391	0	115.07	50.67	39.99	187.75
8011	Jango Fett	2002	422	0	63.27	30.67	29.99	110.97
8012	Super Battle Droid	2002	379	0	52.47	23	34.99	49.96
8014	Clone Walker Battle Pack	2009	72	4	28.54	19.73	11.99	138.03
8015	Assassin Droids Battle Pack	2009	94	5	17.79	12.27	9.99	78.08
8016	Hyena Droid Bomber	2009	232	3	29.71	17.67	19.99	48.62
8017	Darth Vader's TIE Fighter	2009	251	1	116.4	53.33	29.99	288.13
8018	Armored Assault Tank (AAT)	2009	407	7	117.75	46.73	49.99	135.55
8019	Republic Attack Shuttle	2009	636	3	94.71	48.07	59.99	57.88
8028	Mini TIE-Fighter	2008	44	0	6.77	4.53	2.99	126.42
8029	Mini Snowspeeder	2008	66	0	33.09	22.33	0	0
8031	V9 Torrent	2008	66	0	8.75	6.56	3.99	119.30
8033	General Grievous' Starfighter	2009	44	0	9.68	9.13	3.99	142.61
8036	Separatist Shuttle	2009	259	5	33.47	22.6	29.99	11.60
8037	Anakin's Y-wing Starfighter	2009	570	3	76.69	44.38	59.99	27.84
8038	The Battle of Endor	2009	890	12	138.71	96.29	99.99	38.72
8039	Venator-Class Republic Attack Cruiser	2009	1,170	5	295.36	151.68	119.99	146.15
8083	Rebel Trooper Battle Pack	2010	79	4	33.05	12.31	11.99	175.65
8084	Snowtrooper Battle Pack	2010	74	4	18.71	12.45	11.99	56.05
8085	Freeco Speeder	2010	177	2	22.65	16.2	24.99	-9.36
8086	Droid Tri-Fighter	2010	268	3	28.56	14.8	24.99	14.29
8087	TIE Defender	2010	304	2	49.98	34.67	49.99	-0.02
8088	ARC70 Starfighter	2010	396	4	71.59	45.47	59.99	19.34
8089	Hoth Wampa Cave	2010	297	3	57.25	37.39	39.99	43.16
8091	Republic Swamp Speeder	2010	176	5	22.49	16.73	29.99	-25.01
8092	Luke's Landspeeder	2010	163	5	36.13	23.3	24.99	44.58
8093	Plo Koon's Jedi Starfighter	2010	175	2	32.85	19.67	24.99	31.45
8095	General Grievous' Starfighter	2010	454	3	66.67	37.47	49.99	33.37

NUMBER	NAME	YEAR	PIECES	MINIFIGS	NEW	USED	RETAIL	GROWTH%
8096	Emperor Palpatine's Shuttle	2010	592	4	82.81	48.75	59.99	38.04
8097	Slave I	2010	573	3	132.37	78.25	79.99	65.48
8098	Clone Turbo Tank	2010	1,141	6	161	96.67	119.99	34.18
8099	Midi-Scale Imperial Star Destroyer	2010	423	0	39.4	23.13	39.99	.48
8128	Cad Bane's Speeder	2010	318	5	44.87	32.8	49.99	0.24
8129	AT-AT Walker	2010	815	8	234.07	176.2	109.99	112.81
9488	Elite Clone Trooper & Commando Droid Battle Pack	2012	98	4	18.17	11	12.99	39.88
9489	Endor Rebel Trooper & Imperial Trooper Battle Pack	2012	77	4	18.03	11.29	12.99	38.80
9490	Droid Escape	2012	137	4	33.09	20.67	19.99	65.53
9491	Geonosian Cannon	2012	132	4	19.39	14.73	19.99	-3.00
9492	TIE Fighter	2012	413	4	92.02	64.07	54.99	67.34
9493	X-wing Starfighter	2012	560	4	71.52	42.44	59.99	19.22
9494	Anakin's Jedi Interceptor	2012	300	5	58.28	36.93	39.99	45.74
9495	Gold Leader's Y-wing Starfighter	2012	458	3	67.33	42.33	49.99	34.69
9496	Desert Skiff	2012	213	4	33.46	21.87	24.99	33.89
9497	Republic Striker-class Starfighter	2012	376	3	49.37	25.67	44.99	9.74
9498	Saesee Tiin's Jedi Starfighter	2012	244	3	32.27	18.27	29.99	7.60
9499	Gungan Sub	2012	465	4	65.21	44.27	69.99	-6.83
9500	Sith Fury-class Interceptor	2012	748	3	86.09	53.33	89.99	-4.33
9509	Star Wars Advent Calendar	2012	234	10	47.26	23.33	49.99	-5.46
9515	Malevolence	2012	1,101	6	153.75	106.13	119.99	28.14
9516	Jabba's Palace	2012	717	9	149.1	121.53	119.99	24.26
9525	Pre Vizsla's Mandalorian Fighter	2012	403	3	44.33	31.47	49.99	1.32
9526	Palpatine's Arrest	2012	645	6	66.49	51.93	89.99	-26.11
9674	Naboo Starfighter & Naboo	2012	56	1	16.26	8.3	9.99	62.76
9675	Sebulba's Podracer & Tatooine	2012	80	1	14.33	5.8	9.99	43.44
9676	TIE Interceptor & Death Star	2012	65	1	18.65	9.2	9.99	86.69
9677	X-wing Starfighter & Yavin 4	2012	77	1	27.11	11.09	9.99	171.37
9678	Twin-Pod Cloud Car & Bespin	2012	78	1	8.47	2.13	9.99	5.22
9679	AT-ST & Endor	2012	65	1	10.8	7.17	9.99	8.11
TC4	TC4	2012	3	0	29.04	24.6	3.99	627.82
YODA	"Yoda minifig, NY I Heart Torso"	2013	3	1	20.07	0	3.99	403.01

SUPER HEROES

30162	Quinjet	2012	33	0	10.19	10.33	3.99	155.39
30163	Thor and the Cosmic cube	2012	25	1	16.68	9.78	4.99	234.27

NUMBER	NAME	YEAR	PIECES	MINIFIGS	NEW	USED	RETAIL	GROWTH%
30164	Lex Luthor	2012	14	1	26.22	19	3.99	557.14
30165	Hawkeye with equipment	2012	24	1	12	2.62	3.99	200.75
30167	Iron Man vs. Fighting Drone	2013	24	1	10.91	11.67	5.49	98.72
30168	Iron Patriot Gun mounting system	2013	17	1	27	0	3.99	576.69
30302	Spider-Man	2014	45	1	11	0	3.99	175.69
4528	Green Lantern	2012	38	0	18.73	10.07	14.99	24.95
4529	Iron Man	2012	44	0	72.6	29.13	14.99	384.32
4530	The Hulk	2012	39	0	23.78	15	14.99	58.64
4597	Captain America	2012	44	0	38.06	17.13	14.99	153.90
5000022	The Hulk	2012	4	1	31.47	20.93	3.99	688.72
5001623	Jor-El	2013	5	1	14.72	9	3.99	268.92
5002125	Electro	2014	0		99.99	3.99	171.93	
5002126	Martian Manhunter	2014	4	1	14.25	8	3.99	257.14
5002145	Rocket Raccoon	2014	13		0	4.99	81.96	
5004081	Plastic Man	2014	4		0	3.99	281.95	
6862-2	Superman Vs Power Armor Lex	2012	207	3	22.5	18.81	19.99	12.56
6865	Captain America's Avenging Cycle	2012	72	3	25.67	17.67	12.99	97.61
6866	Wolverine's Chopper Showdown	2012	199	3	70.4	44.53	19.99	252.18
6867	Loki's Cosmic Cube Escape	2012	181	3	39.4	19.88	19.99	97.10
6868	Hulk's Helicarrier Breakout	2012	389	4	75.59	49.93	49.99	51.21
6869	Quinjet Aerial Battle	2012	735	5	80.31	51.67	69.99	14.74
6873	Spider-Man's Doc Ock Ambush	2012	295	3	45.76	27.07	29.99	52.58
76002	Superman: Metropolis Showdown	2013	119	2	16.6	7.75	12.99	27.79
76003	Superman: Battle of Smallville	2013	418	5	29.47	29.07	49.99	-41.05
76004	Spider-Man : Spider-Cycle Chase	2013	237	3	21.93	14.13	19.99	9.70
76005	Spider-Man : Daily Bugle Showdown	2013	476	5	40.7	31.07	49.99	8.58
76006	Iron Man: Extremis Sea Port Battle	2013	195	3	21.78	15.6	19.99	8.95
76007	Iron Man: Malibu Mansion Attack	2013	364	5	26.88	27.4	39.99	-32.78
76008	Iron Man vs. The Mandarin: Ultimate Showdown	2013	91	2	12.32	9.8	12.99	-5.16
76009	Superman Black Zero Escape	2013	168	3	16.2	12.27	19.99	8.96
76014	Spider-Trike vs. Electro	2014	70	2	19.88	7.93	12.99	53.04
76015	Doc Ock Truck Heist	2014	237	3	23.37	11.46	19.99	16.91
76016	Spider-Helicopter Rescue	2014	299	4	41.27	29.99	44.99	-8.27
76017	Captain America vs. Hydra	2014	172	3	28.33	21	19.99	41.72
76018	Hulk Lab Smash	2014	398	5	46.81	42.3	49.99	-6.36
76019	Starblaster Showdown	2014	196	3	27.81	28.18	19.99	39.12
76020	Knowhere Escape Mission	2014	433	3	59.76	26.47	39.99	49.44
76021	The Milano Spaceship Rescue	2014	665	5	65.87	56.67	74.99	2.16
76022	X-Men vs. The Sentinel	2014	336	4	46.16	23	49.99	-7.66
Comcon013	Green Lantern (SDCC 2011 exclusive)	2011	5	1	43.87	43.33	3.99	999.50
Comcon014	Batman (SDCC 2011 exclusive)	2011	6	1	42.56	44.4	3.99	966.67
Comcon016	Green Lantern (NYCC 2011 exclusive)	2011	6	1	82.6	37.82	3.99	1970.18
Comcon018	Batman (NYCC 2011 exclusive)	2011	6	1	40.7	79	3.99	920.05
LCP2012	Iron Man & Captain America (2012 Collectors Preview)	2012	7	2	515.07	0	3.99	12809.02

NUMBER	NAME	YEAR	PIECES	MINIFIGS	NEW	USED	RETAIL	GROWTH%
TECHNIC								
3057	Master Builders - Create 'N' Race	2000	105	0	21.62	15	19.99	8.15
41999	4x4 Crawler Exclusive Edition	2013	1,585	0	338.29	298.5	199.99	69.15
42000	Grand Prix Racer	2013	1,141	0	138.02	97.47	129.99	6.18
42001	Mini Off-Roader	2013	100	0	22.29	3.5	12.99	71.59
42002	Hovercraft	2013	170	0	35.13	18.58	19.99	75.74
42004	Mini Backhoe Loader	2013	246	0	41.27	19.25	24.99	65.15
42005	Monster Truck	2013	329	0	63.88	23.95	49.99	27.79
42006	Excavator	2013	720	0	120.27	58.47	79.99	50.36
42007	Moto Cross Bike	2013	253	0	44.5	40.22	39.99	11.28
42008	Service Truck	2013	1,276	0	104.39	84.2	129.99	9.69
42009	Mobile Crane MK II	2013	2,606	0	196.57	167.4	219.99	0.65
42010	Off-road Racer	2013	160	0	26.82	16.33	19.99	34.17
42011	Race Car	2013	158	0	34.47	19.88	19.99	72.44
42020	Twin Rotor Helicopter	2014	145	0	19.89	20	12.99	53.12
42021	Snowmobile	2014	186	0	25.33	20.67	19.99	26.71
42022	Hot Rod	2014	414	0	39.81	31.4	39.99	-0.45
42023	Construction Crew	2014	833	0	82.83	40.48	69.99	18.35
42024	Container Truck	2014	948	0	86.25	53.69	79.99	7.83
42025	Cargo Plane	2014	1,297	0	132.69	112.2	139.99	-5.21
42026	Black Champion Racer	2014	137	0	31.52	0	19.99	57.68
42027	Desert Racer	2014	148	0	30.71	0	19.99	53.63
42028	Bulldozer	2014	617	0	75.84	40.49	49.99	51.71
42029	Customised Pick-Up Truck	2014	1,063	0	93	74.73	99.99	-6.99
42030	VOLVO L350F Front Loader	2014	1,636	0	231.48	320	249.95	-7.39
5206	Speed Computer	2000	19	0	34	21	19.99	70.09
5218	Pneumatic Pack	2000	147	0	90.5	39.43	27.99	223.33
8041	Race Truck	2010	608	0	82.86	53.2	59.99	38.12
8043	Motorized Excavator	2010	1123	0	390.47	258.2	199.99	95.24
8045	Mini Telehandler	2010	117	0	26.58	14.33	10.99	141.86
8046	Helicopter	2010	152	0	39.12	12.53	19.99	95.70
8047	Compact Excavator	2010	252	0	62.33	29.6	24.99	149.42
8048	Buggy	2010	314	0	63.69	39	39.99	59.26
8049	Tractor with Log Loader	2010	525	0	112.18	69.87	59.99	87.00
8051	Motorbike	2010	467	0	140.13	67.6	39.99	250.41
8052	Container Truck	2010	686	0	208.03	77.33	69.99	197.23
8053	Mobile Crane	2010	1,289	0	204.25	118.8	99.99	104.27
8063	Tractor with Trailer	2009	1,100	0	166	93.2	99.99	66.02
8065	Mini Container Truck	2011	119	0	23	12.64	10.99	109.28
8066	Off-Roader	2011	141	0	27.47	16.4	19.99	37.42
8067	Mini Mobile Crane	2011	292	0	50.05	26.33	24.99	100.28
8068	Rescue Helicopter	2011	408	0	56.8	36	39.99	42.04
8069	Backhoe Loader	2011	609	0	81.13	49.95	59.99	35.24
8070	Super Car	2011	1,281	0	221.53	144.33	119.99	84.62
8071	Lift Truck	2011	593	0	72.96	38.4	49.99	45.95
8081	Extreme Cruiser	2011	590	0	122	88.47	59.9	103.67
8109	Flatbed Truck	2011	1,115	0	197.61	142.13	99.99	97.63
8110	Unimog U400	2011	2,047	0	272.32	190.07	199.99	36.17
8236	Bike Burner	2000	60	0	10.38	5.07	5.99	73.29
8237	Formula Force	2000	115	0	11.5	5.93	9.99	15.12
8238	Dueling Dragsters	2000	202	0	7.8	6.53	17.99	-56.64

NUMBER	NAME	YEAR	PIECES	MINIFIGS	NEW	USED	RETAIL	GROWTH%
8240	Slammer Stunt Bike	2001	152	0	19.93	8.44	14.99	32.96
8242	Slammer Turbo	2001	253	0	21.37	21	19.99	6.90
8256	Go-Kart	2009	144	0	67.17	20.8	14.99	348.10
8258	Crane Truck	2009	1,877	0	340.07	235.4	149.99	126.73
8259	Mini Bulldozer	2009	165	0	28.76	19.67	9.99	187.89
8260	Tractor	2009	104	0	25.31	11.8	9.99	153.35
8261	Rally Truck	2009	198	0	28.13	21.92	19.99	40.72
8262	Quad-Bike	2009	308	0	45.4	28.13	39.99	13.53
8263	Snow Groomer	2009	590	0	192.13	105.07	49.99	284.34
8264	Hauler	2009	575	0	157.06	91.93	69.99	124.40
8265	Front Loader	2009	1,061	0	251.33	168.47	79.99	214.20
8270	Rough Terrain Crane	2007	106	0	29.33	19	9.99	193.59
8271	Wheel Loader	2007	200	0	27.33	19	19.99	36.72
8272	Snowmobile	2007	331	0	99.07	45	29.99	230.34
8273	Off Road Truck	2007	805	0	111.39	64	49.99	122.82
8274	Combine Harvester	2007	1,025	0	250.53	136.47	69.99	257.95
8275	Motorized Bulldozer	2007	1,384	0	812.87	327.93	149.99	441.95
8281	Mini Tractor	2006	121	0	33.93	17.33	9.99	239.64
8282	Quad Bike	2006	200	0	28.93	15.67	19.99	44.72
8283	Telehandler	2006	323	0	59.5	29.8	29.99	98.40
8284	Dune Buggy / Tractor	2006	872	0	109.8	79.6	59.99	83.03
8285	Tow Truck	2006	1,877	0	704.6	272.73	119.99	487.22
8287	Motor Box	2006	93	0	73.8	53.25	29.99	146.08
8288	Crawler Crane	2006	800	0	396.07	219.87	49.99	692.30
8289	Fire Truck	2006	1,036	0	155.73	71.13	74.99	107.67
8290	Mini Forklift	2008	89	0	21.69	9.8	7.99	171.46
8291	Dirt Bike	2008	248	0	49.73	30.73	24.99	99.00
8292	Cherry Picker	2008	726	0	186.6	88.8	59.99	211.05
8294	Excavator	2008	720	0	174.4	97.2	59.99	190.72
8295	Telescopic Handler	2008	1,182	0	208.88	117.2	89.99	132.11
8296	Dune Buggy	2008	199	0	36.4	23	19.99	82.09
8297	Off-Roader	2008	1,097	0	269.27	129.47	119.99	124.41
8415	Dump Truck	2005	284	0	53.69	30.5	29.99	79.03
8416	Fork-Lift	2005	729	0	177.56	79	69.99	153.69
8418	Mini Loader	2005	66	0	12.17	8.53	5.99	103.17
8419	Excavator	2005	286	0	50.87	32.6	19.99	154.48
8420	Street Bike	2005	506	0	161.4	65.07	49.99	222.86
8421	Mobile Crane	2005	1,884	0	450.6	224.4	149.99	200.42
8430	Mag Wheel Master	2002	318	0	47	18.3	34.99	34.32
8431	Pneumatic Crane Truck	2002	862	0	161.5	103.88	84.99	90.02
8433	Cool Movers	2004	215	0	30.8	8.71	12.99	137.11
8434	Aircraft	2004	445	0	76.45	40.87	34.99	118.49
8435	4WD	2004	763	0	75.53	47.87	49.99	51.09
8436	Truck	2004	1,027	0	180	90.73	89.99	100.02
8438	Pneumatic Crane Truck	2003	848	0	66	107.33	84.99	-22.34
8441	Fork-Lift Truck	2003	70	0	20	9.6	5.99	233.89
8451	Dump Truck	2003	183	0	40.18	22.87	19.99	101.00
8453	Front-End Loader	2003	214	0	34.53	17.4	19.99	72.74
8454	Rescue Truck	2003	639	0	92.64	55.6	69.99	32.36
8455	Back-Hoe	2003	704	0	231.53	170.4	99.99	131.55
8457	Power Puller	2000	979	1	292.29	229.27	99.99	192.32
8458	Silver Champion	2000	1,431	0	414.2	178.53	169.99	143.66

NUMBER	NAME	YEAR	PIECES	MINIFIGS	NEW	USED	RETAIL	GROWTH%
8464	Pneumatic Front-End Loader	2001	591	0	256.99	95.6	69.99	267.18
8465	Extreme Off-Roader	2001	365	0	73.3	33	39.99	83.30
8466	4X4 Off-Roader	2001	1,102	0	295.87	209.53	119.99	146.58
8509	Swamp	2000	45	0	11.56	8.87	5.99	92.99
8510	Lava	2000	35	0	10.25	6.73	5.99	71.12
8511	Frost	2000	44	0	10.88	7.27	5.99	81.64
8512	Onyx	2000	37	0	8.25	8.07	5.99	37.73
8513	Dust	2000	46	0	14.25	7.4	5.99	137.90
8514	Power	2000	32	0	8.08	8.27	5.99	34.89
8521	Flare	2000	44	0	28.5	13.73	5.99	375.79
8522	Spark	2000	35	0	15	7.86	5.99	150.42
8523	Blaster	2000	88	0	14.2	5.53	14.99	-5.27
8880	Super Car	1994	1,343	0	310.93	236.6	129.99	139.20
9390	Mini Tow Truck	2012	136	0	19.33	7.67	11.99	61.22
9391	Tracked Crane	2012	218	0	42.48	24.11	19.99	112.51
9392	Quad Bike	2012	199	0	52.88	21.2	24.99	111.60
9393	Tractor	2012	353	0	45.35	23.78	39.99	13.40
9394	Jet Plane	2012	499	0	67.04	31.4	49.99	34.11
9395	Pick-Up Tow Truck	2012	954	0	78.83	50.93	69.99	12.63
9396	Helicopter	2012	1,056	0	120.87	83.8	119.99	0.73
9397	Logging Truck	2012	1,308	0	170.59	95.27	139.99	21.86
9398	4x4 Crawler	2012	1,327	0	184.39	127.13	199.99	-7.80

TEENAGE MUTANT NINJA TURTLE

NUMBER	NAME	YEAR	PIECES	MINIFIGS	NEW	USED	RETAIL	GROWTH%
30270	Kraang Laser Turret	2013	36	1	4.83	2.5	3.99	21.05
30271	Mikey's Mini-Shellraiser	2014	47	1	7.49	22.13	4.99	50.10
5002127	Flashback Shredder	2014	0	1	5.65	23	0	
79100	Kraang Lab Escape	2013	90	3	21.32	9.67	12.99	64.13
79101	Shredder's Dragon Bike	2013	198	3	25.98	17.2	24.99	3.96
79102	Stealth Shell in Pursuit	2013	162	3	24.23	12.13	19.99	21.21
79103	Turtle Lair Attack	2013	488	5	60.57	34.07	49.99	21.16
79104	The Shellraiser Street Chase	2013	620	5	45.16	37	59.99	-24.72
79105	Baxter Robot Rampage	2013	397	5	40.61	41.06	39.99	1.55
79115	Turtle Van Takedown	2014	368	4	43.91	38.67	39.99	9.80
79116	Big Rig Snow Getaway	2014	741	6	60.31	0	69.99	3.83
79117	Turtle Lair Invasion	2014	888	6	76.93	73.33	99.99	-23.06
79118	Karai Bike Escape	2014	88	2	13.1	0	12.99	0.85
79119	Mutation Chamber Unleashed	2014	196	3	25.24	11.4	24.99	1.00
79120	T-Rawket Sky Strike	2014	286	4	37.73	0	34.99	7.83
79121	Turtle Sub Undersea Chase	2014	684	5	52.14	0	59.99	3.09
79122	Shredder's Lair Rescue	2014	478	5	53.44	0	49.99	6.90
Leonardo	Shadow Leonardo UK tin edition	2013	7	1	30.55	16.4	0	

THE LEGO MOVIE

NUMBER	NAME	YEAR	PIECES	MINIFIGS	NEW	USED	RETAIL	GROWTH%
30280	The Piece of Resistance	2014	33	1	11.83	5.5	0	
30281	Micro Manager Battle	2014	27	1	10.7	0	0	
30282	Super Secret Police Enforcer	2014	40	1	7.58	6.33	4.99	51.90
5002045	Pyjamas Emmet	2014	4	1	22.71	10.33	0	
5002203	Radio DJ Robot	2014	4	0	11	0	0	
5002204	Western Emmet	2014	6	1	11.96	0	0	
70800	Getaway Glider	2014	104	3	23.14	13	12.99	78.14
70801	Melting Room	2014	122	3	19.7	6.69	12.99	51.66

NUMBER	NAME	YEAR	PIECES	MINIFIGS	NEW	USED	RETAIL	GROWTH%
70802	Bad Cop's Pursuit	2014	314	2	35.33	21.78	29.99	17.81
70803	Cloud Cuckoo Palace	2014	197	3	28.24	21.33	19.99	41.27
70804	Ice Cream Machine	2014	344	3	31.2	0	29.99	4.03
70805	Trash Chomper	2014	389	3	33.76	32.67	29.99	12.57
70806	Castle Cavalry	2014	424	3	35.26	16.48	29.99	17.57
70807	MetalBeard's Duel	2014	412	3	34	37.33	34.99	-2.83
70808	Super Cycle Chase	2014	514	5	47.84	36.13	49.99	-4.30
70809	Lord Business' Evil Lair	2014	738	6	63	46.27	69.99	-9.99
70810	MetalBeard's Sea Cow	2014	2,741	4	234.99	196.93	249.99	-6.00
70811	The Flying Flusher	2014	351	3	41.54	28.39	29.99	38.51
70812	Creative Ambush	2014	473	4	43.07	35	39.99	7.70
70813	Rescue Reinforcements	2014	859	5	74.64	45.5	69.99	6.64
70814	Emmet's Constructo-Mech	2014	707	4	62.98	45	59.99	4.98
70815	Super Secret Police Dropship	2014	854	8	71.18	70.39	79.99	1.01
70816	"Benny's Spaceship, Spaceship, SPACESHIP!"	2014	939	5	90.87	81.07	99.99	-9.12

THE SIMPSONS

NUMBER	NAME	YEAR	PIECES	MINIFIGS	NEW	USED	RETAIL	GROWTH%
71006	The Simpsons House	2014	2,523	6	192.96	180	199.99	-3.52

TOY STORY

NUMBER	NAME	YEAR	PIECES	MINIFIGS	NEW	USED	RETAIL	GROWTH%
30070	Alien Space Ship	2010	32	1	8.84	5.27	3.99	121.55
30071	Army Jeep	2010	37	1	11.19	5.07	2.99	274.25
30072	Woody's Camp Out	2010	18	1	6.33	6.68	0	
30073	Buzz's Mini Ship	2010	23	1	10.08	0	0	
7590	Woody and Buzz to the Rescue	2010	92	2	39.05	21.73	19.99	95.35
7591	Construct-a-Zurg	2010	118	1	20.94	10.67	24.99	6.21
7592	Construct-a-Buzz	2010	205	1	34.56	19.4	24.99	38.30
7593	Buzz's Star Command Spaceship	2010	257	2	38.81	20.13	29.99	29.41
7594	Woody's Roundup!	2010	502	4	49.23	36.13	49.99	.52
7595	Army Men on Patrol	2010	90	4	16.89	14.72	10.99	53.69
7596	Trash Compactor Escape	2010	370	5	52.76	30.2	49.99	5.54
7597	Western Train Chase	2010	584	6	118.89	76.33	79.99	48.63
7598	Pizza Planet Truck Rescue	2010	225	4	47.74	31.8	39.99	19.38
7599	Garbage Truck Getaway	2010	402	4	52.37	28.27	49.99	4.76
7789	Lotso's Dump Truck	2010	129	3	13.12	9.87	19.99	-34.37

NUMBER	NAME	YEAR	PIECES	MINIFIGS	NEW	USED	RETAIL	GROWTH%
TRAINS								
10001	Metroliner	2001	782	11	420.86	229.2	148.99	182.48
10002	Railroad Club Car	2001	293	5	208.47	125.53	37.99	448.75
10013	Open Freight Wagon	2001	121	0	43.73	43.07	16.99	157.39
10014	Caboose	2001	170	0	52.67	36.2	14.99	251.37
10015	Green Passenger Wagon	2001	194	0	56.21	47.07	19.99	181.19
10016	Tanker	2001	128	0	77.86	48.73	19.99	289.49
10017	Hopper Wagon	2001	228	0	61.21	35.53	19.99	206.20
10020	Santa Fe Super Chief	2002	435	2	265.6	203.53	39.99	564.17
10022	Santa Fe Cars - Set II	2002	411	0	273.35	192.69	34.99	681.22
10025	Santa Fe Cars - Set I	2002	326	0	204.4	182.53	34.99	484.17
10133	Burlington Northern Santa Fe	2004	407	2	324.63	192.27	39.99	711.78
10153	Train Motor 9 V	2002	3	0	99.64	47.56	24.99	298.72
10170	TTX Intermodal Double-Stack Car	2005	366	0	132.4	94.47	39.99	231.08
10173	Holiday Train	2006	965	7	702.33	438.13	89.99	680.45
10194	Emerald Night	2009	1,085	3	384.35	266	99.99	284.39
10205	"Large Train Engine with Tender, Black"	2002	232	0	310	108.93	0	
10219	Maersk Train	2011	1,237	3	274.44	208.27	119.9	128.89
10233	Horizon Express	2013	1,351	6	164.39	112.73	129.99	26.46
2159	9V Train Track Starter Collection	2006	24	0	35.47	23.5	29.99	18.27
3740	Small Locomotive	2001	67	0	52.25	32.3	14.99	248.57
3741	Large Locomotive	2001	92	0	100.5	65.8	19.99	402.75
3742	Tender	2001	39	0	55.67	63.67	10.99	406.55
3743	Locomotive Blue Bricks	2001	106	0	42.12	11	6.99	502.58
3744	Locomotive Green Bricks	2001	106	0	31.19	50	6.99	346.21
3747	Locomotive Dark Grey Bricks	2001	106	0	20.88	3.11	6.99	198.71
4206	9V Train Switching Track Collection	2006	27	0	32.33	0	44.99	-28.14
4534	LEGO Express	2002	456	5	257.87	162.53	159.99	61.18
4535	LEGO Express Deluxe	2002	762	5	300.07	196.07	169.99	76.52

GLOSSARY

ABS Plastic: Acrylonitrile Butadiene Styrene; the thermoplastic polymer that LEGO bricks are made out of. A durable and safe product.

AFOL: An acronym that stands for Adult Fan of LEGO. It is the standard term used to refer to LEGO fans who are typically older than the toys key demographic of children. Generally pronounced to rhyme with "hay-foal."

Advanced Building Techniques: LEGO building practices and methods developed over the past 15 years or so that enable the creation of more complex and detailed LEGO models. Some of the major advanced building techniques include Offsetting, Letterings, Studs Not On Top (SNOT), Diagonal Striping, Studs Not In a Row (SNIR), Micro-Striping, Mixed Cylinder Curving.

Battle Pack: A small LEGO set that contains about 100 pieces, mostly found in the *Star Wars* and Castle themes. It usually contains three to five minifigures. They are nicknamed "Army Builders" because of the multitude of minifigures for the price, usually around $10 to $12.

BrickMaster: A LEGO magazine from several years ago that gave subscribers a new polybag set every couple of months, besides the magazine itself. Many of the LEGO polybags ended up being quite rare and collectible.

Buy In Point/Price: The amount paid for a LEGO set. Not every set is bought at Manufacturer's Suggested Retail Prices (MSRP). Many are bought below MSRP at discount or sale price. Some sets are bought after retirement for more than the MSRP.

CAGR (Compound Annual Growth Rate): According to Investopedia.com and Wikepedia.com, it is the year-over-year growth rate of an investment over a specified period of time. CAGR isn't the actual return in reality. It's an imaginary number that describes the rate at which an investment would have grown if it grew at a steady rate. You can think of CAGR as a way to smooth out the returns.

CMFs (Collectible Minifigures): These are small polybag packets that LEGO introduced in 2010 and continues to this day that include one minifigure of various origins. They are differentiated by series and theme. There are usually 16 different minifigures in a series, and there have been 15 different series and theme releases as of this writing.

Completist/Completionist: A person who collects or owns every LEGO item or set within a series, line, or theme. They must have the complete set in order to be satisfied.

Constraction: A LEGO term that describes a hybrid theme or model type that combines traditional "action figure" characteristics with LEGO bricks. These are usually larger Technic or Bionicle-based sets that are larger than traditional LEGO minifigures. They are very playable and look like plastic dolls or figures.

Cuusoo: A Japanese term that means "fantasy" or "imagination." It was a Japanese company and idea that enabled people to submit ideas for products that would be turned into actual retail items. LEGO teamed with Cuusoo and let fans vote on custom LEGO models that could be put into production if a series of approvals were met. The original designer would get paid a 1 percent royalty on sales. The LEGO Cuusoo theme was changed to the LEGO Ideas theme and is one of their most popular lines.

LEGO Dark Ages: The time in life in which a LEGO fan no longer plays or pays attention to LEGO sets. It usually takes place from the mid-teens to late 20s or early 30s. Many times, parenthood or a special LEGO set will bring a person "out of their LEGO Dark Ages." It varies from person to person, but almost every LEGO fan goes through it.

Design by ME (Factory Theme): This was a LEGO theme that enabled fans to design their own sets for purchase. Sometimes, LEGO would use an idea and market the set to the masses. The 10190 Market Street is the best example of this theme's success.

EOL (End of Line): The term used when describing when a set retires from the production and is removed (or sold out) from primary retail sources.

Greebles: According to Wikepedia.com, a greeble is a fine detailing added to the surface of a larger object that makes it appear more complex and, therefore, more visually interesting. It usually gives the audience an impression of increased scale. The detail can be made from simple geometric primitives (such as cylinders, cubes, and rectangles), or more complex shapes, such as pieces of machinery (sprockets, cables, tanks). Greebles are often present on models or drawings of fictional spacecraft or architectural constructs in science fiction and are used in the movie industry (special effects). With LEGO sets, it is small bricks and pieces added to a model to give added dimension and detail, creating more realistic-looking creations. They can be internal or external and are important to many *Star Wars* and Advanced/Large Scale Model sets.

Legos: The improper slang term for LEGO bricks.

Here is a list of simple rules from The LEGO Group's Fair Play brochure that they like to adhere to in order to protect their brand and trademark:

ALWAYS write our trademarks in capital letters.

ALWAYS use a noun after the trademark, e.g. LEGO toys, LEGO values.

NEVER add a possessive "s," plural "s," or hyphen, e.g. LEGO's design, more LEGOs to play with, LEGO-bricks.

NEVER change or adjust the graphical design of a trademark, e.g. change the colors or shape of the LEGO logo.

LEGO Primary Market: Major LEGO retailers such as LEGO brick and mortar and online stores, Target, Toys R Us, Amazon, Walmart, Barnes & Noble, Kmart, and other stores that sell new LEGO sets.

LEGO S@H (Shop At Home): The LEGO online store.

LEGO Secondary Market: Online sites such as eBay.com, BrickClassifieds.com, Bricklink.com, BrickOwl.com and even Amazon.com when selling third-party-owned products. These sites specialize in selling used and resold new LEGO sets and parts.

LEGO VIP Program: LEGO membership program that lets you earn 1 VIP Point for every $1 you spend online or at the LEGO® Store. Once you reach 100 VIP Points, you will receive a $5 reward. You can use those rewards toward your next purchase. Think of it as a 5 percent discount.

LUG: A frequently used acronym, which stands for LEGO Users Group. Originally used to describe a local (or regional) LEGO club that met and interacted primarily in a "real world" context, the term has been extended to include virtual groups of LEGO fans. Many LUGs now also have an online presence, further blurring the line between traditional LUGs and online LEGO fan communities.

Maxifigure: The large, non-typical LEGO figure or character that consists of multiple pieces to complete. It usually is two to three times the size of a conventional LEGO minifigure. Many times, the figure is of an animal, dinosaur or monster.

Microfigure: Very small LEGO figures found in some sets; smaller than the traditional LEGO minifigures. Often found in Minecraft or Superhero sets.

Microset: The smallest LEGO set size in existence and smaller than a miniset.

Minifigure Scale: Any LEGO set or model that a minifigure is capable of fitting into. The size of the set must be in proportion to the minifigure in order to fit into vehicles or buildings.

Miniset: A LEGO set that is sized between a microset and conventional LEGO set. Many of the *Star Wars* themes polybags are minisets.

MISB: An acronym for Mint In Sealed Box. The most desired and valued LEGO box condition.

MOC: An acronym for My Own Creation. MOCs are custom LEGO sets and models developed and built by LEGO fans. They can be 50-piece microsets or 50,000-piece massive models and everything in between.

MSRP: An acronym for Manufacturer's Suggested Retail Price; what a LEGO set costs before discounts are applied.

NIB: An Acronym for New In Box. A LEGO set that has sealed inner packages and has never been built. The box can be opened, unsealed and/or damaged.

Part Out: The process of taking a new LEGO set, cracking it open and selling the pieces for a profit (more than MSRP) on secondary LEGO sites.

Plateau: A term describing when a LEGO set's value levels off and stagnates on the LEGO secondary market. It can decrease or increase or stay the same at that point.

Polybag: The small soft plastic package that many small LEGO sets are encased and sold in.

PPP (Price Per Piece): The ratio of the cost of a new LEGO set (usually at retail/MSRP) to the number of pieces in that set. $0.09 per piece is about average.

ROI (Return On Investment): A performance measure used to evaluate the efficiency of an investment or to compare the efficiency of a number of different investments. To calculate ROI, the benefit (return) of an investment is divided by the cost of the investment; the result is expressed as a percentage or a ratio. More on this in the introduction of the book.

Sleeper/Under the Radar Set: A set that largely goes unnoticed by the LEGO collector community and either retires early or appreciates to high levels or growth rates without much buzz or discussion on major LEGO websites.

Three (or Two) In One Set: A LEGO set, usually from the Creator or Technic theme, that comes with three sets of instructions to build three different models.

UCS (Ultimate Collector Series): A *Star Wars* subtheme of upscale, larger, and highly detailed sets designed for the older LEGO fan and collector. They are some of the largest and most expensive sets that LEGO produces and are based on iconic vehicles and characters.

Vertical Build: A difficult method of LEGO construction. It requires the LEGO builder to look at a set of LEGO instructions from the top down to decipher the building order and method. It is often confusing and is designed for more experienced builders.

WHOOOSH Factor: The ability of a LEGO set to be flown around a room in an imaginary fashion (possibly with man-made engine and laser noises), either by children or adults. It is a gauge of "playability." The more WHOOOSH, the more fun and playable a LEGO set is. The set with a high WHOOOSH Factor is also more sturdy and stable.

WOW Set: Simply, the type of set that when you see it, you say "WOW!" It is the best of the best and a handful of sets meet this requirement.

BIBLIOGRAPHY

Books and Magazines

Beckett, Jeremy, and Beecroft, Simon. *LEGO Star Wars: The Visual Dictionary.* DK Publishing; Har/Toy edition (September 21, 2009).

Breen, Bill, and Robertson, David C. *Brick by Brick: How LEGO Rewrote the Rules of Innovation and Conquered the Global Toy Industry.* Crown Business; Reprint edition (June 24, 2014).

Herman, Sarah. *Building History: The LEGO Group.* Barnsley, South Yorkshire: Pen & Sword Books Ltd, 2012.

Lipkowitz, Daniel. *The LEGO Book.* DK Children; Exp Rev edition (August 20, 2012).

Wilkinson, Philip. *LEGO Architecture: the Visual Guide.* DK; Lea edition (September 1, 2014).

Brick Journal magazine. Edited by Joe Meno, it spotlights all aspects of the LEGO Community, showcasing events, people, and models in every issue, with contributions and how-to articles by top builders worldwide, new product introductions, and more. www.brickjournal.com.

Electronic Media

www.Bricklink.com
www.BrickPicker.com
www.Brickset.com
www.Cuusoo.com
www.History.com
www.Investopedia.com
www.LEGO.com
www.Rebrickable.com
www.Wikipedia.com
www.Wookiepedia.com

Film and Television

Captain Phillips
Star Wars I-VI
Peanuts, Charles M. Shulz
Harry Potter
Legends of Chima: The Animated Series
Indiana Jones
The Cartoon Network
Pirates of the Caribbean
DC Comics
Marvel Comics
Disney
Discovery Channel

INDEX

ABOUT THE AUTHORS

Ed Maciorowski is the co-founder and co-owner of BrickPicker.com. He has been a LEGO collector since 1973, when his parents gave him his first set (710 Wrecker with Car). Ed is now an investor as well, with over 6,000 sets in his collection and a current market value well into the six figures.

He and his brother, Jeff, got the idea to create the online LEGO price and investing guide after Ed discovered that a 10179 Millennium Falcon set he bought for $399 was selling for $800-$1,200 on eBay two years later. The price for that set is now nearly $4,000.

Ed also is a regular contributor in the LEGO-themed magazine, *BLOCKS*.

Jeff Maciorowski is the co-founder and co-owner of BrickPicker.com. He is a senior website engineer for a 40 million dollar market research company and specializes in multiple web technologies, including Cold Fusion, jQuery, Oracle, and mySQL. Jeff built Brickpicker.com from the ground up and it is now the third busiest LEGO-themed website in the world that attracts over five million visitors annually. The site has been featured in the *USA Today* and other digital media outlets (BBC.com, Wired.com). Jeff is also the creator of the recently launched BrickClassifeds.com website, a cost-effective secondary LEGO marketplace.

TOP COLLECTOR GUIDES
JUST **FOR YOU**

Whether you are just getting started or have been collecting for years, our books will help you build, identify, value, and maintain your collections. For more information, visit **KrauseBooks.com**

Krause Publications books can also be found at many booksellers nationwide, and at antiques and hobby shops.

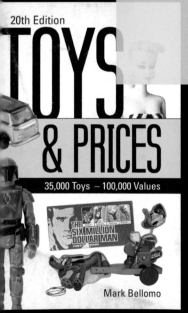
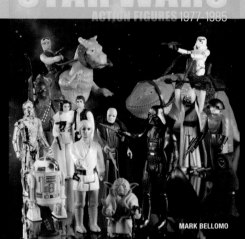
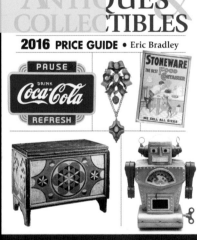

Visit **KrauseBooks.com** – where there's something for everyone

kp **krause publications**
A DIVISION OF F+W, A Content + eCommerce Company
www.krausebooks.com

Antique Trader®
www.antiquetrader.com